KT-403-343

THE HEART OF THE WRITER

Also by Jack Hodges

The Maker of the Omnibus

Robert Louis Stevenson

THE HEART OF THE WRITER

Private and Public Lives of English Writers

JACK HODGES

'The driver was huddled up in a cape . . . His face was a surprise, so kind it was and modest . . . The boy . . . returned punctually at sunset – driven not by Sir Thomas Browne, but by a maiden lady who was full of quiet fun.'

E. M. Forster: THE CELESTIAL OMNIBUS

SINCLAIR-STEVENSON

First published in Great Britain in 1994
by Sinclair-Stevenson
an imprint of Reed Consumer Books Ltd
Michelin House, 81 Fulham Road, London sw3 6rb
and Auckland, Melbourne, Singapore and Toronto

Copyright © 1994 by Jack Hodges

The right of Jack Hodges to be identified as author
of this work has been asserted by him in accordance
with the Copyright, Designs and Patents Act 1988.

A CIP catalogue record for this book
is available at the British Library
isbn 1 85619 379 9

Typeset by CentraCet Limited, Cambridge
Printed and bound in Great Britain by
Mackays of Chatham plc, Chatham, Kent

'. . . the business of the biographer is often to pass slightly over those performances and incidents, which produce vulgar greatness, to lead the thoughts into domestick privacies, and display the minute details of daily life, where exterior appendages are cast aside, and men excel each other only by prudence and virtue.'

SAMUEL JOHNSON

Contents

Contents

Contents

APPENDICES

List of Illustrations

Acknowledgements

O nce more I am grateful to Oriol Bath for allowing me to use her beautiful drawing of the Omnibus, which I commissioned as a bookplate, on the title-page. Indeed, I would find it difficult now to think of these books without it.

I also thank the following owners of copyright material who have kindly given me permission to quote extracts: Constable & Company Ltd. (Andrew Birkin's *J. M. Barrie and the Lost Boys*); The Estate of Francis Kilvert (*Kilvert's Diary* ed. William Plomer, published by Jonathan Cape Ltd.); Peter Owen Publishers London (Margaret Morris's *My Galsworthy Story*); Oxford University Press (Richard Ellmann's *James Joyce*, 1959); Peters Fraser & Dunlop Group Ltd. (Constance Babington Smith's *John Masefield*); R.I.B. Library: Reed Book Services (Christopher Milne's *The Enchanted Places* published by Methuen London, © Christopher Milne 1974; Ann Thwaite's *Waiting for the Party* published by Secker & Warburg Ltd., © Ann Thwaite 1974); Weidenfeld & Nicolson Ltd. (Nigel Nicolson's *Portrait of a Marriage*); The Estate of Vyvyan Holland (*Son of Oscar Wilde*, published by Rupert Hart-Davis).

The various excerpts from books by Vera Brittain are included with the permission of Paul Berry, her literary executor, Virago Press Ltd and Victor Gollancz Ltd.

For any accidental omissions, for any instance where, after every effort, I have been unable to contact the copyright holder, I ask the indulgence of those concerned. Any inadvertent omissions can be corrected in any future editions.

Preface

In *The Maker of the Omnibus* I inquired into creativity by comparing the lives of English writers. The present book may be said to look at the kind of person that makes a writer. It uses the same method but portrays lover and parent instead of child and student. There is a glimpse of the public figure handling distinctions and royal preferment. The book also shows the surprising place that writers hold in a people's affections.

About 1934, in the days of Uncle Mac and David, *Toytown*, and *The Castles of England* by L. du Garde Peach, there was broadcast on Children's Hour a short story by E. M. Forster, 'The Celestial Omnibus'.[1] It had sound effects of carriage wheels, horses' hoofs and thunder, but what I remember most are the trumpeting and great voice of Achilles towards the end. After the war, a copy I came across in a second-hand bookshop recalled the magic of that early impression. Since then, I have got junior boys in a secondary school to enact the story (with Mr Bons in top hat, and a Beecham recording of Beethoven's *Thanksgiving after the Storm*), shared it with A-level students, and told it to an English class in Wandsworth Prison. It is a parable on a child's faith. It is also an allegory of a journey, the destination marked on a signpost pointing up an alley.

The omnibus is a *book*, transporting the boy to his own discovered Mountain of 'every dear passion, every joy'. The driver is every author of power, feeding the imagination. There are none of the lurid persecutors that are found on the pages of Bunyan, although the boy after his first journey is caned by his father and locked up. The disturbing character is Mr Bons, a kind and respectable bibliophil. He accompanies the boy to the alley and aboard the omnibus, which puts him in a different category from the philistine father, but any fuller vision he cannot bear, and when they arrive he cries for his external

1 *The Celestial Omnibus & other Stories*, pub. by Sidgwick & Jackson Ltd. (1911).

world. He suggests the *Pharisee* and, as it has been pointed out to me, the unusual name Bons is an inversion of the word Snob. The alley, lack of patronage, the Company itself, sunrise and sunset, return tickets, Bermondsey gasworks, each is capable of interpretation in this beautiful story matching literary experience and spiritual truths.

In limiting my drivers to English ones, I made at the outset a cut large enough to be significant. For a similar reason, Sir Laurence Olivier removed Queen Margaret from his screen version of *Richard III*. But I excluded the creator of Natásha Rostóva . . . If I found compensation in a small island's finest achievement, this was not Mr Podsnap putting 'the rest of Europe and the whole of Asia, Africa, and America nowhere'. Basic things about writers – such as imagination preventing cruelty (according to Wilde's definition), making them loving parents[1] – are common to all.

On finishing his 'labour of love and lamentations', *Landscape Painting from Giotto to the Present Day*, Lewis Hind was asked whether he would consider doing a similar service for Portrait Painting. His monosyllabic answer was very loud.

Southfields, London
December, 1992

1 See p. 243.

PART ONE
IN LOVE

CHAPTER ONE

Popularity of Marriage

I

Most of our writers married. Even SHAW ignored the warning of his own Jack Tanner – that 'of all human struggles there's none so treacherous and remorseless as the struggle between the artist man and the mother woman'.[1] At forty-two he married Charlotte Payne-Townshend, a year younger: a Fabian with considerable property. St John Ervine, in a moving obituary, described how Shaw always treated her with 'old-world courtesy' and 'never broke the slightest promise to her'.

> The loss of her was irredeemable, far greater than even he had imagined it would be . . . 'If Charlotte were dying,' he said once, 'I know an infallible way to restore her to health.'
> 'And what is that, G.B.S?' I asked.
> 'I should simply go to bed and say that I were ill!'
> And indeed, Charlotte would have come running from the grave to help him. I do not doubt that she was waiting for him this morning when he went away.[2]

At least six writers married three times: Milton, J. B. Priestley, Edmund Blunden, Cyril Connolly, A. J. P. Taylor – even Pugin, who died at forty. RICHARD LOVELL EDGEWORTH was the loving husband of four wives. J. MIDDLETON MURRY claimed he first found sexual fulfilment when he married for the fourth time in his late fifties. BERTRAND RUSSELL married four times. Of ROBERT BOLT's four marriages, two were to the same bride, Sarah Miles. JOHN OSBORNE is happily married to his fifth wife.

MILTON was not removed from domestic reality any more than was Wordsworth. After reunion with his first wife, he took in the whole

---

1 *Man and Superman* (1903): Act I, p. 23.
2 BBC radio: 2 Nov. 1950.

noisy family of in-laws – ten of them, for nearly a year, when they were ruined as result of the Civil War. His third wife, Elizabeth Minshall, is singled out[1] as a particularly courageous woman.

PRIESTLEY's third marriage, when he was fifty-nine, to Jacquetta Hawkes, is described by his biographer as 'the most important love relationship in both their lives'.[2] CONNOLLY's third marriage at fifty-six, to Deidre Craig, resulting in two children, Matthew and Cressida, gave him enormous happiness which he did not try to conceal.

After two broken marriages, each bringing 'great pain', A. J. P. TAYLOR married at seventy Eva Haraszti, a Hungarian. A spokesman from the Hungarian Embassy commented:

. . . a question of two historians who have collaborated in the field of Anglo-Hungarian relations and who feel, perhaps, they would benefit more if they were together.

Seven years later, his 'Diary' in *The London Review of Books* reported Eva having to go into hospital and 'the devastation my wife's absence causes me'.[3] His next entry speaks of her safe return:

There is nothing I like more than taking up my wife's breakfast . . . The essential thing is that she is back with me and my life is once more an uninterrupted round of happiness.[4]

Even conscientious objectors to marriage have succumbed, JOYCE among them. When SHELLEY married Mary in St Mildred's Church in the City on the morning of 30 December 1816, it was not long after the suicide of Harriet, his first wife, and the perhaps even more tragic suicide of Fanny, Mary's half-sister. Godwin gave his daughter away and his short stout wife was there, presumably wearing her green spectacles. It makes the oddest scene – the respective authors of *Political Justice* and *Queen Mab* taking their cues from a priest and repeating after him their vows. Neither man was a stranger to the marriage service, each having gone through it *twice*. When the validity of Shelley's marriage as a minor in the Church of Scotland had been questioned, he and Harriet were remarried on 24 March 1814, in St George's Church, by the Rev. Edward Williams, curate, in the presence of Harriet's father and another witness. GODWIN, at twenty-

---

1 See p. 33.
2 Vincent Brome: *J. B. Priestley* (1988), pp. 375–6.
3 *An Old Man's Diary* (1984), p. 113.
4 *Ibid.*, pp. 121–2.

one, had married Mary Wollstonecraft (then living as Mrs Imlay) in time to legitimize their daughter Mary. His second marriage at forty-five to Mrs Clairmont, a widow with a son and daughter ('Claire'), was far from happy. She made a harsh stepmother; she is said to have introduced herself to her future husband: 'Do I have the pleasure of addressing the immortal Godwin?'[1]

C. S. LEWIS was not alone in marrying for the first time in later life. BACON, at forty-five, married Alice Barnham, who was not yet fourteen; J. S. MILL was the same age but had known his lady twenty-one years. FANNY BURNEY married at forty-one, two years after her resignation from Court; her husband, d'Arblay, was a French emigrant – adjutant-general to Lafayette.

Leonard Woolf tells that when he took his dog for a walk, about the time of his going up to Cambridge, he sometimes met THEODORE WATTS-DUNTON in Putney Park Lane, 'arm-in-arm with a beautiful young lady with whom we had a distant acquaintance, the enormous-eyed, almost Pre-Raphaelite-looking, Clara Reich'.[2] A few years later, the bachelor of seventy-three married. A mystery is here – for it was a sensuous love not on his part alone. They had waited twelve years, two years less than the Tennysons.

II

The following formed marriages with a literary association: Godwin = (1) Mary Wollstonecraft; Shelley = (2) Mary Wollstonecraft Godwin; Browning = Elizabeth Barrett; Leslie Stephen = (1) Harriet Thackeray; William Rossetti = Emma, daughter of Ford Madox Ford; G. M. Trevelyan = Janet, daughter of Mrs Humphry Ward and niece to Matthew Arnold; Leonard Woolf = Virginia, daughter of Leslie Stephen; Harold Nicolson = Victoria Sackville-West; A. A. Milne = Dorothy, daughter of Ernest de Selincourt; Gilbert Cannan = Mary (2), Barrie's ex-wife; J. Middleton Murry = Katherine Mansfield (2); David Cecil = Rachel, daughter of Desmond MacCarthy; Nicholas Monsarrat = Ann; Ted Hughes = (1) Sylvia Plath; Harold Pinter = (2) Lady Antonia Fraser; Michael Holroyd = Margaret Drabble.

1 *DNB*.
2 *Sowing* (1960), pp. 170–1.

Marital links among younger writers have almost become a way of life. Hunter Davies = Margaret Forster; Thomas Hinde = Susan Chitty; Salman Rushdie = Marianne Wiggins; Anthony Thwaite = Ann; Terence de Vere White = (2) Victoria Glendinning (2). Susan Hill is married to the Shakespearean scholar Professor Stanley Wells. Richard Holmes lives with the poet Vicki Feaver.

DESMOND MACCARTHY took pride in his wife being author of *A Nineteenth-Century Childhood* and the novel *A Pier and A Band*. During a luncheon party at home, he exclaimed: 'Yes, Molly, you must go on writing! I have always wanted to be *Mister* Henry Wood!'

CHAPTER TWO

A Passionate Galsworthy

To assess marital happiness is another matter. GALSWORTHY and Ada have always been regarded as ideally happy, despite a childless marriage. More recent evidence suggests that Ada, who from the age of seventeen had followed her mother round all the fashionable resorts in Europe to find a suitable match, and married at twenty-four Galsworthy's cousin whom she divorced, required unlimited pampering.

Five years after her second marriage, Galsworthy, whom she had influenced and encouraged to make writing his career, fell in love with Margaret Morris, a dancer of nineteen. The affair was unconsummated, and provided copy for the last stave, 'Autumn', of *The Dark Flower*.

They met at the Savoy Theatre when, after the first night of Marie Brema's production of Gluck's *Orpheus and Eurydice*, Margaret Morris was invited on the stage by the producer, presented to Beerbohm Tree, and acclaimed by all for her dancing, her choreography, and designs for the costumes and scenery. Galsworthy, then forty-three, 'tall, handsome . . . hair slightly greying at the temples, and an eyeglass',[1] was standing in the wings. Marie Brema introduced him, and they discussed her method of dancing. He compared her friezes of figures to Greek vases come to life. He invited her to tea at 14 Addison Road to meet his wife, to explain more and to tell them her future plans.

She found Ada quite charming. They told her they always had reservations about classical ballet – whether its stylized movements could adequately express human emotion. This was exactly what she had felt. Galsworthy invited her to lunch the following week, to discuss the production of his play *The Little Dream*, and asked her to arrange the dances.

1 Margaret Morris: *My Galsworthy Story* (1967), p. 22.

Brought up in France, her family always poor, Margaret grew to love the peace and beauty of their house: its all-white walls and white paint – an innovation then – its one or two pictures and ubiquitous flowers and books. It had a little garden with a low magnolia tree under the dining-room window.

After a year, the Galsworthys helped her to start The Margaret Morris School of Dance. He told her he had watched her training the children for his play.

'. . . *all* children should learn the ease and grace of movement you can give them, and it should be *the foundation of all training for Drama*.'[1]

She found a room over a milk-shop in High Street, Bloomsbury. They paid her first year's rent, bought lino, curtains, and a second-hand piano, behind which the pupils changed. She put an advertisement in *The Stage*, and Galsworthy attended an audition of would-be pupils. She soon danced with her first group – Margaret Morris and her Dancing Children. Galsworthy, Granville-Barker, Desmond MacCarthy, Henry Ainley, Ethel Smyth, and Ellen Terry were among a list of Patrons printed in her first prospectus.

Within two months the school was housed in a room more than twice the size, over a stained-glass factory in Endell Street. Galsworthy offered to pay what she couldn't afford – and even asked to have some lessons. From their country home in Devon the Galsworthys sent her cream every week. She was now rehearsing the part of Mrs Megan in his play *The Pigeon*. That Christmas she painted a small water-colour of *The Little Dream* and sent it to the Galsworthys. Ada thanked her 'most heartily'. Galsworthy wrote:

My dear Margaret,
That is a very sweet and lovely thing you have made me, and you shall be blessed whenever I look upon it. I'm going to hang it in my new 'study' . . .
Our love to you . . .[2]

He took her to dinner at Kettners. Next day he took her to a theatrical costume-hire place to find clothes for her part as Mrs Megan. In the taxi back to the theatre he said she looked cold and for the first time he put his arm round her. When she buried her face in the soft pile of his overcoat he kissed her, protesting he was too old for her.

1 *Ibid.*, p. 35.
2 *Ibid.*, p. 51.

Galsworthy 'was suddenly revealed as a passionate human being who loved me . . .'

Never for a moment did I think of trying to displace Ada. I knew if it came to choosing between us, it had to be Ada: but *why need there be a choice?*[1]

To avoid publicity, between rehearsals of *The Pigeon* he came to lunch – her family now had a top flat in Wellington Mansions, Castle Street. If the two of them were alone he sat on the opposite side of the table, and when the meal was over he made her sit on the other side of the room. They talked 'for hours' about how they could avoid hurting Ada.

I was so obviously inexperienced . . . that he could not bring himself actually to become my lover.[2]

When Ada asked why Margaret Morris no longer visited Addison Road, Galsworthy made some excuse and then his wife broke down. It was impossible for him to lie to her. He told Margaret that she had said she would not stand between them and that the marriage was unchanged. Margaret wrote to Ada, who replied:

You must not be unhappy, but very happy – first love at your age – can there be anything more holy! And you must not think of me – I am content . . . Yours in love . . .[3]

But they were words. Ada was no Jane Wells who could let her husband love two women at the same time. Rather than endure an 'Eternal Triangle', she would have given him up entirely. When Margaret saw him later that day, he looked 'years older', and from that time they were never alone together. Within a week he took his wife to France.

Another month and he wrote from Beaulieu, addressing her as 'Dear dear child':

. . . I didn't want you to despair. But in very very truth there . . . can be no better for her unless all ends between us. I have watched it day by day . . . such torture and misery . . . So my poor dear it must be Goodbye . . . forget and forgive me![4]

1 Margaret Morris: *My Galsworthy Story* (1967), p. 56.
2 *Ibid.*, pp. 56–7.
3 *Ibid.*, pp. 57–8.
4 *Ibid.*, p. 69.

They corresponded for another eighteen months. In all, sixty-seven letters passed between them. His final letter, from Switzerland, enclosed a cheque for the studio rent – '. . . don't bother to acknowledge it'. She married a painter, J. D. Fergusson.

Much has been made of the reserved and stoical Galsworthy, but Margaret Morris knew another and passionate side, and Ada must have known it also. In his diary from 1910, there occasionally appears a rounded capital A. It has been interpreted as the symbol for when he and Ada made love, which was not very often. Two years later, he had ended the affair with Margaret in a sudden resolve to take Ada first to France and then America, and it is claimed that from this time she turned him out of her bed for good.

But an unpublished version of his dedication to *The Forsyte Saga* reads:

. . . to my Wife, being, in the opinion of its author the best of his work, and the fittest to be dedicated to the dearest and most lovely companion, the most faithful helpmate, and best natural critic a man ever had.[1]

When Quiller-Couch acknowledged the beautiful writing of *The Dark Flower* but confessed, 'I do not like this new book of his at all . . . no book about marriage in which the child is ignored can even begin to be a true book . . .', Galsworthy said in his reply:

I am probably the most happily married man in England. . . . I know . . . the value and beauty of a perfect union.[2]

1 H. V. Marrot: *The Life & Letters of John Galsworthy* (1935), p. 104.
2 21 Oct. 1913: *ibid.*, pp. 382–3.

CHAPTER THREE

Wives who were Eulogized

I

Like Galsworthy, a group of writers have eulogized their wives. After Ann's early death, DONNE declared that his love for her had led him to seek God.[1] Yet from a worldly point of view his marriage to a minor, without her father's consent and which terminated his employment with the Lord Keeper, had been a great disaster.

MILTON's short-lived second marriage was to Katherine Woodcock, who, like his first wife, died after childbirth. She is the subject of his sonnet:

> Methought I saw my late espousèd saint,
> Brought to me, like Alcestis, from the grave . . .

Harriet, the widow whom J. S. MILL married at forty-five, became 'a saint to be worshipped':

For seven and a half years that blessing was mine; for seven and a half only![2] . . . Her memory is to me a religion . . .[3]

LESLIE STEPHEN, an agnostic like Mill, told Julia, who became his second wife, she 'must not be angry if I put you in the place where my Saints ought to be'.[4] ERIC GILL never forgot a dream in which he was walking in heaven with his wife Mary and their children:

---

1 Eliot confided in the Rev. W. F. Stead that Dante's love for Beatrice, passing over into love of God, had also been his experience. But he was referring, not to his wife, to Emily Hale. Lyndall Gordon construes his acceptance of Valerie Fletcher, his second wife, in terms of George Herbert's mystical lyric: 'Love bade me welcome . . .' (*Eliot's New Life* (1988), pp. 244–5).
2 *Autobiography* (1873), p. 240. (It was published posthumously, edited by his stepdaughter, Helen Taylor.)
3 *Ibid, Published from the original MS. in the Columbia University Library* ed. Roger Howson: Preface by John Jacob Coss (1924), p. 170. A restored passage.
4 7 Aug. 1877.

We came upon our Lord . . . And I said to him: 'This is Betty . . . and this is Petra . . . and this is Joanna . . . and this is Gordian . . .,' and he shook hands with them all. And then I said: 'And this is Mary.' And he said: 'Oh, Mary and I are old friends.'[1]

It is only to be expected that STEELE, who said of Lady Elizabeth Hastings that 'to have loved her was a liberal education' – a compliment Thackeray called the finest perhaps ever offered to a woman – would show a respect for his wife and speak of her in a way that was untypical of his day. He called his second wife Mary (his 'dearest Prue') 'the beautifullest object in the world'. Some four hundred letters are extant that he wrote to her, accompanied by occasional guineas, little parcels of tea, or walnuts. In a dedication to one of his volumes he compared her with a guardian angel:

I cannot believe one of them to be more good in inclination, or more charming in form than my wife.

After being married two and a half years, he wrote:

I know no happiness in this life in any degree comparable to the pleasure I have in your person and society.[2]

Six or seven years later, he was writing:

. . . I know no one who deserves so much commendation as yourself, and to whom saying the best things would be so little like flattery . . . But, indeed, though you have every perfection, you have an extravagant fault . . . and that is, that you do not love to dress, to appear, to shine out, even at my request, and to make me proud of you, or rather to indulge the pride I have that you are mine . . .[3]

A few days before BLAKE died, three months before his seventieth birthday, he said to his wife:

'Stay! Keep as you are! *you* have been ever an angel to me: I will draw you!'[4]

– which he proceeded to do.

He had met Catherine Boucher, 'a very pretty brunette', when he was unhappy from a broken courtship. As soon as she saw the red-haired engraver her intuition told her that he would be her husband,

1 *Autobiography* (1940), pp. 208–9 Note.
2 7 Apr. 1710. Quoted by W. M. Thackeray: *The English Humourists of the 18th Century* (1853), p. 138 Note.
3 *Ibid.*, p. 145 Note.
4 Alexander Gilchrist: *Life of William Blake* (1863), i, p. 360.

and she nearly fainted away. They married in Battersea Parish Church on Sunday, 18 August 1782, he twenty-four, she twenty, and being the poor daughter of a market gardener she put a cross for her name. She 'proved herself one of the best wives that ever fell to the lot of a man of genius', wrote Mrs Anne Gilchrist.

They set up house at 23 Green Street, Leicester Fields. We read that she was jealous at first and then the cause was removed. Blake made provision by continuing to work hard at hackwork, but on his father's death two years later he partnered a print shop at 27 Broad Street, and his younger brother Robert came to live with them as his assistant and pupil. One day a quarrel arose between his brother and Kate in front of him. Blake thought she said things that were unjustified:

'Kneel down and beg Robert's pardon directly, or you never see my face again!'

She 'thought it very hard' since she was not at fault.

'Robert, I beg your pardon, I am in the wrong.'
'Young woman, you lie! [Robert retorted.] *I* am in the wrong!'[1]

Within just over two years Robert died, tenderly nursed by William. There was a move to 28 Poland Street, where Blake now instructed his wife as his only pupil. On rejection of *Songs of Innocence* he set about publication himself, saying that Robert in a dream had shown him a new technique – 'illuminated printing'. Next morning Kate spent 1s 10d of their last half-crown on materials. She learnt to pull impressions from a copperplate that had had its background etched away so that only relief lines printed. She helped to tint designs and marginal decoration, then to assemble the pages into covers. Hayley said of her:

. . . she draws, she engraves, & sings delightfully & is so truly the Half of her good Man, that they seem animated by one Soul, & that a soul of indefatigable Industry & Benevolence . . .

At Mrs Mathew's *conversazioni* at Rathbone Place, Nollekens Smith 'often heard' Blake 'read and sing several of his poems', to tunes 'most singularly beautiful'.[2] So they worked side by side singing, often

1 *Ibid*, i, pp. 58–9.
2 *Ibid.*, i, p. 47.

with the presence of children, but these were not their own. The 'songs of happy chear' were complemented five years later by *Songs of Experience*. Nearly all his books were made in this way. His greatest poems and illustrations – except his final masterpieces of the *Job* engravings and the Dante water-colours – would all be done (as were Wells's stories with Jane) in the early years.

When he was thirty-six they moved to 13 Hercules Buildings, Lambeth, a modest bungalow-type building, and it was at the end of its narrow rear garden which boasted a vine that Thomas Butts, the only patron of Blake's imaginative art, found them one day sitting naked in the summer-house.

'Come in!' Blake called. *'It's only Adam and Eve, you know!'*[1]

They had been reciting from *Paradise Lost* with the Garden of Eden around them. Blake taught his wife to see visions, just as he taught her to read, draw and become a skilful engraver. J. T. Smith, who knew both well, said that to this motherless wife 'Blake was at once lover, husband, child'. She would get up in the night when he was inspired to sketch or write, and so agonizing would be the ordeal 'that she had to sit motionless and silent' –

. . . only to stay him mentally, without moving hand or foot: this for hours, and night after night[2]

They had worked through their early struggle of wills and (in Lawrence's phraseology) 'the rainbow stood on the earth' and they 'met to the span of the heavens'.

When Blake was forty-two, the dilettante squire William Hayley gave an invitation to work for him at Felpham, Sussex. Before setting out with sixteen heavy boxes and portfolios, Blake wrote:

My dear & too careful and over-joyous woman has exhausted her strength. Eartham will be my first temple and altar; my wife's like a flame of many colours of precious jewels whenever she hears it named.[3]

The damp in winter affected their health, and he found his 'Corporeal Friend', Hayley, a 'Spiritual Enemy' in art. More frighteningly, Blake was tried at Chichester Quarter Sessions for uttering 'seditious and

1 *Ibid.*, i, p. 115.
2 *Ibid.*, i, p. 316.
3 Letter to Hayley: 16 Sept. 1800.

treasonable expressions' when he had thrown a soldier, John Schofield, out of their garden. His wife too, was involved, for Schofield deposed:

Blake said, My Dear, you would not fight against France – she replyed no, I would for Bonaparte as long as I am able.

Had it been six or so years before, when the invasion scare was greater, and Spy Nozy was watching Coleridge and the Wordsworths, there might have been a different result. The jury found 'William Blake . . . not Guilty . . .' Yet they were three relatively happy years in that cottage by the sea.

They returned to London to take the first floor of 17 South Molton Street. Here they were so poor that they lived on half a guinea a week, excluding rent. These were the years when a quartern loaf reached its famine price of 1s 10d. J. Bronowski reminded us that 'Blake lived in the most violent age of English history'.[1] He 'lived the Industrial Revolution . . . in the decay of his engraver's craft',[2] to which he had served a seven-year apprenticeship. It is not known how they lived for the last ten years at this address. But in all the years of their poverty they were never in debt. She must have been a provident housewife. We are told she was an excellent cook, and 'could even prepare a made dish, when need be'. She humoured him, as Gilchrist's illustration shows:

'The money is going, Mr Blake.' 'Oh, d— the money!' he would shout; 'it's always the money!'[3]

Making no further comment, she would go on serving what there was – until the empty plate reminded him that he must put aside his painting and writing, to work at his engraving.

After their final move to the first floor of 3 Fountain Court, he used to fetch the porter for their dinner from a house at the corner of the Strand. J. T. Smith said that Blake always lit the fire and put on the kettle for breakfast before his 'beloved Kate' awoke. When Blake was sixty-eight, Wordsworth's travelling companion, H. Crabb Robinson, visited them and wrote that she seemed the one woman to make him happy:

1 *A Man Without a Mask: William Blake 1757–1827* (1944), p. 127.
2 *Ibid.*, p. 86.
3 Alexander Gilchrist: *Life of William Blake* (1863), i, p. 313.

She had been formed by him. Indeed, otherwise, she could not have lived with him . . . She had . . . an implicit reverence for her husband.[1]

She must have been in Samuel Palmer's mind when he paid tribute to their home – like an artisan's with its unmistakable signs of hardship. Blake worked in a little bedroom overlooking the river; everything was clean, everything in place.

He ennobled poverty, and, by his conversation and the influence of his genius, made two small rooms in Fountain Court more attractive than the threshold of princes.[2]

She told Smith that on the day of his death he was composing and singing hymns so sweetly that she rose to hear them better, and when she had expressed this to him he looked at her most affectionately and exclaimed:

'My beloved! they are *not mine. No!* they are *not* mine!'[3]

He went on to tell her that after his death they would not be parted and he would always be near to take care of her. Never in their lives did they have our problem about a boundary between the material and the spiritual. He once said death meant no more to him than to pass from one room into another.[4]

THOMAS MOORE married at thirty-one a young actress, Bessie Dyke. 'From . . . the year of his marriage . . . to that of his death,' – over forty years –

this excellent and beautiful person received from him the homage of a lover, enhanced by all the gratitude, all the confidence, which the daily and hourly happiness he enjoyed were sure to inspire.[5]

---

1 *Diary, Reminiscences, & Correspondence* ed. Thomas Sadler (1869), ii, p. 383. 17 Dec. 1825.
2 Letter to Alexander Gilchrist: 23 Aug. 1855.
3 Alexander Gilchrist: *Life of William Blake* (1863), i, p. 361.
4 Hardy, according to St John Ervine, quoted it as his own, and when Ervine quoted it to Shaw, Shaw nodded his head. 'That's how I think of it,' he said. Cf. Tennyson: 'Gone for a minute, my son, from this room into the next . . .' (*The Grandmother*: xxvi.)
5 The Rt. Hon. Lord John Russell, MP: *Memoirs, Journal & Correspondence of Thomas Moore* (1853–6), i, p. xi, Preface.

II

DE QUINCEY married at thirty-one Margaret Simpson, the eighteen-or nineteen-year-old daughter of a substantial Westmorland farmer, his near neighbour at Grasmere. He called her his Electra, 'the dear companion of my later years'. In two passages of his *Confessions* he refers to her 'angelic smiles'.

Paint me . . . a room seventeen feet by twelve, and not more than seven and a-half feet high . . . Make it populous with books; and, furthermore, paint me a good fire; and furniture plain and modest, befitting the unpretending cottage of a scholar. And near the fire paint me a tea-table; and (as it is clear that no creature can come to see one on such a stormy night) place only two cups and saucers on the tea-tray . . . And, as it is very unpleasant to make tea, or to pour it out for one's-self, paint me a lovely young woman sitting at the table. Paint her arms like Aurora's, and her smiles like Hebe's; but no, dear M—! not even in jest let me insinuate that thy power to illuminate my cottage rests upon a tenure so perishable as mere personal beauty, or that the witchcraft of angelic smiles lies within the empire of any earthly pencil . . .[1]

But a year or so after a happy marriage his private means finally collapsed.

For nearly two years I believe that I read nothing and studied nothing.[2]

He sat amongst his five thousand books in Dove Cottage, Grasmere, taking a daily dose of laudanum that had accelerated to 8,000, 10,000 and even 12,000 drops.

Margaret's care of him through the worst years of his opium agonies at Grasmere finds a parallel with Fanny's lifetime and devoted nursing of Stevenson.

For thou thoughtest not much to stoop to humble offices of kindness, and to servile ministrations of tenderest affection; to wipe away for years the unwholesome dews upon the forehead, or to refresh the lips when parched and baked with fever; nor even when thy own peaceful slumbers had by long sympathy become infected with the spectacle of my dread contest with phantoms and shadowy enemies that oftentimes bade me 'sleep no more' – not even then didst thou utter a complaint or any murmur, nor withdraw thy

1 *The Collected Writings of Thomas De Quincey* ed. David Masson (1889–90), iii, pp. 409–10.
2 *Ibid.*, iii, p. 377.

angelic smiles, nor shrink from thy service of love, more than Electra did of old.[1]

Listening to his garbled speech at night, she would turn to him and cry: 'Oh, what do you see, dear? what is it that you see?' For the crocodile he had a special aversion.

So often did this hideous reptile haunt my dreams that many times the very same dream was broken up in the very same way: I heard gentle voices speaking to me . . . and instantly I awoke; it was broad noon, and my children were standing hand in hand, at my bedside, come to show me their coloured shoes, or new frocks, or to let me see them dressed for going out. No experience was so awful to me, and at the same time so pathetic, as this abrupt translation from . . . the unutterable abortions of miscreated gigantic vermin to the sight of infancy and innocent *human* nature.[2]

Somehow realizing that 'death by brain-fever or by lunacy' could not be far away, and 'considering how important my life had become to others besides myself',[3] he 'weaned' himself to three hundred drops, 'with a difficulty that is past all description'. Her life with him often meant separation, first when he was working in London, and then Edinburgh, before the move from Dove Cottage to be with him there. It recalls Tetty having to be away from Johnson, who was toiling in a similar way to De Quincey.

III

SHELLEY dedicated *Queen Mab* to his first wife:

> Whose eyes have I gazed fondly on,
> And loved mankind the more?
> Harriet! on thine – thou wert my purer mind;
> Thou wert the inspiration of my song . . .

Three years later he eloped the second time, and took Mary Wollstonecraft Godwin, together with her stepsister Jane ('Claire'), to the Continent. In Paris Mary reminded Shelley that it was his twenty-second birthday, and when they were on the Rhine Mary celebrated her seventeenth; Jane Clairmont was only sixteen. Claire Tomalin

1 *Ibid.*, iii, p. 377.
2 *Ibid.*, iii, p. 443.
3 *Ibid.*, iii, p. 447.

pays tribute to Shelley's journeys: 'in terms of sheer organizing ability required and fatigue . . . particularly when one thinks of the state of the roads, the inns and transport available'.[1] After six weeks they returned to London and had to be separated to evade their creditors. In a letter at this time, Shelley calls her 'the subtlest and most exquisitely fashioned intelligence . . . among women there is no equal mind to yours!'[2] Next day he writes:

I believe I must become in Mary's hands, what Harriet was in mine . . . how, beyond measure, reverencing and adoring the intelligence that governs me![3]

Francis Thompson corrected Coventry Patmore and said that Shelley 'left a woman not because he was tired of her arms, but because he was tired of her soul'.[4]

Mary went with him without the assurance of marriage that Harriet had been given, and only after two and a half years did that unexpected possibility arise. At first they moved from one lodging to another, largely around Kentish Town, living on post-obit borrowing – her father doing nothing to see, in Shelley's words, 'that . . . a young family, innocent, and benevolent and united, should not be confounded with prostitutes and seducers'.[5] Nine months after their marriage, and now twenty-five, he addresses her in a dedicatory poem to *The Revolt of Islam*:

> So now my summer-task is ended, Mary,
> And I return to thee, mine own heart's home;
> As to his Queen some victor Knight of Faery,
> Earning bright spoils for her enchanted dome;
> Nor thou disdain, that ere my fame become
> A star among the stars of mortal night,
> If it indeed may cleave its natal gloom,
> Its doubtful promise thus I would unite,
> With thy beloved name, thou Child of love and light . . .
>
> They say that thou wert lovely from thy birth
> Of glorious parents thou aspiring Child:
> I wonder not . . .

1 *Shelley & his World* (1980), p. 74.
2 27 Oct. 1814.
3 28 Oct. 1814.
4 *Shelley* (1909), p. 36.
5 Letter to Godwin, 6 Mar. 1816.

Few would now deny that the golden-haired, hazel-eyed daughter of Mary Wollstonecraft and William Godwin, with high forehead, was a more suitable partner than Harriet, the tragic victim of what Richard Garnett regarded as 'the greatest misfortune' of Shelley's life – 'his imprudent marriage'.[1] Shelley told Peacock:

Everyone must know that the partner of my life should be one who can feel poetry and understand philosophy. Harriet is a noble animal, but she can do neither.[2]

At Casa Ricci in Leghorn, when he was nearly twenty-eight, they finished reading Virgil together, and two days later began Lucretius. 'It is not our custom, when we can help it,' Shelley wrote, referring to himself and Mary, 'to divide our pleasures.' He wrote to Peacock:

I want Jones's Greek Grammar very much for Mary, who is deep in Greek.[3]

She was *La Gloriosa donna della mia mente*. But the woman in her missed society more than he. Also, inconsistently, she was jealous of Claire. The death of Mary's third child, Clara, may be compared with the watershed in Harriet's life when Ianthe was born. She blamed Shelley for being caught up with Byron at the time and from then on Mary became, to a certain extent, a conventional wife. She scolded him at the Casa Magni when she was at table with Claire and Jane Williams and he suddenly appeared naked from the beach, crossing the room behind the maid-servant – a disconcerting incident made worse by his breaking cover to explain!

There were his 'Italian Platonics' directed towards Emilia Viviani, a girl like a Greek statue. An acquaintance of the Viviani family had told them of the Governor of Pisa immuring his elder daughter of nineteen in the Convent of St Anna until a suitor who did not want a dowry could be found. Shelley, Mary and Claire visited her many times, and he began a great love poem calling on:

> . . . ye, bright regents, with alternate sway,
> Govern my sphere of being, night and day!
> Thou [= Mary], not disdaining even a borrowed might;
> Thou [= Emilia], not eclipsing a remoter light . . .[4]

1 *DNB*.
2 *Memorials of Shelley* (1860).
3 Edward Dowden: *The Life of Percy Bysshe Shelley* (1886), ii, pp. 333–4.
4 *Epipschydion* (1821) ll. 360–3.

Emilia wrote to Mary:

You seem to me a little cold sometimes . . . but I know that your husband said well when he said that your apparent coldness is only *the ash which covers an affectionate heart*.[1]

With unexpected bathos Emilia married Biondi, the man her father had found.

Towards the end, at Casa Magni, Shelley used to draw their monthly allowance from Leghorn. On his return, he emptied the bag of coins on the floor and, using a fire-shovel and his foot, made a kind of cake which he cut in half with the shovel. One part was for rent and housekeeping, the other again divided between Mary and himself. But that was theoretical. His went to the insatiable Godwin; Claire, unbefriended by Byron, the father of her child; the improvident Hunts – anyone but himself. Raymond Mortimer spoke of De Quincey's 'hatred and contempt for money'. We see the same contempt and disdain in Shelley's use of the fire-shovel and foot.

Two months before he drowned, he probably saved Mary's life. A miscarriage had caused her to lose a great deal of blood.

. . . for seven hours I lay nearly lifeless . . . At length, ice was brought . . . it came before the doctor, so Claire and Jane [Williams] were afraid of using it; but Shelley overruled them, and by an unsparing application of it I was restored.[2]

Recollection of the lectures he had attended at St Bartholomew's Hospital at the time of his lodging in Poland Street had prompted him to make her sit in the ice, preventing further haemorrhage.

Two days later he made perhaps the severest, yet still a gentle, censure of Mary in a letter to John Gisborne:

. . . Italy is more and more delightful to me . . . I only feel the want of those who can feel, and understand me. Whether from proximity and the continuity of domestic intercourse, Mary does not . . . It is the curse of Tantalus that a person possessing such excellent powers and so pure a mind as hers, should not excite the sympathy indispensable to their application to domestic life.[3]

The *cor cordium*, which Trelawny snatched from the funeral pyre, passed at Mary's urgent request from Leigh Hunt to her, and after

1 24 Dec. 1820.
2 Letter to Mrs Gisborne, June 1822.
3 18 June 1822.

her death were found in a copy of *Adonais*, under silk, the ashes she had treasured. To show how far she had come, Matthew Arnold told of her *cri de coeur* when she was choosing a school for her surviving son Percy. Someone had given the advice: 'Oh, send him where they will teach him to think for himself!'

. . . Mrs Shelley answered: 'Teach him to think for himself? Oh my God, teach him rather to think like other people!'[1]

Francis Thompson declared:

. . . few poets were so mated before, and no poet was mated afterwards, until Browning stooped and picked up a fair-coined soul that lay rusting in a pool of tears.[2]

IV

Nine years after marriage, ROBERT BROWNING wrote *By the Fireside*, which contains what may be described as the final expression of love between man and woman:

> My own, see where the years conduct!
> At first, 'twas something our souls
> Should mix as mists do; each is sucked
> Into each now . . .

In his first letter to ELIZABETH BARRETT, he told her: 'I love your verses with all my heart' and added: ' – and I love you too.'[3] Four months afterwards, between 3.0 and 4.30 p.m. on 20 May 1845, they met in her room on the second floor back, at 30 Wimpole Street. She was thirty-nine and he was thirty-three.

Her widowed father, whose wealth was derived from Jamaican estates worked by slaves, had forbidden his eight grown-up sons and three daughters to marry, and was morbidly – if not unnaturally – possessive of Elizabeth, his eldest child. He had created a psychological condition surrounding her delicate health, so that restricted in movement she lived with her curtains drawn. Yet, contrary to legend, when she told her father that Browning had called he did not seem very interested.

1 *Essays in Criticism: Second Series* (1888), pp. 205–6.
2 *Shelley* (1909), p. 38.
3 10 Jan. 1845.

'I do not want to see your literary friends.'

Rosalie Mander draws attention to the inconsistency of Victorian behaviour.[1] For one and a half hours Elizabeth, unchaperoned, received a strange gentleman in her bedroom.

A short time after that meeting Browning had fallen in love and, even though believing her to be an incurable invalid, made her an offer of marriage. It is possible she may not have broken free from her father if he had not, at first, refused her doctors' request for her to winter in Italy. However, when they repeated urgently that to face another English winter would risk her health, he gave written consent provided that, contrary to her wishes, no brother or sister accompanied her. Browning suggested to her that they should go together as man and wife.

There followed what Chesterton called 'possibly the best poem that she produced'.[2] She asked her sister to hire a carriage to take her to Regent's Park and, upon there alighting, she walked a little way on the grass; then, leaning against a tree, she gazed at the sky and foliage denied her so long. Mingled in her thoughts must have been gratitude to her father for encouraging her studies and writing when she was a girl, and his pride in her fame.

On Saturday morning, 12 September 1846, on the arm of Wilson, her maid, she got downstairs and managed to reach a chemist, where she bought some smelling-salts. Together they walked to the cab rank in Marylebone Road to hire a fly for the short journey to St Marylebone Parish Church, where a secret marriage took place. A week later she eloped with Browning for Italy, accompanied by her maid and dog Flush. She never saw her father again. He cut her off, putting her books in store and charging her rental, and when he died over ten years later there were no messages for her. Even her brothers suspected that Browning, whose books brought in nothing, was after her small inherited income and royalties.

She became pregnant within a month of marriage, but this resulted in the first of numerous miscarriages. After a brief stay in Pisa, they moved to Florence for their permanent home: a flat in Casa Guidi, near the Pitti Palace. Before long the invalid of Wimpole Street had responded to her husband's vitality and to the Italian sun. Cheerfully

1 *Mrs Browning* (1980), p. 42.
2 *Robert Browning* (1903), p. 78.

she let herself be dragged uphill in a wine hamper; she ascended mountain peaks at 4.0 a.m., and rode for miles on a donkey. Their only child, Robert ('Pen'), was born when she was forty-three.

They visited England in the year of the Great Exhibition, on the way meeting Tennyson – in Strasbourg – who offered them the use of his house at Twickenham. In London they met Elizabeth's sister Henrietta and brother George, also John Forster, the Carlyles, Rossetti, and Coleridge's daughter Sara. (Afterwards they made yearly visits, always steering clear of the family home.) Next year they met the Ruskins and Kingsley, but only Browning could attend the christening of Hallam Tennyson, Elizabeth being unwell. Browning tossed the baby up in his arms and Tennyson commented: 'Ah, that's as good as a glass of champagne.' In Rome, a year later, they met Thackeray and his daughters, the elder, Anny, now sixteen. 'It was Browning who told us where to go,' she wrote.

One can hardly imagine a more ideal spot for little girls to live than that to which he directed us – to a great apartment over the pastry-cook's in the Palazzo Poniatowski, in the Via Della Croce.[1]

Two years afterwards, Browning appended to his collection of poems *Men and Women* some verses entitled *One Word More: To E.B.B.*, which contain the refrain:

> Take them, Love, the book and me together:
> Where the heart lies, let the brain lie also.

When they discovered the maid Wilson was pregnant by another servant, Ferdinando Romagnoli, the Brownings saw to it that they were married at the British Consulate. The couple remained in their service and in later years Pen continued to employ them. The Brownings found room for Landor, when he was turned out by his family after making over all his property. In Rome they met Joseph Severn, at that time the British Consul aged sixty-seven, and Elizabeth questioned him about the last days of Keats, who had died in his arms.

I made him tell me the most minute details – some very painful.

There was also a visit by Hans Andersen.

Back at Casa Guidi the following year, she found it too tiring to

1 Lady Ritchie: *Chapters from Some Unwritten Memoirs* (1894), p. 178.

walk up and down their verandah as of old. When she was too weak to get up, Browning carried her out on to the balcony so that she could see across to San Felice, at which they had gazed so often. She caught a chill and on Friday, 28 June 1861, Pen went to his mother's bedside; he always said goodnight twice. He asked if she were really better and she assured him: 'Much better.' During the early hours she awoke and Browning fed her with jelly.

Then came . . . the most perfect expression of her love to me within my whole knowledge of her – always smilingly, happily, and with a face like a girl's – and in a few minutes she died in my arms, her head on my cheek . . . Her last word . . . when I asked 'How do you feel?' – '*Beautiful*.'[1]

Browning returned slowly to London, with twelve-year-old Pen. Much of his work was still to come, but he was bereft. Eight years later, when he was fifty-seven, he stayed with Lady Ashburton in Scotland and proposed marriage but she refused him. Whether he was prompted to ease his loneliness or, as he rationalized to her, it was for the sake of Pen, he would never erase his 'very own Ba'. That same year his masterpiece began to appear, in this he invoked 'from the realms of help':

> O lyric Love, half-angel and half-bird
> And all a wonder and a wild desire . . .[2]

V

TENNYSON spoke of Emily Sellwood, for whom he had waited fourteen years:

The peace of God came into my life before the altar when I married her.[3]

Dean INGE applied these words to himself,[4] and thirty-four years after his own wedding TROLLOPE wrote:

Perhaps I ought to name that happy day as the commencement of my better life.

1 Browning's letter to Miss Haworth: 20 July 1861.
2 *The Ring & the Book* (1868–9), i, p. 72.
3 *Alfred Lord Tennyson: A Memoir by his Son* (1897), i, p. 329.
4 See *Vale* (1934), p. 27.

In Fairy Wood, at Somersby, TENNYSON met Emily, a girl of seventeen, walking with his friend Arthur Hallam. He said: 'Are you a Dryad or an Oread wandering here?'[1] He fell in love with her at twenty-six, when she was a bridesmaid at her sister's wedding. For four years they exchanged letters and then Emily's father forbade the correspondence. Henry Sellwood disapproved of Tennyson on the grounds of bohemianism, addiction to port and tobacco, and latitudinarian religious views. (When KINGSLEY asked a future sister-in-law why she objected to his own marriage, she replied: 'My objection is *you*.')

After ten years' separation, the author of *The Princess* was in a position honourably to offer his wife a home. He married when he was over forty, and the same month published his elegy on Arthur Hallam. He had been writing *In Memoriam* since he was twenty-four, and its publication curiously parallels the consummation of his love. Their son wrote:

It was she who became my father's adviser in literary matters . . .[2]

She dealt with his world-wide correspondence. At eighty-three, his last book, *The Death of OEnone*, he dedicated to her:

> There on the top of the down . . .
> I thought to myself I would offer this book to you,
> This, and my love together,
> To you that are seventy-seven,
> With a faith as clear as the heights of the June-blue heaven,
> And a fancy as summer-new
> As the green of the bracken amid the gloom of the heather.

Edmund Gosse, as a boy, eavesdropped on a party where the grown-ups were giving their answers to: 'What is the most beautiful thing in the world?' He remembered KINGSLEY, then grey-haired, solemnly answering: 'My wife's eyes.'

A few months after his marriage, at twenty-five, Kingsley wrote:

I am all naked and *half* without you.

Twenty years later, he wrote:

1 *A Memoir, cit.*, i, p. 148.
2 *Ibid.*, i, p. 331.

I dreamt of you last night in *all* your beauty and loved you. I won't say more for fear the letter should miscarry.[1]

When she was believed to be dying, they agreed together on an epitaph: 'Amavimus, amamus, amabimus.' He left his bed, where *he* was actually the one dying, and evaded his nurse to sit by her for a few moments in a bedroom in another part of the house, holding her hand. 'This is heaven,' he said.[2]

VI

In precarious health and with very limited money, STEVENSON turned his back on family and friends to cross an ocean and a continent so that he might join a married American woman ten years older, who had a grown-up daughter, a ten-year old son, and contemplated divorce. Two years later, at the age of twenty-nine, he married Fanny Osbourne (née Van de Grift), who was nearly forty, at San Francisco. (Belloc walked across America to propose to Elodie Hogan, and she refused him. He went by train and she accepted him.)

Stevenson was to tell his mother that his marriage had been 'the most successful in the world':

She is everything to me: wife, brother, sister, daughter and dear companion; and I would not change to get a goddess or a saint. So far, after four years of matrimony.[3]

After nine years of marriage he wrote the lyric:

> Trusty, dusky, vivid, true,
> With eyes of gold and bramble-dew,
> Steel-true and blade-straight
> The great artificer
> Made my mate . . .
>
> Teacher, tender, comrade, wife,
> A fellow-farer true through life,
> Heart-whole and soul-free
> The august father
> Gave to me.

1 Susan Chitty: *The Beast & the Monk: A Life of Charles Kingsley* (1974), p. 89.
2 *Ibid.*, p. 295.
3 Graham Balfour: *The Life of Robert Louis Stevenson* (1901), i, pp. 205–6.

Two years before he died he wrote:

As I look back, I think my marriage was the best move I ever made in my life. Not only would I do it again; I cannot conceive the idea of doing otherwise.[1]

He had met Fanny when he was twenty-six, while staying at Fontainebleau. Separated from her husband, she had come to the artistic colony with her children to find country lodgings. Four years previously, Stevenson had fallen in love with another married woman, Frances Sitwell (with an even greater age difference). Fearful of similar scandal, his father now withdrew financial help when his son went to California, until Colvin told him of the approaching marriage and that the doctors, after a haemorrhage of the lungs, for the first time had diagnosed consumption. Then Stevenson received a cable assuring him that he could count on £250 a year, and he recognized his father's blessing.

When they came to the family home at 17 Heriot Row, Edinburgh, his mother wrote in her diary:

Fanny fitted into our household from the first.[2]

But the doctors were insistent there should be a move to the Swiss Alps. For fifteen years, against a background of changing scenes, Fanny watched and nursed him. She wrote to Colvin from Bournemouth:

I had to lift Louis in and out of bed ten times in one night. [He refused to use 'invalids' appliances'.] He was quite off his head and would not be contradicted because he was bleeding at the lungs at the same time and got into such furies when I wasn't quick enough.

Sudden attacks when blood would spurt from his mouth were frightening. The strain told on her own health, and during his last years in Samoa her attacks of mental illness caused the roles of nurse and patient to be reversed. There were times when, aggravated by drugs, she had to be held down, raving, to her bed. During those last four years both her children, grandchild, mother-in-law, and cousin on a lengthy stay, made up their household. Stevenson was trying to cheer her from a depression when he suddenly died. She outlived him by twenty years.

1 *Ibid.*, i, p. 176.
2 Quoted by Jenni Calder: *RLS: A Life Study* (1980), p. 150.

VII

On a visit to Galway with their four-year-old son, JOYCE wrote to Nora in Trieste:

One moment I see you like a virgin or madonna . . .

His love was both in the convention and profane:

. . . the next moment I see you shameless, insolent, half naked and obscene!

The letter concluded:

I gave others my pride and joy. To you I give my sin, my folly, my weariness and sadness.[1]

Three days afterwards, in Dublin, he set her firmly in a shrine:

Guide me, my saint, my angel . . . *Everything* that is noble and exalted and deep and true and moving in what I write comes, I believe, from you. O take me into your soul of souls and then I will become indeed the poet of my race . . . My holy love . . . can it be that we are now about to enter the heaven of our life?[2]

On a second absence, following very shortly, he told her that his love was 'really a kind of adoration',[3] and referring to when she had chafed at being separated and to the constant fear of eviction by their landlord, he wrote:

If you leave me I shall live for ever with your memory, holier than God to me. I shall pray to your name.[4]

In one of the letters, he apostrophized her as a mother figure:

O that I could nestle in your womb like a child born of your flesh and blood . . .[5]

They had come together five years previously, when he was twenty-two and Nora Barnacle twenty. He asked her to accompany him on

1 2 Sept. 1909. Richard Ellmann: *James Joyce* (1959), p. 296.
2 5 Sept. 1909: *ibid.*, pp. 296–7.
3 27 Oct. 1909: *ibid.*, p. 315.
4 18 Nov. 1909: *ibid.*, p. 316.
5 5 Sept. 1909: *ibid.*, pp. 296–7.

borrowed money to the Continent, but wanted there to be no doubt about the 'hazardous life' that lay ahead:

My mind rejects the whole present social order and Christianity – home, the recognized virtues, classes of life, and religious doctrines.[1]

On principle, he would not let her wear a ring when she visited her mother with their daughter Lucia; 'to secure the inheritance under will', he married her when she was forty-seven. They remained together thirty-six years, until he died. Their home was a series of lodgings scattered throughout Italy, Switzerland and France. She had to contend not only with great poverty but his erratic life-style, which involved drinking at night and an entire lack of budgeting; while from their thirties he was often incapacitated, on the verge of going blind. She told her sister, echoing Jane Carlyle:

Being married to a writer is a very hard life.[2]

A baker's daughter, she did not even believe in his literary calling – unlike Blake's wife, who was more disadvantaged. He complained to his brother:

. . . she cares nothing for my art.[3] . . . With one entire side of my nature she has no sympathy and will never have any . . .

Yet one evening she misquoted his poem *O, sweetheart, hear you your lover's tale* – which 'made me think for the first time in nine months that I was a genuine poet'.[4] She wanted 'Jim' to give up writing, and thought he should have stuck to singing – 'To think he was once on the same platform with John McCormack!'[5] When he was working on *Finnegans Wake*, she asked:

Why don't you write sensible books that people can understand?[6]

For his part only one of the things that he had told her before they went away did he recant – if by rejecting 'recognized virtues' he meant family. Side by side with his 'boundless ambitions', to her and to their children he was constant, and loved them dearly. Her own moment

1 29 Aug. 1904: *ibid.*, p. 175.
2 *Ibid.*, p. 565.
3 To Stanislaus: 3 Dec. 1904. *Ibid.*, p. 195.
4 Ditto: 12 July 1905. *Ibid.*, p. 210.
5 The occasion was on 27 Aug. 1904, in the Antient Concert Rooms, Dublin.
6 Richard Ellmann: *James Joyce* (1959), p. 603.

of illumination came after his death, in a reply she gave to an interviewer who asked her about other important writers she had known:

Sure, if you've been married to the greatest writer in the world, you don't remember all the little fellows.[1]

VIII

c. s. lewis could not have gone further. He called his wife:

. . . my daughter and my mother, my pupil and my teacher, my subject and my sovereign; and always holding all these in solution, my trusty comrade, friend, shipmate, fellow-soldier. My mistress; but at the same time all that any man friend (and I have had good ones) has ever been to me. Perhaps more.[2]

His was one of the strangest marriages of all – undertaken at fifty-eight to save a woman, much younger, from extradition. There followed three years of ecstatic happiness. The bachelor don met Joy Davidman, writer and mother of two young boys, because she wrote him fan letters. Outspoken – even abrasive – New York Jewish, ex-communist, Christian convert, she was neither liked nor welcomed by many of his friends, who were almost exclusively collegiate and male. Before going back to America, she received a letter from her husband asking for a divorce in order to marry her cousin, who had been looking after the home while she was in Britain. When she returned, a divorced woman, to Oxford with her sons, she wanted British nationality; and the Anglican apologist married her secretively in a register office.

Six months later she had a fall and broke a leg. Terminal cancer was revealed, and it was only then that Lewis committed himself to his true feelings about her. He proclaimed his love by having a bedside wedding sanctified by his Church, and there was a service of divine healing. The disease went into remission and Lewis believed a miracle had taken place. He told Coghill: 'I never expected to have, in my

---

1 Her interview with John Prudhoe in Zurich, 1953: *ibid.*, p. 755.
2 *A Grief Observed* (1961), p. 39.

sixties, the happiness that passed me by in my twenties.'[1] He wrote of it:

For those few years, H. and I feasted on love . . . No cranny of heart or body remained unsatisfied.

Then again she became very ill and died in great pain. He lived three more years. The hitherto celibate man, who for the first time had allowed his emotions to be involved overwhelmingly, now had to reconcile her suffering and their fugitive happiness with his faith in a loving God. He went through his night of the soul.

When you are happy . . . you will be – or so it feels – welcomed with open arms. But go to Him when your need is desperate, when all other help is vain, and what do you find? A door slammed in your face, and a sound of bolting and double bolting on the inside.[2]

Gradually he came to realize that 'you can't see anything properly' with eyes 'blurred with tears . . . you are like the drowning man who can't be helped because he clutches and grabs'.[3] In the year after his death appeared *Letters to Malcolm: Chiefly on Prayer*, the last book prepared by him.

The letter that VIRGINIA WOOLF left on the mantelpiece before she drowned herself is as much a tribute to her as to her husband, for putting on record at such a time the debt she owed and for preserving her dignity as a human being to express it.

Dearest . . . You have given me the greatest possible happiness. You have been in every way all that anyone could be . . . I don't think two people could have been happier than we have been.

It is a story of 'Greater love . . .'

I know that I am spoiling your life, that without me you could work . . .[4]

1 *Letters of C. S. Lewis* ed. with *Memoir* by W. H. Lewis (1966), p. 23.
2 *A Grief Observed* (1961), pp. 9–10.
3 *Ibid.*, pp. 37–8.
4 Leonard Woolf: *The Journey Not the Arrival Matters* (1969), pp. 93–4.

CHAPTER FOUR

Some Courageous and Beautiful Wives

Particularly courageous wives were Bunyan's second and Milton's third. With a nine-year-old blind daughter, Mary, and three younger children, BUNYAN at thirty-one married his 'well-beloved' Elizabeth in the second year of his widowhood. Over a year later, when he was imprisoned for refusing to undertake not to preach again as a separatist, she fought courageously to have his case reviewed at the Assizes.

Elizabeth Minshall, whom MILTON married at fifty-five, took on a totally blind husband with three daughters, aged seventeen, fifteen and eleven, the elder ones fractious to Deborah, the youngest, who had been born a few days before their mother died. Without this discreet and effective woman, perhaps his greatest works four years afterwards would never have appeared.

There were some particularly beautiful wives: Pepys's 'young beauty', Sheridan's 'angel',[1] Jane Welsh Carlyle ('the flower of Haddington'), Watts-Dunton's young lady, and Virginia Woolf. Jane (née Burden), wife of WILLIAM MORRIS, inspired Rossetti to paint a large number of magnificent dream-like pictures belonging to his later phase. Her multiple portrait, life-sized, in warm crayon, 'with curled-up lips and amorous hair',[2] looked down on the young Beerbohm as the front door of No. 2 The Pines closed behind him. 'A remarkable woman,' said Watts-Dunton, 'a most remarkable woman; superior to Morris intellectually, she reached a greater mental height than he was capable of, yet few knew it.' He told 'how she had acquired French and Italian with the greatest ease and felicity'.

When Morris had met her she possessed very few educational advantages; yet she very quickly made good her shortcomings. When reminded that H. Buxton Forman had written that he had seen beautiful women in all quarters

---

1 i.e. his first wife, née Elizabeth Ann Linley.
2 Max Beerbohm: *And Even Now* (1920), p. 62.

of the globe, 'but never one so strangely lovely and majestic as Mrs Morris', Watts-Dunton remarked, 'She was the most lovely woman I have ever known, her beauty was incredible.'[1]

As an elderly lady she was brought to visit Mrs Sassoon, but six-year-old Siegfried stayed under the table.

Minny Thackeray, who married LESLIE STEPHEN, had grown into a beauty, her bronze hair setting off a delicate complexion. His second wife, Mrs Julia Duckworth, was one of the most beautiful women in England – as a girl, she was chosen for Burne-Jones's *Annunciation*. When MALCOLM MUGGERIDGE first visited his in-laws, he was immediately struck by the beauty of his aunt, BEATRICE WEBB, 'a beauty of bone rather than of flesh . . . so reminiscent of Kitty's'.[2] A. J. P. TAYLOR called Kitty Muggeridge 'staggeringly beautiful'.[3]

1 Theodore Watts-Dunton: *Old Familiar Faces* (1916), p. 10.
2 *Chronicles of Wasted Time* (1972–3), i, p. 147.
3 *A Personal History* (1983), p. 110.

CHAPTER FIVE
Lucky Marriages

I

Contrary to a popular view on artists generally, there does not seem hard support for the premiss that writers make bad or unfaithful marriage partners. MRS GASKELL, in addition to tending to a creditable literary career, never failed to support her husband, a Unitarian minister, in his pastoral work. Of their six children four daughters lived to grow up.

Although of an unsociable and inequable disposition, the Rev. William Gaskell had as emancipated a view of women as did the father of Beatrice Webb. He not only encouraged his wife to write but, unlike other husbands before the Married Women's Property Act, he allowed her complete control of her earnings. She was free to stay often with a continually increasing circle of friends – she stayed at Haworth Parsonage with Charlotte Brontë – and to make long visits to Italy, France and Germany.

Three years after Sir Andrew Clark had confirmed a very serious condition of the lungs, JOHN RICHARD GREEN at forty married Alice Stopford, herself a historian. Five years after their marriage, Sir Andrew had to tell her that her husband was terminally ill.

That night Green happened to say: 'I have so much work to do! If I could only finish my work!'[1] To relieve his anxiety his wife spent the night in drawing up a scheme which he began to carry out next day. Instead of the six weeks prognosticated by his physician, he survived nearly two more years. Unable to hold his pen, he dictated to her the revisions and conclusion of *The Making of England*. When this had been published, *The Conquest of England* went on until he said, 'Now I am weak, and can work no more.'[2] Enough had been done to enable her to bring it out a few months later.

1 *Letters of John Richard Green* ed. Leslie Stephen (1901), p. 398.
2 *Ibid.*, p. 401.

Before his marriage, in his first moments of success with his *Short History*, he had said: 'I know what men will say of me, "He died learning."' After Green's death, Humphry Ward added that they would also say:

He died loving.[1]

Sir Launder Brunton told Mrs Green that what had kept him alive was his dread of separation from her.

According to J. Dover Wilson, whose friendship with G. M. TREVELYAN extended sixty years and was 'so close that he always seemed to regard me as his son', Janet was 'the perfect wife for her serious-minded George'. She tramped with him all over Italy when he was writing his Garibaldi books.

She was 'endowed' with her Uncle Matthew Arnold's 'refusal to take things too seriously, however serious he might think them'. When Dover Wilson first met her at Trinity, she had already contracted the paralysis which was in the end to keep her in her chair.

But the spirit could never be in chains; it remained sweet and cheerful, even merry, as it must always have been. To her husband it was agony to watch the progress of the disease. He endured it with Meredithian stoicism . . .

Dover Wilson remembered being with them at the time of Janet's eightieth birthday, when suddenly he uttered a terrible cry ringing through the house: 'We ought to die when we are eighty! We ought to die when we are eighty!'[2] And Janet sat smiling in her chair.

MASEFIELD was a happily married man – 'abnormally human', as a visiting American journalist disappointedly recorded. 'The days that make us happy make us wise,' the poet said.

He had met Constance de la Cherois Crommelin when he was twenty-three, at one of Laurence Binyon's dinner parties. After four years at Cambridge, she was now a teacher at Miss Lawrence's school at Brighton (soon to become Roedean). She was eleven and a half years older than Masefield, whose formal education had finished on the Conway training ship. He told his sister Norah in a letter:

My lady is slightly older than I am, which, with such a bun-headed person as myself, is a jolly good thing.[3]

1 *Ibid.*, p. 402.
2 *Milestones on the Dover Road* (1969), pp. 30–1.
3 Undated: Constance Babington Smith: *John Masefield: A Life* (1978), p. 75.

Binyon was anxious about the age gap and felt responsible, but when Constance had misgivings Masefield wrote to her:

About this question of age, please believe me dearie that it *cannot* make any difference to my dear love of you.[1]

She gave birth to their second child, a son, when she was forty-three.

When his wife's looks began to fail he became infatuated with Elizabeth Robins, another much older woman, whom he actually called 'Mother'; she called him her 'little son'. But he admitted even to her:

She is my genius. I am only a pen. Her pen at my best, I hope; but all my talent comes from her.[2]

His attraction to other talented women and his worship of them never began a 'triangular' situation. He accepted his wife's guidance with regard to Lillah, Granville-Barker's wife:

I don't *think*, if I were you, I should go on dining with Mrs Barker any more. I fancy she rather loves having bevies of men round her when she is alone . . . This is said in jealousy *for* you, and for the regard that I want people to have for you . . .[3]

By the time of World War I, when Masefield was thirty-seven, Constance recorded in her diary:

When we were saying how kind our friends were to us, [Jan] said 'It's because we love each other so, that people like us.'[4]

At this time also, she was 'greatly surprised and moved' when he presented a new sonnet series to her:

It was wonderful having them, and they in themselves are most moving and beautiful.[5]

When he was fifty-four, Constance, now sixty-six, had a successful operation for a brain tumour. She lived until ninety-three and, in her last illness, tended by a nurse, the aged man insisted on doing what he could to help her. Nevill Coghill recalled that Masefield always passed the butter to his wife before anyone else had the chance to.

1 7 Apr. 1903: *ibid.*, p. 80.
2 Undated letter to Elizabeth Robins, quoted by Babington Smith: *ibid.*, p. 100.
3 Undated letter: *ibid.*, p. 95.
4 14 Jan. 1915: *ibid.*, p. 119.
5 7 Feb. 1915: *ibid.*, p. 121.

II

ALDOUS HUXLEY's marriage to Maria Nys was a very lucky one. Raymond Mortimer said:

She was his eyes, as Dorothy Wordsworth was her brother's . . .[1]

She was a Belgian refugee of barely eighteen, and Huxley met her at Garsington when he was twenty-two. He proposed on the lawn. During two ensuing years when working at the Air Board and at Eton, while she taught French in a furnished room, he never had second thoughts. Years later, she wrote to their married son:

Why, why in the world did Aldous choose me out of the many prettier, wittier, richer etc young girls? Why in the world did he come back to fetch me after two long years . . . ? Knowing all the time . . . that he could never teach me to write poetry or remember what I read in a book or spel . . .[2] He could sense . . . I was a steady one, and I could sense that I would be entirely devoted to his service for the rest of our lives.[3]

A year following their marriage, she had a dangerous time at the birth of this only child and she was advised not to have another.

Already, by Matthew's first birthday, they had adopted a life-style that would take them round the world and find them settling mainly in Florence, then Sanary, and finally California, with stays in Paris, Switzerland, the Albany, Spain, Mexico and New York in between. Packing her things in Sanary, Maria said:

We *may* go away . . . 'For long?' Who can tell? We're Gypsies.[4]

But they were gypsies of the sun, who spoke many languages without a foreign accent, and friends such as Edward Sackville-West (his pupil at Eton) and Raymond Mortimer tracked them down. When they lived at Suresnes, eight-year-old Matthew, who was on holiday from his school near Godalming, travelled by himself in a small plane from

1 'Huxley: divided spirit': *The Sunday Times* review of Sybille Bedford's *Aldous Huxley*, i (1973).
2 Letter to Matthew Huxley, 1952: Sybille Bedford: *Aldous Huxley: A Biography* (1973–4), i, p. 95.
3 Ditto: *ibid.*, ii, pp. 135–6.
4 *Ibid.*, i, p. 327.

Croydon. An Italian maid, Rina, was with them seven years till she married. There were Giulia, the cook, and a Tuscan girl, Camilla.

The pace was relaxed, harmonious, yet in a way simple – granted the 'Sun, roses, fruit, warmth'. They breakfasted late and then he went to his room to fulfil the three-yearly contracts of his publisher, Chatto & Windus. At one o'clock there was sunbathing – on the roof at Villa Huley. To Sophie, their seven-year-old niece, they were 'a couple out of a fairy tale', and she watched them swim out slowly, side by side, 'with straw hats on, discussing important subjects'.[1] In the afternoon he painted. After tea there was more work before a further swim or baths. They dined in immaculate white cottons. Their day finished listening to the gramophone as they swung in garden hammocks. When thirty-year-old Matthew informed them of his approaching wedding, Huxley wrote to him:

After thirty years of it, I can say I am definitely for matrimony . . .[2]

His biographer writes that for thirty-six years, in sickness and in health, Maria 'resolved . . . that he should be spared concerns extraneous to his work and thoughts, should be free, above all should feel free, of any domestic and practical demands'.[3] She even went so far as to compromise herself in his short-lived affairs, by parcelling the book that he would send instead of flowers. Only one of these romances was different, and this was with Nancy Cunard, when he was twenty-eight. Maria packed, to impel him to make up his mind. She packed all night, and absently and miserably he sometimes lent a hand. In the morning, exhausted, she threw everything unpacked out of the window; then suddenly, without breakfast or further ado, they left England together for Italy.

With their newly found pleasure in motoring, they toured the 'richness' of that land – at the wheel Maria, the competent driver, not he, because of his eyes – travelling over a million miles without ever an accident. In hotel registers she entered 'chauffeur' under profession; she was also 'his personal relationship interpreter', the archetypical woman who relied on intuition where he employed thought. Often unwell, not helped by pregnancies which had to be terminated, she typed his books, although hastily with some mistakes; she preserved

1 *Ibid.*, i, p. 236.
2 9 Dec. 1949: *ibid.*, ii, p. 111.
3 *Ibid.*, i, p. 118.

his friendships and guarded his working time. She read aloud to him *Ape and Essence* for four and a quarter hours. They were so close that after her death he spoke of 'amputation'.[1]

When Huxley was fifty-seven, she was seriously ill. A cyst, found to be malignant, was removed, and the prognosis kept from him. She wrote to her sister Jeanne:

You do know for how many years we've loved Aldous and known his goodness and his sweetness and his honesty – but you also know how tiring, in spite of all this, he was to live with . . . Well now . . . his attitude is not the same . . . he even decides his own decisions . . . he also *offers* his services, whereas up to now he has always been content to offer a little money rather than to pay with his person, or rather with his soul . . . My illness . . . has been both the starting point and the arrival of this development.[2]

But the process began four years earlier, when she had written to the same sister:

. . . he assured me that he never misses his brilliant friends . . . He doesn't want conversational fireworks any more . . . Aldous . . . has become a very remarkable human being . . .[3]

It was not a subjective idea of hers. Raymond Mortimer, discussing the climate of the Los Angeles region and its enervating effect upon the critical faculty, wrote:

. . . his character took on a new beauty. He had always been brave, generous and kind. Now, thanks chiefly to Maria, he became far more human and approachable . . . [he] became himself absolutely selfless . . . a saint.[4]

When Huxley was sixty, Maria insisted of a French specialist that her condition be confided to *her*, for her husband had a book to finish and peace of mind was essential. The same night, while Huxley was in the hotel, laid low by a new attack of bronchitis, she told her sister and brother-in-law in their home that she mustn't be the one to die first – that relentlessly, bit by bit, she had to fight so that he would have her with him all his life. A year after her death and now sixty-one, he married Laura Archera, twenty years younger. He wrote to his son and daughter-in-law:

1 *Ibid.*, i, p. 152.
2 Apr. 1952: Sybille Bedford: *Aldous Huxley: A Biography* (1973–4), ii, p. 131.
3 19 Mar. 1947: *ibid.*, ii, p. 80.
4 Review of Bedford: *op. cit.*: *The Sunday Times*: 15 Sept. 1974.

I had a sense for a time that I was being unfaithful to that memory. But tenderness, I discover, is the best memorial to tenderness.[1]

Four years later, a malignant tumour on the back of his tongue responded to a radium-needle treatment. Two and three years afterwards, other tumours appeared on his neck. He died on the day President Kennedy was assassinated, and Laura helped him, telling him to let go, as he had helped Maria.

III

Cyril Connolly said of Eileen (née O'Shaughnessy), the wife of ORWELL during his creative period:

Very charming . . . intelligent . . . and she loved him . . . and although she didn't wear make-up or anything like that, she was very pretty, and totally worthy of him as a wife; he was very proud of her.[2]

Orwell had met her through the landlady of his Parliament Hill flat when Eileen was studying at University College for a higher degree in Educational Psychology, and she accepted the ways of this lonely and enigmatic man. A £500 advance for *The Road to Wigan Pier* enabled him to take the plunge. He told Geoffrey Gorer, who had written to him after *Burmese Days*:

I should never be economically justified in marrying so might as well be unjustified now as later . . . it will always be hand to mouth as I don't see myself ever writing a best-seller.[3]

He got things back to front – driving with his bride to church, and there carrying her in his arms from the gate to the porch.

Gorer said that the only times he ever saw Orwell happy were during the first year of marriage. Paul Potts, a poet whom Orwell had befriended, spoke of 'a real marriage, not perfect' –

But nothing except her death, that came so suddenly and too early, would have broken it up.[4]

---

1 19 Mar. 1956: *op. cit.*, ii, p. 213.
2 Melvyn Bragg's BBC *Omnibus* production. Quoted by Bernard Crick: *George Orwell: A Life* (1980), p. 173.
3 May 1936. Bernard Crick: *George Orwell: A Life* (1980), p. 199.
4 *Dante Called You Beatrice* (1960), p. 75.

They made their first home at Wallington – he thirty-three, and she two years older. The tiny cottage, which they rented for 7s 6d a week, had a corrugated iron roof, no bathroom, and a privy in the garden. He banged his head on the beams. From a little shop in one of the two ground-floor rooms, Eileen served small groceries, and sweets to village children. When she visited her favourite brother, Orwell grumbled because the serving of these ha'p'orths interrupted his writing of *The Road to Wigan Pier*. He dug the fair-sized garden for vegetables and built a coop for chickens and geese. Across the road he leased a patch of ground to keep a couple of goats.

After a little over six months, he joined the militia of the Workers' Party of Marxist Unification[1] in the Spanish Civil War. Two more months, and Eileen went to work in the office of the Independent Labour Party in Barcelona. She found him at Monflorite, attending a field hospital with a poisoned hand, and spent three days near the front. Shortly after she left, he wrote:

Dearest, you really are a wonderful wife. When I saw the cigars my heart melted away.[2]

She was at his side a whole week at Tarragona, when he had the narrow escape of a sniper's bullet through his throat. Discharged from the POUM, he rejoined Eileen at Barcelona during a police purge and they tried to get a friend out of prison at considerable risk to themselves.

Back at Wallington, a tubercular lesion on his lung began to haemorrhage badly. He was taken into Preston Hall, Aylesford, for nearly six months, and Eileen made the difficult and costly journey fortnightly. A fellow patient recalled 'Mrs Blair' as 'a charming lady who was much interested in us'.[3] On the outbreak of war she took a job in the Censorship Department in Whitehall, coming to Wallington at weekends, while Orwell finished *Inside the Whale*.

In May 1940, they shut up The Stores and moved into a two-room, fourth-floor flat with no lift, above 18 Dorset Chambers, Chagford Street, near Regent's Park. His diary the following month contains an entry:

1 Partido Obrero de Unificacion Marxista (POUM).
2 Feb. 1937: Bernard Crick: *George Orwell: A Life* (1980), p. 218.
3 *Ibid.*, p. 242.

Thinking always of my island in the Hebrides, which I suppose I shall never possess or see.[1]

The loss of her favourite brother, attending the wounded at Dunkirk, caused Eileen to be depressed for perhaps eighteen months and their friends the Fyvels noticed her 'tired and drawn . . . drably and untidily dressed'.[2] Orwell and T. R. Fyvel had been introduced to each other earlier that year by their mutual publisher, Frederick Warburg. Fyvel had 'a strong feeling' that Eileen 'did not really like pubs but . . . loyally sat alongside Orwell, sipping her beer'.[3]

After about a year they moved to a flat in St John's Wood, and after another year to a larger one in Maida Vale, at 10A Mortimer Crescent, where Fyvel described them living 'in reasonable discomfort'. Just before the last move, Eileen had transferred to the Ministry of Food, where, along with Lettice Cooper, she helped prepare radio broadcasts for The Kitchen Front. The wife of Johnson specially admired *The Rambler*; Orwell's wife was particularly fond of *Animal Farm*, which they used to discuss and plan as they lay in bed, a thing that had not happened with his other writing.[4]

With no children of their own, Orwell wanted to adopt a baby, but Eileen had been less inclined to give up her job. Now she relented, and the baby boy captivated them both. The month he arrived their flat was bombed by a 'doodle-bug', and they were lent a flat at 106 George Street before they rented 276 Canonbury Square.

A curious feature of their marriage was that while she always showed concern about his health, he seems to have ascribed any disquieting signs in her merely to work fatigue or war strain. Not that he was ever less cavalier towards himself. Despite such signs, nine months after they had received the baby he went abroad as a war correspondent. In just over a fortnight he was taken ill and, still forty-one, sent *Notes for My Literary Executor* for his wife to witness.

But Eileen had died under anaesthetic. Receiving the wire, two days delayed, he discharged himself from the hospital in Cologne and, wearing an army greatcoat, returned to London. He found an unfinished letter:

1 T. R. Fyvel: *George Orwell: a personal memoir* (1982), p. 154.
2 *Ibid.*, p. 105.
3 *Ibid.*, p. 118.
4 See letter to Dorothy Plowman, 19 Feb. 1946: *The Collected Essays, Journalism & Letters of George Orwell* ed. Sonia Orwell & Ian Angus (1968), iv, p. 104.

Dearest, I'm just going to have the operation . . .

She had feared cancer even before Richard's adoption, but did not tell him.

I wanted you to go away peacefully.[1]

There is the legend, created by less intimate friends, of a non-committal 'You know my wife has died' – 'Such a shame . . . a good old stick.'[2] But Gorer and Potts declare that he mourned visibly, with anguish. During that first week Potts heard him call two women by Eileen's name. Two others say that his tears, if brief, could not be checked. On going back to Europe, in Paris he met Malcolm Mugger-idge, who attempted 'some lame conversational remarks by way of sympathy; but he brushed them aside'. Muggeridge believed that under Orwell's 'enormous reticence', which his sister Avril said was inherited from their father, he was 'absolutely shattered'.[3] Fyvel said that his friend never fully recovered from the blow. A year afterwards, Orwell wrote to a woman to whom he had proposed:

I was sometimes unfaithful to Eileen, and I also treated her very badly, and I think she treated me badly too at times, but it was a real marriage in the sense that we had been through awful struggles together and she understood all about my work, etc.[4]

Intent on keeping the child, he found a nurse-cum-housekeeper in Susan Watts, who, married and aged twenty-five, was more like a younger sister. When she asked him about the wardrobe full of Eileen's clothes, it was as though he could not bear to consider them.

According to Bernard Crick, within little more than a year Orwell had proposed to at least four women. He had a brief affair with Sonia Brownell, who was then with Connolly on *Horizon*. At this stage she turned down his proposal, although 'very, very fond of him'. He proposed to beautiful Celia Kirwan, Koestler's sister-in-law. Then there was Anne Popham. All refused 'gently', remaining his friends. Christmas 1945 he and Richard spent with the Koestlers, and to a

---

1 23–4 Mar. 1945.
2 Bernard Crick: *George Orwell: A Life* (1980), p. 327. See letter to Stafford Cottman, 25 Apr. 1946: 'It was an awful shame . . .' (*The Collected Essays, Journalism & Letters, cit.*, iv, p. 149).
3 Malcolm Muggeridge: *Chronicles of Wasted Time* (1972–3), ii, p. 232.
4 1946. Bernard Crick: *George Orwell: A Life* (1980), p. 332.

discussion about the qualities one would like to possess, Orwell contributed: 'I should like to be irresistible to women.'[1]

His six-year-old dream of a 'Hebridean island which I shall now probably never see' was realized after all, through David Astor, who as a boy had spent summer holidays on Jura and found him Bramhill – an abandoned farmhouse with outbuildings. According to Fyvel, Orwell fled to Bramhill not only to write *Nineteen Eighty-Four* but because London life had become no longer tenable: the loneliness of his widower's life was 'deeply disturbing'.[2] Susan arrived with Richard, not expecting to find Orwell's younger sister Avril already there. Avril disapproved of Susan calling him 'George' rather than 'Eric', his real name. She disapproved of Richard waking her brother by tickling his feet as Susan had taught him. She disapproved of Susan. When Susan's communist friend, David Holbrook, visited with permission, the two men had a violent row and, after a heated exchange with Avril, Susan went away with Holbrook.

Orwell's tenure of the dream home came to an abrupt end when he went into Cotswold Sanatorium at the beginning of 1949. He had always seemed optimistic he would survive, and as Potts said:

Under his influence all his friends stopped taking the doctors seriously.

In August that year, Orwell wrote to Warburg:

As I warned you I might do, I intend getting married again [to Sonia] when I am once again in the land of the living, if I ever am. I suppose everyone will be horrified, but apart from other considerations I really think I should stay alive longer if I were married.[3]

Two more weeks and he moved into University College Hospital, his typewriter taken firmly away.

His second proposal to Sonia Brownell had been successful, and they were married in hospital on 13 October 1949: he forty-six, she thirty-one. Not wishing to be married in a dressing-gown, he had asked Malcolm Muggeridge and Anthony Powell to find him a smoking-jacket and Sonia bought it for them to give, and then they forgot whether it had been 'crimson corduroy' or 'mauve velvet'.[4]

1 *Ibid.*, p. 334.
2 *George Orwell: a personal memoir* (1982), p. 151.
3 22 Aug. 1949. *The Collected Essays, Journalism & Letters of George Orwell* ed. Sonia Orwell & Ian Angus (1968), iv, pp. 505–6.
4 Bernard Crick: *George Orwell: A Life* (1980), p. 403.

After the ceremony, Sonia and a small party were entertained by David Astor to a wedding luncheon at the Ritz; then a signed menu was brought back to the sick man. In the New Year there were plans for him to fly with Sonia to a Swiss sanatorium, and Malcolm Muggeridge noticed a fishing-rod at the foot of the hospital bed. But on the night of 21 January 1950 Orwell sustained a lung haemorrhage and died immediately, before Sonia could be found.

IV

DAPHNE DU MAURIER and Major 'Boy' Browning ('Tommy') set off for their honeymoon by boat, like her two characters in *The Loving Spirit* – confirming Wilde's theory that 'Life imitates art'.[1] Only three months before, the thirty-five-year-old guardsman had sailed his yacht down to Fowey in the hope of meeting the twenty-four-year-old author. He cruised up and down in front of her house until she accepted his invitation to go on board. *She* proposed.

Michael Thornton wrote:

It was a very strange union that somehow worked against all the odds.[2]

Both had known previous loves, and these not their last. Her own divided make-up meant that three of hers were women. She functioned better at her writing when solitary in Cornwall – while he, Lieutenant-General during the war, and then Comptroller of the Queen's household, was in London and abroad. Yet their marriage lasted over thirty-two years and he died, tenderly nursed, at Menabilly.

EMLYN WILLIAMS, whose second volume of autobiography[3] revealed a complex man, had no plans for a third, which would have taken in his subsequent marriage and the birth of two sons. He was able to explain:

A happy marriage doesn't make for riveting reading.

---

1 'The Decay of Lying': *Intentions: 1st Collected Edn. of the Works of Oscar Wilde* (1908), viii, p. 40.
2 *The Observer*: 23 Apr. 1989.
3 *Emlyn* (1973).

CHAPTER SIX
Unlikely Marriages

I

Garrick, remembering perhaps a slight from Tetty's satirical tongue, described her to Boswell, as 'very fat, with a bosom of more than ordinary protuberance, with swelled cheeks, of a florid red, produced by thick painting, and increased by the liberal use of cordials . . .'[1] JOHNSON told Topham Beauclerk, 'with much gravity':

'Sir, it was a love-marriage upon both sides.'[2]

He was twenty-five when he married the forty-six-year-old widow, who had a grown-up daughter and two sons. She brought a dowry of £600–£700. They had been acquainted for three years, going back a year or so before her first husband, a mercer, died.

According to William Shaw, she was still 'young and handsome',[3] and her portrait – painted a few years previously – in which she has blonde hair and carries her head high, bears this out. It was Johnson's physical and nervous peculiarities that alarmed her sons. She told her daughter: 'this is the most sensible man that I ever saw in my life.'[4] He was to tell Mrs Thrale that Tetty could argue a point so well she was useful to have on your side, and when they read comedy together she was 'better than any body he ever heard'. The incongruity lies in the age gap, the same number of years as in the fleeting marriage of George Eliot.

The wedding took place on 9 July 1736, at Derby – by reason of her family's opposition – and the future bride and bridegroom set out from Birmingham on horseback. He told Boswell:

1 James Boswell: *The Life of Samuel Johnson, LL D* (1791), i, p. 46.
2 *Ibid.*, i, p 44.
3 *Memoirs of the Life & Writings of the Late Dr Samuel Johnson* (1785), pp. 25–6.
4 Boswell: *op. cit.* i, p. 43.

'Sir, she had read the old romances, and had got into her head the fantastical notion that a woman of spirit should use her lover like a dog. So, Sir, at first she told me that I rode too fast, and she could not keep up with me; and, when I rode a little slower, she passed me, and complained that I lagged behind. I was not to be made the slave of caprice; and I resolved to begin as I meant to end. I therefore pushed on briskly, till I was fairly out of her sight. The road lay between two hedges, so I was sure she could not miss it; and I contrived that she should soon come up with me. When she did, I observed her to be in tears.[1]

His venture to set up his own schoool, on his wife's capital, failed. The only pupils Boswell knew about were Garrick, Garrick's brother, and another boy, Offely. They used to listen at the door of his bedroom, and peep through the keyhole, to make fun of his pet-names Tetty or Tetsey for the mature woman he adored.

Intending 'to try his fate with a tragedy', he 'rode and tied' with Garrick to London. After a few months he fetched his wife from Lichfield, and at first they took lodgings in Woodstock Street near Hanover Square. Her life with him meant poverty until death, and for long periods he had to be away from her side. In disillusionment, she became an alcoholic and finally an opium-eater, spending much of her time in bed. Unable now to satisfy him physically, she pleaded the need for 'country air', and he rented for her a humble dwelling in Hampstead where he would visit two or three days in the week. Whatever his personal hardship, he saw she had a maid, and the substantial house at 17 Gough Square, which stretched his means to the limit, was largely for her. To make herself more youthful, if she ventured in company she wore make-up and garish clothes. They continued to have admiration and affection for each other. She did not attend the first night of *Irene*, put on when Garrick took over Drury Lane, but she said, after a few numbers of *The Rambler* had appeared:

'I thought very well of you before, but I did not imagine you could have written any thing equal to this.[2]

Boswell wrote:

. . . she must have had a superiority of understanding and talents, as she certainly inspired him with a more than ordinary passion . . .[3]

1 Boswell: *op. cit.* i, p. 44
2 *Ibid.*, i, p. 113. *Aetat.* 41: 1750.
3 *Ibid.*,i, p. 44.

She died when he was forty-two, three years before the publication of his *Dictionary* which brought him fame. In his letter to Lord Chesterfield he said:

The notice which you have been pleased to take of my labours, had it been early, had been kind; but it has been delayed . . . till I am solitary, and cannot impart it . . .[1]

If now he wanted to study, he could not read in rooms where she had sat. He took his books up to the garret, 'because in that room only, I never saw Mrs Johnson'. He preserved her wedding-ring 'in a little round wooden box'. A month after her death, he prayed that he might 'remember with thankfulness the blessings so long enjoyed by me in the society of my departed wife; make me so think on her precepts and example, that I may imitate whatever was in her life acceptable in thy sight, and avoid all by which she offended'.[2] He kept 'the anniversary of my Tetty's death, with prayer and tears in the morning'.

In the evening I prayed for her conditionally, if it were lawful.[3]

He remembered that he might have practised more 'joint devotion, patient exhortation, and mild instruction'.

Like Carlyle, Shaw, Nicolson, he was devastated by his loneliness, but they were older men. He attempted 'to seek a new wife without any derogation from dear Tetty's memory'[4] – probably Hill Boothby. When he was sixty, and 'saw the sea at Brighthelmston I wished for her to have seen it with me'.[5] Six years later, on a visit to the Palais Bourbon, he recorded in his small paper-book:

The sight of palaces, and other great buildings, leaves no very distinct images, unless to those who talk of them. As I entered, my wife was in my mind: she would have been pleased. Having now nobody to please, I am little pleased.[6]

At seventy-two, he wrote in his diary:

This is the day on which, in 1752, dear Tetty died. I have now uttered a prayer of repentance and contrition; perhaps Tetty knows that I prayed for

1 [7] Feb. 1755. Ibid., i, p. 142. Aetat. 45.
2 25 Apr. 1752. *Prayers & Meditations Composed by Samuel Johnson, LL D & Published from his Manuscripts, by George Strahan, AM* (1785), p. 11.
3 28 Mar. 1753.
4 Easter. 22 Apr. 1753.
5 28 Mar. 1770.
6 17 Oct. 1775. James Boswell: *The Life of Samuel Johnson, LL D* (1791), i, p. 505.

her. Perhaps Tetty is now praying for me. God help me . . . We were married almost seventeen years, and have now been parted thirty.[1]

A few months before he died, he 'laid . . . a stone over Tetty' in the church of St Peter and St Paul, Bromley, Kent. He arranged for a Mr Ryland to cut her epitaph:

> Hic conduntur reliquiae
> ELIZABETHAE
> Antiqua Jarvisiorum gente,
> Peatlingae, apud Leicestrienses, ortae;
> Formosae, cultae, ingeniosae, piae;
> Uxoris, primis nuptiis, HENRICI PORTER,
> Secundis, SAMUELIS JOHNSON:
> Qui multum amatam, diuque defletam
> Hoc lapide contexit.
> Obiit Londini, Mense Mart.
> A.D. MDCCLII.[2]

DISRAELI, at thirty-four, married the widow of Wyndham Lewis, who was twelve years older. It had been to the Wyndham Lewises that he owed his first parliamentary seat. 'Dizzy married me for my money,' said Mary Ann, 'but if he had the chance again, he would marry me for love.' Every anniversary he wrote her a short verse. Following a moment of triumph in the House – his domestic franchise stealing Liberal thunder and leaving even Gladstone bemused – he dropped into the Carlton Club but declined an invitation to supper. Mary told T. E. Kebbel about it with simple pride:

I had got him a raised pie from Fortnum and Mason's, and a bottle of champagne, and he ate half the pie and drank all the champagne, and then he said, 'Well, my dear, you are more like a mistress than a wife.'[3]

She was seventy-seven.

Every fortnight she cut his hair and preserved the trimmings in a small sealed packet, hundreds of which he discovered after her death.

---

1 28 Mar. 1782. *Prayers & Meditations Composed by Samuel Johnson, LL D & Published from his Manuscripts, by George Strahan, AM* (1785), p. 207.
2 'Here lie the remains of Elizabeth, descended from the ancient house of Jarvis at Peatling in Leicestershire; a Woman of beauty, elegance, ingenuity, and piety. Her first Husband was Henry Porter; her second, Samuel Johnson, who having loved her much, and lamented her long, laid this stone upon her. She died in March. 1752.' (Johnson's own translation given to his stepdaughter, Lucy Porter: 2 Dec. 1784. *The Letters of Samuel Johnson* ed. R. W. Chapman [1952], iii, p. 252.)
3 T. E. Kebbel: *Lord Beaconsfield & Other Tory Memories* (1907), p. 40.

She died of cancer of the stomach after long illness; they had been together thirty-three years. 'She believed in me,' he said, 'when men despised me.' During the rest of his life his writing-paper had mourning edges. He said to Lady Bradford:

It is strange, but I always used to think that the Queen persisting in these emblems of woe, indulged in a morbid sentiment; and yet it has become my lot, and seemingly an irresistible one.[1]

II

As CHARLOTTE BRONTË lay exhausted, her pregnancy aggravated by a severe chill, she saw her husband praying softly by her side and whispered: 'Oh, I am not going to die, am I? He will not separate us, we have been so happy!'[2] Her married life lasted nine months, and she was not quite thirty-nine when she died.

The Rev. Arthur Bell Nicholls's feelings for her had been immediate, yet he was her father's curate for seven and a half years before that Monday, 13 December 1852, when, having come to tea and sat with him between eight and nine o'clock, he opened the parlour door 'as if going'. She described it all to her closest friend, Ellen Nussey:

I expected the clash of the front-door. He stopped in the passage: he tapped [on the dining-room door]: like lightning it flashed on me what was coming. He entered – he stood before me. What his words were you can guess; his manner – you can hardly realise – never can I forget it. Shaking from head to foot, looking deadly pale, speaking low, vehemently yet with difficulty – he made me for the first time feel what it costs a man to declare affection where he doubts response. The spectacle of one ordinarily so statue-like, thus trembling, stirred, and overcome, gave me a kind of strange shock. He spoke of suffering he had borne for months . . . and craved leave for some hope. I could only entreat him to leave me then and promise a reply on the morrow. I asked him if he had spoken to papa. He said, he dared not. I think I half led, half put him out of the room.

When he had gone, she immediately told her father.

Agitation and anger disproportionate to the occasion ensued; if I had *loved* Mr Nicholls and had heard such epithets applied to him as were used, it would have transported me past my patience; as it was, my blood boiled with a

1 Quoted by André Maurois: *Disraeli: A Picture of the Victorian Age* (1927), p. 249.
2 E. C. Gaskell: *The Life of Charlotte Brontë* (1857), ii, p. 324.

sense of injustice, but papa worked himself into a state not to be trifled with, the veins on his temples started up like whipcord, and his eyes became suddenly bloodshot. I made haste to promise that Mr Nicholls should on the morrow have a distinct refusal.

She told her friend that she had written to him 'and got his note'.

. . . Papa's vehement antipathy to the bare thought of anyone thinking of me as a wife, and Mr Nicholls's distress, both give me pain. Attachment to Mr Nicholls you are aware I never entertained, but the poignant pity inspired by his state on Monday evening, by the hurried revelation of his sufferings for many months, is something galling and irksome. That he cared something for me, and wanted me to care for him, I have long suspected, but I did not know the degree and strength of his feelings.[1]

It was decided that the Rev. P. Brontë's conscientious and reliable curate must go. In the village they all thought that Charlotte had 'disdainfully refused' him, and a generous subscription was collected in token of respect. Now, five months after his proposal, he was leaving. At first, she had thought it best to stay out of sight.

But perceiving that he stayed long before going out at the gate, and remembering his long grief, I took courage and went out trembling and miserable. I found him leaning against the garden door in a paroxysm of anguish, sobbing as women never sob. Of course I went straight to him. Very few words were interchanged, those few barely articulate. Several things I should have liked to ask him were swept entirely from my memory. Poor fellow! But he wanted such hope and such encouragement as I could not give him. Still I trust he must know now that I am not cruelly blind and indifferent to his constancy and grief.[2]

He wrote a few times and at last she replied. A secret correspondence ensued. Gradually the Rev. P. Brontë's violent opposition was broken down. Catherine Winkworth wrote of a conversation at this time when Charlotte had said:

'. . . it is a great thing to be the first object with anyone . . . But, Katie, it has cost me a good deal to come to this.'

'You will have to care for his things, instead of his caring for yours, is that it?'

'. . . But those are not everything, and I cannot conceal from myself that he is *not* intellectual; there are many places into which he could not follow me

1 15 Dec. 1852. *The Brontës: Their Lives, Friendships & Correspondence* (The Shakespeare Head Press, 1932), iv, pp. 29–30.
2 27 May 1853. *Ibid.*, iv, pp. 68–9.

intellectually . . . He is a Puseyite and very stiff . . . I shall never let him make me a bigot . . .'

'Perhaps . . . you may do something to introduce him to goodness in sects where he has thought it could not be.'

'That is what I hope; he has a most sincere love of goodness wherever he sees it. I think if he could come to know Mr Gaskell[1] it would change his feeling.'[2]

There is doubt about the timing of her father's announcement that he would not be attending the wedding. (Thirteen years previously, Wordsworth could not face his daughter Dora's nuptials.) Villagers who saw the little party come out of church said she looked 'like a snowdrop'.[3]

On her two months' honeymoon in Ireland to meet his family, Charlotte wrote to Margaret Wooler, who had given her old pupil away at the church:

I trust I feel thankful to God for having enabled me to make what seems a right choice – and I pray to be enabled to repay as I ought the affectionate devotion of a truthful, honourable, unboastful man.[4]

She admitted to Catherine Winkworth that her husband was 'not a poet or a poetical man', but described his tact when she wished to take in her own way 'the Atlantic coming in all white foam':

I did not want to talk – but I *did* want to look and be silent. Having hinted a petition, licence was not refused – covered with a rug to keep off the spray, I was allowed to sit where I chose – and he only interrupted me when he thought I crept too near the edge of the cliff.[5]

This picture of a solicitous and ministering male is paralleled in MME D'ARBLAY's description of life at The Hermitage, Great Bookham. Fanny wrote to her father in her first year of marriage:

Here we are tranquil, undisturbed, and undisturbing . . . He works in his garden, or studies English and mathematics, while I write. When I work at my needle, he reads to me; and we enjoy the beautiful country around us in long and romantic strolls, during which he carries under his arm a portable garden-chair . . . that I may rest as I proceed.[6]

1 A Unitarian minister. Charlotte was then staying with the Gaskells.
2 Letter to Emma Shaen: 8 May 1854. *The Brontës: Their Lives, Friendships & Correspondence* (The Shakespeare Head Press, 1932), iv, pp. 122–3.
3 E. C. Gaskell: *The Life of Charlotte Brontë* (1857), ii, p. 316.
4 10 July 1854. *The Shakespeare Head Brontë cit.*, iv, p. 135.
5 27 July 1854. *Ibid.*, iv, pp. 137–8.
6 22 Mar. 1794. *Diary & Letters of Madame d'Arblay* ed. by her Niece (1842–6), vi, p. 22.

Fanny had long been persuaded that marriage for her was 'a state of too much hazard . . . to draw me from my individual plans and purposes'. She remembered at thirteen being asked when she intended to marry, and solemnly replying: 'When I think I shall be happier than I am in being single.' No 'wonder' could have exceeded her own that her partner in middle life proved to be a Frenchman – 'a prejudice certainly, impertinent and very John Bullish, and very arrogant . . .'[1]

On account of M. d'Arblay's property – 'whatever it was' – having been confiscated by the Convention, Dr Burney had written to his daughter prudently, 'not to entangle herself in a wild and romantic attachment'. He acknowledged 'a very amiable and accomplished man', but one who was 'a mere soldier of fortune'. From the beginning, however, unlike the Rev. P. Brontë, he assured her that 'M. d'Arblay will be always received by me with the utmost attention and respect'.[2] In a 'Memorandum',[3] Fanny records that her father 'gave way' and 'sent, though reluctantly, a consent'. He, too, did not attend his daughter's wedding, but six weeks afterwards, on hearing that 'M. d'Arblay is not only his own architect, but intends being his own gardener', had 'the honour to send him Miller's Gardeners' Dictionary'.[4] Next year he was godfather at his grandson's christening, and the little Alexander Charles was given his grandfather's name.

The Peace of Amiens, which saw Wordsworth and Dorothy crossing the Channel to visit Annette, also saw Fanny with her eight-year-old son joining M. d'Arblay in Paris. In attempting to gain his half-pay on the retired list of French officers, he had been required at the Alien Office to give an undertaking not to return for one year. The resumption of war, however, meant that Fanny was to be exiled for ten years 'under the dominion of Bonaparte'. M. d'Arblay, having made his stand never to fight against England, obtained employment as a civil servant. Then, when Alexander reached military age, she managed to bring him back to England.

After Napoleon's abdication, Louis XVIII appointed M. d'Arblay an officer in the Corps de Gardes du Roi, and two months later he was rewarded with his old rank, Maréchal de Camp. The following

1 *Ibid.*, vi, pp. 14–16.
2 May 1793. *Ibid.*. v, pp. 426–8.
3 7 May 1825. *Ibid.*, v, p. 429.
4 Letter to Mme d'Arblay: 12 Sept. 1793. *Ibid.*, vi, p. 4.

year, at the beginning of the Hundred Days, there was not at first, writes Fanny, 'any change in our way of life'.

. . . we even resumed our delightful airings in the Bois de Boulogne, whither the General drove me every morning in a light calèche . . .[1]

But when it became obvious that Napoleon would attempt Paris, there came 'one of the most dreadful days of my existence'.[2] After M. d'Arblay had come to her and 'in the most kindly, soothing terms, called upon me to *give him an example of courage*', she saw him from a window, past sixty years of age –

just mounting his war-horse, a noble animal, of which he was singularly fond, but which at this moment I viewed with acutest terror, for it seemed loaded with pistols, and equipped completely for immediate service on the field of battle . . .[3]

Fanny yielded to his wishes to flee with others to Brussels. As the wife of an officer in the King's Bodyguard, in actual service, she might, he had feared, be seized as a hostage and treated the worse for being English.

At sixty-three, she proved her devotion and loyalty in a heroic way. On hearing that her husband had suffered an injury, she travelled from Brussels to Trèves to be with him. She had been warned of the anarchy in the aftermath of Waterloo, with the Prussian army pursuing vanquished French soldiers and both parties turned into desperate marauders. She went without escort by an unplanned succession of diligences, the last one 'a queer German carriage'. A journey of some 225 miles took her six days.

Her marriage, like Johnson's, meant periods when they had to be apart, but at seventy-three, bereaved for seven years of 'the truest of partners' – '*mon très cher ami*' – she wrote:

. . . never, never was union more blessed and felicitous; though, after the first eight years of unmingled happiness, it was assailed by many calamities, chiefly of separation or illness, yet mentally unbroken.[4]

1 *Ibid.*, vii, p. 68.
2 *Ibid.*, vii, p. 78.
3 *Ibid.*, vii, pp. 80–1.
4 'Memorandum' *cit.*: *ibid.*, v, p. 429.

CHAPTER SEVEN

In the Teeth of Convention

I

To the credit of Pepys, Boswell, and Sheridan, each married for love. PEPYS's marriage, at twenty-two, to Elizabeth Marchant de St Michel, a fifteen- or sixteen-year-old penniless beauty, the daughter of a French Huguenot refugee, was unusual in its day for not being put forward by either set of parents.

When he was nearly twenty-seven, on the eve of his momentous journey as Montague's private secretary to bring back Charles II, he writes:

I went home to bed, very sad in mind to part with my wife . . .[1]

Nearly thirty-two, he writes that cross words as they lay in bed caused him to strike her such a blow over the eye 'as the poor wretch did cry out . . . but her spirit was such as to endeavour to bite and scratch me'. He, 'coying' with her, sent for butter and parsley, and he was 'vexed at my heart to think what I had done'.[2] Over two years later, we read:

. . . mightily pleased with my wife's trill.[3]

In her last year she had a tooth drawn, and when he was brought the message that all was well –

So I home to comfort her . . .[4]

Pepys spent a lot more on his own clothes than on hers, and he flirted with servants not only at home. In St Dunstan's –

1 *Diary*: 16 Mar. 1660.
2 *Ibid.*, 19 Dec. 1664.
3 *Ibid.*, 11 Mar. 1667.
4 *Ibid.*, 18 May 1669.

I heard an able sermon . . . and stood by a pretty, modest maid, whom I did labour to take by the hand and the body but she would not, but got further and further from me. And at last I could perceive her to take pins out of her pocket to prick me if I should touch her again; which seeing I did forbear, and was glad I did spy her design. And then I fell to gaze upon another pretty maid in a pew close to me, and she on me; and I did go about to take her by the hand, which she suffered a little and then withdrew. So the sermon ended and the church broke up, and my amours ended also, and so took coach and home, and there took up my wife, and to Islington with her . . .[1]

She caught him embracing Deb when after supper he was having his hair combed,[2] but there is no doubt that the marriage on the whole was happy. She died at twenty-nine when he was thirty-six, and she never saw him reach the pinnacle of his fame as Secretary to the Admiralty.

Before BOSWELL married at twenty-nine his first cousin, Margaret Montgomerie, he had fallen in love with a Roman Catholic actress, become infected at least twice with gonorrhea, had conducted an affair in Scotland with Peggy Doig, who was probably a servant, and one in London with the handsome actress 'Louisa'. He had enjoyed a liaison with Mrs Dodds, a young grass widow. Now, to the chagrin of the eighth Laird of Auchinleck, the only woman his son had ever wanted to marry possessed neither lands nor money. The disappointed man married again on his son's wedding-day.

Boswell's home-loving wife thought it incongruous that her advocate husband should spend some of his holidays with Johnson in London – and Boswell's father thought the same. When Johnson accepted the younger man's challenge to accompany him on a Highland tour, she remarked with nice antithesis that though she had seen many 'a bear led by a man, she had never before seen a man led by a bear'.

Eight years after their marriage she became seriously infected with TB, and about this time Boswell seemed unable to enlarge his prospects either in parliament or law. He resorted again to prostitutes and began to depend on drink. He inherited the Auchinleck estate when he was forty-two, and made a good laird. But London was still the place 'which I was so madly fond of' twenty-four years ago, and at forty-six, having been called to the English bar, he moved his

1 *Ibid.*, 18 Aug. 1667.
2 *Ibid.*, 25 Oct. 1668.

family to the capital. His practice now virtually ceased and, although Johnson was dead, Margaret saw her husband's twin fascination at work in his prolonged preparation of *The Life*.

As her condition deteriorated she was brought back to Auchinleck according to her wish. Unexpectedly, under the influence of Lord Lonsdale, Boswell at forty-eight obtained the recordership of Carlisle, and with his wife's blessing returned to London to be at his patron's call. Soon after, on hearing her condition might be critical, he posted back with his boys in sixty-four hours and a quarter but they were too late. Nineteen carriages followed her hearse. She did not see his masterpiece, any more than Johnson's wife had seen the *Dictionary*. During his few remaining years the five children of his marriage loved him deeply when he continued to think himself a failure.

SHERIDAN was only twenty when he caused a Bath scandal by eloping with seventeen-year-old Elizabeth Ann Linley – famous for her beauty and soprano voice. They went through a form of marriage near Calais. Two years later they married in Marylebone Church. He had fought two duels, and now broke with his father and a legal career. She adored him. Six years later, Fanny Burney in the company of her father and Joshua Reynolds met them after the success of *The Rivals* and *The School for Scandal*. Fanny was 'absolutely charmed' at the sight of Mrs Sheridan, and wrote:

Mr Sheridan has a very fine figure . . . He is tall . . . I like him vastly, and think him every way worthy his beautiful companion . . . they are extremely happy in each other . . .[1]

She died of TB when he was forty, and three years later he married Hester Jane Ogle, the twenty-year-old daughter to the Dean of Westminster ('My sweet Hecca', 'My own dear bit of brown Holland') by whom he had another son. His latter years were clouded by his circulatory complaints and his wife's cancer (although she succeeded him by just over a year), and by debts and the loss of his Stafford seat.

J. S. MILL continued his friendship with Mrs Taylor when his father, like Stevenson's over first Mrs Sitwell and then Mrs Osbourne (before Louis made her his wife), strongly disapproved. But James Mill had formed his son's intellectual life and been instrumental in

1 *Diary & Letters of Madame d'Arblay* ed. by her Niece (1842–6), i, pp. 167, 170–1.

shaping his career; it must therefore say much for J. S. Mill's depth of affection and his independence of will. When eventually Mrs Taylor was widowed and he married her, it led to his complete estrangement from his mother and sisters. He spoke of her not only as one who had a saintly character,[1] but 'one who was greatly the superior' of both himself and Carlyle –

. . . who was more a poet than he, and more a thinker than I – whose own mind and nature included his, and infinitely more.[2]

II

In all but legal form, GEORGE ELIOT's life with G. H. Lewes, continuing twenty-four years until he died, was a happy and successful marriage. After their return from the Continent she began to insist that those who wrote personal letters to her should address them to 'Mrs Lewes'. She told Mrs Peter Taylor that she had ceased 'to be "Miss Evans" . . . having held myself under all the responsibilities of a married woman'.

. . . and when I tell you that we have a great boy of eighteen at home who calls me 'mother', as well as two other boys, almost as tall, who write to me under the same name, you will understand that the point is not one of mere egoism . . . when I request that anyone who has a regard for me will cease to speak of me by my maiden name.[3]

She had met Lewes when she was thirty-two – he in a state of dejection, his home hopelessly broken up. Ten years earlier, at twenty-four, he had married Agnes Jervis and they had lived in The Phalanstery – a commune in Queen's Road, Bayswater – with Leigh Hunt's eldest son Thornton, his wife, and two other couples. Thornton Hunt had set it up the previous year, inspired by the works of Pierre Fourier. But casualties happened as when Shelley had followed the teaching of Godwin. Agnes bore two children by Thornton, and Lewes ceased to regard her as his wife. She bore four of Thornton's children, all registered in Lewes's name. Lewes provided Swiss

---

1 See p. 11.
2 *Autobiography: Published from the original MS. in the Columbia University Library* ed. Roger Howson: Preface by John Jacob Coss (1924), p. 124. A restored passage.
3 Letter: 1 Apr. 1861.

schooling for the three boys, and gave Agnes £100 a year. Such magnanimity meant, in legal terms, he had condoned her adultery.

Convinced that Lewes and Agnes could never repair their marriage, George Eliot determined to live openly with him. Nearly three years after their first meeting, they went to Germany together and there was malicious gossip from people ignorant of the facts. She answered Mrs Bray's taunt, and that of the society of her day:

Women who are content with light and easily broken ties, do *not* act as I have done. They obtain what they desire and are still invited to dinner.[1]

It was Lewes who suggested she should try fiction, and he compared *Amos Barton* with *The Vicar of Wakefield* when submitting it to Blackwood. She used her pen-name shortly afterwards. All her great work was done with Lewes's intelligent encouragement. His own diary refers to 'deep wedded happiness'. He cushioned her from everyday practicalities; he even kept from her the few unfavourable reviews.

Five months after Lewes's death, she wrote to her friend of ten years, a banker who held her investments:

I am in dreadful need of your counsel. Please come to me when you can – morning, afternoon, or evening.

John Cross arrived next evening, and 'from this time forward I saw George Eliot constantly'. A year and a half later, she became a married woman to this man twenty years her junior. On their honeymoon, in the heat of Venice, he suffered a sudden mental derangement and jumped from their hotel balcony into the Grand Canal. Gondoliers quickly came to his rescue, and a doctor prescribed chloral. There is no evidence such an attack recurred. He lived to be eighty-four.

But six months after her marriage she died, having lived just under three weeks in the stately Cheyne Walk home which now bears her plaque. The loss of Lewes was mortal.

III

W. H. DAVIES, when he was over fifty, met Emma one Friday at 11.0 p.m. near Marble Arch and took her home.

1 4 Sept. 1855.

Her age was twenty-three, but with her short skirt and a soft, saucy-looking little velvet cap with tassels, she did not look a day more than fifteen.[1]

The previous year he had decided 'to find a woman to share my life',[2] and had lived first with Bella who stole his clock, and then Louise who drank. Both were prostitutes. On this particular night, he had made up his mind 'to make a great effort . . . to find a young woman who was not too demoralised to be saved from the streets . . .'[3]

Unknown to him, Emma was in search of a father for her unborn child, and it was only a matter of weeks when she lost blood. A police ambulance took her to hospital, where her six-month pregnancy was terminated. Meanwhile, Davies had gone down with VD and suspected Emma. He started to improve after a quarter-mile walk of heroic will-power to see and touch Marble Arch, but the doctor warned: 'If anything like this occurs to you again, you are doomed.' Then, in spite of the disparity in their ages and even though she had lost her child, Emma returned.

They moved to an eight-roomed house in the country where she showed herself a natural home-maker, with proverbial green fingers in the garden. He now discovered a sore the size of a pin's head, and the doctor said: 'If it is what I fear, you are in for a long and dangerous illness.'[4] Davies could not understand how Emma herself did not appear to be suffering, and for the first time felt bitter towards her. That evening, he said their marriage would have to be postponed until she saw to her own health. The silence in the room was terrible, 'her poor little white face' twitching, and he sent her to bed alone. When a thunderstorm broke, and knowing she would be afraid, he got in beside her and she nuzzled close. She said in the morning:

. . . when I saw you lying at my side, with an arm outstretched, like Christ on the Cross – I took shelter at once, and all my fears were gone.[5]

The doctor's prognosis failed to come to pass. And Davies had suspected Emma, not the culprit Louise!

1 W. H. Davies: *Young Emma* (1980), p. 58. Posthumously published, it was written in 1924 when Emma was 24.
2 *Ibid.*, p. 18.
3 *Ibid.*, p. 55.
4 *Ibid.*, p. 100.
5 *Ibid.*, p. 129.

I had understood that a venereal disease showed itself within ten or fourteen days after intercourse, and it was nearly three weeks after my adventure with the woman, when I met young Emma . . .[1]

It was *he* who had put *her* at risk, and mercifully she had escaped intact. When he had been very poor, he did not marry because he had 'too much thought for a woman to do that'.[2] Now, with this simple, childish wife, who joined him in pillow-fights and liked asking riddles, he was 'in the presence of a great heart and an affectionate spirit'.[3]

1 *Ibid.*, p. 154.
2 *Ibid.*, p. 132.
3 *Ibid.*, p. 119.

CHAPTER EIGHT

In the Teeth of Experience

There are cases where a writer who has experienced a harrowing marriage enjoys a complete reversal on marrying again. MEREDITH's marriage to Mrs Nicolls, a widow seven years older, when he was twenty-one, was a 'blunder – no sun warmed my roof-tree'. To his second wife, Marie (née Vulliamy), whom he married at thirty-six, he was devoted. She was a 'capital wife', his 'help-meet', and copied out chapters of *Vittoria*.

ELIOT married for the second time when he was nearly sixty-nine. Almost eight years previously he had appointed Valerie Fletcher, then twenty-two, as his secretary at Faber's, and now for exactly eight years she was to be his wife. She had become infatuated with his poetry from the age of fourteen. 'It was extraordinary', she said, 'that I felt I just *had* to get to Tom, to work with him.'[1] It seems that he did not prepare John Hayward, his companion in Carlyle Mansions, sufficiently, if at all, for this dramatic change. Nor did he his other close friend of this period, Mary Trevelyan, who had actually proposed to him twice. Both felt themselves victims of his 'aboulie', and were affected for the rest of their lives.

Eliot told his American publisher, Robert Giroux: 'I'm the luckiest man in the world.' He told another friend, Dr Joseph Chiari: 'I don't deserve such happiness.'[2] Chiari comments:

He spent his last years caught between the enchantment of newly found love and the fear that he might not be given enough time to reward, through happiness, the one who had so transformed his life.

Eliot said to him 'many times, that without Valerie he would not have survived the harsh bouts of illness which afflicted the last eight years of his life . . .'[3]

1 Interview in *The Observer*: 20 Feb. 1972. Quoted by Peter Ackroyd: *T. S. Eliot* (1984), p. 298.
2 Joseph Chiari: *T. S. Eliot: A Memoir* (1982), p. 28.
3 *Ibid.*, p. 55.

The reticent man was seen holding hands when many people were present. He told one reporter: 'I am thinking of taking up dancing lessons again.' He told another:

Love reciprocated is always rejuvenating. Now I feel younger at seventy than I did at sixty . . . An experience like mine makes all the more difference because of its contrast with the past.[1]

He wrote his wife a poem, but apart from certain scenes in *The Elder Statesman* his creative life was over. He rationed his days as director at Faber's, also his own writing time, so that they could walk together in Kensington Gardens. He confided to Pound that his childhood and his second marriage were the only times in his life when he had been happy.

After seven very unhappy years, EVELYN WAUGH married a Catholic girl, Laura Herbert, when he was thirty-three. They honeymooned in Italy, and she made 'a lovely wife'.

She brought him great happiness and they made a good team.[2]

She had the life-style of the Irish peasantry, when Evelyn may have sometimes pined for a more elegant partner, but she was 'the only one to keep him in place, and understood him perfectly'.[3] His biographer states that when he 'was in a tiresome mood and "went too far" Laura would sharply call him to order – with effect':

. . . Laura was a devotedly patient wife. But she was not his 'doormat' as many people believed. She was perfectly able to stand up for herself . . . If it had been otherwise . . . Evelyn would not have loved her as he did.[4]

There is nothing to suggest he was ever unfaithful to her.

1 Interview with Henry Hewes in *The Saturday Review*: 13 Sept 1958.
2 Auberon Waugh: *Arena*, BBC2, Apr. 1987.
3 *Ibid.*
4 Christopher Sykes: *Evelyn Waugh: A Biography* (1975), p. 450.

CHAPTER NINE

The Forming of the Rainbow

I

The marriages of Pepys, Carlyle, and D. H. Lawrence saw sparks perpetually flying, yet mutual devotion was very real. The LAWRENCES' marriage was summed up by Frieda:

We fought our battles outright to the bitter end. Then there was peace, such peace . . . To understand what happened between us, one must have . . . thrown away as much as we did and gained as much, and have known this fulfilment of body and soul.[1]

'Things happened quickly' after they had met. When Lawrence said they must go away together, Frieda Weekley, the German wife of his professor at Nottingham, 'was frightened'. She knew how terrible such a thing would be for her husband, who trusted her. She left her son with his father, and took her two little girls to their grandparents in London.

He seemed to have lifted me body and soul out of all my past life. This young man of twenty-six . . . And we had known each other barely for six weeks.[2]

They left for Germany, to begin their wandering life together and apart. They walked across the Alps. At Gorgnano in Italy, the daughter of the aristocratic von Richthofen learnt to wash sheets and cook with large copper pans. Lawrence taught her to be tidy and less wasteful. They married at a registrar's office in Kensington when he was twenty-eight and his tubercular tendencies were already apparent.

Sometimes he was jealous as, for example, over her friendship with Middleton Murry. At Zennor in Cornwall, Katherine Mansfield saw him beat Frieda's 'head and face and breast' and pull out her hair, yet

1 *'Not I, But The Wind . . . .'* (1934), p. 34.
2 *Ibid.*, pp. 5–6.

in half an hour they were '*mutually* remembering a certain . . . very extravagant macaroni cheese they had once eaten'.[1] Sometimes she faced a rival – Mabel Dodge, the rich American woman at Taos. But whenever they parted, they always came together again. That was how Lawrence saw the 'Rainbow' being formed – a man and woman adapting their separateness until they created, in the phrase of André Maurois, a single 'jewel of trust and peace'.

Robert Nichols called Frieda, despite her birth, 'one of life's natural squatters, a gypsy and totally unpractical'. Aldous Huxley called her 'incredibly stupid – the most maddening woman I think I ever came across'.

Nevertheless, she was the only sort of woman with whom D.H.L. could live . . .[2] I have seen him on two occasions rise from what I thought was his death-bed, when Frieda, who had been away, came back after a short absence.[3]

II

Over a period twice as long, there were many more times when CARLYLE and Jane chose to be apart. On his 'annual migrations' to Scotsbrig, lasting two months as a rule, only rarely did she accompany him. He did not take her on his tour of Ireland, nor on his two visits to Germany. A critical time was his capitulation, in middle age, to Lady Ashburton, when Jane felt herself cast in the role of a dependant. After her death, he spoke of 'our . . . hard battle against fate; hard but not quite unvictorious, when she left me, as in her car of heaven's fire'.[4]

But the picture most of us have – of a widower suffering remorse: 'Oh that I had you yet but for five minutes beside me, to tell you all!' – is insufficient. He was only too painfully aware of what was happening while she was alive. J. A. Froude, who has been accused

1 Letter to Ottoline Morrell: 17 May 1916.
2 Letter to Dr Henry Head and his wife, 8 Mar 1930. Sybille Bedford: *Aldous Huxley: A Biography* (1973–4), i, p. 225.
3 *Ibid.*, i, p. 264.
4 'Jane Welsh Carlyle': *Reminiscences* by Thomas Carlyle, ed. J. A. Froude (1881), ii, p. 172.

of being 'prejudiced in favour of Jane and against Carlyle',[1] said 'his was the soft heart, and hers the stern one'.[2]

God bless thee, my poor little darling. I think we shall be happier some time, and oh, how happy if God will! (2 November 1835)

Oh Jeannie, would thou wert happier! Would I could make thee happy! (5 April 1841)

In the mutual misery we often are in, we do not know how dear we are to one another. (1841)

. . . know well always that I cannot deliberately mean anything that is harmful to you, unjust, painful to you. Indeliberately I do enough of such things without meaning them. (26 March 1842)

Courage, my poor little Jeannie! Ah me! Had I been other, for you too it might have been all easier. But I was not other: I was even this . . . let us both cry for help to be better for each other . . . (9 April 1842)

At the time of 'that black business', her dislike – even jealousy – of Lady Harriet (who became Lady Ashburton), he wrote:

. . . dear Goody . . . let us . . . pray . . . that we *may* be . . . helpful, not hindersome to one another . . . For *thy* great unwearied goodness, and true ever-watchful affection, mixed as it is with human infirmity, oh, my dearest, woe to me for ever if I could forget it . . . (7 July 1846)

Oh, my Jeannie! my own true Jeannie! bravest little life-companion, hitherto, into what courses are we tending? (14 August 1846)

Edward Irving had first taken him to see her 'on a summer evening after sunset . . . the beautifullest young creature I had ever beheld, sparkling with grace and talent . . .'[3] Jane Welsh had been a pupil of Irving, for whom she had an early passion and whom Carlyle so deeply admired. The attractive looks of the well-to-do doctor's daughter caused her to be sought by many. But she was a poet, extremely knowledgeable of literature, reading Virgil as a child. It was the lonely and impecunious scholar who won the prize in his thirty-first year, when she was twenty-five. During their five-year courtship by letter, he admitted 'his strange dark humours'.

In the early years of marriage, 'on summer mornings after breakfast

1 Ian Campbell: 'Thomas Carlyle': *Writers at Home: National Trust Studies* (1985), p. 74.
2 J. A. Froude: *Thomas Carlyle: A History of his Life in London 1834–1881* (1884), ii, p. 171.
3 Journal: 5 May 1866.

. . . [she] used very often to come up to the little dressing-room where I was shaving and seat herself on a chair behind me, for the privilege of a little further talk' before 'I took to my work, and probably we did not meet much again till dinner'.[1]

He continued to use pet-names when writing to her: 'my dear Bairn', 'my dear little Janekin', 'dear life partner! dear little Goody of me', 'my poor little Protectress!' As Nora held for Joyce, and Joy for C. S. Lewis, a maternal role too, so he wrote to Jane when she had gone to Folkestone:

. . . I am dreadfully low-spirited, and feel like a child *wishing Mammy back*.[2]

He accompanied her birthday present with a 'notekin' –

. . . a little jewel-box . . . Blessings on thee with it! I wish I had diamonds to fill the places with for my little wifie.[3]

I send thee a poor little card-case . . . God bless thee, and know thou always, in spite of the chimaeras and illusions, that thou art dearer to me than any earthly creature.[4]

Twenty-four years into marriage, it was a five-pound note for Christmas, with –

The Prophecy of a Wash-stand to the Neatest of all women. Blessings on her bonny face, and be it ever blithe to me, as it is dear, blithe or not.

When she left on the table for 'the Noble Lord' her 'Budget of a Femme Incomprise',[5] occupying several pages and mocking the stance he took whenever money was discussed, he read it 'with great laughter' and wrote on it: 'my . . . cleverest of women . . . and thy *30l* more shall be granted, thy bits of debts paid, and thy will be done'.[6] He was very tender when her mother died, and again when it came home to him that she was really ill – no more public vehicles: she must have her own brougham. He took care of her canaries when she was away, and her dog Nero ran with him at night 'through the Brompton solitudes . . . merry as a maltman'.

1 *Ibid.*, 30 Nov. 1867.
2 J. A. Froude: *Thomas Carlyle: A History of his Life in London 1834–1881* (1884), ii, p. 249.
3 13 July 1844: *ibid.*, i, p. 345.
4 13 July 1846: *ibid.*, i, p. 383.
5 12 Feb. 1855.
6 See Froude *op. cit.*, ii, pp. 162–70.

She for her part honoured his genius and was his best, if severest, critic. She suffered the painters and workmen while he was away because he couldn't bear the inconvenience – 'Oh! my dear little Jeannie . . . how you have lain between me and these annoyances, and wrapt me like a cloak against them!' In the spring that she died, she told him to lie on the sofa but not to sleep, and going to her piano – which she had not done for at least ten years – she got out the Thomson Burns book and gave him all his old favourites, 'with an honest geniality and unobtrusively beautiful perfection of heart and hand – which I have never seen equalled . . .'[1]

But however much their arc quivered, it could not strengthen because of the way they were constituted. Both suffered from dyspepsia and insomnia. He was domineering and irritable, she 'far too sharp-tempered, but true to the bone'.[2] There were times when, because of his obstinacy, she felt like a 'keeper in a mad-house' and, fearing for her sanity, contemplated separation. His friend, J. A. Froude, said:

It was only in his letters that he showed what was really in his heart.[3]

He had Orwell's massive reticence. Froude said again:

His misfortune was . . . he had no perception.[4]

Following an injury when she was thrown by a cab, Jane's lower jaw weakened – and the resulting facial expression he associated with stupidity. One morning when she was in great pain, he stood leaning on the mantelpiece and looking at her. 'Jane, ye had better shut your mouth.' He added she should be thankful her accident was no worse – to which she made a spirited reply. Sometimes he gave rein to his impulses like a naughty child. During a three months' absence an ailing Jane had the house redecorated, with furniture mended at minimum cost, herself covering chairs and sofas, stitching carpets and curtains, also arranging his library the way he once said he should like it to be. Three days after his return, the woman next door played her

---

1 Journal: 30 Dec. 1867.
2 His letter to Jane: July–Aug. 1857. Cf. Froude: '. . . a tongue, when she was angry, like a cat's, which would take the skin off at a touch'. (*Op. cit.*, i, p. 180.)
3 *Ibid.*, ii, p. 52. (See also, i, p. 79.) Cf. Froude: 'The real Carlyle is . . . in [the Journal], for it contains his dialogues with his own heart.' (*Ibid.*, i, p. 420.)
4 *Ibid.*, ii, p. 242. (See also, i, p. 385; ii, p. 272.)

piano and he insisted he should have a room made on the roof. When the prohibitive cost was pointed out, he had the rooms altered below.

After the Ashburton chapter, what Froude calls 'the fine edge' of their feeling for each other suffered. She even suspected he wrote his letters for a biographer.[1] Once, she upbraided him for coming with a lighted cigar in his mouth to kiss her before leaving, when, as he explained (in the inevitable letter), he wanted to whisper he had given the maid half a crown. Again like Orwell with Eileen, he made little of her complaints – 'If Carlyle wakes once in a night,' she told Froude, 'he will complain . . . for a week. I wake thirty times every night, but that is nothing.'[2] Her rare capacity for friendship made its moan to Mrs Tennyson:

Wouldn't I like to go and visit you if that man would leave his eternal *Frederick* and come along! *He* goes nowhere, sees nobody . . .[3]

On the evening after the day Carlyle delivered his inaugural address as Lord Rector of Edinburgh University,[4] she came into the room at the Forsters' flourishing a telegram from Professor Tyndall announcing its great success. 'The radiance of her enjoyment', wrote Dickens, 'was upon her all night.' After forty years, it was testimony to a kind of rainbow.

Three weeks later, on picking up a pet dog run over in Hyde Park, she got back in her brougham and presently the coachman saw her sitting there dead, the dog on her knees.

Carlyle never recovered completely.

. . . but no full gust of tears came . . . I cannot weep . . . God enable me to live out my poor remnant of days in a manner she would have applauded. Hers – as known to me only – were all very noble, a life of hidden beauty, all given to me as part of my own.[5]

He shuffled through fifteen more years – a partial recluse in dressing-gown, nightcap and slippers, his beard unkempt and blue eyes filmed. When the season was clement, he took a 'final pipe' in the 'Patch of Garden' before retiring. At seventy-two, he wrote in his Journal:

1 See J. A. Froude: *Thomas Carlyle: A History of his Life in London 1834–1881* (1884), ii, p. 233.
2 *Ibid.*, ii, p. 234.
3 21 Jan. 1857.
4 The ceremony was on Mon., 2 Apr. 1866.
5 Journal: 5 May 1866.

Her little Gooseberry bush (brought hither from her Father's Grave, *his only*, at that time): her Hawthorn, Ash-tree, &c., all from loved scenes of childhood, are in vigorous bud again, almost in leaf . . .[1]

1 27 Feb. 1868.

PART TWO
THE PAINS OF LOVE

CHAPTER ONE

The Private Catastrophe

Perhaps the most bizarre example of a writer in domestic torment is when T. S. ELIOT's first wife tracked him down to a *Sunday Times* book exhibition. Throughout his lecture she stood, holding up high their dog Polly. At the end, she was first in the audience to reach his table and the little dog jumped up and down excitedly. She asked if he would come back. He autographed his last three books that she held in her hand and hurriedly left – 'I cannot talk to you now!' As with Hardy and Emma, it is sad to think of the early promise. Eliot had written to his father:

She has everything to give that I want, and she gives it. I owe her everything.[1]

He was twenty-six, on a travelling scholarship at Oxford, when he met the vivacious Vivienne Haigh-Wood ('Vivien'), six months older than himself. They married at Hampstead Register Office, a week after he left University. After a brief honeymoon at Eastbourne, he met her parents and for the first time may have learned that she had a history of nervous illness. Quite soon she became seriously ill and he nursed her – coping as he did for eighteen years virtually single-handed. At the end of the first year, he said he had been through 'the most awful nightmare of anxiety that the mind of man could conceive'.[2] They moved to a small flat at 18 Crawford Mansions, and he started renting a country cottage in summer.

When he began at the bank, Vivien persuaded him to accompany her to a dance hall in Queensway on Sunday afternoons. Brigit Patmore sometimes went with them and has described one occasion when, coming away, they stopped at a chemist's 'for aspirin or something'. Vivien thought she could do what Karsavina did in a

---

1 Quoted by Lyndall Gordon: *Eliot's Early Years* (1977), p. 79.
2 Letter to his brother, Henry Ware Eliot, Jr., Sept. 1916. *Ibid.*, p. 75.

ballet and, holding on to the counter with one hand, stretched out the other to Eliot, who not at all put out studied her feet while he supported her 'with real tenderness'.[1]

That autumn his former teacher, Bertrand Russell, seduced her; he may have done so the first year, when they had shared his flat in Bury Street and Eliot was teaching at High Wycombe Grammar School. Russell had also taken her to Torquay for convalescence since Eliot was not free to do so himself. Three years after marriage, they lived in a cottage lent by Russell at Marlow.

I . . . endeavoured to help them in their troubles until I discovered that their troubles were what they enjoyed.[2]

The following summer, at Bosham, Eliot began his practice of joining her usually at weekends. He rationalized their periodic living apart, saying that Vivien made significant improvement when he was not there. At Christmas, his bronchitis caused their roles of nurse and patient to be reversed. There was a move to a less-cramped flat at 9 Clarence Gate Gardens; then the strain of nursing her father caused Vivien to collapse and Eliot, himself looking exhausted, left gatherings early to be with her. At thirty-three, he had a nervous breakdown. A specialist advised him to go away alone, for three months, and not exert his mind at all. The bank gave him leave of absence. Taking a month at Margate, in a shelter on the promenade he wrote 'The Fire Sermon' from *The Waste Land*. He left for Lausanne, to be under an analyst recommended by Ottoline Morrell and Julian Huxley, while Vivien went to a sanatorium outside Paris.

The following year, editing *Criterion* and working at the bank, as well as caring for a hysterical and accusatory wife, he wrote to John Quinn:

I have not even time to go to a dentist or to have my hair cut . . . I am worn out. I cannot go on.[3]

In a cable to Quinn he said that his affairs were in complete chaos. Those close to him saw a man fearful of poverty and near breaking-point once more. After the Woolfs called one day at the flat, he was barely able to see them out.

1 *My Friends When Young: the memoirs of Brigit Patmore* ed. Derek Patmore (1968), p. 85.
2 *The Autobiography of Bertrand Russell* (1967–9), ii, p. 19.
3 12 Mar. 1923. Lyndall Gordon: *Eliot's Early Years* (1977), p. 124.

He tried to settle her alone in a cottage at Fishbourne, but in a matter of three weeks she wasted away on a very severe diet medically prescribed. Seven or eight times she came near to dying. Two specialists came down from London, and a local doctor called twice daily. Eliot had taken three weeks' holiday from the bank, and another fortnight. She accused Ottoline Morrell and the Sitwells of 'disloyalty' because, in urging him to leave the bank, he would not then be able to pay her very high medical bills.

There were times she acknowledged 'my savage and rebellious conduct'. Over a year previously, at Bosham, she had devoted a great deal of time to the launching of *Criterion* and, even now, she contributed anonymous prose sketches, sometimes in collaboration with Eliot. When he was thirty-six, she fell into a 'fearful abyss':[1] her body utterly prostrate, only her mind active and intense. Eliot sought Leonard Woolf's experience with Virginia. He told Russell 'living with me has done her so much damage',[2] and that perhaps it would be best if they parted. He feared the possessiveness of his wife's instability:

As to Tom's *mind*, I am his mind.[3]

She noticeably improved, but became afflicted with shingles. After their move to 57 Chester Terrace, Aldous Huxley described her mottled face and the house smelling like a hospital. Peter Ackroyd explains that ether was used at that time as a tranquillizer, and Vivien would rub it over her body.

Next year she travelled between sanatoria abroad, Eliot sometimes accompanying her. A fellow-patient described her unkempt appearance and her walking lost and very sad, almost as if in a trance. The following year she helped nurse her dying father at St Leonard's, and Eliot stayed with her for a few weeks, commuting to and from Faber's. He was now baptized into the Anglican Church, a significant step in his life, but Vivien did not attend. When he was thirty-nine a dinner party celebrated her return from a Paris sanatorium, and she started an argument with him in the presence of the Joyces and Fabers. Some months later, she suffered from the delusion that he was having an

---

1 24 Nov. 1934: the diaries of Vivien Eliot. Peter Ackroyd: *T. S. Eliot* (1984), p. 149.
2 *The Autobiography of Bertrand Russell* (1967–9), ii, p. 174.
3 Vivien's letter to Jack Hutchinson, inserted in her Diary: 8 Dec. 1935. Quoted by Gordon, *op. cit.*, p. 79 Note, and Ackroyd, *op. cit.*, p. 150.

affair with Ottoline Morrell. Any party was liable to be pierced by her screaming at him. The rumour went around that Eliot was now habitually drunk.

They moved back to Clarence Gate Gardens, switching in a few months from numbers 98 to 177 and then 68. Perhaps not surprisingly, she wanted to know if it was 'accident' that they moved so often, but Virigina Woolf, noting other remarks, saw her question as a sign of paranoia. Edith Sitwell greeted her in Oxford Street and her reply was schizophrenic:

No, no . . . You have mistaken me *again* for that *terrible* woman who is so like me.[1]

At forty-two, Eliot lectured at University College and they were described as 'a forlorn pair'[2] – Vivien wearing a scarf across her mouth and plucking continually at his sleeve.

She did not want him to accept the one-year Charles Eliot Norton professorship at Harvard but, unknown to her, he had decided on a permanent separation. For the last time they walked together, before his ship left. From America he instructed his solicitors to draw up a Deed of Separation. Over there he renewed his acquaintance with Emily Hale, whom he had courted in Harvard days and to whom he had sent roses from England before meeting Vivien.

On his return he stayed for several months at Frank Morley's farm in Surrey, and then he became a paying guest at the presbytery of Father Cheetham, who appointed him the following year Vicar's Warden of St Stephen's, Gloucester Road. Meanwhile Vivien decorated the flat and when he did not come became panic-stricken, at first taking to her bed. She feared he had met with an accident, and the Fabers did their best to reassure her. Eventually there was a formal meeting between them in the presence of solicitors.

He sat near me and I held his hand, but he never looked at me.[3]

An allowance was paid through her bank. None of her family passed judgment at the time. She again accused Virigina Woolf and Ottoline Morrell of having affairs with her husband. She even carried a joke

1 John Pearson: *Façades: Edith, Osbert, & Sacheverell Sitwell* (1978), pp. 277–8.
2 Quoted by Peter Ackroyd: *T. S. Eliot* (1984), p. 184.
3 *The Diaries of Virginia Woolf*, iv, 21 July 1933.

knife in her handbag, which some of their friends took to be real. Eliot always believed she was sane, but talked herself into insanity.

She seemed to me like a child of 6 with an immensely clever and precocious mind . . .[1]

She waited at 68 Clarence Gate Gardens, refusing to sign any 'blackmailing paper'[2] and writing to him many times. She tried catching him at Faber's, but while his secretary engaged her he was slipping from the building. She signed her Christmas cards as from them both. Through a Court order he had his books removed from the flat. She went to Oxford, the scene of their meeting and courting. She attended a production of *Sweeney Agonistes* at The Westminster. When she became aware of an attempt to commit her, she went to Paris. Then, when he was forty-seven, she caught up with him at *The Sunday Times* book exhibition and that was the last time they met. She saw *Murder in the Cathedral* at The Mercury seven times.

When Eliot was fifty, she became a resident in a private mental hospital in Finsbury Park and he must have given consent, although not eligible as one of the two signatories. Apparently she attempted escape. After eight years, news of her death came very early in the morning at Carlyle Mansions where he was living. In a state of shock, Eliot cried, 'Oh God! Oh God!' and his companion John Hayward in a wheelchair, a sufferer from muscular dystrophy, helped him. Eliot went with her brother to the burial.

Emily Hale, who had waited so long, supposed there would be no barrier now to his marrying her. A shattered man explained that his love for her was spiritual. Mary Trevelyan believed he deliberately chose ten years' penance for the guilt he felt towards Vivien. Joseph Chiari, his friend from 1943 – 'younger than he by quite a stretch of years' – wrote:

. . . the destructive, de-humanising suffering of a person with whom he had been closely linked affected him deeply . . . he . . . constantly asked himself how far what had happened was his fault and, like Harry Monchensey in *The Family Reunion*, whether he himself was not truly responsible for her death-in-life.[3]

1 Letter to Russell: *The Autobiography of Bertrand Russell* (1967–9), ii, p. 174.
2 The diaries of Vivien Eliot: 20 Jan. 1934. Quoted by Peter Ackroyd: *T. S. Eliot* (1984), p. 208; also by Lyndall Gordon: *Eliot's New Life* (1988), p. 70.
3 *T. S. Eliot: A Memoir* (1982), p. 52.

He wrote no more poetry, outside the verse of his plays (and a dedicatory poem). 'Tall, gaunt, of pallid hue and tensely withdrawn from anything reminiscent of the flesh',[1] he lectured in America, before an operation for hernia and the extraction of the remainder of his teeth. But there was to be more, an unexpected epilogue of marital delight.[2]

EVELYN WAUGH's wife left him for another man a year after their marriage.

I did not know it was possible to be so miserable and live.

He was converted to Roman Catholicism at twenty-six, when he was suicidal. He filed a petition for divorce but it took years before he received a dispensation from Rome.

---

1 Hans Meyerhoff in *The Partisan Review*, Jan. 1948. Quoted by Peter Ackroyd: *T. S. Eliot* (1984), p. 285.
2 See pp. 63–4.

CHAPTER TWO

A Living Sorrow

When THACKERAY was forty-five, a year after the publication of *The Newcomes*, Whitwell Elwin, on a walk from Piccadilly to Brompton, urged him to describe a 'domestic family, enjoying calm, domestic felicity'.

Thackeray replied pathetically, 'How can I describe that sort of domestic calm? I have never seen it. I have lived all my life in Bohemia.'[1]

His formidable Irish mother-in-law had used every means, largely foul, to prevent his marrying, at twenty-five, the petite, demure, eighteen-year-old redhead Isabella Shawe. His four years of happiness with 'Puss', 'dear Trot', his 'dearest little Wife', can be seen reflected in all his major books. They lost their middle child at eight months old – a date that Thackeray always marked in his diary. After the birth of a third daughter, 'the little woman' remained unnaturally 'low' and 'absent'. When he was taking his family from London to Cork, she flung herself into the sea from the water-closet and was twenty minutes floating on her back, paddling with her hands, before the ship's boat saw her. Next night she made further attempts on her own life, so that in bed he 'had a riband round her waist, & to my waist, and this always woke me if she moved'.[2]

After two months she was admitted into Esquirol's Maison de Santé, at Ivry, outside Paris.[3] The last time Thackeray visited, he took her for a walk across the fields to a 'little gudgeon house on the river' and, during dinner, she suddenly flung herself into his arms and kissed him. The waiter came in at that precise moment, which made

---

1 *Some Eighteenth-Century Men of Letters: Biographical Essays* by the Rev. Whitwell Elwin . . . with a *Memoir* ed. by his son Warwick Elwin (1902), i, pp. 156–7.
2 Letter to his Mother, 4–5 Oct. 1840: *The Letters & Private Papers of William Makepeace Thackeray* ed. Gordon N. Ray (1945–6), i, p. 483.
3 Joyce's daughter was a patient there in 1936, under Dr Achille Delmas.

her laugh – 'the first time these six months'[1] – and at once Thackeray brought her home. Unfortunately, progress was not maintained. For about six weeks he looked after her entirely by himself – an experience which caused him to refer to Lamb as 'Saint Charles'. Thackeray almost broke down, until he hired a woman who did it all 'cheerfully' for ten francs a week. On the baby's birthday he had to prompt her mother and then she kissed her, but showed no other emotion. He told Mrs Procter he was 'quite beaten down': there was nothing the matter with her except 'silence and sluggishness'.

She is not unhappy . . . smiling and [looks] about sixteen years old.[2]

He opened his heart to FitzGerald:

They are not half the children without their mother – A man's grief is very selfish . . . it's our comforts we mourn.[3]

Thackeray's mother, who took an individual line over medicine, advocating homoeopathic doctors, now recommended hydropathy, and he interviewed Dr Weincke. They began a 'frightfully complicated' system which involved sweating for four hours, followed by baths and walks, taking up most of the day. For three months he was with his wife at a sanatorium near Boppard on the Rhine, under the care of a famous water-doctor. Treatment began at 5 a.m. with sweating in blankets; at 8 a.m. they poured buckets of water over her; at 12 a.m. there was 'an enormous douche' for five minutes; at 5 p.m. more sweating and ice-cold water. At first, she was apprehensive of the 'immense sluicing' and he went in with her. He gave a description to FitzGerald:

Mrs Thack in the condition of our first parins, before they took to eating apples, and the great Titmarsh with . . . a petticoat lent him by his mother, and far too scanty to cover that immense posterior . . . with wh. nature has furnished him.[4]

Then came the usual relapses. Although Thackeray put his young wife away, he was constantly trying to find more congenial and

1 Letter to Mrs Procter, 5 Apr. 1841: *The Letters & Private Papers of William Makepeace Thackeray* ed. Gordon N. Ray (1945–6), ii, p. 15.
2 28 May–5 June 1841: *ibid.*, ii, p. 23.
3 9 Mar. 1842: *ibid.*, ii, p. 43.
4 13 Sept.Oct. 1841: *ibid.*, ii, p. 36.

therapeutic places for her. He now tried Dr Puzin at Chaillot, and visited her continually.

. . . it makes my heart sick to be parted from her.

Thackeray didn't know anywhere in London where he could install her to be so comfortable. His friend Procter, who was a Lunacy Commissioner '& knows them all', took him to his favourite place, 'which makes me quite sick to think of even now'.[1]

The children were looked after by Thackeray's mother in France, while he wrote and lived in London clubland. 'Q' said no one knew better the world between Kensington and Cornhill, the big houses, the clubs, the newspaper offices, the taverns, but Thackeray did not really know his England.

His loyalty never faltered:

My dearest Mammy . . . Ah! there was more nobleness and simplicity in that little woman that neither of you knew, than I've seen in most people in this world.[2]

When he was beginning *Vanity Fair*, he instructed his mother to let the children visit their mother often and to pay for a coach if it rained. After three years' devoted struggle, an awful realization began to dawn:

My dear Aunt [Mrs Ritchie] . . . my wife is provokingly well – so well I mean, that I can't understand why she should not be quite well. I begin to fear now that the poor dear little soul will never be entirely restored to us.[3]

She was with Dr Puzin for over three years, before the final move when she was brought to England and placed in the care of Mrs Bakewell, 'an excellent worthy woman' in Camberwell, who made a remarkable difference to 'the poor little woman's appearance' and kept her clean. Now thirty-four, Thackeray visited her 'almost every other day'. He told Mr Pryme:

I am engaged to dine with my wife on Thursday; and as it is the only free day I have this week I must not disappoint her. But those little parties are over very early . . .[4]

1 Letter to his Mother, 25–30 Sept. 1842: *ibid.*, ii, p. 81.
2 11? June 1842: *ibid.*, ii, p. 53.
3 13 Oct. 1843: *ibid.*, ii, p. 125.
4 Dec. 1845?: *ibid.*, ii, p. 223.

He described, for his mother, 'the three Camberwell ladies . . . my wife, Mrs Gloyne and Mrs Bakewell – one mending the right hand breeches pocket another the left the third a hole in my coat-tail!'[1] Sometimes he took her to the theatre – 'in a private box and she enjoys herself in her little way . . .' But after a day's work, his visits made 'poor holiday making'.[2]

At thirty-seven, he wrote to his sister-in-law, Jane, remembering 'how tenderly you always loved her . . . that dear artless sweet creature who charmed us both so'. It is as though he writes an epitaph:

What a whir of life I've seen since then, but never her better I think: whose reason it pleased God to destroy before her body: and who cares for none of us now . . .[3]

During his first American lecture tour, when he was forty-one, he advised his mother, who had the girls, that it were best if they did not write to their own mother, for such letters could only grieve her and he did not want them to receive an irrational reply.

If she could get well . . . she might come back and be a sister to the girls – God bless her. Her intelligence has slept during the time theirs was developing. I doubt whether she ought to come back; and whether, Fate having put that awful 12 years barrier and death between us, it would be happy for her to be reinstated into our world.[4]

It sounds peculiarly like *Act* III of Barrie's *Mary Rose*:

CAMERON: You must be prepared to find her – different.
MRS MORLAND: We are all different. Her age –
CAMERON: I mean, Mrs Morland, different from what you expect. She iss not different as we are different. They will be saying she iss just as she was on the day she went away. These five-and-twenty years, she will be thinking they were just an hour in which Mr Blake and I had left her in some incomprehensible jest . . .
MR MORLAND: Do you think she should have come back, Mr Cameron?

Two years later, he answered an inquiry from his Cambridge friend, the Rev. John Allen:

The poor dear little wife who you remember is very well . . . though cut off for 15 years from husband & children. She does not miss them though: and

1 6 Mar. 1846: *ibid.*, ii, p. 231.
2 Letter to his Mother, Mar. 1846: *ibid.*, ii, p. 233.
3 19 Sept. 1848: *ibid.*, ii, p. 431.
4 26 Jan. 1853: *ibid.*, iii, p. 187.

the care of her serves to maintain a very worthy old couple who treat her with the utmost kindness and watchfulness – so that her illness serves for some good.[1]

At forty-six, he observed to Mrs Baxter: 'A man without a woman is a lonely wretch.'[2] Unlike Leonard Woolf, whose loved one returned to him for long lucid intervals, Thackeray's deprivation of his 'little woman' was total. She spent fifty-three years in psychosis, living on long after him.

Mrs Fuller (Anne Thackeray's daughter, Hester) remembered her grandmother playing Irish jigs to her on the piano.

I do not think that she knew that my mother was her daughter or that I was her grandchild.[3]

She always wore the engagement ring which had a diamond set between two opals. Before presenting it to her, Thackeray had shown it excitedly to a friend, who pointed out that the black enamel setting meant it was intended to be a bereavement ring.

1 7 Feb. 1855. *The Letters & Private Papers of William Makepeace Thackeray* ed. Gordon N. Ray (1945–6), iii, p. 419.
2 10–23 Apr. 1858. *Ibid.*, iv, p. 81.
3 *Ibid.*, i, p. clxv.

CHAPTER THREE

Sacrificial Marriages

I

After four years' unrequited love for Mary Evans during his student days, COLERIDGE at twenty-three married Sara Fricker, Southey's sister-in-law, 'at St Mary's Redcliff, poor Chatterton's church!'

> The thought gave a tinge of melancholy to the solemn joy which I felt, united to the woman whom I love best of all created beings . . . *Mrs Coleridge!* I like to write the name.[1]

Over eleven years on, he assured De Quincey 'that his marriage was not his own deliberate act, but was in a manner forced upon his sense of honour by the scrupulous Southey, who insisted that he had gone too far in his attentions to Miss Fricker for any honourable retreat'. She had expected Southey to marry her, and this might explain Southey's pressure on Coleridge. But De Quincey adds:

> . . . a neutral spectator of the parties protested to me, that, if ever in his life he had seen a man . . . what he would have called desperately in love, Coleridge, in relation to Miss F., was that man.[2]

As their marriage progressed and disillusionment set in, she held up Southey and the 'methodical tenor of his daily labours' as an example to her husband, a self-confessed 'to-morrower' – who it is now known had physical cause. In just after a year, helped by good friends, they settled at Nether Stowey. He began a programme of early-morning gardening, reviewing, and Sunday preaching in the Unitarian Chapel at Bridgwater. He made her a skivvy by having Charles Lloyd as a lodger and inviting, at various times, to their five-roomed cottage

---

1 Letter to Thomas Poole: Wed. even., 7 Oct. 1795. *Letters of Samuel Taylor Coleridge* ed. Ernest Hartley Coleridge (1895), i, p. 136.
2 'Samuel Taylor Coleridge': *Selections Grave & Gay* (1853–71), ii, p. 167.

(with kitchen but no oven) Wordsworth and his sister Dorothy, Southey, Lamb, Hazlitt, and Cottle the bookseller; a maid, Nanny, also slept in.

Lamb, at twenty-two, came in the summer following their own arrival. Coleridge wrote to Southey:

Charles Lamb has been with me for a week . . . The second day after Wordsworth came to me, dear Sara accidentally emptied a skillet of boiling milk on my foot, which confined me during the whole time of C. Lamb's stay and still prevents me from all *walks* longer than a furlong.[1]

Hazlitt, just twenty, stayed three weeks. On his second day, Wordsworth arrived from Bristol and, having sat down, 'instantly began to make havoc of the half of a Cheshire cheese on the table'. He looked through the window, observing: 'How beautifully the sun sets on that yellow bank!'[2] Hazlitt said of Coleridge:

His genius at that time had angelic wings, and fed on manna. He talked on for ever; and you wished him to talk on for ever.[3]

According to De Quincey, when the Wordsworths settled at Alfoxden, and a young lady 'intellectually . . . very much superior to Mrs Coleridge' became 'a daily companion of Coleridge's walks . . . that superiority . . . in winning Coleridge's regard and society, could not but be deeply mortifying to a young wife . . . Mrs Coleridge, not having the same relish for long walks and rural scenery . . . was condemned to a daily renewal of this trial'.

. . . often it would happen that the walking party returned drenched with rain; in which case, the young lady, with a laughing gaiety . . . would run up to Mrs Coleridge's wardrobe, array herself, without leave asked, in Mrs Coleridge's dresses . . . In all this, she took no liberty that she would not most readily have granted in return; she confided too unthinkingly in what she regarded as the natural privileges of friendship . . . Mrs Coleridge . . . felt herself no longer the entire mistress of her own house; she held a divided empire; and it barbed the arrow to her womanly feelings that Coleridge treated any sallies of resentment which might sometimes escape her as narrow-mindedness.

1 July 1797.
2 'My First Acquaintance with Poets'.
3 *Lectures on the English Poets* (1818), p. 330.

Presumably, Nanny – and Charles Lloyd – 'began to drop expressions which alternately implied pity for her as an injured woman, or contempt for her as a very tame one'.[1]

It was the time when Coleridge wrote *The Rime of the Ancient Mariner*, *Kubla Khan*, *Frost at Midnight*, the first part of *Christabel*, the poems on which his poetical reputation rests. He ends his *Fears in Solitude*:

> And now, beloved Stowey! . . .
> . . . hidden from my view,
> Is my own lowly cottage, where my babe
> And my babe's mother dwell in peace! With light
> And quickened footsteps thitherward I tend,
> . . . all my heart
> Is softened, and made worthy to indulge
> Love, and the thoughts that yearn for human kind.

Later that year, when the Wordsworths – who had become so important to him – left Alfoxden, he went with them abroad for ten months to improve his knowledge of the German language and literature. While he was away, Sara and the children went back to Bristol to live with her mother. On arrival at Hamburg, Coleridge wrote in a letter:

Good-night, my dear, dear Sara! – *every night when I go to bed and every morning when I rise*, I will think with yearning love of you and of my blessed babies! . . . My dear Sara! I think of you with affection and a desire to be home, and . . . will be, I trust, your husband faithful unto death.[2]

Six months on, their second child Berkeley died of smallpox, and he wrote from Göttingen where he had recently matriculated:

It is one of the discomforts of my absence, my dearest Love! that we feel the same calamities at different times – I would fain write words of consolation to you; yet I know that I shall only fan into new activity the pang which was growing dead and dull in your heart . . . when in moments of fretfulness and imbecility I am disposed to anger or reproach, it will, I trust, be always a restoring thought – 'We have wept over the same little one, – and with whom I am angry? With her who so patiently and unweariedly sustained my poor and sickly infant through his long pains – with her, who, if I too should be

---

1 'Samuel Taylor Coleridge': *Selections Grave & Gay* (1853–71), ii, pp. 167–9.
2 19 Sept. 1798: *Letters of Samuel Taylor Coleridge* ed. Ernest Hartley Coleridge (1895), i, p. 261.

called away, would stay in the deep anguish over my death-pillow! who would never forget me!"[1]

Three months after his return, journeying at Wordsworth's invitation to see the Lake District, he met Sarah Hutchinson, the 'Asra' of his poems, his passionate and hopeless love. Again an important woman in his life was to be the sister-in-law of a friend, this time Wordsworth, whose marriage to Mary Hutchinson would sharpen the contrast of his own.

Dorothy found for the Coleridges Greta Hall at Keswick, and there Derwent was born, but Mrs Coleridge was unhappy, separated from familiar ties. Coleridge, at twenty-nine, told Southey:

For what is life, gangrened, as it is with me, in its very vitals, domestic tranquillity?[2]

And again:

Never, I suppose, did the stern match-maker bring together two minds so utterly contrariant in their primary and organical constitution.[3]

De Quincey said:

My own impression is, that neither Coleridge nor Lord Byron could have failed, eventually, to quarrel with *any* wife . . .[4]

At a later time, Coleridge made him a confidant:

What he had to complain of was simply incompatibility of temper and disposition.

Without comprehension 'of her husband's intellectual powers' and 'hearing from everybody that Coleridge was a man of most extraordinary endowments . . . she naturally looked to see, at least, an ordinary measure of worldly consequence attend upon their exercise.[5]

Yet early in 1802 they both made certain promises to each other, and in the letter above Coleridge was able to inform Southey:

I rejoice . . . that now for a long time there has been more love and concord in my house than I have known for years before.

1 8 Apr. 1799: *ibid.*, i, pp. 284, 287.
2 31 Dec. 1801: *ibid.*, i, p. 366.
3 29 July 1802: *ibid.*, i, pp. 389–90.
4 'Samuel Taylor Coleridge': *Selections Grave & Gay* (1853–71), ii, p. 169.
5 *Ibid.*, ii, pp. 166–7.

Coleridge's making up his mind 'to a very awful step' of separation had alarmed Mrs Coleridge and 'wounded her pride'. She was 'made *serious*, and for the first time since our marriage she felt and acted as beseemed a wife and a mother to a husband and the father of her children'.

She promised to set about an alteration in her external manners and looks and language, and to fight against her inveterate habits of puny thwarting and unintermitting dyspathy, this immediately, and to do her best endeavours to cherish other feelings. I, on my part, promised to be more attentive to all her feelings of pride, etc., etc., and to try to correct my habits of impetuous censure. We have both kept our promises . . . and . . . I have the most confident hopes that this happy revolution in our domestic affairs will be permanent . . . Believe me, if you were here, it would give you a *deep* delight to observe the difference of our minutely conduct towards each other, from that which, I fear, could not but have disturbed your comfort when you were here last. Enough. But I am sure you have not felt it tedious.[1]

At the end of the year a daughter, Sara, was born.

The following August, he set out on a Scots tour with Wordsworth and Dorothy. He left them after fifteen days, and in eight more walked 263 miles in an attempt to conquer his opium habit by violent exercise. The Southeys now joined the Coleridges at Greta Hall and made it their permanent home. Coleridge, at thirty-one, physically and emotionally racked, and to escape from a love denied to him through his religious principles, left England.

While waiting at Portsmouth 'with great anxiety for the arrival of the Speedwell', which was to sail with 'The Leviathan, Man of War, our convoy', he wrote:

My dear Sara! the attentive and excellent mother of my children . . . what we have been to each other, our understandings will not permit our hearts to forget! God knows, I weep tears of blood, but so it is! For I greatly esteem and honour you. Heaven knows if I can leave you really comfortable in your circumstances I shall meet Death with a face, which . . . would rather shock than comfort you to imagine.[2]

For, with all his troubles, he kept up till death an insurance that enabled her to receive about £2,500.[3] He sailed for Malta, then went

1 29 July 1802. *Letters of Samuel Taylor Coleridge* ed. Ernest Hartley Coleridge (1895), i, pp. 389–90.
2 1 Apr. 1804: *ibid.*, ii, p. 468.
3 Leslie Stephen: *DNB*.

to Rome, and was absent for two and a half years. Long before, he had said that 'a residence of two years in a mild and even climate will, with God's blessing, give me a new lease in a better constitution'. Meanwhile, Southey must have braced himself for providing, by authorship alone, for his extended household.

On his return, Coleridge first sought work in London – at the Foreign Office and at *The Courier*. He wrote from No. 348 Strand:

My dear Sara . . . I have had application from the R. Institute for a course of lectures, which I am much disposed to accept both for money and reputation . . . If I finally accept . . . I must return by the middle of November, but propose to take you and Hartley with me, as we may be sure of rooms either in Mr Stuart's house at Knightsbridge, or in the Strand . . .

My heart aches so cruelly that I do not dare trust myself to the writing of any tenderness either to you, my dear, or to our dear children. Be assured, I feel with deep though sad affection toward you, and hold your character in general in more than mere esteem – in reverence . . .

My grateful love to Southey . . . And may God Almighty preserve you, my dear! and your faithful, though long absent husband . . .[1]

Broken in health, he arrived in Keswick, where two weeks convinced him that separation from his wife was inevitable.

That Christmas Day, on a visit to Wordsworth at Coleorton, Coleridge wrote:

My dear Sara . . . All here love him [Hartley] most dearly; and your namesake [Sarah Hutchinson] takes upon her all the duties of his mother and darling friend, with all the mother's love and fondness. He is very fond of *her* . . . We all wish you a merry Christmas and many following ones . . .
. . . believe me anxiously and for ever,
Your sincere friend . . .[2]

The following year the £150 annuity, which he had received from the brothers Wedgwood since 1798 and which for years had gone to Mrs Coleridge and her mother, was reduced.

De Quincey's association with Coleridge began ten months later, at Bridgwater:

I had received directions for finding out the house where Coleridge was visiting; and, in riding down a main street . . . I noticed a gateway corresponding to the description given me.

1 16 Sept. (1806): *Letters of Samuel Taylor Coleridge* ed. Ernest Hartley Coleridge (1895), ii, pp. 507–9.
2 25 Dec. 1806. *Ibid.*, ii, p. 510.

Coleridge was standing under it, 'in a deep reverie'.[1] He led De Quincey to a drawing-room and rang the bell for refreshments. De Quincey relates that 'for about three hours' Coleridge 'had continued to talk', when 'the door opened, and a lady entered . . .'

Coleridge paused upon her entrance; his features, however, announced no particular complacency, and did not relax into a smile. In a frigid tone he said, whilst turning to me, 'Mrs Coleridge'; in some slight way he then presented me to her: I bowed; and the lady almost immediately retired. From this short but ungenial scene, I gathered, what I afterward learned redundantly, that Coleridge's marriage had not been a very happy one.[2]

Several weeks after, Coleridge 'came with his family to the Bristol Hot-Wells, at which, by accident, I was then visiting'.

On calling upon him, I found that he had been engaged by the Royal Institute to lecture . . . during the coming winter of 1807–8, and consequently, was embarrassed about the mode of conveying his family to Keswick.[3]

Two months later De Quincey escorted in a post-chaise Mrs Coleridge with her two sons, Hartley, eleven,[4] and Derwent seven, and Sara, 'her beautiful little daughter, about five', to Grasmere and the Wordsworths. Having spent the night at Dove Cottage, Mrs Coleridge and her children pursued their journey northward to Keswick.

A year later Coleridge, now separated from his wife, who remained at Keswick with their daughter, was domiciled with the Wordsworths at Allan Bank, Grasmere. Hartley and Derwent attended a small boarding school in Ambleside and spent every weekend with their father. In the small room near the front door, Sarah Hutchinson helped him as his secretary on *The Friend*, but when she went to her brother in Wales for a long rest the production was abandoned. Coleridge appeared only briefly, for meals. He never went out. Dorothy recorded:

This beautiful valley seems a blank to him.

At thirty-nine, shortly before his Six Lectures on the Drama at Willis's Rooms, he wrote to Mrs Coleridge from 71 Berners Street:

1 'Samuel Taylor Coleridge': *Selections Grave & Gay* (1853–71), ii, p. 156.
2 *Ibid.*, ii, pp. 164–5.
3 'William Wordsworth': *Ibid.*, ii, p. 232.
4 Hartley's diminutive size may have led De Quincey to believe him 'aged nine'.

My dear Love, – Everything is going on so very well, so much beyond my expectation . . . The last receipt for the insurance is now before me, the date the 4th of May. Be assured that before April is past, you shall *receive* both receipts and the one for the present year, in a frank.

. . . Ever since I have been in town, I have never taken any stimulus of any kind, till the moment of my getting into bed, except a glass of British white wine after dinner, and from three to four glasses of port when I have dined out . . .

As soon as ever I have settled the lecture room . . . I will the very first thing pay the insurance and send off a parcel of books for Hartley, Derwent, and dear Sara, whom I kissed seven times in the shape of her pretty letterlet . . .

God bless you and your affectionate husband . . .[1]

Three days later:

My dear Sara . . . If I can procure the money, I will attempt to purchase Nobs, and send him down to Keswick by short journeys for Herbert [Southey] and Derwent to ride upon, provided you can get the field next us . . .[2]

While his tragedy *Remorse* was running successfully at Drury Lane, he wrote:

My dear Sara . . . the main business of [this letter] is to desire you to draw upon Brent and Co., No. 103 Bishopsgate Street Within, for an hundred pounds, at a month's date from the drawing, or, if that be objected to, for three weeks, only let me know which. In the course of a month I have no hesitation in promising you another hundred, and I hope likewise before Midsummer, if God grant me life, to repay you whatever you have expended for the children . . .[3]

Next year, still only forty-one, he confessed to Cottle 'the tremendous effects' of laudanum-taking on himself:

. . . for ten years the anguish of my spirit has been indescribable . . . the consciousness of my GUILT worse, far worse than all . . . Had I but a few hundred pounds, but £200 – half to send to Mrs Coleridge, and half to place myself in a private madhouse . . . where a medical attendant could be constantly with me for two or three months . . . then there might be hope.[4]

1 21 Apr. 1812: *Letters of Samuel Taylor Coleridge* ed. Ernest Hartley Coleridge (1895), ii, pp. 579–80, 583.
2 24 Apr. 1812: *ibid.*, ii, p. 584.
3 (20 Jan.), 18(13): *ibid.*, ii, p. 603.
4 26 Apr. 1814: *ibid.*, ii, pp. 617–8.

His long-tried friends remained faithful to him. He resided with Josiah Wade and then with the Morgans. For the last eighteen years of his life he was sheltered by James and Anne Gillman at No. 3 The Grove, Highgate, and thanks to their inexhaustible patience the drug was regulated and just about brought under control.

Dorothy Wordsworth observed of the marriage:

Mrs C . . . is very much to be pitied, for when one party is ill matched the other necessarily must be so too.[1]

II

KIPLING married Caroline Balestier as a tribute to her brother Wolcott, an American publisher and writer with whom he had collaborated.

When Kipling had been living with his parents in Earl's Court Road he pursued a boyhood sweetheart, Flo Garrard, and, wounded, by her rejection, formed an obsessive friendship with the young American. After they too had differences, Kipling left England for a voyage round the world. An urgent message from Caroline that her brother was seriously ill brought Kipling's immediate return, only to find him already dead. He married her eight days after landing. Henry James in middle age had also been a warm friend of Wolcott, and attended the funeral at Dresden. He gave away the bride at All Souls, Langham Place – Caroline from the New World to Kipling from India. 'An odd little marriage,' he called it.

She was like a mother, looking after the business side, her role similar to those played by the wives of Chesterton and Wells. She guarded him from anything that might distract his writing, but there was little understanding of the deepest part of him or his work. Like Chesterton with Frances, Kipling became entirely dependent upon his wife. He told Lady Milner that even if he had wanted to run away he couldn't, because Carrie would have to look out the train and book the ticket. Mrs Cabot saw him waiting at a railway station while his wife checked the bags, and when she inquired where they were staying, he didn't know – he was only 'a cork on the water' when Carrie was with

1 To Mary Hutchinson, 29 Apr. 1801: *The Letters of William & Dorothy Wordsworth* ed. C. L. Shaver, Mary Moorman, Alan G. Hill (1967–79), i, p. 330.

him. He had no illusions about his recovery during the critical time he had pneumonia:

. . . I owe my life to Carrie. R. K.[1]

She curtailed his visitors, and the only telephone at Bateman's was in her bedroom. The devoted man confided to a friend his need sometimes to escape and be with others. Towards the end her possessiveness became neurotic, and she threatened to take her life. Like Stevenson's wife, she was jealous even of her daughter.[2]

Loyalty and sacrifice lay at the heart of C. S. LEWIS's relations with Janie Moore ('Minto'). There had been a pact with Paddy, his roommate at Keble, that should either be slain at the Front the survivor would care for the other's parent – in Lewis's case, a widowed father; in Paddy's, a mother estranged from her husband and left with a young daughter, Maureen. When his friend was killed, Lewis for over thirty years, until Mrs Moore's senility and death, remained true to his pledge.

As a woman in her mid-forties, she mothered the nineteen-year-old cadet, soon a lieutenant, when his father in Ireland seemed not to care that his son was being posted abroad and, a year later, was returning wounded. On resuming his studies and solely dependent on his father's allowance, he paid her rent on a succession of lodgings around Oxford if her husband failed to send a remittance. So began the life which had to be hidden from College authorities – not only while he was an undergraduate but when he became a Fellow at Magdalen. He visited Minto daily in their 'joint ménage' and she referred to him as her adopted son. She revelled in hyper-activity and told visitors: 'He is as good as an extra maid in the house.[3] On one occasion she had him humping a wringer on a bus to the centre of Oxford and back, in an unsuccessful attempt to exchange it for a lawnmower. When he was thirty-one, together with his brother and Minto he bought The Kilns, a cottage standing in eight acres, and this became their

1 Kipling's postscript in Caroline's diary, 31 Dec. 1899: Lord Birkenhead: *Rudyard Kipling* (1978), p. 203.
2 There are other similarities with the Stevenson story: the fondness of both Stevenson and Kipling for unconventional clothes (witness Kipling's knickerbockers and sombrero hat in Brattleboro); and the drunken, penniless Beatty, Kipling's brother-in-law, provides a curious parallel to the dependent, drinking, dishonest Joe Strong, Stevenson's stepson-in-law.
3 *Letters of C. S. Lewis* ed., with a *Memoir*, by W. H. Lewis (1966), p. 16.

permanent home. Once, two Fellows of Magdalen called unexpectedly and were startled to find Maureen, not Lewis, answering the door. At the beginning of Minto's decline, his assiduous attention and care caused him to suffer a serious breakdown.

His brother and friends saw only 'a mysterious self-imposed slavery':

The thing most puzzling . . . was Mrs Moore's extreme unsuitability as a companion for him. She was a woman of very limited mind . . . She . . . interfered constantly with his work, and imposed upon him a heavy burden of minor domestic tasks.[1]

Lewis described such bondage as the more or less common twentieth-century adaptation of Courtly Love.[2] He never forgot her affection when he had been in such desperate need and, while others saw only a domineering and difficult woman, he had a vision of 'the unbearable beauty of her face'. For his biographer has identified her as that 'Lady . . . Sarah Smith' who 'lived at Golders Green' – now 'one of the great ones', lackeyed by *a thousand liveried angels* and preceded by 'youthful shapes' of singing boys and girls who danced and threw flowers before her. On earth –

Every young man or boy that met her became her son – even if it was only the boy that brought the meat to her back door. Every girl that met her was her daughter . . . Every beast and bird that came near her had its place in her love.[3]

A. N. Wilson suggests it would be 'amazing' if their long relationship 'was entirely asexual'.[4]

1 *Ibid.*, p. 12.
2 See *The Allegory of Love: A Study in Medieval Tradition (1936)*, p. 7.
3 *The Great Divorce: A Dream* (1945), pp. 97–9.
4 *C. S. Lewis: A Biography* (1990), p. xvi.

CHAPTER FOUR
Intellectually Incompatible

I

Intellectual incompatibility, it seems, has been the weakness of a certain number of literary marriages: those of Coleridge, Shelley, Dickens, Ruskin, Dorothy L. Sayers . . . Johnson put it:

A man of sense and education should meet a suitable companion in a wife. It was a miserable thing when the conversation could only be such as, whether the mutton should be boiled or roasted, and probably a dispute about that.[1]

The solution of Sir Thomas More, Blake, and Shelley was to 'form' their wives after their own pattern. MORE, at twenty-seven, married Jane Colt whom Erasmus described to Von Hutten as 'wholly uneducated' and 'brought up with her parents in the country':

He taught her books. He taught her music, and formed[2] her into a companion for his life.

Erasmus compared More's household to Plato's Academy adapted on Christian lines. After six years his *cara uxorcula* died; then he married a widow, Alice Middleton, seven years older than himself. He made his second wife learn the harp, cithern, and guitar, 'and practise before him every day'.[3]

II

SHELLEY was nineteen when he eloped with Harriet Westbrook, a sixteen-year-old pupil of Mrs Fenning's Academy for Young Ladies,

---

1 James Boswell: *The Life of Samuel Johnson, LL D* (1791), i, p. 344. *Aetat.* 61: 1770.
2 Compare H. Crabb Robinson on Blake and his wife: 'She had been formed by him . . .' (p. 16).
3 Letter of Erasmus to Ulrich Von Hutten, 23 July 1519: trans. Froude.

on Clapham Common. Petite, with plentiful light-brown curls and 'the tint of the blush rose shining through the lily',[1] she was Venus elect (had the school dared) at its *fête champêtre*. They were married in Edinburgh on 28 August 1811, Shelley being described in the records of Register House as 'farmer, Sussex'.

His boyhood love for his beautiful cousin, Harriet Grove, had gone unrequited, opposed by her parents because of his opinions taken from Godwin on marriage and religion. He told his friend Hogg:

She married! Married to a clod of earth; she will become as insensible herself; all those fine capabilities will moulder . . .[2]

He explained 'the circumstances which caused my marriage' in a letter to his 'soul's sister', Miss Hitchener – the Sussex schoolmistress, feminist, republican, aged twenty-nine, whom he had met on a visit to relatives:

Some time ago, when my sister was at Mrs Fenning's school, she contracted an intimacy with Harriet. At that period I attentively watched over my sister, designing, if possible, to add her to the list of the good, the disinterested, the free . . . I called on [Harriet] . . . designing that *her* advancement should keep pace with, and possibly accelerate, that of my sister . . . The frequency of her letters became greater during my stay in Wales . . . They contained complaints of the irrational conduct of her relatives, and the misery of living where she could love no one . . . I arrived in London. I was shocked at observing the alteration of her looks . . . She had become violently attached to me . . . It was impossible to avoid being much affected; I promised to unite my fate to hers . . . Blame me if thou wilt, dearest friend, for *still* thou art dearest to me . . . If Harriet be not, at sixteen, all that you are at a more advanced age, assist me to mould a really noble soul into all that can make its nobleness useful and lovely. Lovely it is now, or I am the weakest slave to error.[3]

From Edinburgh they began their wanderings that would fill the time they lived together – what Harriet described to a friend as 'the happiest and *longest* (crowded) two years of my life'.

His father had stopped his quarterly allowance of fifty pounds and, at York, he sought the mediation of the Duke of Norfolk. When they arrived at Keswick, where they rented Chesnut Cottage, they were *'so poor as to be actually in danger of every day being deprived of the necessaries of*

1 Thomas Love Peacock: *Memorials of Shelley* (1860).
2 Letter, 11 Jan. 1811. Edward Dowden: *The Life of Percy Bysshe Shelley* (1886), i, p. 101.
3 Letter, 26 Oct. 1811 (?). *Ibid.*, i, pp. 174–5.

life',[1] before his father reinstated the allowance, the same amount as Mr Westbrook was allowing Harriet: £200 a year.

At Calvert's cottage, Shelley first met Southey, who lent him books and got a reduction in their rent, supplying linen from his wife's store to make this possible. Harriet told one of the Southey family that the garden was not let with their part of the house, but 'the people let us run about in it, whenever Percy and I are tired of sitting in the house'. Claire Tomalin reminds us that 'many of the characters in Shelley's life story are children'.[2] Southey wrote to Grosvenor Bedford:

Here is a man at Keswick . . . just what I was in 1794. His name is Shelley, son to the member of Shoreham; with £6000 a year entailed upon him, and as much more in his father's power to cut off . . . I dare say it will not be very long before I shall succeed in convincing him that he may be a true philosopher, and do a great deal of good, with £6000 a year, the thought of which troubles him a great deal more at present than ever the want of sixpence . . . did me.[3]

Southey later invited them to Greta Hall.

After three months or so among the Lakes, Harriet was helping her husband distribute his *Address to the Irish People* in the cause of Catholic Emancipation. From their lodgings on the first floor of No. 7 Sackville Street, Dublin, she wrote to Miss Hitchener:

I am sure you would laugh were you to see us give the pamphlets. We throw them out of window, and give them to men that we pass in the streets. For myself I am ready to die of laughter when it is done, and Percy looks so grave. Yesterday he put one into a woman's hood of a cloak; she knew nothing of it, and we passed her. I could hardly get on, my muscles were so irritated.[4]

She began to speak in the same way that he spoke, and about the same things. Just before they had left for Ireland, she wrote to Miss Hitchener:

I am Irish . . . I have witnessed too much of John Bull, and I am ashamed of him. Till I am disappointed in the brothers and sisters of my affection, I will claim kindred with those brave sons of the ocean . . .[5]

1 Shelley's letter to T. C. Medwin, 20 Mar. 1812. Thomas Medwin: *The Life of Percy Bysshe Shelley* (1847), i, p. 375.
2 *Shelley and his World* (1980), p. 61.
3 4 Jan. 1812. Edward Dowden: *The Life of Percy Bysshe Shelley* (1886), i, p. 211.
4 27 Feb. 1812. *Ibid.*, i, p. 250.
5 29 Jan. 1812. *Ibid.*, i, p. 246.

Over there, she, like Shelley, became vegetarian.

At Tremadoc in North Wales, where Shelley gave money and time to support a land reclamation project, he described himself to Hogg:

. . . when I come home to Harriet I am the happiest of the happy.[1]

She loved singing old Irish songs, and sent away for 'Robin Adair' and 'Kate of Kearney'. She was now even learning Latin.

I do not teach her grammatically, but by the less laborious method of teaching her the English of Latin words, intending afterwards to give her a general idea of grammar.[2]

To obtain further subscriptions for the land reclamation scheme upon which the livelihood of many workers and their families depended, they went to London and there he first met Godwin. As Harriet watched Godwin and Shelley talk, she thought of Socrates and one of his disciples.

After their return, eighteen-year-old Fanny, Godwin's stepdaughter, wrote him a letter, describing Harriet as 'a fine lady'. Shelley replied playfully and then continued:

But to be serious . . . How is Harriet a fine lady? You . . . accuse her . . . of this offence – to me the most unpardonable of all. The ease and simplicity of her habits, the unassuming plainness of her address, the uncalculated connection of her thought and speech, have ever formed, in my eyes, her greatest charms; and none of these are compatible with fashionable life . . .[3]

He wrote to Hogg:

I continue vegetable; Harriet means to be slightly animal, until the arrival of Spring.[4]

When they heard of fourteen Luddites executed at York, they started a subscription in London for the widows and orphans. Harriet wrote to Hookham (later the publisher of *Queen Mab*):

Put down my sister's name, Mr Shelley's, and mine for two guineas each.[5]

After the birth of their first child, Ianthe, it particularly distressed Shelley that Harried hired a nurse and did not suckle the child herself.

---

1 Letter: 7 Feb. 1813.
2 Edward Dowden: *The Life of Percy Bysshe Shelley* (1886), i, p. 321.
3 *Ibid.*, i, p. 328.
4 27 Dec. 1812, *Ibid.*, i, p. 322.
5 *Ibid.*, i, p. 323.

She stopped reading aloud those didactic works of a high moral tone which had amused Hogg on visiting them. If he called now and a walk was proposed, she 'commonly conducted us to some fashionable bonnet-shop'. The schoolgirl so anxious to please had grown into a woman demanding her carriage and plate, with no further aspirations to extending her education.

At Bracknell they took High Elms, to be near the Boinvilles whom they had met in London. According to Peacock, 'Shelley was surrounded by a numerous society, all in a great measure of his own opinions in relation to religion and politics', but each having 'some predominant crochet'. When Peacock 'was sometimes irreverent enough to laugh at the fervour with which opinions . . . were battled for', he notes:

Harriet Shelley was always ready to laugh with me, and we thereby lost caste.[1]

In this third year of marriage, Shelley's attaining his majority made no difference to their financial position. Probably to escape their creditors, they took a trip to Edinburgh, their carriage providing an easy journey and Peacock occupying a fourth place. They stayed about six weeks at 36 Frederick Street – a happy time for Harriet – before returning to London.

But the centre was not holding. Shelley stayed a month apart from Harriet, with the Boinvilles.

I have escaped, in the society of all that philosophy and friendship combine . . . my heart sickens at . . . that necessity which will quickly divide me from the delightful tranquillity of this happy home . . .[2]

Mrs Boinville wrote to Hogg:

Shelley is again a widower; his beauteous half went to town on Thursday . . .[3]

Three months later, Harriet went with their child to her father's house at Bath. Thornton Hunt said that she left her husband of her own accord. Shelley wrote frequently informing her where he was.

Any hope for reconciliation died after he met Mary in Godwin's

1 *Memorials of Shelley* (1860).
2 Letter to Hogg, 16 Mar. 1814. Edward Dowden: *The Life of Percy Bysshe Shelley* (1886), i, p. 408.
3 18 Apr. 1814. *Ibid.*, i, p. 410.

house in Skinner Street. He entreated Harriet to come to London, where he explained his newly found happiness. The shock that she was to be, as it were, a sister or daughter, while a sixteen-year-old supplanted the legal bond, caused her to collapse and suffer a miscarriage. Devotedly he helped to nurse her. He saw his actions totally consistent with what he and Mary believed, with what Mary's mother had pioneered and her father taught, about sexual freedom. Mary had been conceived out of wedlock, her half-sister Fanny Imlay ('Godwin') was also illegitimate, and Mary and her stepsister Jane Clairmont ('Claire') were to bear illegitimate children. Only momentarily did he break – when Godwin, in the role of his father, shut the door of his house against him. Then there was a Regency tableau when he came with laudanum and pistol, threatening suicide.

After his elopement with Mary to the Continent, he sent a letter which did not receive a reply:

My dearest Harriet,
   . . . I write to show that I do not forget you; I write to urge you to come to Switzerland, where you will at last find one firm and constant friend, to whom your interests will be always dear – by whom your feelings will never wilfully be injured. From none can you expect this but me . . . With love to my sweet little Ianthe, ever most affectionately yours . . .[1]

Six weeks following, they returned with no money, and Mary and sixteen-year-old Claire sat for two hours in a coach outside Harriet's lodgings while Shelley persuaded her to provide their fares.

While Shelley was still twenty-two, his grandfather died. The future heir sat outside with Milton's *Comus* while the will was read. As he wrote to Godwin:

My grandfather had left me the option of receiving a life estate in some very large sum (I think £140,000) on condition that I would prolong the entail . . . Longdill [Shelley's solicitor] considered [these conditions] very favourable to me, and urged me by all means to grasp at the offer.[2]

In accordance with his principles that entailment was morally wrong, he disinherited himself in favour of his brother, in exchange for an annuity of £1,000 out of which he paid £50 a quarter to Harriet. His father settled most of his debts, and Shelley sent £200 to clear

1 13 Aug. 1814. *Ibid.*, i, p. 449.
2 7 Jan. 1816. *Ibid.*, i, pp. 539–40.

Harriet's. With her own father's annuity, she now had a yearly income of £400.

During the next two years, Harriet turned to a mutual acquaintance, Major Ryan, who left her when his regiment sailed for India. Shelley and Mary convinced themselves she had formed the liaison before they themselves had eloped. Now, driven from her father's house, she may have sought the protection of a groom. When Shelley and Mary returned from a four-month stay in Geneva, it was first to learn that the gentle Fanny, feeling herself unwanted, had taken an overdose of laudanum at twenty-three. Then, hearing that Westbrook had disowned his own daughter, Shelley tried to trace her. Within three months, Harriet's body, advanced in pregnancy and revealing a valuable ring on her finger, was found in the Serpentine, to be buried without memorial under the name Harriet Smith. She was twenty-one.

Probably Shelley never saw her last letter, written to him care of her sister Eliza, in which she made a desperate plea:

My dear Bysshe, let me conjure you by the remembrance of our days of happiness to grant my last wish [to let Ianthe stay with Eliza] . . . I never could refuse you and if you had never left me I might have lived . . . There is your beautiful boy, oh! be careful of him, and his love may prove one day a rich reward . . .[1]

At twenty-five, he wrote some variant lines for *The Revolt of Islam*:

> One whom I found was dear but false to me.
> *The other's heart was like a heart of stone.*

But he told Peacock, as they walked in Bisham Wood, that he intended to take 'a great glass of ale every night . . . to deaden my feelings',[2] and later explained that those feelings had to do with Harriet.

III

Like Shelley with Harriet, RUSKIN married Ephie Gray thinking he might influence her and make of her the wife he wanted.

---

1 9 Nov. 1816. Quoted by Claire Tomalin: *Shelley & his World* (1980), p. 61.
2 Thomas Love Peacock: *Memorials of Shelley* (1860).

I was grieved and disappointed at finding I could not change her, and she was humiliated and irritated at finding she could not change me.[1]

He seems not to have allowed that marriage meant some compromise with 'the artist man'. He told Dr Acland, when it was all over:

I found . . . that the more I gave, the less I was thanked – and I would not allow the main work of my life to be interfered with. I would not spend my days in leaving cards, nor my nights in leaning against the walls of drawing rooms. Effie found my society not enough for her happiness – and was angry with me for not being entertaining, when I came to her to find rest.[2]

Kingsley, nearly three years before the Dickenses separated, met them dining out. He found DICKENS 'a really genial lovable man, with an eye like a hawk':

Not high bred but excellent company, and very sensible. But Mrs Dickens! Oh the fat vulgar vacancy![3]

It is difficult to believe that Catherine (née Hogarth), with whom Dickens lived for twenty-two years and who, over a period of fifteen, bore him ten children, could have been utterly incompatible. Their struggle, too, was in part the Shavian one of 'artist man' and 'mother woman'. Even their children were aware of it. 'I am certain', his eldest son used to say, 'that the children of my father's brain were much more real to him at times than we were.' At forty-five, infatuated with Ellen Ternan, an actress of eighteen, Dickens invited Wilkie Collins to accompany him on a tour:

I want to escape from myself . . . my blankness is inconceivable – indescribable – my misery, amazing.[4]

He ordered a small bed in his dressing-room and wrote to his wife's maid, Anne, telling her to have the communicating door to the bedroom sealed by a carpenter. She was instructed not to gossip. Kate spent hours sobbing, and Forster found him 'inaccessible' to friendly advice. His daughter said:

My father was like a madman when my mother left home . . . He did not care a damn what happened to any of us.[5]

1 Quoted by J. H. Whitehouse: *Vindication of Ruskin* (1950), p. 15.
2 May 1854. Jeffrey Spear: *TLS*, 10 Feb. 1978.
3 Apr. 1855. Susan Chitty: *The Beast & the Monk: A Life of Charles Kingsley* (1974), p. 174.
4 29 Aug. 1857.
5 Gladys Storey: *Dickens and Daughter* (1939), p. 94.

An establishment was provided for Ellen at Windsor Lodge, Peckham, and delicacies were sent when she was off-colour. The liaison lasted twelve years until he died. He left her £1,000 in his will.

The friends of Dickens, like Shelley's friends, felt sorry for the wife at the time of her rejection. She was forty-three, and had to leave behind five sons, their ages ranging from six to thirteen, and two daughters eighteen and nineteen. Forster put through the legal separation, in which Kate received a settlement for £600 a year and a small house on the edge of Camden Town. Their eldest boy, Charley, now twenty-one, went with her. Her youngest sister, Georgina, who had been in the Dickenses' household ever since the tragic death of Mary Hogarth,[1] stayed on at Gad's Hill, even befriending Ellen.

By contrast, CONAN DOYLE did not hurt Touie (née Louise Hawkins), who had contracted TB. Twelve years into their marriage he met Jean Leckie, a singer, and six years after that meeting his two daughters became frightened of their kindly father now so strange and unpredictable. The children suffered, like those of Dickens.

Following the death of Touie in three more years, nervous illness put paid to work for eight months. Shortly after, at forty-eight, he married Jean at St Margaret's, Westminster. Among the guests were Barrie, Jerome, Bram Stoker; also George Edalji, for whom he had obtained a pardon from a prison sentence and who now presented his benefactor with one-volume editions of Shakespeare and Tennyson. Two more sons and a daughter were born.

IV

DOROTHY L. SAYERS told John Cournos that she was 'a really rather primitive woman'.[2] Vera Brittain, who liked her, said that her unconcealed passion for Sir Hugh Allen, who conducted the Oxford Bach Choir of which they were members, was a standing joke in Somerville.

. . . she sat among the mezzo-contraltos and gazed at him with wide, adoring eyes as though she were in church worshipping her only God. But a realistic sense of humour always saved her from becoming ridiculous, and at the

1 See p. 140.
2 27 Oct. 1924. James Brabazon: *Dorothy L. Sayers: The Life of a Courageous Woman* (1981), p. 94.

Going-Down Play given by her Year . . . she caricatured her idol with triumphant accuracy and zest.[1]

She made for herself a 'ravishing little cap . . . in black ribbon and net', and told her parents that she had been invited to his organ loft in New College Chapel.

She worked for a year as secretary to Eric Whelpton, who was running an Educational Bureau in Normandy. He believed she 'was certainly madly in love with me' but, according to James Brabazon, Whelpton 'found it hard to respond to Dorothy's concept of flirtation as a game'.[2] In London, at twenty-eight, and writing *Whose Body?*, she met John Cournos, 'who spells Art with a capital A'. She would have married him had he been the marrying kind. He wanted to be 'free to live and love naturally' and, after it was all over, she wrote:

I could not be content with less than your love and your children and our happy acknowledgement of each other to the world.[3]

When she was nearly thirty-three, she married in a registrar's office Oswald Atherton Fleming ('Mac'), a divorced Scot. A captain in World War I, who had been gassed and shell-shocked, he liked to be called Major. He was a crime and motor-racing reporter on *The News of the World*, a post he held two more years until his health began to deteriorate and he became progressively difficult. Mac had drunken spells, and she who had told John Cournos

If I could have found a man to my measure, I could have put a torch to the world,

became the disillusioned bread-winner. After twenty-four years the marriage ended with his death, and almost casually she gave the urn containing Mac's ashes to the local doctor who happened to be going where her husband had wanted them scattered. (Frank BENNETT put Arnold's on the luggage rack of the train, and sat beneath them on his way back to Burslem.)

1 *Testament of Youth* (1933), p. 106.
2 *Dorothy L. Sayers: The Life of a Courageous Woman* (1981), p. 80.
3 27 Oct. 1924. *Ibid.*, p. 72.

CHAPTER FIVE
Companionable Marriages

I

SCOTT's marriage, at twenty-six, to Charlotte Carpenter 'fell something short of love in all its fervour . . . folk who have been nearly drowned in bathing rarely venturing a second time out of their depth'. This allusion and others, made in his last journal, are to the one passionate love affair of his life. From the age of nineteen he had unsuccessfully courted Williamina Belsches, of a higher social class. After many vicissitudes the affair ended with her engagement to a rich young landowner, and one year later Scott married on the rebound, as it were. In his journal he states that, though his broken heart had been pieced together, 'the crack will remain to my dying day'.

Charlotte bore him two sons and two daughters, but does not seem to have shared his imaginative life. Their marriage is usually described as happy, qualified by 'companionable'. He spoke of their love increasing. His 'thirty years' companion' had become 'the sharer of my thoughts and counsels'.[1] Ten days after her death, he wrote:

. . . the solitude seemed so absolute – my poor Charlotte would have been in the room half-a-score of times to see if the fire burned, and to ask a hundred kind questions. Well, that is over – and if it cannot be forgotten, must be remembered with patience.[2]

II

Already Secretary of the Bank of England, and author of *The Golden Age* and *Dream Days*, KENNETH GRAHAME at forty married Elspeth

1 Diary, 16 May 1826. J. G. Lockhart: *Memoirs of the Life of Sir Walter Scott, Bart.* (1837–8), vi, p. 299.
2 Diary, 26 May 1826. *Ibid.*, vi, p. 305.

The Pains of Love

Thomson, three years younger. As hostess for her stepfather she had entertained literary and artistic celebrities. As a child she received Mark Twain who had called when her parents were out; at ten she struck up a friendship with Tennyson. The initiative for their marriage came from her.

Significantly, during their engagement Grahame had taken to hiding his emotions under phonetically spelt letters reminiscent of Swift's *Journal to Stella*.[1] She refused to wear an engagement ring, and the later eccentric married in old muslin while an expensive wedding-dress remained unpacked. Three days of the honeymoon were spent at St Ives and then they returned to Fowey and his friends the Quiller-Couches, also his bachelor friend Edward Atkinson. But she did not share the passion that they and her husband had for boats. More seriously, she and 'Q' did not get on.

Although Elspeth immediately became pregnant, all was not well with their physical relationship. Within a month of their marriage, Mrs Thomas Hardy replied to her urgent request for help and advice:

I can scarcely think that love proper and enduring, is in the nature of men . . . Keeping separate a good deal is a wise plan in crises . . . If he belongs to the public in any way, years of devotion count for nothing . . . it is really a pity to have any ideals in the first place.[2]

For six years – uncreative ones for Grahame, who likewise had suffered shock and disappointment – their first home was 16 Durham Villas, Campden Hill. His friend, Graham Robertson, tells of Kenneth's special room 'like a nursery' with books outnumbered by toys. They were everywhere – 'intriguing, fascinating toys which could hardly have been conducive to study'.[3] Yet Peter Green believes that if Grahame had not married Elspeth, it is extremely unlikely whether *The Wind in the Willows* would ever have been written:

. . . driven in on himself, badly bruised by contact with adult passion, Grahame turned . . . to the world of symbol and myth.[4]

The blurb Grahame wrote contains the phrase: 'clean of the clash of sex'.

1 Compare the cypher letters of Swinburne and his cousin Mary Leith (née Gordon). See p. 119.
2 20 Aug. 1899. Peter Green: *Kenneth Grahame: A Study of his Life, Work & Times* (1959), pp. 220–1.
3 Patrick Chalmers: *Kenneth Grahame: Life, Letters & Unpublished Work* (1933), p. 97.
4 Green: *op. cit.*, p. 265.

Elspeth tried at first to recreate the social parties of her family home, but Grahame, who (like Ruskin) had no small-talk, preferred the company of his few intimate friends. Frustrated in an ideal union, they idealized their handicapped and only son Alistair ('Mouse') who could not possibly fulfil their expectations of him.

Towards the end of their fifth year of marriage, Elspeth who had suffered most of the time from nervous illness, left London for a long cure at Woodhall Spa in Lincolnshire, and a few months later Grahame went alone to Spain. Their little boy stayed with relatives at Broadstairs. Grahame had only reached the Pyrenees when a telegram informed him that Mouse was seriously ill with peritonitis. Both parents rushed to be at his side during a successful operation. Elspeth then went back to her Spa for perhaps another six months while Grahame returned to the Bank.[1] After two years they moved to Cookham Dene where he had been brought up as a child. In an examination of the chapter 'Wayfarers All' in *The Wind in the Willows*, his biographer suggests that Grahame came near to leaving Elspeth the following year.[2]

When Grahame was fifty and retired from the Bank, he took Elspeth to Italy, but they did not go again for twelve years in spite of the fact that, in his late twenties and thirties, Italy had been his passion. He had fixed on his house in Kensington a blue-and-white plaque of a Madonna and Child by della Robbia that he bought on the first of his yearly visits. Conjecture can only be made that Elspeth, probably through no fault of her own, could neither compete against nor complement his essential solitariness.

It was easier to go a-building among those dream-cities where no limitations were imposed, and one was sole architect, with a free hand.[3]

Like the Barries, they were of no help to each other. In Grahame's retirement a large part of him seemed in danger of atrophy, and after *The Wind in the Willows* his remaining twenty-five years were virtually uncreative. Professor Hamilton, who spent a weekend after they had come to Boham's, found that with Elspeth doing most of the talking Grahame would be silent for more than an hour. But as soon as the

---

1 Elspeth's nervous illness, and the Bank, sound curiously like Eliot's circumstances.
2 Green: *op. cit.*, p. 255.
3 'The Roman Road': *The Golden Age* (1895) p. 127.

two men set on a country walk, Grahame broke into 'an easy current of cheery conversation'.[1]

Their visiting American friends, the Purveses, were amused and taken aback that Grahame and his wife (like the Hardys) lived in separate parts of the house and took it for granted their guests would follow the same 'nocturnal separation of the sexes'. When Mouse had gone to The Old Malthouse School, Grahame walked for hours alone on the Berkshire Downs. In spite of their affluence, Elspeth now dressed in shabby clothes. She rose about eleven, and still showed nervous symptoms by lying on a divan, sipping hot water, for much of her time. Grahame denied she allowed mouse-nests to form in her larder.

After Alistair's death,[2] they seemed to find a new companionship revisiting Italy. They finally moved to Church Cottage, Pangbourne, where Grahame refused to have a telephone. Here, Elspeth's meanness over food (she had always eaten very little) reached new heights and the pair often had lunch out of a paper bag on the porch. Malcolm Elwin met them in the house of Sir Harold Hartley, and 'gathered that Mr Grahame had long since learned that it was a waste of time and energy to attempt to express any opinion in his wife's company.[3]

1 Peter Green: *Kenneth Grahame: A Study of his Life, Work & Times* (1959), p. 302.
2 See pp. 302–3.
3 Green: *op. cit.*, pp. 341–2.

CHAPTER SIX
Doomed

I

FRANCES HODGSON's escalating success enabled her to indulge a restless temperament and lead an individual life-style, unusual for her time, after she was married.

She was fifteen when her mother had brought their family to New Market, Tennessee. Their nearest neighbours were the family of the only doctor, kindly John Burnett. His eighteen-year-old son, Swan, permanently limping from an accident to his leg, waited seven years before he could persuade Frances to marry him. By then he had qualified in medicine, but it was her literary work that made it possible for him to study as an oculist in Paris, where they spent eighteen months with their first child.

Established as a best-selling author with *That Lass o' Lowrie*, Frances found that her achievement of ten books in six years caused strains in their marriage. She no longer saw in Swan – who negotiated with her publishers – the crippled boy to whom she had lent Dickens, Thackeray, and Tennyson. He spoke as if to 'a kind of pen-driving machine':

How did you get on this morning? How much did you do? Is your story nearly finished? How much longer will it take you?[1]

Their married life became a succession of long periods living apart. When her two sons, Lionel and Vivian, were twelve and eleven, she brought them to England for Queen Victoria's Golden Jubilee and then on to Paris and Florence. After sixteen months away the boys went to their father in Washington while she went to Boston, where her dramatised version of *Little Lord Fauntleroy* was running.

It was on a visit to London when she was thirty-nine that Frances began seeing a great deal of Stephen Townesend, who was ten years

1 Ann Thwaite: *Waiting for the Party: The Life of Frances Hodgson Burnett* (1974), p. 67.

younger than she. He wanted a career in the theatre but, facing disapproval from his clerical family, had qualified as a surgeon. Now, at twenty-nine, he in turn was to be helped by Frances to achieving his ambition. She began by employing him as her business manager. He made himself indispensable when she had a fall from a horse, then again during the tragic illness followed by the early death of Lionel at sixteen. He became her lover. She wrote to Vivian in Washington:

Of course Uncle Stephen takes care of my business . . . but . . . I feel as if I was the one who had to take care of him. He is so delicate and nervous and irritable, poor boy. But I have to remember when he seems to be unreasonable, that he was never anything but *perfect* to Lionel, and that he was his comfort and strength and beloved to the last minute.[1]

She produced Stephen in the role of Joe Hurst in her play *The Showman's Daughter* at the Royalty Theatre in London. Meanwhile Swan was still concerning himself with her business affairs in America.

At forty-three, she made her thirteenth Atlantic crossing (there were to be thirty-three in all) and her husband inquired of Scribner:

Did Mrs Burnett leave her London Banker's address with you? She left it with us but it has been misplaced.[2]

She was in London when Swan left her house in Washington and moved into one of his own. About this time she was seeing more of Israel Zangwill than of Stephen. At forty-eight, she started divorce proceedings against Swan. She wrote to Vivian at Harvard:

I have put it merely upon the ground of 'Desertion', which Dr Burnett himself made quite simple by leaving my house of his own will. I have always thought he did this with intention.[3]

She now moved from 63 Portland Place and rented Maytham Hall, Rolvenden, with 'seventeen or eighteen bedrooms, stables, two entrance lodges to the park and a square tower on the roof, from which we can see the English Channel'.[4] Henry James had recently established himself less than ten miles away at Lamb House, Rye.

Then, at fifty, Frances secretly married Stephen, probably in Genoa. Within three months she was writing to her sister Edith:

He talks about my 'duties as a wife' as if I had married him of my own accord – as if I had not been forced and blackguarded and blackmailed into it . . . It

1 *Ibid.*, pp. 139–40.
2 *Ibid.*, p. 150.
3 *Ibid.*, p. 176.
4 *Ibid.*, p. 179.

is my duty to make my property over to him – to live alone at Maytham except when he wishes to bring down a hospital nurse or so . . .

Her marital image as a 'pen-driving machine' was repeated –

It is my duty to work very hard and above all to *love* him very much and insist on his writing plays with me.[1]

Stephen claimed she had seduced him from the beginning. For months Frances was suicidal:

Oh, God, if I have ever done a good deed in my life, kill me before the day is over.

She wrote to Vivian:

Understand that when I say your father never assumed a single responsibility of manhood, I know another who has assumed even fewer and has done more evil.[2]

In the village they used to say that Stephen came down for his money and then was off on his cob. The Maude little girls stayed at Maytham and Pamela recalled later that Mr Townesend always seemed 'so alone', playing on the pianola. She couldn't remember that Frances and he ever spoke to each other.

The following year, Stephen visited Frances in an American sanatorium and she told him she could not struggle with his temperament any longer. Ann Thwaite thinks it 'likely' that Frances bought him off with her English royalties.[3]

II

HAZLITT's misanthropy – a word used by Coleridge and De Quincey in describing him – was not likely to lead to a satisfactory and lasting relationship. As a young man he was disappointed by Miss Railton and perhaps by Dorothy Wordsworth. There was a discreditable, and still somewhat mysterious, episode at Keswick when he chastised a local girl and a large mob came looking for him. He hid at Greta Hall

1 Ann Thwaite: *Waiting for the Party: The Life of Frances Hodgson Burnett* (1974), pp. 191–2.
2 *Ibid.*, p. 193.
3 *Ibid.*, p. 203.

until Coleridge and Southey deemed it wise to send him scurrying across the hills to Grasmere and Wordsworth.

His marriage at thirty to Miss Sarah Stoddart held for eleven years, and then he lived chiefly apart until their Scots divorce when he was forty-four. He now fell in love with Miss Walker, the landlord's teenage daughter at his lodgings. The gloomy man was transformed – he rhapsodized about her to all, regardless of their inevitable boredom and laughs. De Quincey, who judged him fairly stringently, wrote:

> . . . I do maintain that a passion capable of stifling and transcending what was so prominent in his own nature was . . . a noble affection . . . I must reverence a man, be he what he may otherwise, who shows himself capable of profound love.[1]

But while accepting his gifts, she was paying her attentions to another resident and, suspicions aroused, Hazlitt followed her one Sunday to her rendezvous. In his *Liber Amoris; or, The New Pygmalion*, he 'whistled her down the wind'. Nothing was hid. Again, De Quincey saw 'no indelicacy in such an act':

> It was an explosion of frenzy . . . the sole necessity for *him* was to empty his over-burdened spirit.[2]

At forty-six, he married a widow, Mrs Bridgewater, but soon afterwards set out to make a tour of picture-galleries in Europe, which he had always promised himself. When he wrote to bring her home two years later, she declared, hardly surprisingly, that their parting was for ever. He died of cancer of the stomach at fifty-two, with Lamb one of those at his bedside. His last words, according to his son, were: 'Well, I have had a happy life.'[3]

Frances Hodgson Burnett wrote of everybody waiting for 'the Party'[4] which never materializes, and her biographer in her title applied it to Frances. It is hard to think of Hazlitt as being blessed either – unless the remark alluded to his writing life, and his surviving son whom he loved.

---

1 *The Collected Writings of Thomas De Quincey* ed. David Masson (1889–90), iii, p. 80.
2 *Ibid.*, xi, p. 346.
3 *DNB*.
4 Cf. Maugham, repeating at nearly ninety-two: '. . . life's been rather like a party that was very nice to start with but has become rather noisy as time went on. And I'm not at all sorry to go home.' (Robin Maugham: *Conversations with Willie* [Amer. edn. 1978], p. 183.)

CHAPTER SEVEN

Unmarried

I

That a minority did not marry need not imply they were unaffected by the opposite sex.

When Mr Walmesbury, a plasterer in Shoreditch, was asked about his lodger, he said that seventeen-year-old CHATTERTON 'did not dislike the ladies'. Chatterton's sister said that at Bristol he had addressed a poem to Miss Rumsey and they began a corresponding acquaintance; also that he had frequently walked 'the Colledge green with the young girls that statedly paraded there to shew their finery'.[1] A postscript in a letter to his sister from London reads:

I am this minute pierced through the heart, by the black eye of a young lady, driving along in a hackney coach. – I am quite in love: if my love lasts till that time, you shall hear of it in my next.[2]

He boasted, at fifteen, to a schoolfriend who had emigrated to America:

I have been violently in love these three-and-twenty times since your departure, and not a few times came off victorious.[3]

Not attempting to justify the many passages in Chatterton's writings 'not only immoral but bordering upon a libertinism gross and unpardonable', James Thistlethwaite, another old schoolfellow, believed them 'to have originated rather from a warmth of imagination,

1 Letter to Croft: 22 Sept. 1778. The Rev. Sir Herbert Croft: *Love & Madness. A Story Too True* (1780), p. 146.
2 30 May 1770. *Ibid.*, p. 182.
3 To Mr Baker, Charlestown, S. Carolina: 6 Mar. 1768. David Masson: *Chatterton: A Story of the Year 1770* (1874), p. 20.

aided by a vain affectation of singularity, than from any natural depravity . . .'[1]

SAMUEL ROGERS confided to his friend Lady Jersey, 'If I had a wife, I should have somebody to care about.' She taunted him whether this suppositious wife would not care for somebody else. André Maurois comments that 'an aesthete lives his life in slow-motion and marriage means too abrupt a decision'.[2]

Rogers was one of the very few literary people whom Mrs Dickens liked – one of the very few to whom she signed letters 'Yours very affectionately' – and he in turn was extremely nice to her. However, she still did not qualify for one of his celebrated breakfasts. The unhappy and brilliant Mrs Norton, at the sensational trial of Lord Melbourne v. Captain Norton, entered on the arm of Rogers. When Charlotte Brontë was invited to breakfast, she found one of his other two guests 'a very beautiful and fashionable woman'.[3] The Tennysons, bringing their baby Hallam, paid him a visit when he was eighty-nine. Rogers said, bowing: 'Mrs Tennyson, I made one great mistake in my life, I never married!'[4]

JANE AUSTEN, aged nearly twenty-seven, received a proposal of mar riage from Harris Bigg-Wither, a friend of the family, and it seems that, after acceptance, she next day or sooner refused him. Her nephew, 'unable to assign name, or date, or place', affirmed another 'passage of romance . . . on sufficient authority'.[5] One of five versions, all derived ultimately from her sister Cassandra, holds that they met a young clergyman at Sidmouth when visiting his brother, a doctor, and that he and Jane fell in love but he died shortly after. Constance Pilgrim makes a fascinating case that the affair lasted longer and went far deeper than is generally thought.[6] On the testimony of Jane's friend, Mrs Barrett, that Anne Elliott in *Persuasion* is Jane herself, she identifies the unknown suitor with a young sea officer, who went down with his ship – the shy, estimable John Wordsworth, younger brother of the poet.

1 *The Works of Thomas Chatterton, containing his life by G. Gregory, DD* ed. Robert Southey (1803), i, p. xlix.
2 *Byron* (1930), p. 139.
3 Letter to the Rev. Patrick Brontë: 26 June 1851.
4 *Alfred Lord Tennyson: A Memoir by his Son* (1897), i, p. 361.
5 Quoted by Constance Pilgrim: *Dear Jane: A Biographical Study of Jane Austen* (1971), p. 18.
6 *Op. cit.*

KEATS's material prospects and health made it virtually impossible for him to marry. His engagement to Fanny Brawne, daughter of the family who came to live next door at Wentworth Place, was secret – he twenty-four and she nineteen. Together with his other friends, Fanny and her mother nursed him through his last year. Fanny prepared his clothes and lined a travelling cap with silk when he went, on his doctor's advice, to Italy. She gave him a knife, a lock of her hair, and a pocket book.

Matthew Arnold commented that a man who wrote such love letters was 'probably predestined . . . to misfortune in his love affairs'.[1] John Drinkwater thought:

Better indeed, for Keats's happiness, to die at twenty-five than to wear his life out with the feather-headed Fanny.[2]

Both views are unexpectedly harsh. No more than any other man would Arnold have wanted his own love letters 'put into the microscope of a Coterie',[3] and Keats has the last word when he wrote to Fanny about six months before he died:

A person in health as you are can have no conception of the horrors that nerves and a temper like mine go through.[4]

His strong sense of humour can be found. He tells her to come 'this evening, without fail – when you must not mind about my speaking in a low tone for I am ordered to do so though I *can* speak out'.[5] There is the passage:

When I send this round I shall be in the front parlour watching to see you show yourself for a minute in the garden. How illness stands as a barrier betwixt me and you! . . . I must make myself as good a Philosopher as possible . . . 'If I should die,' said I to myself, 'I have left no immortal work behind me – nothing to make my friends proud of my memory – but I have lov'd the principle of beauty in all things, and if I had had time I would have made myself remember'd.'[6]

From Kentish Town, while lodging with Leigh Hunt, he writes:

1 *Essays in Criticism: Second Series* (1888), p. 103.
2 *The Outline of Literature* (1923–4), ii, p. 389.
3 July 1820? *The Letters of John Keats* ed. Maurice Buxton Forman (1931), ii, p. 545.
4 Aug. 1820? *Ibid.*, ii, p. 548.
5 4 Feb. 1820? *Ibid.*, ii, p. 498.
6 Feb. 1820? *Ibid.*, ii, p. 510.

For this week past I have been employed in marking the most beautiful passages in Spenser, intending it for you, and comforting myself in being somehow occupied to give you however small a pleasure.[1]

His letters to her speak without reserve of the 'misery' of 'an intellect in splints'.[2] He says in one:

You always concentrate my whole senses.[3]

Perhaps Arnold was offended lest the *sensuous* poet had become the *sensual* man (although it was fashionable to use one word):

I have seen you the whole time in your shepherdess dress. How my senses have ached at it![4]

Keats's first editor, Harry Buxton Forman, held a different opinion of Fanny Brawne from Drinkwater's:

I fully believe that she was warmly attached to Keats and mourned his loss long and bitterly. Time, the healer of most wounds, healed that of Fanny Brawne sufficiently to admit of her marriage when Keats had been ten years dead . . . She was a contributor to *Blackwood's Magazine*; and I have in my possession a manuscript tale called *Nickel Liszt* translated by her from the German, showing some literary skill.[5]

II

The woman who shared with a vicarious thrill SWINBURNE'S excitement at being beaten, and who believed it attributable solely to memories of Eton, was his cousin Mary Leith (née Gordon). They were first cousins, their mothers being sisters, and their fathers first cousins, being sons of two brothers who were themselves first cousins to Swinburne's maternal grandmother, the Countess of Ashburnham. It was a closed situation like one in his novels.

Mary, as a small child, had come so frequently to East Dene on the Isle of Wight, from her neighbouring home Northcourt, that she seemed like another younger sister to Swinburne's four. She grew into

1 Tuesday Aftn. May 1820? *Ibid.*, ii, p. 532.
2 To Mrs Brawne: 24 Oct. (1820). *Ibid.*, ii, p. 567.
3 Mar. 1820? *Ibid.*, ii, p. 519.
4 Tuesday Morn., May 1820. *Ibid.*, ii, p. 534.
5 Biographical Memoranda included by his son: *ibid.*, i, p. lv.

a tomboy whose main passion was riding, and became more like a younger brother.

At twenty-six, he had stayed with his aunt and cousin at Northcourt, and on failure to persuade Mary to marry him (in spite of the incest) he not only took to excessive alcohol but to prostitutional flagellation.

> It will grow not again, this fruit of my heart . . .
> It will grow not again, it is ruined at root . . .
>
> I will go back to the great sweet mother,
> Mother and lover of men, the sea . . .
> O fair white mother . . .
> Born without sister, born without brother,
> Set free my soul as thy soul is free.[1]

When he was fifty-four she replied to his letter, using their childhood code, and praised his unpublished *Flogging Block*. She hoped it might be said of the birch, as of Eton, 'Florebit'. The following year, after her husband died, she took tea with her cousin at The Pines, and in her thank-you letter expressed how upset she was that 'the timehonoured & traditional pode of nunishment is disused at Eton'.[2] After Swinburne's death, she declared in her biography:

. . . that there was never . . . an ounce of sentiment between us. Any idea of the kind would have been an insult to our brother-and-sister footing.[3]

But Jean Overton Fuller, who unearthed the letters at the British Museum, believes that Mary was his *femme inspiratrice*: she was not only the prototype of *Dolores* and present in more than one character in *Lesbia Brandon*, but without her 'we should not have had his *Atalanta in Calydon*'.[4]

The only other woman (so far as is known) for whom he had felt a secret passion was Elizabeth Siddal, Rossetti's wife, who posed for the drowning Ophelia in the painting by Millais. She had red hair like his own, and Swinburne used to come and read the Elizabethan playwrights to her at Chatham Place.

She was a wonderful as well as most loveable creature.

1 'The Triumph of Time' (written 1864): *Poems & Ballads* (1866).
2 2 Feb. 1893.
3 *The Boyhood of Algernon Charles Swinburne* (1917), pp. 4–5.
4 *Swinburne: A Critical Biography* (1968), p. 278.

He had dined with Lizzy and Rossetti at the Sablonière restaurant near Leicester Square on the night she took an overdose of laudanum, and attended the inquest to testify that Rossetti and she had been on good terms. He may have been present when Rossetti buried the poems to Lizzie in her coffin.

As young men, Cowper, Alexander Cruden, and Lamb were all crossed in love. It put Cruden away for the first time, and was probably the reason for Lamb's six weeks' stay 'in a madhouse at Haxton'. It may have been a factor in Cowper's first attack of madness. Swift's complicated love for Stella, and for Vanessa, is reserved for that appropriate Part.[1]

1 See pp. 182–92.

CHAPTER EIGHT
Forbidden Fruit

I

Thackeray and Barrie each loved a married woman. Both men were in their late thirties; both had tragic marriages. Each was a friend of the respective husband, acting openly (and indiscreetly) as if such behaviour were perfectly normal and acceptable – which was no more true for Thackeray in a Victorian society than for Barrie in an Edwardian one. What may seem even stranger today is that neither man sought physical satisfaction. With Barrie it seems likely there was an impediment anyway, and what Thackeray said –

(I mean that any wrong was out of the question on our children's account)[1]

– rings peculiarly true.

THACKERAY's attachment to the wife of his Cambridge friend, the Rev. William Brookfield, when he had given up all hope of his own wife recovering her sanity, did not find favour with her until he had become the celebrated author of *Vanity Fair* and then she presently confided, what he had already surmised, that her husband's unkindness made her unhappy. Because his long-standing friend acquiesced in their friendship, he believed his position privileged and when Brookfield eventually insisted it must end, Thackeray lost his self-control.

He was forty. It was a grief greater than any he had known since his wife's loss of reason. Five years previously, he had set up a London home for his two little daughters. Now, vainly, he tried to console himself in travel. He wrote to his closest confidantes, knowing it would get back to Jane:

---

1 To Kate Perry: Sept.? 1851. *The Letters & Private Papers of William Makepeace Thackeray* ed. Gordon N. Ray (1945–6), iv, p. 431.

Her husband is a good fellow and does love her: and I think of his constant fondness for me . . . and how cruelly I've stabbed him and outraged him with my words . . .[1]

In the welter of his emotions he wrote again:

But that I knew I was safe

– and here was the allusion already quoted about the children –

I suppose I should have broken away myself . . . I wish that I had never loved her. I have been played with by a woman, and flung over at a beck from the lord and master – that's what I feel . . .[2]

Two more months or so, and there is a reminiscence of Dan Peggotty:

But will it soothe my dear to know that I'm always here, and that I admire her, bless her, love her? I'll keep that light . . . though she mayn't be there to see it: and who knows but some day she may come again & knock at the door . . .[3]

II

BARRIE's attachment to Sylvia Llewelyn Davies began when he was living with his wife. Sylvia, the daughter of George du Maurier, was married to a young barrister, Arthur Llewelyn Davies. Barrie met 'the most beautiful creature he had ever seen'[4] at a dinner party. She was secreting the after-dinner sweets into her silk reticule and told him they were 'for Peter', aged one, her other sons being George and Jack, four and three. Then it dawned that they were the boys wearing red tam-o'-shanters he had met in Kensington Gardens. Eventually there were five, including Michael and Nico.

Now he would come back with them and his great St Bernard dog, and continue his stories in their home – without any invitation from the father – and stay till their bedtime. Sylvia and his wife became good friends and, what was more surprising, Arthur agreed to a split holiday seven years later. Sylvia and two boys accompanied the Barries to Normandy, while Arthur took the others to his parents'

1 To Mrs Elliot & Kate Perry, 26 Sept. 1851: *ibid.*, iv., p. 429.
2 To Kate Perry, Sept.? 1851: *ibid.*, iv, p. 431.
3 To Mrs Elliot & Kate Perry, Nov. 1851: *ibid.*, iv, p. 433.
4 Janet Dunbar: *J. M. Barrie: The Man Behind the Image* (1970), p. 114.

home at Kirby. Barrie called Sylvia by her second name, addressing her in his letters 'Dearest Jocelyn' and signing himself 'Your loving'.

For greater economy Arthur moved his family to Berkhamsted, twenty-five miles away, but it made no difference to Barrie's involvement. How deeply the father resented such intrusion is all conjecture. Their nurse, and Jack as he grew into adolescence, probably reflected their own feelings when they said that Arthur's sense of irritation was endured only for her sake. Sylvia, so patently devoted to her husband, took innocent delight in the luxury that Barrie's riches provided, and their promise of future security gave peace of mind when tragic illness befell. But Peter, looking back, was convinced that whatever bitterness may have rankled, 'the kindness . . . of which J. M. B. gave such overwhelming proof' from the time of Arthur's illness, 'far more than outweighed all that'.[1]

A year after that split holiday, Arthur suffered the affliction of a sarcoma in his face, which meant an operation to remove half his upper jaw and palate. Immediately Barrie cancelled all other arrangements, insisted on the best treatment and let it be understood that he would pay the enormous medical bill. Every day for six weeks he made himself available in the sick-room. Arthur wrote to nine-year-old Peter:

Mr Barrie is now sitting here with me reading the newspaper . . . Don't you think Mr Barrie is a very good friend to all of us?[2]

Afterwards Barrie brought the suffering man home in his chauffeur-driven open Lanchester. Sylvia wrote to six-year-old Michael:

Mr Barrie is our fairy prince, much the best fairy prince that was ever born because he is *real*.[3]

Three months later, the sarcoma recurred and again Barrie was by his bedside. Arthur wrote to his father:

Barrie's unfailing kindness and tact are a great support to us both.[4]

Now unable to speak, Arthur passed across pencil notes which have been preserved. One is just two words:

1 The Peter Davies collection of personal papers: *ibid.*, p. 152.
2 14 June 1906: Andrew Birkin: *J. M. Barrie & the Lost Boys* (1979), p. 137.
3 'For June the 16th, My Michael's 6th birthday': *ibid.*, p. 138.
4 21 Sept. 1906: Janet Dunbar: *J. M. Barrie: The Man Behind the Image* (1970) p. 159.

Dear Jimmy.

Another – 'Do write more things other than plays' – Peter in his maturity thought intended as a compliment:

His conversation was often on a much higher plane, and doubtless rose to its highest in his talks with the dying Arthur.[1]

When the end came, Barrie assumed financial responsibility for the widowed mother and five boys. Two and a half years later, Sylvia collapsed and cancer was diagnosed. Barrie, recently divorced, resumed the role he had performed at the bedside of Arthur. She was forty-four.

Peter, twelve at the time, remembered Barrie breaking the news of her death despairingly, and how 'they sat and blubbered together'.[2] Jack, fifteen, recalled being taken into a room where Barrie, who was alone, told him that his mother had promised to marry him and she had worn his ring. Jack believed his mother had said it only because she knew she was dying. But Barrie maintained the same story to Nico's wife sixteen years later, when he gave her a diamond and sapphire ring which he said he had given to Sylvia – 'as we would have been married had your mother lived'.[3]

In her will, he was appointed the second of four trustees and guardians, and next to her mother. Sylvia wrote:

J. M. B. I know will do everything in his power to help our boys – to advise, to comfort, to sympathize in all their joys and sorrows.[4]

An earlier version spoke of him as 'the best friend in the whole world'. After her death he wrote once a year, on her birthday, 'giving an account of his stewardship, telling her how the boys were shaping, and what they had done'.[5]

1 His papers *cit.*: Andrew Birkin: *J.M.Barrie & the Lost Boys* (1979), p. 148.
2 *Ibid.*, Also, Janet Dunbar: *J.M.Barrie: The Man Behind the Image* (1970), p. 191.
3 Birkin: *op. cit.*, p. 191.
4 Dunbar: *op. cit.*, p. 191.
5 Denis Mackail: *The Story of J. M. B.: a biography* (1941), p. 480.

CHAPTER NINE

Sexual Repression and Deprivation

GODWIN, after his marriage to Mary Wollstonecraft, took separate apartments in the Polygon, Somers Town – twenty doors from his own house. His theory was that too close an intimacy brought mutual weariness.

The shock of disappointment on his wedding-night was confided by CARLYLE to his mother two days later – the interval of time she had specified. A few days more and he wrote for guidance from his brother Jack, a medical student at Edinburgh. Years afterwards, when he heard from a friend that gossip in the London Clubs was branding him impotent, he assured him it was untrue, but the wounding must have gone deep. When he came across sexual innuendoes of another kind, made about his hero Frederick, he wrote:

. . . the present Editor does not . . . value the rumour at a pin's fee. '. . . But are there no obscene details at all, then? grumbles the disappointed idle public . . . much depraved in every way. Thus, too, you will observe of dogs: two dogs, at meeting, run, first of all, to the shameful parts of the constitution; institute a strict examination, more or less satisfactory, in that department. That once settled, their interest in ulterior matters seems pretty much to die away . . .' Enough, oh, enough![1]

The rumour surfaced again, after his death, when Froude raised the possibility. A more recent biographer, admitting that the Carlyles' affection for each other took a physical form in 'whispers and embraces', cites 'the early retreat to separate beds and rooms', and opines that 'sexual intercourse played little or no role . . . during almost forty years of marriage'.[2] Different interpretations[3] of the

1 *History of Frederick the Great* (1858–65), iv, p. 415.
2 Fred Kaplan: *Thomas Carlyle: A Biography* (1983), p. 119.
3 '. . . some internal evidence in the lives of both husband and wife tends to make the suggestion [of impotence] not merely frivolous or malevolent'. (W. R. Bett: *The Infirmities of Genius* [1952], p. 14.) Cf. '. . . their physical attraction for each other is inescapable to any student of the letters written after 1826'. (Ian Campbell: *Thomas Carlyle* [1974], p. 61.)

same internal evidence cause him to be put here rather than in the next chapter.

In CHESTERTON's marriage, if the opinion of his brother's widow be accepted, shortcoming lay in his wife. She said that Frances shrank from her husband's touch on their wedding-night and screamed at his physical embrace. The story has been put forward to explain his reckless indulgence in food and drink, for he was not corpulent at the time of marriage. A *TLS* contributor writes that if Chesterton suffered in a virtually sexless union, 'like many another man he married his belly when he could not have a wife, and fathered his own guts'.[1] The explanation omits one important fact, that Frances had an operation in the hope of future children.

Jessie Chambers, with whom LAWRENCE had a close relationship from boyhood to early manhood, was the prototype of the sexually frigid Miriam in *Sons and Lovers*. But Jessie said it was *Lawrence* who was puritanically afraid of sensual experience.

1 17 Aug. 1973.

CHAPTER TEN

Sexual Impediment

After six years of marriage, Effie secured annulment since 'the said JOHN RUSKIN was incapable of consummating the same by reason of incurable impotency'. A few months later, she married Millais.

There is a story that Ruskin's study of Greek statues had led him to believe that all nude women were anatomically perfect, and that his aesthetic expectations were cheated on his wedding-night.

It may be thought strange that I *could* abstain from a woman who to most people was so attractive. On the contrary there were certain circumstances in her person which completely checked it.[1]

Effie, entreating her father to assist her release, wrote that Ruskin had told her 'his true reason' for refusing to consummate the marriage '(and this to me is as villainous as all the rest) that he had imagined women were quite different to what he saw I was, and that the reason he did not make me his wife was because he was disgusted with my person the first evening . . .'[2]

His version to one of his closest friends, Dr Acland, pushes physical relations to one side:

I never attempted to make her my wife the first night – and afterwards we talked together – and agreed that we would not, for some time consummate marriage; as we both wanted to travel freely – and I particularly wanted my wife to be able to climb Alps with me, and had heard many fearful things of the consequence of bridal tours.[3]

KINGSLEY requested his own future wife should remain for the first month in his arms 'a virgin bride, a sister only'. But his motive had

1 Ruskin's statement written out for his lawyers. Quoted by Mary Lutyens: *Millais & the Ruskins* (1967), p. 191.
2 7 Mar. 1854.
3 May 1854. Quoted by Jeffrey Spear: *TLS*, 10 Feb. 1978.

been entirely different. This was no more than a postponement to make their sexual gratification more enjoyable:

> . . . when we lie naked in each other's arms . . . toying with each other's limbs . . . Shall we not feel . . . that those thrilling writhings are but dim shadows of a union which shall be perfect?[1]

RUSKIN, in the statement written out for his lawyers at the time of the annulment, admitted:

> For my part I married in order to have a companion – not for passion's sake . . .[2]

J. K. Jerome introduced the actress Mary Ansell to BARRIE, both in their thirties, and when it went wrong felt guilt. She confided subsequently to friends such as Wells and Compton Mackenzie the shock of her honeymoon, for Barrie was impotent. There is, however, contradictory evidence that she confided to Hilda Trevelyan she had enjoyed 'normal marital relations'[3] in the early days of marriage.

Barrie neglected his wife. Like the Hardys, the couple reached the stage of non-communication. After fifteen years, Barrie's gardener at Black Lake Cottage told him Mary was having an affair with GILBERT CANNAN, twenty years her junior. She wanted a divorce in order to marry him and, when nothing could move her, Barrie gave in. Her second marriage proved no more successful.

1 1843. Letter quoted by Susan Chitty: *The Beast & the Monk: A Life of Charles Kingsley* (1974), p. 81.
2 Quoted by Mary Lutyens: *Millais & the Ruskins* (1967), p. 190.
3 Andrew Birkin: *J. M. Barrie & the Lost Boys* (1979), p. 180.

CHAPTER ELEVEN

Magnanimity

In a similar situation, both Barrie and Bennett acted with incredible generosity. When BARRIE heard Mary was alone, that Black Lake Cottage – the country home which she had retained – was sold, and the money he had given her gone, he sent someone to ask her to meet him so that he could give her financial assistance. Her pride stood in the way. He wrote:

It would be silly of us not to meet, and indeed I wanted to go to you all yesterday. I thought perhaps you would rather come here, and of course whichever you prefer, but that is your only option as I mean to see you whether the idea scares you or not. Painful in a way the first time but surely it need not be so afterwards. How about coming here on Wednesday to lunch at 1.30.

It would be hard to find greater magnanimity than his closing sentence:

But just one thing I should like to say, because no one else can know it so well as I, that never in this world would a young literary man have started with better chances than Mr Cannan when he had you at the helm.[1]

Barrie arranged an allowance to be paid her, and she later lived chiefly in France. She came to his bedside when he lay dying, and stood looking down on the unconscious man. He bequeathed to 'my dear Mary Cannan with my affectionate regards'[2] £1,000 and an annuity of £600 during her life, free of income tax.

When his wife after fourteen years took a young lover, BENNETT settled £2,000 upon her, tax-free for life. It crippled him from the time the tax man pursued him. He found himself travelling third class.

1 15 Mar. 1917. Janet Dunbar: *J. M. Barrie: The Man Behind the Image* (1970), pp. 218–9.
2 *Ibid.*, p. 302.

CHAPTER TWELVE
Bad Men to Marry

H ARDY had been attracted to many girls in his youth. He was discovered 'making violent approaches' at a Christmas party to his cousin Rebecca, and turned out of the house. He was engaged to his cousin, Tryphena Sparks, one of the prototypes for Sue Bridehead in *Jude the Obscure*.

At thirty-four he married Emma Lavinia, whom he had met while working on a church in Cornwall. For three years they were sublimely happy, she with her literary ambition and helping in his work.

We faced by chance ways after that . . .

Their marriage lasted forty years. After he had built Max Gate, she often remained in the country for the three months every year which he spent (like Wordsworth) in London – frequenting his club, the opera, concerts and parties. At fifty-three, he met Mrs Florence Henniker, a more considerable prototype for his character Sue Bridehead. A novelist in her late thirties, she had a military husband and was the daughter of Richard Monckton Milnes. She seems to have proved more conventional in their personal relations than Hardy had at first supposed. It was not with Emma he wrote poetry now, but the poet Rosamund Tomson. Shut out of his creative life, and neglected as wife, Emma started abusing not only him but his whole family in her diary.

Lewis Hind reminisces how he called at Max Gate and Hardy told him he was firmly resolved to write no more novels.

I believe that he was about to tell me why . . . when Mrs Hardy – his former wife – entered the room. Said Mrs Hardy to me – 'Oh, I want to show you my water-colours.' And I, being weak, and courteous to the nieces of archdeacons, was wafted away. So my interview with Thomas Hardy ended.[1]

1 *Authors & I* (1921), p. 116.

At about sixty-seven, Hardy met Florence Emily Dugdale, in her late twenties, a writer of children's books and articles. Two years later, he was taking her to the seaside at Aldeburgh, 'as she is so very delicate'. Next year he managed to get her to become an accepted visitor at Max Gate – her own family thinking her his secretary. Shortly after this time, Emma was to suffer agonizingly from gall-stones. Their marriage had reached the pass that they met only at dinner and then did not speak. She died when he was seventy-two. Within a month, Florence was installed at Max Gate. Hardy, remorseful at Emma's uncomforted pain, venerated her memory.

> She opened the door of the West to me . . .
> She opened the door of Romance to me . . .
> She opened the door of a Love to me . . .
> She opens the door of the Past to me . . .[1]

He spoke of 'her who loyally loved me', and even the discovery of her diaries made no difference. Florence found Emma everywhere. Not one piece of furniture was to be moved. Unaccompanied by Florence, Hardy visited St Juliot on the anniversary of his first meeting Emma there.

The following year, aware of local gossip and innuendoes from her own family, Florence felt she should 'have some position of authority at Max Gate',[2] and Hardy married her. She was thirty-six, making an age gap of two more years: the same for Eliot's second marriage. Hardy hoped 'the union of two rather melancholy temperaments may result in cheerfulness'.[3] It was not to be. When Wessex died, Florence wrote:

Of course he was merely a dog, and not a good dog always, but *thousands* (actually thousands) of afternoons and evenings I would have been alone but for him . . .[4]

BENNETT's wife, at Comarques, found companionship in two dogs, and various rabbits, cats, and ducks. When Bennett complained that the noise of the ducks interrupted his work, she went to the under-gardener, who suggested she replace the females with drakes. The

---

1 'She Opened the Door', written 1913: *Human Shows, Far Phantasies, Songs & Trifles* (1925).
2 Florence to Rebekah Owen: 9 Feb. 1914. Robert Gittings: *The Older Hardy* (1978), p. 159.
3 To Frederick Harrison: 17 Feb. 1914. *Ibid.*, p. 160.
4 26 Dec. 1926. *Friends of a Lifetime: Letters to Sydney Carlyle Cockerell* ed. Viola Meynell (1940), p. 314.

French woman who scoured Essex, insisting on *drakes*, aroused considerable comment.

Since HARDY said, 'I was a young man till I was 40 or 50,' perhaps we should think of him at this time as being middle-aged. Sassoon told Laurence Whistler a confidence Florence had imparted to Sydney Cockerell, that Hardy remained potent as a lover until a few years before his death.[1] She looks very pensive in photographs with him.

BENNETT at forty married his French secretary, Marguerite Soulié, who was thirty-two, tall and slim, with long black hair, a year after Eleanor Green, the beautiful young American redhead, had refused him. Within as little time as four years, he did not take her to America to share his triumph – something she never forgave. He neglected her, as Barrie neglected Mary. Their relationship lasted about the same length of time, and Bennett secured a legal separation.

In his last years 'a dazzling blonde' of thirty-something, Dorothy Cheston, became his mistress because the flowers he brought her every day were wilted and she took pity on a man who, despite success, could so easily be cheated by florists.[2] That is what we always thought, but Frank Swinnerton tells of an unsuccessful actress seeking help in her career; of Wells, when Bennett died, refusing to come down from the flat above:

'No! I *won't*! She's a bitch, and she killed Arnold.'[3]

Furthermore, Swinnerton recounts how she took him into the bedroom to see his friend's body, and wrenched a ring from Bennett's finger.

There was no suggestion that the ring was to be a treasured keepsake. She was appropriating something she fancied.[4]

These sometimes tragic images seize upon the mind, but they are not typical of writers as a whole.

1 Laurence Whistler: *TLS*, 2 May 1975.
2 Dorothy Cheston Bennett: *Arnold Bennett: A Portrait done at Home* (1935), pp. 56, 59.
3 *Arnold Bennett: A Last Word* (1978), p. 88.
4 *Ibid.*, p. 86.

PART THREE
COMPLICATED LOVE

CHAPTER ONE

Original Marriages

I

Some writers who could be said to have made curious matrimonial arrangements found these worked surprisingly well. BEATRICE and SIDNEY WEBB married in their early thirties. Their wedding rings were inscribed *pro bono publico*. They spent their honeymoon inspecting trade societies in Ireland and attending the Trade Union Congress in Glasgow.

They were together over fifty years, until Beatrice died. On one of his visits to Passfield Corner, Malcolm Muggeridge 'on Monday morning . . . peeped in at them':

> He was seated at a desk . . . pen strokes steady, stance assured. She was prowling about the room . . . There they were, planning our future . . .[1]

In their mid-seventies they visited Russia and three years later, in their last major book, *Soviet Communism: a New Civilisation*, the doctrine of 'gradualism' which they had held so long seemed to be abandoned.

After being five years happily married, HAROLD NICOLSON and VICTORIA SACKVILLE-WEST loved members of their own sex and each was habitually unfaithful to the other. Harold referred to Vita's affairs as 'your muddles', she to his as 'your fun'.[2] The creators of the great garden at Sissinghurst created for themselves a married life that suited both perfectly and lasted forty-nine years. Harold spent the week in London and they reunited at weekends. Their younger son, Nigel, has told how they 'berthed like sister-ships' – for tea, the tour of the garden, the 'succession of privacies'.[3] When apart, they wrote to each

---

1 *Chronicles of Wasted Time* (1972–3), i, pp. 149–50.
2 *Portrait of a Marriage* (1973), p. 187 (Amer. edn., p. 207).
3 *Ibid.*, p. 226 (Amer. edn., pp. 256–7).

other every day from the time of their engagement in 1911 until Vita's death in 1962, and each kept all the other's letters.

Sixteen years after they were married, in a debate on BBC radio they concluded that a successful marriage was 'the greatest of human benefits', that it must be based on 'a common sense of values' and that 'modesty, good humour and, above all, occupation' were the only things that would 'stave off marital nerves'.[1] Vita wrote to her husband that they had 'never interfered with each other, never been jealous of each other':

And now we love each other . . . more agonizingly, since we see the inevitable end.[2]

The day she died, Harold wrote in his *Diary*:

I pick some of her favourite flowers and lay them on the bed.[3]

About three weeks after, he put: 'Oh, Vita, I have wept buckets for you.' Nigel says: 'I was awed by his desolation . . .'[4]

JOHN BETJEMAN at twenty-seven married Penelope Chetwode, daughter of a field-marshal. They had a son and a daughter. Before he was forty-eight, he and his wife began to live separate lives. Lady Betjeman said:

If we live entirely together, we have terrific rows . . . Fundamentally we are very fond of each other.[5]

In the mid-1950s he began dividing his time between The Mead, Wantage, and a flat in Cloth Fair.

1 *Ibid.*, p. 189 (Amer. edn., p. 210)..
2 1960. *Ibid.*, p. 227 (Amer. edn., p. 257)..
3 *Diaries & Letters 1945–1962* ed. Nigel Nicolson (1968), p. 415.
4 *Portrait of a Marriage* (1973), p. 227 (Amer. edn., p. 258).
5 Graham Lord: *The Sunday Express*, 18 Aug. 1974.

CHAPTER TWO

Third Parties

I

DOROTHY WORDSWORTH lived with her brother, continuously from the Racedown and Alfoxden days, for nearly fifty-five years – seven years longer than his wife. Their relations have never been fully determined. She would enter in her *Journal*:

After dinner we made a pillow of my shoulder, I read to him and my Beloved slept . . .[1]

Or again:

. . . we sate . . . at the window – I on a chair and William with his hand on my shoulder. We were deep in Silence and Love, a blessed hour.[2]

The removal at a later date of certain passages gave grounds to F. W. Bateson for his incest theory.[3]

She accompanied her brother to Scarborough for the wedding, having 'long loved Mary Hutchinson as a Sister' and looked 'forward with perfect happiness to this Connection between us'. The highly emotional woman recorded that she slept with William's wedding-ring on her finger the night before. But happy as she was, she half-dreaded 'that concentration of all tender feelings . . . which will come upon me on the wedding morning'.[4] She did not attend the ceremony. When she saw the party returning from the church,

I could stand it no longer and threw myself on the bed . . . till I met my beloved William and fell upon his bosom.[5]

1 17 March 1802: *Journals of Dorothy Wordsworth* ed. Mary Moorman (1971), pp. 102–3.
2 2 June 1802: *ibid.*, p. 130.
3 *Wordsworth: a re-interpretation* (1954; revised 1956).
4 To Mrs John Marshall, 29 Sept. 1802: *The Letters of William & Dorothy Wordsworth*, i, 'The Early Years' ed. Chester L. Shaver (1967), p. 377.
5 4 Oct., 1802. *Journals cit.*, p. 154.

Beyond dispute are the facts that without reservation she had been prepared to share their home with Annette and Caroline, and that she lived with William and Mary and, for long periods, Mary's sister, Sarah Hutchinson, in happy agreement.

In her major work Mary Moorman dismissed the attempt to read 'morbid implications' in passages of Wordsworth's poetry such as:

> . . . my sister, and my friend,
> Or something dearer still, if . . .
> . . . in the heart of love
> There be a dearer name.[1]

Hunter Davies cites the marriage as spoiling 'incest theories', although he acknowledges that 'someone could argue . . . it provides proof of guilt'.[2] But in a letter to the *TLS*, Jonathan Wordsworth withdrew from 'the lofty position' adopted on this subject in his letter of the previous month. He had been looking again at the MS. of Dorothy's *Grasmere Journal* and was 'almost certain' that he could make out the following words under one of Mr Bateson's deletions:

Had such a sweet baby last night! – the very image of his father. Wm is writing to Annette, as he thinks we might go to France for a bit. When we get back he has it in mind to marry dear Mary for the look of things. Poor Coleridge is terribly jealous! He says he thinks dear Sara is never going to give him a child, and he's written her a long gloomy poem all about joy. Secretly I think he wants me to have a little Samuel as well as my William! – and why not indeed, if Wm is going to get married?[3]

The Wordsworth story is being revealed in serial form. In 1977, a bundle of thirty-five letters between Wordsworth and Mary came to light. It would be difficult to read them and believe with Dorothy (if indeed she wrote it) that his marriage was 'for the look of things'. Wordsworth writes:

O Mary I love you with a passion . . . which grows till I tremble to think of its strength . . .[4]

1 *William Wordsworth: A Biography: The Early Years* (1957), p. 282.
2 *William Wordsworth: A Biography* (1980), p. 139.
3 21 May 1976.
4 11 Aug. 1810: *The Love Letters of William & Mary Wordsworth* ed. Beth Darlington (1982), p. 62.

. . . my longing to have thee in my arms was so great, and the feelings of my heart so delicious, that my whole frame was over powered with Love & longing . . .[1]

. . . every hour of absence now is a grievous loss . . . the fever of thought & longing & affection & desire is strengthening in me . . . Last night I *suffered* . . .[2]

A letter by Dorothy, dated thirteen years after the marriage and addressed to Bernard Barton Esq., who had sent some verses to Wordsworth, gives a peep at her standing:

Sir,

As Mr Wordsworth (my Brother) is gone from home, and as I do not know how long his absence may be, I take the liberty of writing to inform you that your letter addressed to him at Rydal Mount has reached the place of its destination. In the absence of my Brother and Mrs Wordsworth I am accustomed to open his letters, and therefore have had the pleasure of perusing yours . . .[3]

When a turbulent and demanding Dorothy had become dependent upon their loving care, there was never any suggestion she should be put away.

SHELLEY's marriage with Harriet was threatened by the presence of his friend Hogg, of Miss Hitchener – who in less than five months metamorphosed from his 'soul's sister' into 'the Brown Demon' – and, more injuriously and constantly, of his sister-in-law Eliza. On the day Miss Hitchener was going to depart, Hogg claimed that he walked in St James's Park 'with the brown demon on my right arm and the black diamond on my left'. Shelley repeated a domestic triangle when he eloped with Mary, taking Claire. Indeed, after Claire had given birth to Byron's child the Shelleys found Allegra something of an embarrassment, hints being made that Shelley was the father.

J. S. MILL began an intellectual friendship with Mrs Taylor when he was introduced at twenty-two. Until they married, over twenty years later, he was an assiduous visitor, occasionally travelling with her alone, which provoked its share of scandal. With considerable magnanimity her husband seems to have accepted that he could not be her intellectual companion, and on the occasions when Mill dined twice weekly with her in London *he* dined out.

1 Mon. 11.0 a.m., 1 June 1812. Ibid., p. 210.
2 3–4 June 1812. *Ibid.*, p. 229.
3 27 Dec. 1815: unpublished. (In the possession of author Jack Hodges.)

II

A number of writers – Blake,[1] Dickens, Joyce – had a younger brother sharing their household in the early years of marriage. DICKENS never experienced a *solitude à deux*. Even when he was newly married, his sister-in-law Mary Hogarth was squeezed into their three rooms at Furnival's Inn. She, as well as his sixteen-year-old brother, was with them at Doughty Street. It was there Frederick fetched the doctor when Mary suddenly collapsed and died after they had all returned from a happy evening at the theatre. Dickens slipped her ring on his little finger, where it remained. He wrote the epitaph for her grave:

YOUNG, BEAUTIFUL, AND GOOD
GOD IN HIS MERCY
NUMBERED HER WITH HIS ANGELS
AT THE EARLY AGE OF
SEVENTEEN.

Three years later, uncertain of his book's adaptation as a play, Dickens entrusted his wife to Frederick for the first night of *The Old Curiosity Shop* at the Adelphi.

After the first visit to America, another sister-in-law, Georgina, was permanently adopted into the household and, sixteen years later when Kate was sent away, rumours that her own sister had taken her place deflected the scandal of Ellen Ternan. Kate did not speak to Georgina for twenty-one years. Dickens's daughter, Kate Perugini, believed in her old age that a sister-in-law living in the home was 'the greatest mistake'.[2]

In the very first year of his marriage, JOYCE had a wishful scheme that Stanislaus, who worshipped the genius of his older brother and could be depended upon, might share with Nora and himself a small cottage outside Dublin. At the end of the year, when there was another post as English teacher at the Scuola Berlitz, James was able to get him to leave an obscure clerkship in Dublin and come to Trieste, where he had a room next to theirs in their lodgings. As soon

1 See p. 13.
2 Gladys Storey: *Dickens and Daughter* (1939), p. 24.

as he arrived, it was arranged he should pay for household expenses – in fact, before long, James signed the pay-roll for both at the school and pocketed the combined salaries. Not long after, Stanislaus was with them in another lodging where James, coming home late and drunk, had to go through his brother's room in order to reach his own and Nora's. Sometimes, roused from his sleep in disgust and angry that alcohol was helping to ruin his brother's eyes, Stanislaus beat him in frustration. On 12 September 1908 Stanislaus recorded in his diary that he had saved his brother and Nora six times from starvation.[1] It was the classic story of giver taken for granted and resented. Stanislaus began to find himself left to eat alone; even his young nephew taunted him in the street that the family, because of him, 'had no dinner today'. After another two years, tired of humiliation and exploitation, he lived apart; but when Joyce came to apologize, Stanislaus, torn by the loss of their friendship, joined them once more and, as he wrote to his father, 'The mistake began again.'[2] The brothers were of opposite types: Stanislaus a Puritan (as defined by Chesterton),[3] and James a Catholic. When Joyce took his family to Paris, he asked if Stanislaus might replace him at the Università di Trieste. Stanislaus married at forty-two, and called his son James.

When C. S. LEWIS married late in life, he and Joy would not consider his elder brother – who had made his home with him after retirement and acted as secretary – living anywhere else. Major Warren, with considerable reservations at first, came to speak of the house as being enriched by the presence of Jack's wife; after her death, while not comparing his own sorrow with his brother's, he said, 'I still miss her sadly.'

BENNETT and Marguerite did not spend their honeymoon alone. Before the wedding-day was fixed, he had invited the Marriotts from Chelsea days to spend the summer at Les Sablons. They naturally offered to postpone their visit. Bennett sent a postcard: 'On the contrary, I shall need you all the more.'[4]

1 Richard Ellmann: *James Joyce* (1959), p. 278.
2 1910: letter not sent. *Ibid.*, p. 313.
3 'The [Puritan] is always screwing himself up to see truth; the [Catholic] is often content that truth is there. The Puritan is only strong enough to stiffen; the Catholic is strong enough to relax.' (*George Bernard Shaw* [1910], p. 107.)
4 Dudley Barker: *Writer by Trade: A View of Arnold Bennett* (1966), p. 135.

III

MASEFIELD'S marriage came in the middle of his wife's twenty-four-year intimacy with Isobel – the gauche, defensive and physically unattractive sister of Roger Fry. Yet Constance had seen qualities sufficient to make her give up a secure teaching post at Brighton and join Isobel in running their own school in Marylebone Road. A month before her marriage, Constance set down in a notebook that she wanted 'always to cherish, honour and protect' her.

I will try always to have leisure for her every day . . . I must always be as tender as I can.[1]

She planned that they would share a meal daily if possible.

It was an unusual wedding for, instead of the bride's family, Isobel was in charge. Invitations went out in her name and on the day she was publicly weeping. The following year, when Masefield had to leave their home in Greenwich to work on *The Manchester Guardian*, Constance and their baby lived most of the time with Isobel. On his return, Constance still had her teaching and often stayed with her friend. A move to Little Venice was made in the interests of the school and Constance's friendship. Six years after their marriage the Masefields, jointly with Isobel, took as a country retreat the Rectory Farm, Great Hampden. When the school in Marylebone closed down, they followed Isobel to Hampstead and their daughter Judith joined the morning classes she was now giving.

Then, in the eleventh year of their marriage, the Masefields settled at Lollingdon Farm, while Isobel remained in Hampstead 'absorbed' in social work. She visited them once for a short time, although Judith spent the summer term of 1917 at the 'farm school' Isobel had started near Aylesbury. Constance now told her husband that, much as she still loved Isobel, she got 'nothing from her that is any comfort to my soul'.[2]

VERA BRITTAIN at twenty-nine married George Catlin, an American professor of politics, and they spent the first year at Ithaca

1 June 1903. Constance Babington Smith: *John Masefield: A Life* (1978), p. 82 Note.
2 Undated letter. *Ibid.*, p. 120.

University. She then resumed her freelance journalism in England while her husband stayed on lecturing. She called theirs a 'semi-detached marriage'.[1] After continual to-ing and fro-ing the States, a home was set up at 19 Glebe Place, Chelsea, when she was thirty-four, and WINIFRED HOLTBY came to live with them. The unusual domestic arrangement which suited them so well gave rise, Vera was assured, 'to a plentiful crop of rumours'. Their friends, at any rate, appeared 'singularly unaffected by our local "reputation"'.[2]

1 *Testament of Experience* (1957), p. 39.
2 *Testament of Friendship* (1940), pp. 291–2.

CHAPTER THREE
Ménage à trois

I

Only the close friends of WILKIE COLLINS – men such as Dickens, Lehmann, Charles Ward – knew a little of his two semi-permanent liaisons that overlapped. His meeting with the attractive young widow Caroline Groves inspired the dramatic encounter in *The Woman in White*. He lived with her over a total period of forty years, and adopted her daughter Harriet, who became his invaluable secretary. After some fourteen or sixteen years, Caroline gave him an ultimatum – to marry her or she would marry a younger man.[1] Collins refused.

Two years after her second marriage (which he attended), Caroline returned to find that her rival, a considerably younger mistress – the dark, good-looking Martha Rudd – had borne his child. The more sophisticated Caroline now became the novelist's housekeeper, continuing to act as hostess when he entertained his male friends, while Martha, living nearby as 'Mrs Dawson', gave him two more children. Collins never married. Both women were provided for equally, and arrangements made for all the children, in his sadly mismanaged will. Kate Dickens, who married his brother Charles, reflected Victorian mores when she said of Wilkie: '. . . he was as bad as he could be', adding: 'yet the gentlest and most kind-hearted of men'.

It seems certain that by the time of WILLIAM MORRIS's joint tenancy of Kelmscott Manor, ROSSETTI, who so often had painted the beautiful Jane, was deeply in love. Her reciprocation of his feelings may have been the cause of her melancholy and frequent ill health.

Morris, at thirty-seven, was no Forsyte to regard his wife as property and, in spite of his hurt, pursued his principles here as in all

---

1 Cf. Rebecca West's ultimatum to Wells, p. 150.

else, trying to persevere in the old friendship. After his first visit to Iceland that same summer, he wrote to Mrs Coronio, a trusted friend:

I know clearer now perhaps than then what a blessing and help last year's journey was to me; what horrors it saved me from.

He wrote again:

Rossetti has set himself down at Kelmscott as if he never meant to go away, and not only does that keep me away from that harbour of refuge (because it is really a farce our meeting when we can help it) but also he has all sorts of ways so unsympathetic with the sweet simply old place . . . O how I long to keep the world from narrowing on me, and to look at things, bigly and kindly.[1]

The personal habits of the two men – Rossetti a laudanum drinker, and Morris an early riser – were now as diverse as those of Byron and Shelley. After two more years Rossetti left permanently, and Morris purchased the much-loved house which he immortalized in *News from Nowhere*.

EDITH NESBIT and her husband Hubert Bland employed, as housekeeper and general aide, Alice Hoatson, who had left her job on *Sylvie's Home Journal* to join them. Two of the later Bland children, Rosamund[2] and John, were Alice's and Edith had no choice but to accept them. The ambiguous Ida Baker lived with the MURRYS at Hampstead and Menton.

II

Almost immediately, Lady Wellcome's marriage to MAUGHAM had to compete against his friendship with Gerald Haxton which was to dominate the greater part of his creative life. She told Beverley Nichols that Gerald had dedicated his whole life to getting her out.[3] Syrie was the daughter of Dr Barnado, and she met Maugham when he was in his late thirties – she a little younger. Appalled at being cited as co-respondent by her husband, Maugham at forty-two married her in the middle of World War I. They had one child, Liza.

1 *The Letters of William Morris to his Family & Friends* ed. Philip Henderson (1950), pp. xlvi–xlvii.
2 See p. 149.
3 Beverley Nichols: *A Case of Human Bondage* (1966), p. 140.

Maugham joined up as a driver and dresser in a Red Cross ambulance unit, and in France met Gerald Haxton, an American orderly in his early twenties. Soon after the war Maugham took him as his companion to the Far East, and each year they went on a long journey together. Meanwhile Syrie achieved international fame as an interior decorator, and she created a tasteful house in the King's Road with her own money. She arranged a completely self-contained flat for her husband in the hope that he would feel free to visit her. But Gerald had been barred from England after a charge of gross indecency in a Covent Garden hotel, and Maugham could seldom be persuaded to come alone.

Her misfortune was to go on loving him. She now designed a long white villa in Le Touquet and had it purpose-built so that Maugham and Gerald could live in the upstairs rooms while her room and the living rooms were on the ground floor. Barbara Black thought that this was her last attempt at accepting Gerald.[1] Beverley Nichols stayed one weekend and, with Gertie Millar, Noël Coward and other guests, saw a smiling Syrie go to her husband, holding out her arms. With one word, 'Darling!' she asked to be kissed, and Maugham publicly turned away. There was a row about laundry bills which she was giving to her guests, but she had paid for everything else. When Nichols returned to London, Syrie, verging on breakdown, accompanied him.

She saw her lawyers and threatened to cite Gerald in divorce proceedings. The marriage had lasted twelve years. Maugham claimed that before their final parting he wrote a letter to her in which he conceded: 'Do not think that I am not grateful for all your love.' Three years after the divorce he bought Villa Mauresque on the French Riviera.

When he was eighty he reported meeting her at the Dorchester, the year before she died. She told him their divorce had been a mistake, to which he had countered that their getting married, 'that had been the mistake'.[2] His final work, *Looking Back*, was seen by Nichols, Rebecca West, Cecil Beaton, Sacheverell Sitwell and others as a libel on the memory of a beautiful and intelligent lady. It was as though

1 Robin Maugham: *Conversations with Willie: Recollections of W. Somerset Maugham* (Amer. edn. 1978), p. 45.
2 *Ibid.*, p. 101.

Gerald had worked on Maugham – always a tender father – to believe that Liza was not his own.

The deep love between LYTTON STRACHEY and Dora Carrington was not disturbed by her marriage to Ralph Partridge. Lytton, physically attracted to her husband in spite of intellectual differences, continued to live in her home. This complicated chapter of Bloomsbury was accepted naturally by the principal characters.

The night before Lytton died, he had a crisis and they went to fetch her. She was found unconscious in the garage, the car engine running. She wrote in her diary entitled 'Her Book':

It is ironical that Lytton by that early attack at 6'ock saved my life, when I gave my life for his. he should give it back. [1]

Seven weeks afterwards, the Woolfs drove down; there was a moment when Dora kissed Virginia and burst into tears.

'There is nothing left for me to do. I did everything for Lytton . . . Lytton was like a father to me. He taught me everything I know. He read poetry and French to me.' [2]

The following morning she put on his yellow dressing-gown and shot herself, bungling it, and died with much pain.

When A. J. P. TAYLOR contemplated at seventy his third marriage, he was sharing a house in Regent's Park with his first wife, Margaret, whose health was declining. After the marriage he and his wife lived in a house on Hampstead Heath.

Naturally she was upset when I treated Margaret as a friend, though certainly not as a rival wife.

He records that within two years Margaret died 'at peace with all the world, including me and Eva'. [3] KINGSLEY AMIS lives at Primrose Hill with his first ex-wife and her current husband.

1 Michael Holroyd: *Lytton Stratchey: A Critical Biography* (1967–8), ii, p. 709.
2 Leonard Woolf: *Downhill All the Way* (1967), p. 252.
3 *A Personal History* (1983), p. 267.

CHAPTER FOUR

The Wells Saga

W ELLS'S saga to make what he called his 'Lover-Shadow'
flesh, had at its heart for more than midway the courage of
Jane.

> She stuck to me so sturdily that in the end I stuck to myself. I do not know
> what I should have been without her. She stabilized my life. She gave it a
> home and dignity. She preserved its continuity . . . I do not think she
> believed very strongly in my beliefs. She accepted them, but she could have
> done without them.[1]

DYLAN THOMAS called Caitlin 'his cattle-anchor, his sheet-anchor'.[2]

WELLS started conventionally enough, being married at twenty-five
to his cousin Isabel Mary Wells at Wandsworth Parish Church. Six
years earlier, studying at South Kensington, he had taken lodgings
with Aunt Mary and her at 181 Euston Road. More recently, he had
been invited to move in again when he was renting an attic room in
Bloomsbury. It sounds like *Mr Polly*, but Miriam has a 'rather lean
and insufficient body'[3] and Isabel was beautiful.

A year after his marriage, a 'valiant little figure' joined his biology
class carrying 'her schoolgirl satchel of books and a very old-fashioned
unwieldy microscope'. His new pupil was Amy Catherine Robbins,
but he came to call her Jane. She redrew his diagrams for a second
edition of *Textbook of Biology*. In just over another year, he left Isabel
and went to live with Jane in rooms in Mornington Crescent – 'with
less than fifty pounds between us and absolute disaster'.[4] She became
his second wife, who managed his success through the years of
wonderful stories beginning with *The Time-Machine*.

When he was thirty, perhaps influenced by Gissing, with whom

---

1 Unpublished Introduction, written in 1928, to *The Book of Catherine Wells. H. G. Wells in
Love: Postscript to an Experiment in Autobiography* ed. G. P. Wells (1984), pp. 35–6.
2 Caitlin Thomas with George Tremlett: *Caitlin: A Warring Absence* (1986), p. 154.
3 *The History of Mr Polly* (1910), p. 161.
4 Unpublished Introduction to *The Book of Catherine Wells. Op. cit.*, p. 27.

they spent a holiday in Rome, he began to suffer from 'domestic claustrophobia'. He tells of visiting Isabel at Virginia Water, of spending the day and seeking her embraces, while she hushed as it were a child and asked: 'How can things like that be?' Bicycling away, he 'felt as though all purpose had been drained . . . and nothing remained worth while'.[1]

He underwent a breakdown and for two months remained a patient in Dr Hick's house at Romsey. Then Jane and he moved to Sandgate, where they built Spade House and she bore him two sons. Gip, their first-born, cost his mother a fight of twenty-four hours for them both.

. . . and then it was, I fear, that the seed of her death was sown in her.[2]

Gip appears in *The Magic Shop*.

Just past forty, Wells asked his wife to condone the polygamy that he taught. She was 'a world-interested woman to my world-interested man . . . a match for the colour of my own mind'.[3] With 'her relative fragility', she had to bide the successive cycles of his loves – one young woman after another.

At forty-one, he was invited by the 'Fabian Nursery' to give three lectures and came under fierce public attack as an advocate of free love. Among the young women who 'assumed attitudes of disciple-ship'[4] was Rosamund Bland, plucked from a railway compartment at Paddington and prepared to run off with him. To Shaw, who endeavoured to play peacemaker between Rosamund's father, a foun-der member of the Society, and himself, Wells wrote:

What an unmitigated middle-Victorian ass you are . . . You dont understand & you cant understand the right & wrongs of the case in which you stick your maiden judgment . . . Now go on being amusing . . .

That same year he broke from the Fabians.

Immediately, he turned to twenty-two-year-old Amber Reeves, whose mother was head of the Women's Section. Amber had a first-class Cambridge degree and called him 'Master', while he was 'entrusted with her own special name of "Dusa" . . . short for

1 *Experiment in Autobiography* (1934), ii, p. 432.
2 Unpublished Introduction to *The Book of Catherine Wells, cit.*, p. 29.
3 *H. G. Wells in Love: Postscript to an Experiment in Autobiography* ed. G. P. Wells (1984), p. 198.
4 *Ibid.*, p. 68.

Medusa'.[1] He invited her often to Spade House. Next year she was pregnant at her request, and he carried her off to Le Touquet. When she married a suitor, Wells provided a cottage. Her father was heard to exclaim: 'That blackguard Wells!' Meanwhile Wells sent for Jane to come over.

With those cheerful youngsters about, I could go for walks, race, bathe, and get back across the gap of feeling that had opened between Jane and myself.[2]

He began *The History of Mr Polly*. Jane and he sold Spade House and took No. 17 Church Row, Hampstead. He also took a tiny flat in Candover Street 'for purposes of work, and nervous relief',[3] and there Dusa came – among the others.

At forty-five, he began his three-year liaison with Elizabeth Gräfin von Arnim ('Little e'), mother of five, later the Countess Russell. They holidayed together in Italy. When they were out one day, they saw in their *Times* a letter from Mrs Humphry Ward deploring Rebecca West and the younger generation, so they stripped under the trees and 'made love all over Mrs Humphry Ward . . . lit a match and burnt her'.[4]

A year later, running concurrently at first, began his ten-year love affair with Rebecca West who was twenty-one. He took a house a dozen miles from Easton Glebe so that he could live at home as well. Then their ménage came to be constantly moved around. Sometimes they were lovers and sometimes friends. Towards the end he began a friendship with Margaret Sanger, an American in her mid-thirties. At this time of overwork and exhaustion, Rebecca said: 'He went round and round like a rat in a maze.' She gave him an ultimatum: marry her and leave Jane, go on with Jane but guarantee her £3,000 a year – or say goodbye.

That year he went to Geneva to see the League of Nations Assembly at work. He took the opportunity of fulfilling a rendezvous with thirty-six-year-old Odette Keun, who had sent him her book describing her adventures in Bolshevik Russia and declared her love. On his arrival at her hotel, she had given instructions to send him up to her room. He found himself in dim light 'with a dark slender young

1 *Ibid.*, pp. 74–5.
2 *Ibid.*, p. 81.
3 *Ibid.*, p. 84.
4 *Ibid.*, p. 89.

woman in a flimsy wrap'.[1] Without seeing each other more clearly, they at once went to bed together. Two weeks later, he rented a farmhouse at Grasse and proceeded to build Lou Pidou in the vicinity. Jane gave Odette a picture by C. R. W. Nevinson. *The World of William Clissold* was dedicated to Odette. But when his son Frank sent a telegram that Jane was dying of cancer, he replied tenderly and came at once. During the following six months he assembled *The Book of Catherine Wells*.

I cannot tell how much I owe her. But indeed my wife was neither Jane, which was her working and practically developed self, nor Catherine, which was the name of her personal reverie and of her literary life. She was both of them and many more as the lights about her changed.[2]

Her death was catastrophic for it took away the base of the triangle which contained his emotions.

He went back to Odette. Then he rediscovered 'the very human' Moura Budberg, whom he had met many years previously in Gorki's flat and who had been his guide in Petersburg. Now she came to the Reichstag where he was lecturing, and greeted him: 'Aige-gee'.[3] He remembered what it was to be really in love. Passionate hate replaced passionate love for Odette. When he was sixty-six and Moura thirty-nine, they spent a holiday in Austria. He had a 'diabolic row' with Odette. At sixty-eight, he was groom in a 'symbolic wedding' with Moura. He said: 'You only look a fool if you fall in love with a *young* woman.' She said: 'I'm not going to marry. He only *thinks* I am, I'm not such a fool.' The strange ceremony was enacted at the Quo Vadis restaurant in Soho, with Max Beerbohm, Harold Nicolson, David Low, and Lady Cunard among the guests. *The Croquet Player* was dedicated to Moura, and I possess a copy of *Mind at the End of its Tether* inscribed: 'With all the Love in the world to my beloved Moura Mutual. Nov 19th'.

Isabel, Jane, Violet Hunt, Dorothy Richardson, Rosamund, Dusa, Little e, Rebecca, Margaret, Odette, Moura – so the pageant of beauties passes and bewilders. They move around a pink, peppery, little man, who had a squeaky voice and a sense of fun – inclined to

1 *H. G. Wells in Love: Postscript to an Experiment in Autobiography* ed. G. P. Wells (1984), p. 125.
2 Unpublished Introduction, written in 1928, to *The Book of Catherine Wells*. *Ibid.*, p. 26.
3 *Ibid.*, p. 140.

think himself 'less obsessed by these desires . . . than the average man'[1] – but whose mind had an international impact perhaps greater than Shaw's. Maugham thought to ask one of Wells's mistresses what it was that had attracted her to him. 'His body smelt of honey,' she said.

1 *H. G. Wells in Love: Postscript to an Experiment in Autobiography* ed. G. P. Wells (1984), p. 52.

CHAPTER FIVE
'The passions . . . his guide'

I

BYRON's marriage was a one-year incident in a love life as bewildering and complicated as Wells's, but Wells returned to Jane when she was dying, and Byron was heartless towards Claire Clairmont and their child Allegra. Unlike Wells, he was bisexual. His amours encompassed nine named mistresses (of his Italian concubines he calculated 'at least two hundred of one sort or another – perhaps more, for I have not lately kept the recount'), one wife, and four or more passionate affairs with known boys. Over a life extending twice the length, Wells had at least seven mistresses and two wives. Yet Byron declared, quite truthfully, he had never seduced any woman. His advances were made only when he knew they would be reciprocated.

'The passions', to quote from the diary of Byron's wife, 'have been his guide from childhood.' He was only nine when he became 'utterly, devotedly fond' of Mary Duff – 'my first of flames, before most people begin to burn'.[1] He was 'bewildered to assign any cause for his precocity of affection'.[2] Perhaps it lay in his being in charge of a widowed, unstable mother and a promiscuous nurse.

When he was twelve, it was thirteen-year-old Margaret Parker –

I do not recollect scarcely anything equal to the *transparent* beauty of my cousin . . . she looked as if she had been made out of a rainbow . . . I could not sleep – I could not eat – I could not rest . . .[3]

Tragically this lovely girl died two years later. At fifteen, he missed a term at Harrow on account of seventeen-year-old Mary Ann Cha-

1 *Journal*: 17 Nov. 1813.
2 *Ibid.*: 26 Nov. 1813.
3 Ravenna *Journal*, 'Detached Thoughts' (1821–2): *The Letters & Journals* ed. Leslie A. Marchand (1973–82), ix, p. 40.

worth. He was staying at Newstead for the summer holiday and used to ride over to Annesley every morning until the Chaworths let him have his own bedroom. One evening in the hall, he overheard Mary upstairs expressing scorn for 'that lame boy' to her maid. He ran out, and all the way to Newstead. The next morning, he came back, pretending he had not heard. His mother wrote to Hanson:

. . . I cannot get him to return to school . . . He has no indisposition . . . but love, desperate love . . . the boy is distractedly in love with Miss Chaworth.[1]

On the publication of *Childe Harold*, at twenty-four, 'I awoke one morning and found myself famous.'[2] One of those pressing to meet him was Lady Caroline Lamb, the twenty-seven-year-old wife of the future prime minister. After she had made his acquaintance, she wrote in her journal:

Mad, bad, and dangerous to know.

She was no novice. Within a month they were lovers. She then made her adultery so public that within another month he wished to withdraw. She sent him a present of her pubic hair:

Caroline Byron – next to Thyrsa [his Trinity choirboy Edlestone] dearest & most faithful.

She disguised herself as a page to bring him her letters. She ran away, and her mother and mother-in-law besought Byron to find her and take her to her husband (a situation which hugely amused the Prince Regent). Six months after he had broken off their affair she met him at Lady Heathcote's ball, and tried to wound herself first with a knife or broken glass, and then she used scissors.

Meanwhile, he had enjoyed at Eywood the 'autumnal charms' of Lady Oxford, now forty.

I never felt a stronger passion; which she returned with equal ardour.[3]

Married against her will, the Hoppner beauty and blue-stocking 'had bestowed her favours on many', and for some months she, Byron and her children scrambled in the woods and splashed on the water

1 Oct. 1803.
2 10 March 1812.
3 Medwin's quotation of Byron. *Journal of Correspondence & Conversations between Lord Byron & the Countess of Blessington* (Cincinnati: 1851), p. 141.

together. Thirteen-year-old Lady Charlotte presented him with two curls which he afterwards treasured.

He was still twenty-five on that early Sunday afternoon, 27 June 1813, when his half-sister Augusta took her place on the roundabout. She was twenty-nine, mother of a large family and Lady of the Bedchamber to the Queen, and had come to London to escape her husband's creditors. Byron and Augusta had seen little of each other since early childhood, and André Maurois suggests:

They were not safeguarded against love, like normal brothers and sisters, by the wear-and-tear of their affection.[1]

A Calvinistic childhood, and ancestral crimes he believed to be in his blood, led Byron to call his intimate relations with Augusta 'incest'. He wrote to Moore that he was 'in a far more serious, and entirely new, scrape than any of the last twelvemonths . . .'[2]

He even shocked Lady Melbourne, who had been his confidante since the affair with her daughter-in-law, Lady Caroline. To divert him from 'the brink of a precipice', she encouraged him to form a new liaison – with Lady Frances Webster, wife of a Cambridge contemporary who had asked him to be godfather to his son. The complacent husband invited him twice to Aston Hall; and when Byron received them at Newstead, Lady Frances came to him at two in the morning: 'I am entirely at your *mercy* . . .' But she added: 'I cannot bear the reflection hereafter.' He wrote to Lady Melbourne to tell her –

Was I wrong? – I spared her . . .[3]

The following year, Augusta gave birth to Medora[4] and after two months with them at Hastings, Byron proposed the second time to Annabella Millbanke, Lady Melbourne's niece. He confided to her aunt that Augusta 'wished me much to marry – because it was the only chance of redemption for two persons . . .'[5] He had met Annabella the previous year, while he had been carrying on with her cousin Lady Caroline. Then twenty-one, she disapproved of 'all the women absurdly courting him' and thought she could help him

1 *Byron* (1930), p. 174.
2 Postscript to letter: 22 Aug. 1813.
3 17 Oct. 1813.
4 See p. 294–5.
5 4 Oct. 1814.

reform. She attended lectures on theology and science, and he nicknamed her 'Princess of Parallelograms'. He had never known 'a woman whom I *esteemed* so much'. She had turned him down, 'believing that he never will be the object of that strong affection which would make me happy in domestic life'. Now she resolved 'to make your happiness my first object in life . . . I will *trust* to you . . .'

According to Annabella in her Journal, on their way to Halnaby Hall for their honeymoon the bells were ringing at Durham and he commented sarcastically: 'Ringing for our happiness, I suppose?' He began a sadistic taunting:

'How is it possible a woman of your sense could form the wild hope of reforming *me*? Enough . . . that you are my wife for me to hate you . . . you will find that you have married a devil . . . It *must* come to a separation!'

He laughed, and she thought it a sick joke. When they arrived in the snow, he did not help her from the carriage. The butler later remembered her looking very young, lonely and listless, in an 'attitude of despair'.[1]

That night he woke up crying: 'Good God, I am surely in Hell!' In the morning he received a letter from Augusta. He read out the beginning: 'Dearest, first, and best of human beings . . .' and asked Annabella what she thought of it. He had alternating moods of tenderness when he called her 'a good kind Pip . . . the best wife in the world'. Of other times – when he said he was a fallen angel, that evil was too strong and he would strangle their child – she recorded:

Then for the first time in my life I knew what it was to be alone with God.

Before going to London they stayed at Six Mile Bottom with Augusta. On the way he was passionately affectionate:

'You married me to make me happy, didn't you? Well, then, you do make me happy.'

That same evening he told her: 'Now I have *her*, you will find I can do without *you* . . .' At 13 Piccadilly Terrace he now tormented them both, and when he saw them uniting and protecting each other would send his wife upstairs – 'We don't want *you* my charmer!' Peter Quennell writes that 'in the humiliations to which he subjected the

1 Harriet Martineau: 'Lady Noël Byron': *Biographical Sketches* (New York: 1869), p. 285.

two women he committed the final and most excruciating assault against his own moral nature'.[1]

Annabella said she would like a painting of him looking at Medora, for his expression then was tender again and 'quite lovely'. He found occasion to tell her: 'You know that is my child' – and, to prove it, worked out the times when Captain Leigh had been away. While his wife was pregnant he had relations with a Drury Lane actress, Susan Boyce. During her labour she thought he threw soda-water bottles against the ceiling below. John Cam said the noise was Byron's usual way of opening bottles – smashing off their necks with a poker.

The baby was christened Augusta Ada. Early in the new year, leaving instructions for her own doctor to report on her husband's state of mind, mother and child set out for Kirkby Mallory, her parents' home, while Byron stayed behind with Augusta. When Dr Le Mann discovered 'nothing like settled lunacy' but only 'an irritability of temper', Byron in her eyes had no excuse. He now pleaded:

Dearest Pip – I wish you would make it up . . .[2]

In fear that the child might be taken from her, she revealed to her lawyers what was to be used only as a last resort: probably her suspicions of incest and, perhaps too, an act of anal intercourse committed during her last month of pregnancy.

Innuendoes had been whispered in the drawing-rooms ever since his publication of *The Giaour* and *The Bride of Abydos*.

> I grant *my* love imperfect, all
> That mortals by the name miscall;
> Then deem it evil, what thou wilt;
> But say, oh say, *hers* was not guilt![3]

On 8 April 1816, Lady Jersey courageously invited Byron and his half-sister to a ball. Mrs George Lamb cut Augusta. As soon as Byron appeared, titled and fashionable ladies left the room in droves. Men avoided his hand. The pale figure, with arms folded, leant against a mantelpiece facing them with disdain.

A week later, nineteen-year-old Claire Clairmont – Mary Shelley's stepsister – succeeded in achieving at last an assignation.[4] The

1 *Byron* (revised edn. 1974), p. 212.
2 26 Feb. 1816.
3 *The Giaour* (1813), ll. 1141–4.
4 See pp. 295–6.

following week, two days before Byron left England for good, he signed the deed of separation and missed by ten minutes the arrival of the Duchess of Devonshire's bailiffs concerning non-payment of rent.

II

Byron was to tell Rogers that Venice 'is a very good place for women', and next year in the Frezzaria he took lodgings in the house of a draper, where he fell in love with his wife, Marianna Segati. She was twenty-two, had large black eyes and hair 'of the curl and colour of Lady Jersey's'. He wrote to Moore that one night a girl of about nineteen came by appointment and told him 'she was married to the brother of my *amorosa*'. Marianna then burst in, and

after making a most polite curtsey to her sister-in-law and to me, without a single word seizes her said sister-in-law by the hair, and bestows upon her some sixteen slaps, which would have made your ear ache only to hear their echo.

After the visitor had rushed away, Byron restrained Marianna, who 'fairly went into fits in my arms'. An hour later, 'Signor Segati . . . finds me with his wife fainting upon the sofa'. There was no scene – 'how they settled it, I know not, but settle it they did'. That summer, after he had made an appropriate payment to the husband, Marianna joined him in a *villeggiatura* beside the Brenta.

I verily believe we are one of the happiest unlawful couples on this side of the Alps.

One evening he was riding with Hobhouse, who had come from Rome to join him, when they noticed among a group of peasants 'two girls as the prettiest we had seen for some time'. They met them again at their hut, and the younger girl took alarm at Hobhouse because she was unmarried, 'for here no woman will do anything under adultery'. Byron's partner, tall and thin, not his usual type, was Margarita Cogni (whom he called 'La Fornarina') – from the Venetian slums. She told him:

. . . all married women did it: but that her husband (a baker) was somewhat ferocious.

In his life at the *villeggiatura*, Marianna (his Antelope) remained for a time his 'regular *Amica*', but subsequently her position became subservient to that of Margarita (his 'gentle tigress'), who came and went as she pleased. In any altercation between the two women, Margarita would exclaim:

You are his *Donna*, and *I* am his *Donna*; *your* husband is a cuckold, and *mine* is another . . . If he prefers what is mine to what is yours, is it my fault? Do not think to speak to me without a reply because you happen to be richer than I am.[1]

When he leased the Palazzo Mocenigo on the Grand Canal, La Fornarina, having quitted her husband, took over the role of housekeeper, terrorizing servants Tita and Fletcher alike.

. . . the expenses were reduced not less than half, and everybody did their duty better.

One night a storm had delayed his return from the Lido, and he found her waiting on the steps – 'her great black eyes flashing through her tears, and the long dark hair, which was streaming, drenched with rain'.

I was told by the servants that she had only been prevented from coming in a boat to look after me, by the refusal of all the Gondoliers of the Canal to put out . . . and that then she sate down . . . in all the thickest of the Squall, and would neither be removed nor comforted. Her joy at seeing me again . . . gave me the idea of a tigress over her recovered Cubs.[2]

After a visit to the Palazzo Mocenigo, Shelley disapproved of Byron's association with 'women . . . the most contemptible . . . the most ignorant, the most disgusting . . .'[3] One feels that T. E. Lawrence, in spite of his composition, would have understood the attraction of such barbaric loyalty.

An instalment remained, set apart by its quality.

1 Letter to John Murray: 1 Aug. 1819.
2 *Ibid.*
3 Letter to Peacock: 22 Dec. 1818.

CHAPTER SIX
Cavaliere Servente

BYRON was thirty-one when he met the Countess Teresa in a Venetian salon. She was nineteen, with auburn curls, and had been married one year to Count Guiccioli, a wealthy eccentric of fifty-eight. Byron wrote to her:

. . . my only and last love . . . You sometimes tell me that I have been your *first* real love – and I assure you that you shall be my last Passion.[1]

It was to be his most successful love affair and, lasting four years, his longest.

She became ill at Ravenna and wanted him with her. Byron's carriages and retinue rumbled from the Palazzo Mocenigo. He wrote to Hobhouse:

I am . . . tired of promiscuous concubinage and now have the opportunity of settling for life.

She already called him 'mio Byron'. In the same letter, he explained she had called it out 'in an audible key' which 'horrified a correct company at the Benzona's'.[2]

On Byron's arrival her husband invited him to their palazzo. Byron recommended a physician from Venice and was her most attentive nurse. She responded 'most *gallantly* in every sense of the word' and he secured accomplices in her household for the renewal of their love. Instead of 'a stiletto in my gizzard some fine afternoon' which he half expected, her husband carried him 'out in his Coach and Six like Whittington and his Cat'.[3] Byron followed them to Bologna. He wrote to Hobhouse:

1 22 Apr. 1819.
2 6 Apr. 1819.
3 To John Murray: 29 June 1819.

. . . I can't say that I don't feel the degradation . . . I like women – God he knows – but the more the system here developes upon me – the worse it seems – after Turkey too – here the *polygamy* is all on the female side.[1]

The Count even left her in his sole charge. Byron then challenged Italian convention by taking her back to Venice to his palazzo, and then to his villa at La Mira on the Brenta. When the Count presently appeared and offered his wife an ultimatum – husband or lover – and she chose lover, Byron wrote that 'he actually came to *me*, crying about it . . .'[2] Byron restored the *status quo* by persuading her, 'with the greatest difficulty',[3] to return to Ravenna with her husband.

To restore Teresa's declining health it was her father, Count Gamba, who now sent for Byron, with the husband's permission, and this succeeding year was one of Byron's happiest and most productive when he went back to Ravenna as the accepted *cavaliere servente* in the Guiccioli household. Accompanied by Fletcher, his devoted servant; Lega Zambelli, the steward; Tita, the Venetian gondolier; and perhaps as many as eleven other servants, as well as his menagerie of ten horses, eight enormous dogs, three monkeys, five cats, an eagle, a crow and a falcon (Shelley was to meet also five peacocks, two guinea-hens and an Egyptian crane on the grand staircase), he took a floor of the Palazzo Guiccioli which for more than a year was to be his home.

The Gambas, father and son, now drew him into a secret revolutionary society – the *Carbonari*. He was watched by government spies and his post-bag examined, but he still managed to store a secret cache of bayonets, muskets and cartridges. Perhaps this incensed his land-lord, Count Guiccioli, to demand of his wife once again to choose. Teresa complained:

It is hard that I should be the only woman in Romagna who is not to have her *amico* . . .

This time it went to the Pope, and man and wife were formally separated with the proviso that Teresa was to live in her father's villa. Byron stayed put at Guiccioli's palazzo, and at eight every evening he visited Teresa with her father's permission. He said he made love by the stroke of the clock. The fear of a would-be assassin never materialized.

1 3 Oct. 1819.
2 To Hobhouse: 20 Nov. 1819.
3 To Douglas Kinnaird: 16 Nov. 1819.

In a wave of Papal repression the Gambas and Teresa moved to Florence, but Byron stayed on another three months. At this time Shelley visited him and found him 'greatly improved' from the Venice days 'in genius, in temper, in moral views, in health, in happiness' – all of which he ascribed to the influence of the Countess Guiccioli. Byron was becoming 'a virtuous man'.[1] On Shelley's suggestion Byron brought the Gambas and Teresa to Pisa. Shelley found a house for the Gambas and the Palazzo Lanfranchi for Byron. The Florentine police reported:

Byron goes to Pisa solely for the beautiful daughter of Count Gamba.

A few months afterwards, Byron and Pietro Gamba (the son), Shelley, Medwin, Trelawny and others, described by the police as 'his company of assassins', were riding towards the city, Teresa in her carriage, when there was an affray with a Sergeant-Major Masi who was in a hurry to get past. It led to one of the Gambas' servants stabbing Masi outside the Palazzo Lanfranchi, for which the footman and innocent Tita were arrested.

On the authorities advising the Gambas to leave, Byron took a villa at Montenero, near Leghorn, for them and the Countess. Leigh Hunt arrived from England just after another heated exchange, started this time between Byron's coachman and the Gambas' cook, resulting in knives drawn and Pietro Gamba wounded by one of his own servants. Hunt recorded that the would-be assassin was still outside when Byron and his friends went to take their customary ride in the evening, and that Teresa had urged 'Bairon' to hold back. Next day Shelley settled the Hunts on the ground floor of the Palazzo Lanfranchi, where Byron and Teresa presently retired for peace and quiet, the Gambas having been expelled.

After Shelley's death, they moved to the Casa Saluzzo in the village of Albaro overlooking Genoa, where the Gambas had fled, and the Hunts with Mary Shelley shared the neighbouring Casa Negroto. Medwin records that Lord Byron was certainly very much attracted to Teresa, 'without being actually in love'. As they sat under the orange tree, Byron called her 'Piccinina'. But he was now restive in domesticity.

A spy for the Austrians wrote:

1 Letter to Mary Shelley: 8 Aug. 1821. Quoted by Edward Dowden: *The Life of Percy Bysshe Shelley* (1886), ii, p. 421.

Mylord has at length decided to leave for Genoa. It is said that he is already tired of his new favourite, the Guiccioli. He has expressed his intent . . . of going on to Athens to purchase adoration from the Greeks.

One day Byron asked Teresa to sit for a miniature. She sensed he was thinking of mementoes and parting, and her eyes filled with tears. Byron spoke to Lady Blessington tenderly of Teresa and the sacrifices she had made:

. . . she must know that I am sincerely attached to her; but the truth is, my habits are not those requisite to form the happiness of any woman: I am worn out in feelings . . .[1]

He was preparing actively for Greece. When her brother, Pietro (who was accompanying him), broke the news, Teresa wrote: '. . . a death sentence would have seemed less terrible'. She said she would follow. Byron wrote to Douglas Kinnaird:

Of course the idea is ridiculous . . . if she makes a scene . . . we shall have another romance – and tale of ill usage and abandonment – and Lady Caroling – and Lady Byroning . . . there never was a man who gave up so much to women – and all I have gained by it has been the character of treating them harshly . . . If I left a woman for another woman – she might have cause to complain – but really – when a man merely wishes to go on a great duty for a good cause – this selfishness on the part of the 'feminie' is rather too much.[2]

On the day before he sailed, she was with him between 3.0 and 5.0 p.m. Next day she sat on the terrace beside Mary Shelley, with *The Hercules* far below and Byron aboard. Pale and faltering, she had to be led to her father's coach to go back home to Ravenna, for Count Gamba's passport had been returned to him. They had to stop midday, she was so unwell. She wrote a letter which was never sent:

I have promised more than I can perform, and you have asked of me what is beyond my strength . . . I feel as if I were dying, Byron have pity on me . . .

She was not yet twenty-four.

1 Marguerite Gardiner, Countess of Blessington: *A Journal of Conversations with Lord Byron* (1834), p. 70.
2 21 May 1823.

CHAPTER SEVEN
Tangled Web

I

Virginia Woolf told Vanessa that KATHERINE MANSFIELD seemed to have 'gone every sort of hog since she was 17'.[1] Like Byron and Maugham, she was bisexual. She was nineteen, back in her home town of Wellington after Queen's College, Harley Street, when she recorded in her *Journal* what seems to be her first sexual experience with a man. It has been suggested that her marriage at twenty was 'perhaps a desperate attempt by Katherine, racked by guilt since her affairs in Wellington, to prove herself a normal woman – a man's woman'.[2]

Her loves were as numerous as '*All* those houses, *all* those flats, *all* those rooms'[3] which she and Murry were to take and withdraw from. Yet two years before she died, she acknowledged:

I've *acted* my sins, and then excused them or put them away with . . . 'it was all experience'. But it hasn't *all* been experience. There *is* waste – destruction, too.[4]

On the strength of her vignettes in the Melbourne *Native Companion*, she came back to England to write when she was still nineteen. During the voyage she went ashore with a passenger at Montevideo and later thought she had been drugged and made pregnant – which proved a false alarm. Within a month of arriving at Beauchamp Lodge, a hostel for music students, in Little Venice, she became secretly engaged to her compatriot, nineteen-year-old Garnet Trowell – after writing love-letters for six years to his twin brother, Tom. On his family banishing

---

1 Letter to Vanessa Bell: 21 June 1917.
2 Antony Alpers: *The Life of Katherine Mansfield* (1980), p. 91.
3 ? Jan 1917. *Katherine Mansfield's Letters to John Middleton Murry 1913–1922* ed. J. M. Murry (1951), p. 91.
4 31 Oct. 1920. *Ibid.*, p. 579.

her from their home when she said she and Garnet were already lovers, she disappeared from the hostel and, after only two or three weeks' acquaintance, married George Bowden, teacher of singing and elocution, who was thirty-one. Claire Tomalin ascribes the hurry to the fact 'she was pregnant with Garnet's baby'.[1] She left Bowden on their wedding-night, and after a week joined Garnet, who was playing in the orchestra of a touring opera company; she became a member of the chorus. Whether she told him of her marriage or whether he heard independently is not clear. After a month, in a flat in Maida Vale, she wrote to him in vain.

Her mother, now travelling to England, took her to a pension in Wörishofen, and after a fortnight returned to Wellington, where she cut her from her will. Katherine suffered a miscarriage when she lifted up high a heavy case. At this time she had the fateful love affair with Sobieniowski, which left her 'with a hideous new sexual problem'.[2] She went back to her husband to 'try and make it work', and even collaborated with him in a concert, successfully acting some of her sketches. She showed him her German stories and he recommended, very wisely, that she pass them to A. R. Orage, editor of a political weekly, *The New Age*.

After a serious operation she refused his assistance further, and accepted an offer of a flat for the winter at 131 Cheyne Walk by a painter friend of her editor. Here she had love affairs with a young schoolteacher, William Orton, and an attractive young City worker, Francis Heinemann. When the painter returned, she found a flat at 69 Clovelly Mansions. Other affairs followed with J. M. Kennedy, a fellow contributor on *The New Age*, Geza Silberer, a thirty-four-year-old Viennese journalist, and another 'Man' of whom she wrote in her *Journal*:

We made love . . . like two wild beasts.[3]

He was perhaps Walter Rippman, her ex-German teacher from Queen's College. There was another false 'pregnancy'. Orage and Beatrice Hastings visited her and disapproved of her promiscuity

1 *Katherine Mansfield: A Secret Life* (1987), p. 64.
2 *Ibid.*, p. 75.
3 6 Sept. 1911. *Journal of Katherine Mansfield* ed. J. Middleton Murry (1954), p. 46.

(perhaps the affair with Kennedy). She replied: 'What does it matter? I don't love him.'[1]

II

Katherine was twenty-two when she met JOHN MIDDLETON MURRY, supposed to be still at Oxford and who was editor of the stylish *Rhythm*. A month later, Murry, looking for another room, was invited to be her lodger. She became Assistant Editor, giving up *The New Age*. Gilbert Cannan called them The Tigers because of a woodcut in the first number. Murry abbreviated it later to Tig for Katherine, and then Wig. After another month, according to Katherine, 'we got into this bed and we laughed and we laughed and we laughed . . . and since that time we have always slept together'.[2] She said later that their relationship had been 'child love'.

Next year saw the folding of *Rhythm* and of its successor, *The Blue Review*. She and Murry went to Paris, but they returned when he was offered the post of art critic to *The Westminster Gazette*. Soon after the new year he was declared bankrupt. Their means were so straightened that they rented two rooms at 102 Edith Grove, Chelsea, where they had a mattress on the floor. Both went down with 'pleurisy' almost immediately. In Katherine's case her TB may already have set in. The Lawrences, who had met them in the office of *Rhythm*, visited them, and in July the Murrys attended their wedding. Frieda gave to Katherine her former wedding-ring, which she put on and never removed. During World War I, Murry, like Lawrence, Aldous Huxley and Leonard Woolf, was rejected, in his case through eyesight.

But Katherine wanted a lover who would '[nurse?] me, love me, hold me, comfort me'[3] – and told Murry she was leaving him. She turned to Francis Carco, whom she had met in Paris. She went to the war zone, where he found her a room.

The act of love seemed somehow quite incidental . . ..[4]

1 Antony Alpers: *The Life of Katherine Mansfield* (1980), p. 134.
2 H. S. Ede: *Savage Messiah* (1931), p. 140. Quoted by Alpers, *ibid.*, p. 141.
3 *Journal of Katherine Mansfield* ed. J. Middleton Murry (1954), p. 61. 30 Aug. 1914.
4 *Ibid.*, p. 78. 20 Feb. 1915.

While she was away, Murry went down with flu and was nursed by Lawrence, who repressed his physical feelings towards him.[1] Katherine now went to Carco's vacant flat on the Quai aux Fleurs, where she wrote *The Aloe* (from which *Prelude* emerged two years later). Murry wrote to her:

. . . you'll stick to me; not so much because you love me, which you do, but because you know that you are more the real you, the good you, with me.[2]

On her next return to Paris, she departed hurriedly when she heard the concierge referring to her as 'la maîtresse de Francis Carco'. She persuaded Murry to winter at Bandol in the South of France. It was then *his* turn to leave her.

In April 1916, the Murrys lived in a group of cottages the Lawrences had found at Higher Tregerthen near Zennor, in Cornwall. They had already lived briefly with them in The Triangle, Chesham, at the beginning of the war, and then only three miles away at Rose Tree Cottage, but the association was pierced by violent quarrels between Frieda and Lawrence as his TB progressed. Katherine wrote to Beatrice Hastings that the Lawrences 'are both too rough for me to enjoy playing with'.[3] After only two months the Murrys moved thirty miles away to Mylor, and then Katherine invited herself to Garsington. Later that year they moved into The Ark – J. M. Keynes's house, 3 Gower Street – sharing it with Dorothy Brett and Dora Carrington. Murry wrote to Lady Ottoline:

. . . I begin to suspect I am in love with you.[4]

At this same time Katherine had a relationship with Bertrand Russell, who has commented:

My feelings for her were ambivalent: I adored her passionately, but was repelled by her dark hatreds.[5]

The Murrys were playing what Claire Tomalin calls 'an elaborate game of hide-and-seek'[6] which would leave Katherine more dependent on Murry as well as on Ida Baker, her schoolfriend.

1 See D. H. Lawrence: *Aaron's Rod* (1922), pp. 101–2.
2 25 Mar. 1915.
3 4 May 1916.
4 22 Sept. 1916.
5 Note he attached to her letters, in 1949.
6 *Katherine Mansfield: A Secret Life* (1987), p. 154.

At the end of that year,[1] her doctor diagnosed consumption and advised her to winter in the South of France. Within two months of her arrival, she experienced her first haemorrhage. Ida joined her at Bandol. On Katherine deciding to come home in the early spring, they were stranded for three weeks in Paris under shellfire. When the authorities permitted their return to England, Murry, instead of embracing her, held a handkerchief to his mouth for fear of infection.

Nevertheless, next month, four days after her divorce, he married her at Kensington Register Office. In late summer they moved for the first time into their own house – The Elephant, 2 Portland Villas, East Heath Road, overlooking the Vale of Health, Hampstead. Specialists who were consulted strongly recommended a sanatorium, but Dr Sorapure, who now became her doctor, understood that it was her writing which gave her the will to live. He was also the first to diagnose her arthritis as of gonococcal origin. She went with Ida to San Remo. There, after a visit from her father and in deep depression, she sent some bitter verses to Murry, who earlier that year had been appointed editor of *The Athenaeum*.

> Someone came to me and said
> Forget, forget that you've been wed.
> Who's your man to leave you be
> Ill and cold in a far country?
> Who's the husband – who's the stone
> Could leave a child like you alone? . . .[2]

A 'shattered' Murry came over, and they agreed they must never part again; but then, accompanied by Ida, Katherine went to a private nursing home in Menton.

Lawrence now ended a relationship she valued.

I loved him . . . Oh, there is something so lovable in him & . . . his passionate eagerness for life – that is what one loves so.[3]

It has been suggested[4] that, wounded because his affectionate letters did not always receive a reply and that she had begun to write to

1 1917.
2 *The New Husband*: i. 4 Dec. 1919. *Katherine Mansfield's Letters to John Middleton Murry 1913–1922* ed. J. M. Murry (1951), p. 427.
3 To Dorothy Brett: 27 Oct. 1918.
4 Claire Tomalin: *Katherine Mansfield: A Secret Life* (1987), pp. 187–8.

Frieda, or perhaps because Murry was rejecting his articles and she seemed to be implicated, he turned on her in phthisical rage.

I loathe you. You revolt me stewing in your consumption . . . You are a loathsome reptile – I hope you will die.[1]

Murry, at her urging, swore to hit him if they should meet. She came back to Hampstead. They entertained the Eliots to dinner. But Murry seemed unable to help her in her suffering. His affections seemed to lie with Dorothy Brett.

The following month she and Ida returned to Menton. Sobieniowski approached Murry with the suggestion that a packet of her letters might be worth £40. She wrote to her husband:

It is imbecile and odious that you should be so troubled.[2]

Ida paid, and Katherine on their receipt destroyed them. She told Murry:

I have of you what I want – a relationship which is unique but it is not what the world understands by marriage . . . I am a writer first.[3]

Murry now wound up the declining *Athenaeum* and joined her. She wrote to Ida, who had gone to pack up in Portland Villas:

Elizabeth Bibesco has shown signs of life again . . . He'll never break off these affairs . . . I wish he'd take one *on* really seriously – and leave me.[4]

In the spring he had to leave her again to give a series of lectures at Oxford. Then in June the Murrys moved into the Chalet des Sapins, Montana-sur-Sierre, not far from her cousin Elizabeth[5] at Randogne. Murry wrote articles for *The Nation* and the *TLS* – he wrote a review of *Women in Love* – while Katherine enjoyed her most fruitful period, completing *At the Bay* and *The Garden Party*, which enabled her to pay her doctor's bills. In a letter to her father, she acknowledged that his allowance of £300 a year was 'an extreme concession', and that her husband 'was the one who ought to provide for me'.[6] Even when Murry had been promoted to Chief Censor in the last year of the war,

1 Received 7 Feb. 1920.
2 16 Sept. 1920. *Letters, cit.*, p. 536.
3 12 Dec. 1920. *Ibid.*, p. 621.
4 Ida Baker: *Katherine Mansfield: The Memories of LM* (1971), p. 162.
5 'Elizabeth' (née Mary Beauchamp) had eloped with von Arnim, had become Wells's mistress, and had recently divorced Bertrand Russell's elder brother, the 2nd Earl.
6 1 Nov. 1921.

husband and wife kept their money affairs 'entirely separate', and when he was *The Athenaeum* editor it was the same.

He doesn't give me a penny and he never has.[1]

In Switzerland she had need to ask cousin Elizabeth for a loan.

Against the advice of Murry, and accompanied by Ida, she left the chalet in the new year for Paris – lured by Dr Manoukhin claiming a new (and expensive) cure for TB. After a week or so Murry joined her and Ida was sent away. In their hotel she wrote *The Fly* and, in response to an article that Murry had written on *Ulysses*, Joyce visited them. After five months they returned to Randogne-sur-Sierre, but within days she was writing secretly to Ida:

I am almost as ill as ever I was, in every way. I want you if you can come . . . We should have to deceive Jack . . . He helps me all he can but he can't help me really . . . It would have to come entirely from you.[2]

Murry later speaks of their agreement on a temporary separation at this time, he staying at Randogne and she (with Ida) moving to Sierre.

After five weeks Katherine drew up a will. There was to be a book for Lawrence (which he never received). On the same day in Wellington, Lawrence sent a one-word postcard: 'Ricordi.' She also deposited at her bank a farewell letter to 'Dearest Bogey':

All my manuscripts I leave entirely to you to do what you like with . . . In fact, my dearest dear, I leave everything to you – to the secret you whose lips I kissed this morning. In spite of everything – how happy we have been! I feel no other lovers have walked the earth more joyfully – in spite of all.[3]

Accompanied by Murry and Ida, she now travelled to Dorothy Brett's house, 6 Pond Street, Hampstead, and Murry for a few days had a room next door. During her stay she saw many people, including Dr Sorapure, her father twice and her sisters, Edward Garnett, Wyndham Lewis. In five more weeks she left London, with Ida. She had more treatments by Manoukhin in Paris, but they left her only able to

---

1 To Murry's brother, Richard: Jan. 1921. Cf. her letter to Murry of 21 May 1918: 'No, my precious. Don't send me the money now. I'll ask when I want it . . . It's just *like you* to give like this.' (*Katherine Mansfield's Letters to John Middleton Murry 1913–1922* ed. J. M. Murry [1951], p. 255.)
2 *c.* 8 June 1922. Ida Baker: *Katherine Mansfield: The Memories of LM* (1971), pp. 200–1.
3 7 Aug. 1922. *Katherine Mansfield: Selected Letters* ed. Vincent O'Sullivan (1989), p. 267.

creep. She faced the fact: 'Nearly all my improved health is pretence
– acting.'[1]

III

Reminiscent of Aldous Huxley and his penchant for alternative
medicine, she had heard of George Gurdjieff and his Institute for the
Harmonious Development of Man. Like Stevenson, she wanted 'the
power to live a full, adult, living, breathing life in close contact with
what I love – the earth . . . the sea – the sun.'[2] She left Ida in Paris
and went to Le Prieuré des Basses Loges, at Avon, on the edge of the
Forest of Fontainebleau. It was her last journey.

Alpers suggests that in this community of sixty people she returned
to the family life she had known as a child and, leaving the teachings
aside, he contradicts the charge that the kindly, practical Gurdjieff
was avaricious and a fraud:

If Gurdjieff had considered his own interest he would hardly have taken the
risk of a bad press – which he got – by having a famous writer die of
tuberculosis at the Institute within the first year of its existence.[3]

Although conditions were Spartan, she didn't spend a single day in
bed. The 'beautiful, wonderful creature' described by Edna Smith[4] –
'exquisite' was the word Frieda had used – now peeled vegetables in
the kitchen, watched the dancing in the living-room, and sat in her
gallery above the cowshed. She was the lady in a fur coat, for she
wore it all the time because of intense cold. Orage, who had been so
important to her, was also there, having quitted *The New Age*. She saw
him every day. 'The tangled web'[5] of her life, which she said was
'worn to tearing point'[6] before she was twenty-two, seems to have
begun a process of unravelling. According to Orage, she had a kind of
mystic experience – 'as if she had been on Sinai'.[7]

1 *Journal of Katherine Mansfield* ed. J. Middleton Murry (1927), p. 248. 10 Oct. 1922.
2 *Ibid*, p. 250. 10 Oct. 1922.
3 *The Life of Katherine Mansfield* (1980), p. 378.
4 Letter to friend, 1928.
5 To Margaret Wishart: Autumn 1909. Alpers: *op. cit.*, p. 101.
6 *Journal of Katherine Mansfield* ed. J. Middleton Murry (1954), p. 46.: 6 Sept. 1911.
7 'Talks with Katherine Mansfield': *The Century Magazine*, Nov. 1924. Quoted by Alpers:
op. cit., pp. 380–1.

When Murry came in the new year, it pleased her that he took a brush in the study-house and worked with the others at the painting of the glass. The same evening, going ahead of him slowly upstairs, she had a sudden fit of coughing. Inside her room blood poured from her mouth. He got her on the couch conscious, and rushed for help. Two doctors came almost immediately, but in a few minutes she died – aged thirty-four. Murry was loyal to her memory, just as in life she to her family had been loyal about him.

CHAPTER EIGHT
A Manly Part

I

It seems incredible how BURNS, like Byron, could have been so busy in 'the drama' of his loves and so prolific in his poetry.

His first poem, written at fourteen, was 'Handsome Nell', and is said to have been addressed to Nelly Kilpatrick, 'a bewitching creature' of thirteen, who sang as she worked beside him – 'You know our country custom of coupling a man and a woman together as Partners in the labors of Harvest'.

. . . the tones of her voice made my heartstrings thrill like an Eolian harp; and . . . my pulse beat such a furious ratann when I looked and fingered over her hand, to pick out the nettle-stings and thistles.[1]

Two years later, he went to a country dancing school 'in absolute defiance' of his father's commands. At seventeen, he was learning 'Mensuration, Surveying . . . &c.' in Kirkoswald when he fell in love with 'a charming Fillette' who 'overset my Trigonomertry, and set me off in a tangent'. The family now moved from the poor soil of Mount Oliphant to a more oppressive landlord at Lochlea.

I saw my father's situation entailed on me perpetual labour . . . My heart was compleatly tinder, and was eternally lighted up by some Goddess or other . . . I spent the evening in the way after my heart.[2]

At twenty-one, he fell more deeply in love with 'my dearest E', perhaps Ellison (or Alison) Begbie, a servant girl on a neighbouring farm. He wrote three poems to her and proposed marriage but she refused him. Soon afterwards he suffered a near nervous breakdown.

At twenty-two, he went to Irvine to enter an abortive flax-dressing

1 Autobiographical letter to Dr John Moore: 2 Aug. 1787.
2 *Ibid.*

business, and while he was there formed 'a bosom-friendship' with Richard Brown, a young sailor, that 'did me a mischief'.

He was the only man I ever saw who was a greater fool than myself when *woman* was the presiding star; but he spoke of a certain fashionable failing with levity which hitherto I had regarded with horror.[1]

According to his brother, all Robert's 'connexions' until this time 'were governed by the strictest rules of virtue and modesty'.[2]

II

When Burns was twenty-six, a servant girl, Betty (or Lizzie) Paton, at Mossgiel farm, where the family had moved now the father was dead, bore him his first child. The lovers received a public rebuke before the Kirk Session and Burns paid the fine of a guinea. The same year, he made pregnant twenty-year-old Jean Armour – 'the jewel for me' of the 'six proper young belles' of Mauchline. Before she gave birth he acknowledged her in writing as his wife, since mutual consent, followed by consummation, constituted in Scots law a legal marriage.

I would gladly have covered my Inamorata from the darts of Calumny with the conjugal Shield . . .[3]

But her father, one of the Auld Lichts that we meet again in those memories of Barrie's mother, forced her to return the document and renege on her word.

What she thinks of her conduct now, I don't know; one thing I know, she has made me compleatly miserable. – Never man lov'd, or rather ador'd, a woman more than I did her . . . My poor, dear, unfortunate Jean! how happy I have been in her arms! . . .[4]

She named him to the Kirk Session. He now sought to clarify his position and, since she would not have him for her husband, he did penance on three Sundays to receive a certificate that he was a bachelor.

Meanwhile he was preparing an edition of his poems – his 'last

1 *Ibid.*
2 'Gilbert's Narrative': letter of Gilbert Burns to Mrs Dunlop.
3 Note for Robert Riddell, added to copy of letter (Apr. 1789) to John Arnot.
4 To David Brice, 12 June 1786.

foolish action' – to raise his passage money to Jamaica, where he had
been offered a post as plantation manager. One speculates on 'what
might have been' had he gone – the poet who wrote:

> Man's inhumanity to man
> Makes countless thousands mourn.

Or:

> . . . A Man's a Man for a' that:
> For a' that, an' a' that . . .

He got as far as assigning his interest in Mossgiel, together with the
profits and copyright of the poems, to his brother for the support of
his daughter by Betty Paton. He wrote from hiding:

Armour has got a warrant to throw me in jail till I find security for an
enormous sum . . . I have run into all kinds of dissipation . . . and other
mischief, to drive her out of my head . . .[1]

The wounded lover had turned to Mary Campbell. On the banks of
the Ayr they exchanged bibles as a mark of betrothment. She agreed
to accompany him to Jamaica.

> The golden hours, on angel wings,
> Flew o'er me and my dearie;
> For dear to me, as light and life,
> Was my sweet Highland Mary . . .
>
> But O, fell Death's untimely frost,
> That nipt my flower sae early!
> Now green's the sod and cauld's the clay,
> That wraps my Highland Mary!

There may have been a flirtation with Betty Miller ('Eliza'), one of the
'belles of Mauchline'.

The Kilmarnock edition won him the friendship of Mrs Dunlop,
who was descended from an uncle of Wallace. She became his
confidante, a motherly figure, like Lady Melbourne for Byron. More
immediately, his sudden fame led to 'some of the first Gentlemen in
the county' offering to befriend him against Armour's injunction.
Instead of emigration, he set out for Edinburgh to negotiate a second
edition.

1 To John Richmond, 30 July 1786.

At Edinr I was in a new world: I mingled among many classes of men, but all of them new to me . . .[1]

The fifteen-year-old Scott saw him at Professor Fergusson's and afterwards remembered his 'perfect self-confidence, without the slightest presumption' among 'the most learned of their time'.[2] But if his poems caused ladies to open doors that previously would have been closed, his charisma inspired rapture. The Duchess of Gordon said he was the only man who 'carried her off her feet'.

During the following unsettled year of journeys that took him over much of Scotland, he linked his arm with Isabella Lindsay on a walking tour and presented her with his picture.

Sweet Isabella Lindsay, may Peace dwell in thy bosom, uninterrupted except by the tumultuous throbbings of rapturous Love!

His relations with Margaret Chalmers got as far as an offer of marriage, but, as she confided to Thomas Campbell, she was already engaged.

The name I register in my heart's core is Peggy Chalmers.[3]

Back in Edinburgh, he conducted a correspondence with Agnes Craig M'Lehose ('my dearest Nancy'), a young grass widow with three small children. She begged him to be satisfied with the 'warmest, tenderest friendship'. He declared he 'loves to madness and feels to torture'. They signed themselves by Arcadian names: Clarinda and Sylvander. He had a lock of her hair put in his ring and vowed he 'will love her to death', which she understood to be a promise that he would wait for her until her husband died. He still found time to write verses to Janet, his 'rosebud', the twelve-year-old daughter of William Cruickshank, at whose house he was staying.

Meanwhile Meg Cameron swore out a writ against him for support of her child, and he wrote that Jean Armour was to be 'in for it again'. The following year, at twenty-nine, to the charge of 'perfidious treachery' from Mrs M'Lehose, he went through a formal ceremony of marriage with 'my Jean', the mother of his second set of twins.[4]

1 Autobiographical letter to Dr John Moore: 2 Aug. 1787.
2 J. G. Lockhart: *Memoirs of the Life of Sir Walter Scott, Bart.* (1837–8), i, p. 138.
3 Letter to Mrs M'Lehose: 10 Jan. 1788.
4 The second set died one week, and three weeks, after birth.

They accepted a rebuke before the Kirk Session and Burns gave another customary guinea to the poor. He wrote to Peggy Chalmers:

. . . I had a long and much-loved fellow-creature's happiness or misery in my determination, and I durst not trifle with so important a deposit.[1]

Two months later, a servant girl, Jenny Clow, bore him a son.

III

They may have 'much caressed' him in Edinburgh but 'the efforts made for his relief were extremely trifling'.[2] Burns rented Ellisland farm, Dumfriesshire, where he installed his wife at the end of the year. Lockhart reported the poet as saying that the first winter he spent at Ellisland was the happiest period of his life – 'for the first time under a roof of his own, with his wife and children about him'.[3] His wife now superintended the farm as he had obtained subsidiary employment as an exciseman. Within two years they made their final move to Dumfries, with the Excise as their sole and improved means of support. They even kept a servant, but 'a life of literary leisure with a decent competence' would never be his.

He had a love affair with Anne Park when his wife returned home to Mauchline on a visit. Another illegitimate child was born. She was christened Elizabeth like his other two daughters, and Mrs Burns brought her up with her other children, including the two sons, Francis Wallace and William Nicol (James Glencairn and Maxwell were still to come). Anne, a blonde barmaid, was the last of his mistresses to bear a name. Betty, Meg, Jenny, Anne . . . W. R. Bett wrote:

Those who followed her have remained intriguingly innominate: a shadowy, mysterious, sorry train of girls who knowingly played with fire because their hearts could not say no.[4]

He made acquaintance with the Riddels. Maria was under twenty and a beauty who attempted verse. Burns sent her some smuggled

1 16 Sept. 1788.
2 J. G. Lockhart: *Memoirs of the Life of Sir Walter Scott, Bart.* (1837–8), i, p. 138.
3 *Life of Robert Burns* (1828), p. 255.
4 *The Infirmities of Genius* (1952), p. 146.

French gloves obtained in his capacity as exciseman. Their house had a fine library, but her husband encouraged excessive drinking. When Burns was nearly thirty-five, he behaved uncharacteristically to Mrs Riddel and they broke with him. It is said that the gentlemen had planned a frolic to enact the Rape of the Sabines. Burns carried out his part (taking up Maria?) and 'was stupefied to find himself alone'. He wrote, allowing for Dr Currie's doctored text:

Your husband, who insisted on my drinking more than I chose, has no right to blame me . . . But to you, Madam, I have much to apologize . . . to be rude to a woman, when in my senses, was impossible with me.[1]

During the next two years he composed several songs to Chloris – Mrs Whelpdale, who was married and deserted at seventeen.

In the penultimate year of his life the death of a daughter, Elizabeth Riddel, nearly two, greatly distressed him. In his last month, on hearing he was at Brow, where she also had gone as a convalescent for sea-bathing, Maria Riddel invited him to dine with her and sent her carriage. As he entered the room, 'pale, emaciated, & . . . feeble', he asked: 'Well, madam, have you any commands for the other world?' A week before he died, he wrote to Mrs Dunlop:

Your friendship with which for many years you honored me was a friendship dearest to my soul . . .

He told Jean not to be afraid:

I'll be more respected a hundred years after I am dead than I am at present.

As with Poe, the memory of him suffered at the hands of his earliest biographers. Leslie Stephen reminded us that Burns was 'never heartless':

. . . he did his best to support his children . . . was a good father and brother . . . in spite of overwhelming difficulties and many weaknesses . . . he struggled hard to 'act a manly part' through life.[2]

1 Dec. 1793.
2 DNB.

CHAPTER NINE

A Cell of Good Living

W hat Cockerell understated as ERIC GILL's 'tendency to be preoccupied with sex'[1] made his life and work of a piece. Gill saw 'the influence of erotic appetite' even in successful lettering;[2] he became a sculptor when his wife was pregnant with their third child:

. . . as I couldn't have all I wanted in one way I determined to see what I could do about it in another – I fashioned a woman of *stone*.[3]

A middle-aged man, desiring his young model, he composed an aesthetic:

And the draughtsman also is a lover . . . He must love not only the thing seen but the thing made also.[4]

Accordingly he drew her successfully by fulfilling his desire. The Catholic convert, confronted by his Church's timidity on sex, preached the 'erotic mysticism' which ('heaven forbid') he denied: he spoke of a picture, '"nudes, no less"', as 'a kind of ikon – a holy image';[5] he proclaimed 'good at the root of all our desiring', and posed whether 'those organs . . . the very root of scandal' were not 'redeemed and made dear'.[6]

He was a seventeen-year-old art student at Chichester when he fell in love with Ethel Moore ('Ettie') – four years older – called Mary after the Gills were received into the Roman Catholic Church. She was the daughter of the Cathedral sacristan, and they married when he was twenty-one. At Hammersmith two years later, when she was

1 To Katharine Adams, 1941. Quoted by Fiona MacCarthy: *Eric Gill* (1989), p. 78.
2 'Lettering, masonry – these are not trades for eunuchs . . .' (*Autobiography* [1940], p. 122).
3 *Ibid.*, p. 158.
4 *Drawings from Life* (1940): Introduction, p. v.
5 *Ibid.*, p. x.
6 *Autobiography* (1940), pp. 224–5.

carrying their second child, he asked their servant, Lizzie, to lie with him: which, he recorded in his diary, happened several times. The following year he went to Chartres for Easter with 'a young Fabian woman', Lillian Meacham – sending a postcard to Ettie: reminiscent of Shelley's letter to Harriet when he eloped with Mary Godwin.

At Ditchling, Gill and his wife, Hilary Pepler, Desmond Chute, and some of the other craftsmen working in community, became Tertiaries of the Third Order of St Dominic. Gill wore the habit, and a cord of chastity. At the same time, the man Sir John Rothenstein described as 'one of those exceptional beings who try to live their lives in accordance with their intellectual convictions'[1] records in his diary incestuous relations not only with his pubescent daughters but his sisters; these relations with his married sister, Gladys, continued throughout his life. His biographer expresses the paradox that his children knew a happy childhood and became 'well-adjusted married women', themselves with large families. She relates the incest to his 'notion of owning all the females in his household'.[2] His sexual feelings towards his daughters perhaps explain the rift with his intimate friend, Hilary Pepler, whose son had fallen in love with Gill's eldest child. His own reason for moving was publicity:

. . . our Dominican friends . . . made us a show place. What we had thought of as a rather secret enterprise, and essentially a company of craftsmen living by their work . . . our clerical friends thought of as a public spectacle of Christian family life.[3]

Perhaps Gill was sensitive of the discrepancies.

At Capel-y-ffin, in 'a hidden valley of the Black Mountains', three sets of parents and seven children, as well as cats, dogs, goats, ducks, geese, and two magpies, joined a family already installed in a 'semi-ruinous' monastery. Here Gill began the pattern of including in his household a resident priest, and a resident mistress – Elizabeth Bill. She, too, became a Tertiary of the Order. He was forty-two. It was the time of his collaboration with Robert Gibbings at the Golden Cockerel Press. There were now his entanglements with Moira, Robert's wife, and also with Beatrice Warde, the sophisticated friend of Stanley Morrison. In the final move to Pigotts, Mary Reeves, the

1 Eric Gill: *First Nudes: With an Introduction by Sir John Rothenstein* (1954).
2 Fiona MacCarthy: *Eric Gill* (1989), p. 156.
3 *Autobiography* (1940), p. 210.

schoolmistress, succeeded Elizabeth Bill. This period also saw his most passionate love affair with Daisy Hawkins, the housekeeper's daughter, whom his wife – exercising her authority for the first time – eventually dispatched to Capel-y-ffin.

Mary (like Wells's Jane) remained constant. She, and the girls as they grew older, knitted and wove and made cheese; that was what Gill wanted them to do:

Marvellous girls – how hard and loyally they worked with their mother . . . the baking and brewing and milking and butter-making . . . cooking and cleaning . . .[1]

Mary (like Emily Brontë) baked good bread. But she was no cypher. His surviving daughter remembered at least one heated discussion behind closed doors. With hindsight, she thought at times 'things must have got pretty anarchic' and her mother must have known pain which she concealed. When Mary was about fifty, she wrote:

I am simply bubbling all over with pride at the thought of being your wife.[2]

At the end of his Requiem Mass, she went to the head of the body exposed in the coffin and with her finger transmitted a kiss.

As *outré* as Joyce, with a life-style overriding even more taboos, Gill, like him, remained 'deeply in love with the mother of my children', and held dear 'family', 'home', and 'parental love'. At the end of his life he wrote:

. . . the work which I have chiefly tried to do . . . is this: to make a cell of good living in the chaos of our world.

Above all things, he hoped he 'had done something towards reintegrating bed and board, the small farm and the workshop, the home and the school, earth and heaven'.[3] To fail with such stakes could not have been altogether inglorious.

1 *Ibid.*, p. 218.
2 21 Feb. 1928. Fiona MacCarthy: *Eric Gill* (1989), p. 208.
3 *Autobiography* (1940), p. 282.

CHAPTER TEN

Sexless Love

I

S WIFT wrote in his letter to Dr Tisdall:[1]
. . . time takes off from the lustre of virgins in all other eyes but
mine.[2]

Because her letters have survived, more is known of Swift's relations
with Esther Vanhomrigh ('Vanessa') than with Esther Johnson
('Stella') – 'whose name', in Macaulay's phrase, 'is inseparably associated with his in a sad and mysterious way'.

On Sunday, 28 January 1728, at about eight o'clock at night, a
servant brought to the Deanery a note telling him of Stella's death.
Swift recorded:

She expired about six in the evening of this day, the truest, most virtuous,
and valuable friend, that I, or perhaps any other person ever was blessed
with.

She was forty-seven. As soon as he was left alone, he resolved, 'for
my own satisfaction, to say something of her life and character'. He
entitled his paper: *On the Death of Mrs Johnson*. He was sixty. Wells, at
the same age, wrote on Jane, in his introduction to *The Book of Catherine
Wells*.

'I knew her from six years old,' Swift began, 'and had some share
in her education.' At twenty-two, he was secretary to Sir William
Temple, his mother's relative or acquaintance, at Moor Park, Surrey,
and the child was a member of the household. It has been suggested
that she was Temple's illegitimate daughter. It has even been put
forward that he was Temple's natural son.

1 See p. 184.
2 *The Correspondence of Jonathan Swift* ed. Harold Williams (1963–5), i, p. 46.

She was sickly from her childhood until about the age of fifteen: But then grew into perfect health, and was looked upon as one of the most beautiful, graceful, and agreeable young women in London, only a little too fat. Her hair was blacker than a raven, and every feature of her face in perfection.

Meanwhile he had taken his MA at Oxford, taken Temple's answer to William III on a constitutional question to do with parliament, and taken holy orders. On Temple's sudden death he received £100, and Stella the lease of some lands in Ireland.

I prevailed with her and her dear friend and companion [Rebecca Dingley – fifteen years older than Stella] . . . to draw what money they had into Ireland . . . Money was then at ten *per cent.* in Ireland . . . and all necessaries of life at half the price. They complied with my advice, and soon after came over; but I happening to continue some time longer in England, they were much discouraged to live in Dublin, where they were wholly strangers. She was at that time about nineteen years old . . . But the adventure looked so like a frolic, the censure held, for some time, as if there were a secret history in such a removal; which, however, soon blew off by her excellent conduct . . . and they both lived together until this day . . . Thus far I wrote the same night between eleven and twelve.

He had reached the point in his narrative when he received several livings in the Irish Church.

Miss Jane Waring gained a brief immortality at this time by judging his income enough for two. Unconvinced of her premise, he presented his terms:

Are you in a condition to manage domestic affairs, with an income of less (perhaps) than three hundred pounds a year? Have you such an inclination to my person and humour, as to comply with my desires and way of living, and endeavour to make us both as happy as you can? Will you be ready to engage in those methods I shall direct for the improvement of your mind, so as to make us entertaining company for each other, without being miserable when we are neither visiting nor visited? . . . Shall the place wherever your husband is thrown be more welcome than courts or cities without him? . . . These are the questions I have always resolved to propose to her with whom I meant to pass my life; and whenever you can heartily answer them in the affirmative, I shall be blessed to have you in my arms, without regarding whether your person be beautiful, or your fortune large. Cleanliness in the first, and competency in the other, is all I look for.[1]

1 4 May 1700. *The Correspondence of Jonathan Swift* ed. Harold Williams (1963–5), i, pp. 35–6.

She retreated hastily into the wings.

During his absences, Stella and Rebecca lived in his houses at Dublin and Laracor, and when he was in Ireland they took lodgings in his neighbourhood. Once, perhaps twice, they joined him in England. When Swift was thirty-six, Dr William Tisdall, a clergyman in Dublin, contemplated marriage to Stella. Swift, prepared to act as intermediary, replied to Tisdall:

. . . if my fortunes and humour served me to think of that state, I should certainly, among all persons on earth, make your choice; because I never saw that person whose conversation I entirely valued but hers . . . nor shall any consideration of my own misfortune of losing so good a friend and companion as her, prevail on me, against her interest and settlement in the world, since it is held so necessary and convenient a thing for ladies to marry; . . . and must add, that though it hath come in my way to converse with persons of the first rank, and of that sex, more than is usual to men of my level, and of our function; yet I have nowhere met with a humour, a wit, or conversation so agreeable, a better portion of good sense, or a truer judgment of men and things . . . I give you joy of your good fortunes, and envy very much your prudence and temper, and love of peace and settlement, the reverse of which has been the great uneasiness of my life, and is like to continue so . . .[1]

Thomas Sheridan said the refusal came from Stella.

Swift drew up a treaty permitting Mrs Anne Long 'to give herself the Reputation of being one of his Acquaintance; which no other Lady shall presume to do, upon any Pretence whatsoever, without his especial Leave and License first had and obtained'. On her death two years later, he wrote:

She was the most beautifull Person of the Age, she live in, of great Honr and Virtue, infinite Sweetness and Generosity of Temper, and true good Sense.

Michael Foot has corrected the image of a chauvinist 'monster':

He adored the company of women and they adored his; he was one of the very first to insist that women should have the same education as men . . .[2]

When the bereaved man resumed his narrative next day, Stella's accomplishments – 'the most and finest . . . of any Person I ever knew of either Sex' – were his theme.

1 20 Apr. 1704. *Ibid.*, i, pp. 45–6.
2 *Debts of Honour* (1980), p. 217.

Never was any of her sex born with better gifts of the mind, or more improved them by reading and conversation . . . I cannot call to mind that I ever once heard her make a wrong judgment of persons, books, or affairs . . . There seemed to be a combination among all that knew her, to treat her with a dignity much beyond her rank . . . Mr Addison, when he was in Ireland, being introduced to her, immediately found her out; and, if he had not soon after left the kingdom, assured me he would have used all endeavours to cultivate her friendship . . . All of us, who had the happiness of her friendship, agreed unanimously, that, in an afternoon or evening's conversation, she never failed before we parted of delivering the best thing that was said in the company.

January 29th, My Head achs, and I can write no more.

January 30th, Tuesday.
This is the night of the funeral, which my sickness will not suffer me to attend. It is now nine at night, and I am removed into another apartment, that I may not see the light in the church, which is just over against the window of my bed-chamber.

She was but little versed in the common topics of female chat . . .

She was well versed in the Greek and Roman story . . . She spoke French perfectly . . . She had read carefully all the best books of travel . . . She understood the Platonic and Epicurean philosophy . . . She understood the nature of government, and could point out all the errors of Hobbes, both in that and religion. She had a good insight into physic, and knew somewhat of anatomy . . . Neither was it easy to find a more proper or impartial judge, whose advice an author might better rely on,[1] if he intended to send a thing into the world, provided it was on a subject that came within the compass of her knowledge.

But her charity to the poor was a duty not to be diminished . . .

The 'ribald priest' of Macaulay noted with approval:

It was not safe nor prudent, in her presence, to offend in the least word against modesty . . .'

Stella's accomplishments were sung in his birthday verse to her:

> No Length of Time can make you quit
> Honour and Virtue, Sense and Wit,
> Thus you may still be young to me,
> While I can better *hear* than *see*.

And when she visited him in his sickness:

1 Cf. Barrie writing to Mary with regard to Cannan. See p. 129.

Her Hearers are amaz'd from whence
Proceeds that Fund of Wit and Sense;
Which though her Modesty would shroud,
Breaks like the Sun behind a Cloud . . .

In his mid-forties, when he became the chief political writer of Harley's new Tory ministry, he wrote the intimate letters to Stella and Rebecca, published posthumously under *Journal to Stella* and which suggest a clear intention of marriage. If Stella and he were secretly married, the compact was merely formal, for they continued to live apart and Stella used her maiden name in her will. The evidence is inconclusive. Thomas Sheridan had a story that Swift found Stella depressed and, learning the cause through a common friend, declared himself too old and poor to marry, but consented to the ceremony which would at least prevent his marrying anyone else. Denis Johnston's more recent theory[1] that Swift was Stella's uncle explains why he could not live with her as man and wife and apparently she never complained. It explains why they never met alone, and why he demanded her removal from the Deanery before she died.

His *Journal* often mentions Mrs Vanhomrigh, with whom he frequently dined and at whose lodgings he kept his 'best gown and periwig' when at Chelsea. But it seldom mentions her daughter, Esther (Vanessa), with whom an intimacy sprang up. After her mother's death, he was prepared to stand surety for Vanessa's borrowing. He even wrote:

I did not imagine you had been under Difficultyes, I am sure my whole Fortune should go to remove them.[2]

He told her: '. . . I hate anything that looks like a Secret'[3] – and was careful their relationship should be *secretive*:

You should not have come by Wantage for a thousand Pound. you used to bray you were very discreet; where is it gone? . . . When I am there [in Ireland] I will write you as soon as I can conveniently, but it shall be allways under a Cover; and if you write to me, let some other direct it, and I beg you will write nothing that is particular, but what may be seen . . .[4]

1 *In Search of Swift* (Dublin 1959), pp. 217–21.
2 ? End of 1714: *The Correspondence of Jonathan Swift* ed. Harold Williams (1963–5), ii, p. 148.
3 (? Dec. 1716). *Ibid.*, ii, p. 239.
4 12 Aug. 1714: *ibid.*, ii, p. 123.

When she told him her intention of returning to Ireland with her sister, Mary, he warned her:

. . . I shall see you very seldom. It is not a Place for any Freedom, but where everything is known in a Week, and magnifyed a hundred Degrees.[1]

. . . I would not have gone to Kildrohod to see you for all the World. I ever told you, you wanted Discretion . . . Nor shall you know where I am till I come, & then I will see you.[2]

She tried a moral argument:

you once had a maxime (which was to act what was right and not mind what they world said) I wish you would keep to it now pray what can be wrong in seeing and advising an unhappy young woman . . .[3]

Her next letter he probably called 'spleenatick':

tis impossible to describe what I have suffer'd since I saw you last, I am sure I could have bore the Rack much better than those killing, killing, words of yours. some times I have resolved to die without seeing you more . . . when I begin to complain then you are angry, and there is something in your look so awful, that it strikes me dumb.[4]

He teased her about writing 'the History of Cad – and – [Vanessa] . . . through all its steps from the beginning to this time':

I believe it would do well in Verse . . . It ought to be an exact Chronicle of 12 Years; from the time of spilling the Coffee to drinking of Coffee . . .[5]

Horace Walpole discovered an ulterior meaning to *Coffee*: 'I think it plain he lay with her.'[6] When Swift was fifty-four, he gave her 'the best Maxim I know':

. . . to drink your Coffee when you . . . can, and when you cannot, to be easy without it. Thus much I sympathise with you that I am not chearfull enough to write, for I believe Coffee once a week is necessary to that.[7]

1 *Ibid.*
2 5 Nov. 1714: *ibid.*, ii, p. 142.
3 Dublin (? Dec.) 1714: *ibid.*, ii, pp. 148–9.
4 Dublin 1714: *ibid.*, ii, p. 150.
5 12 Aug. 1720: *ibid.*, ii, p. 356.
6 An interpretation refuted by Archbishop Bernard in his introduction to *The Correspondence* ed. F. Elrington Ball (1910–14).
7 13 July 1722: *The Correspondence of Jonathan Swift* ed. Harold Williams (1963–5), ii, p. 430.

Cadenus and Vanessa, published after her death, describes at first a master–pupil relationship. When Vanessa startles Cadenus by confessing love, he urges a more excellent way:

> Love . . .
> . . . his Dignity and Age
> Forbid *Cadenus* to engage.
> But Friendship in its greatest Height,
> A constant, rational Delight,
> On Virtue's Basis fix'd to last,
> When Love's Allurements long are past;
> Which gently warms, but cannot burn;
> He gladly offers in return,
> With Gratitude, Respect, Esteem:
> With that Devotion we bestow,
> When Goddesses appear below.[1]

Is this the secret of Macaulay's 'perjured lover'? Perhaps the store that Swift, and the Pope circle, set by friendship has been undervalued in his story. Swift wrote to Pope:

I have often wish'd that God Almighty would be so easy to the weakness of mankind as to let old friends be acquainted in another state; and if I were to write an Utopia for heaven, that would be one of my schemes.[2]

At several times he wrote to Vanessa:

I shall be glad to hear from you, not as you are a Londoner but a Friend.[3]

I say all this out of the perfect Esteem and Friendship I have for you.[4]

. . . Friendship or Tenderness . . . I will allways continue to the utmost.[5]

One thing I differ from you in; that I do not quarrell with my best Friends; I believe you have ten angry passages in your Letter . . .[6]

She tried to compel him – the worst tactic she could have chosen:

once more I advise you if you have any regard for your quiete to allter your behaviour quickly . . . I here tell you that I have determined to try all manner of humain artes to reclaim you and if all those fail I am resolved to have

---

1 Written in summer 1712. Published 1727.
2 Dublin, 12 Oct 1727: *The Works of Alexander Pope* ed. William Warburton (1751), ix, p. 92.
3 8 June 1714: *The Correspondence of Jonathan Swift* ed. Harold Williams (1963–5), ii, p. 26.
4 12 Aug. 1714: *ibid.*, ii, p. 123.
5 (? End of 1714): *ibid.*, ii, p. 148.
6 13 July 1722: *ibid.*, ii, p. 429.

recourse to the black one . . . pray think calmely of it is it not much better to come of your self than to be brought by force . . .[1]

She settled at Marlay Abbey, near Celbridge, where Mary, her sister, died. Once, she opened his letter and found another, by accident or design:

. . . and that a love letter . . . upon my word when I see you I have a vast deall to say to you about that letter I have asked you all the questions I used ten thousand times and don't find them answered at all to my satisfaction.[2]

She used cheek:

– Cad . . . I am mightily pleased to hear you talke of being in a huff 'tis the first time you ever told me so I wish I could see you in one.[3]

She cajoled:

. . . I know your good nature such that you cannot see any humaine creature miserable without being sensibly touched yett what can I do I must either unload my heart and tell you all its griefs or sink under the unexpressable distress I now suffer by your progidious neglect of me.[4]

She let him see how badly she was hurt:

Tis now ten long weeks since I saw you and in all that time I have never received but one lettr from you and a little note with an excuse . . . with the utmost distress and confusion I behold my self the cause of uneasie reflections to you yet I can not comfort you but here declair that tis not in the power of arte time or accident to lessen the unexpressible passion which I have . . . don't suffer me to live a life like a languishing Death which is the only life I can leade if you have lost any of your tenderness for me.[5]

Only her wretchedness remained:

. . . I have worn out my days in sighing and my nights with watching and thinking . . . oh that I could hope to see you here or that I could go to you I was born with violent passions which terminate all in one that unexpressible passion I have for you . . .[6]

. . . I find the more I think the more unhappy I am . . .[7]

1 (? 1719–20): *ibid.*, ii, p. 335.
2 Cell Bridg (27 or 28 July) 1720: *ibid.*, ii, p. 352.
3 1720: *ibid.*, ii, p. 354.
4 (? Nov.–early Dec. 1720): *ibid.*, ii, pp. 362–3.
5 (? Nov.–early Dec. 1720): *ibid.*, ii, p. 363.
6 (? Nov.–early Dec. 1720): *ibid.*, ii, pp. 363–4.
7 (July 1721): *ibid.*, ii, p. 394.

Unlike Johnson, Macaulay, Thackeray, unlike Stella and Pope, she saw both faces:

. . . could I know your thoughts (which no humane creature is capable of geussing at because never any one liveing thought like you) . . . some times you strike me with that prodigious awe I tremble with fear at other times a charming compassion shines through your countynance, which revives my soul . . .[1]

He advised her to 'quit this scoundrel Island'.[2]

Vanessa's mind being less cultivated than Stella's, he anticipated the Shelleyan desire to mould and improve:

. . . I have the same Respect esteem and Kindness for you I ever professed to have . . . especially if you go on to read and still further improve Your Mind and the Talents that Nature have given you . . .[3]

He told her: 'Remembr I still enjoyn you Reading and Exercise for the Improvement of your Mind and Health of your Body, and' – unlike Shelley – 'grow less Romantick, and talk and act like a Man of the World.'[4]

She makes an allusion to Gulliver's misadventure with the monkey, which shows she had read Chapter V of the Voyage to Brobdingnag, but the rest of her words are pitiful:

. . . I do declair that I have so little Joy in life that I don't care how soon mine ends . . . your letters are all the joy I have on Earth . . . Cad think of me and pitty me.[5]

The following year, when he was fifty-five, she wrote either to Stella or himself asking if they were married. He rode to Celbridge, threw down the letter, and turned on his heel. The shock is said to have killed her.[6] She was thirty-five. Her will, previously in his favour, had been revoked.

Not unlike Hardy, who wrote poems on Emma after she had died, Swift now published *Cadenus and Vanessa*, and hid himself in southern Ireland. Stella was shocked at the disclosure, which may have hastened her own death. But when someone remarked that her rival

1 (? Nov.–early Dec. 1720): *ibid.*, ii, p. 364.
2 5 July 1721: *ibid.*, ii, p. 393.
3 15 Oct. 1720: *ibid.*, ii, p. 360.
4 Cloghr, 1 June 1722: *ibid.*, ii, p. 427.
5 (June 1722): *ibid.*, ii, p. 429.
6 2 June 1723.

must have been a remarkable woman for him to have written so beautifully, she made the most celebrated of all her *bons mots*:

That doesn't surprise me for we all know the Dean could write beautifully about a broomstick.

Drinkwater said:

Swift had the moon's mysteriousness in that he had one face for the world and another, not to be seen save by her [Stella], for the woman he loved.[1]

But Pope saw that side of him always, and so did Vanessa at first. He never sent a letter to Stella but he began another the same day. Every year he

> Resolvd my annual Verse to pay
> By Duty bound, on *Stella*'s Day . . .

Sometimes he was playful:

> Stella this Day is thirty four,
> (We shan't dispute a Year or more)
> However Stella, be not troubled,
> Since first I saw Thee at Sixteen
> The brightest Virgin on the Green . . .

Sometimes he was penitent, as in the verses 'Written on the Day of her Birth . . . when I was sick in bed':

> Whatever base returns you find
> From me, Dear Stella, still be kind.
> In your own heart you'll reap the fruit,
> Tho' I continue still a brute.
> But when I once am out of pain,
> I promise to be good again . . .

At fifty-three, he sent appropriate verses when she had visited him again in his sickness:

> Say, *Stella*, was *Prometheus* blind,
> And forming you, mistook your kind?
> No: 'Twas for you alone he stole
> The Fire that forms a manly Soul;
> Then to compleat it ev'ry way,
> He molded it with Female Clay:
> To that you owe the nobler Flame,
> To this, the Beauty of your Frame.

1 *The Outline of Literature* (1923-4), i, p. 277.

The year after Vanessa's death, Stella was dying. Swift left Pope's villa at Twickenham abruptly, yet could not bear to be present in the 'very midst of grief' at Dublin. He scarcely dared open his letters. After her death he lived another eighteen years. Dr Tuke of Dublin had a lock of Stella's hair, enclosed in paper on which was written in the Dean's hand: 'Only a woman's hair.' Even Thackeray conceded that 'to have had so much love, he must have given some . . .'[1]

II

Stella's mysterious role in the life of Swift has something in common with ELIOT's life and the part played by Emily Hale. Eliot met her as a family friend when he was an undergraduate at Harvard and she was seventeen. After his year at the Sorbonne, they played in a family theatrical together. Then, when he went to Germany and Oxford, it was thought he would return and marry her. Instead came his marriage with Vivien in England – for him, as for Shelley and his marriage with Harriet, the greatest mistake of his life. Yet what his biographer calls 'his focus of torment'[2] was to prove one of the two important sources of his inspiration.

At thirty-six and now an Assistant Professor of Speech and Drama, Emily wrote to him for advice on material in her classes. Before their first reunion, which was in America at the time he intended to separate from Vivien, Eliot had a dream with a Dante and Beatrice scenario in which Emily forgave his betrayal. During the following thirty years he wrote to her more than a thousand letters[3] – on average, one every ten days. They met only at rare intervals.

She is *La Figlia*, 'the hyacinth girl' in *The Waste Land*, the 'Lady of silences' in *Ash Wednesday*. She is in the imagery of 'the rose-garden' and 'the lotos' in *Burnt Norton*. She is in the characters Mary and Agatha in *The Family Reunion*, and Celia in *The Cocktail Party*.

1 *The English Humourists of the Eighteenth Century: A Series of Lectures* (1853), p. 53.
2 Lyndall Gordon: *Eliot's New Life* (1988), p. 148.
3 Eliot's letters to Emily Hale are sealed until 12 Oct. 2019. In 1957 she bequeathed them to Princeton University, and in 1963 asked him, unsuccessfully, to reconsider the time set for public access – 50 years after the death of the survivor. In the same year, perhaps as a consequence of her request, it is thought he destroyed the letters that she had written to him.

After his failure to marry her on the death of Vivien, she still hoped that one day he would. Then, after some years, when she received his letter announcing his second marriage, she had a nervous breakdown which debilitated her. (Stella suffered also, when she learned of Vanessa.) But Emily does not seem to have blamed Valerie Eliot; she even praised her devoted nursing of him. Eliot's biographer writes:

His rejection of Emily Hale finally broke the dream that had given the rare moments of radiance to his poetry.[1]

An actress of considerable talent in college productions, Emily performed the veiled and celibate role that Eliot had given her through to the end. It was a very human feeling that she would have liked his readers to know, while she was alive, that she had played a part in the poet's story.

In discussing DICKENS's relations with Ellen Ternan, Peter Ackroyd suggests that the undeniably obsessed man may have realized 'one of his most enduring fictional fantasies. That of sexless marriage with a young, idealised virgin.'[2]

III

RUSKIN, at sixty-eight, confided to Mary Gladstone when she told him she was about to be married:

I don't like married women; I like sibyls and children and vestals.[3]

His heart was 'broken . . . when I was a boy'. In his seventeenth year he fell in love with Adèle Domecq, 'a graceful oval-faced blonde of fifteen', the daughter of his father's partner. She and three younger sisters came to stay.

. . . my parents . . . had never seen me in the least interested or anxious about girls . . . these four girls . . . of course reduced me to a mere heap of white ashes in four days . . .[4] My mother, who looked upon the idea of my marrying a Roman Catholic as too monstrous . . . and preposterous . . .

1 Lyndall Gordon: *Eliot's New Life* (1988), p. 148.
2 *Dickens* (1990), p. 916.
3 1887.
4 *Praeterita* (1886–8), i, pp. 328–9.

hoped, when the Domecqs went back . . . we might see no more of them . . .[1]

Many years later, his father told Burne-Jones he would never forget the day he and his son had taken Adèle to the ship, or the agony of his son. Ruskin's aged mother commented:

Yes, any trouble that has happened to him since then was nothing compared to that.[2]

Dr Evans writes that Ruskin at seventeen still depended upon his mother to guard him from suffering, 'yet it was she who had brought this worst suffering of all upon him'.

. . . the bright mirror of his mind was for ever flawed . . . his very capacity for love was twisted and withered . . .[3]

They met again when Adèle was eighteen, but

The May-frost that had struck John Ruskin had killed the blossom of his love for Adèle; he could remember his love for her as a child, but it could not grow with her maturity into love for her as a woman. Henceforth he was only able to love young girls . . .[4]

In his middle life 'another net of Love' was woven around ten-year-old Rose La Touche, when he gave drawing lessons to her and her family. He described her then as having 'eyes rather deep blue' and 'lips perfectly lovely in profile'.

. . . the hair, perhaps more graceful in short curl round the forehead, and softer than one sees often in the close-bound tresses above the neck.

At the time that his preaching of socialist ideals came under attack, which affected his work, he wrote to his friend, Charles Norton:

I don't in the least know what might have been the end of it, if a little child (only 13 last summer) hadn't put her fingers on the helm at the right time, and chose to make a pet of herself for me . . .[5]

With shades of Barrie, he wrote to Georgina Burne-Jones:

Do I want to keep her from growing up? Of course I do.

1 *Ibid.*, i, p. 333.
2 *Memorials of Burne-Jones* (1904), i, p. 271.
3 Joan Evans: *John Ruskin* (1954), p. 50.
4 *Ibid.*, p. 64.
5 25 Feb. 1861.

When the headmistress invited him to Winnington, he told the girls of his love for Rose, and Dr Evans suggests that some of them 'may have suffered more than he knew from these vicarious flirtations'.[1]

He declared himself on her seventeenth birthday, when he was nearly forty-seven. Her parents were outraged, principally because he had lost his religious faith. Eventually Rose told him he must wait until she came of age. He wrote to Mrs Cowper:

They took the child away from me – practically four years ago (when she was 13) – and since that day . . . I have never had one happy hour – All my work has been wrecked – All my usefulness taken from me.[2]

Rose was as precariously balanced as he, and soon fell ill mentally and physically. The affair dragged on fifteen years until she died.

On such evidence as the autobiographical *The Glimpse*, written more than twelve months after BENNETT married, it has been suggested that his 'sexual desire paused for many years at a delight – warmly cherished though never indulged – in little girls'.[3] BARRIE worshipped motherhood as a spiritual image, as a state almost divorced from the physical acts of procreation and delivery. The elderly Nico, the last survivor of the Five Boys, said:

Of all the men I have ever known, Barrie was . . . the least interested in sex . . .[4]

DODGSON found aesthetic peace and escape in photographing his child-friends. To one of the few who had given him a woman-friendship as well as a child-friendship, he wrote:

About nine out of ten, I think, of my child-friendships get shipwrecked at the critical point, 'where the stream and river meet', and the child-friends, once so affectionate, become uninteresting acquaintances, whom I have no wish to set eyes on again.[5]

He may have been in love with Ellen Terry. In this he was not, of course, alone. Shaw, before his marriage, courted her passionately by correspondence (as, later, he did Mrs Patrick Campbell). Dodgson had followed Ellen Terry's progress from her little Mamillius and Puck, at

1 *John Ruskin* (1954), p. 280.
2 Oct. 1866.
3 Dudley Barker: *Writer by Trade: A View of Arnold Bennett* (1966), p. 40.
4 Andrew Birkin: *J. M. Barrie & the Lost Boys* (1979), p. xii.
5 Stuart Dodgson Collingwood: *The Life & Letters of Lewis Carroll* (1898), pp. 367–9.

the age of eight, but they did not meet until he was nearly thirty-two. She, nearly seventeen then, had already separated from Watts. The following summer Dodgson took the first of his photographs of her. 'I can imagine no more delightful occupation than brushing Ellen Terry's hair!'[1] he said. She, for her part, remembered him in her *Memoirs*:

He was as fond of me as he could be of anyone over the age of ten.[2]

1 Langford Reed: *The Life of Lewis Carroll* (1932), p. 90.
2 *Ellen Terry's Memoirs* ed. Edith Craig & C. St John (1933), p. 18.

CHAPTER ELEVEN
Friendships of Deep Affection

I

GIBBON formed an enduring friendship with a young Swiss. It started when his father, to disentangle him from his youthful conversion to Rome, dispatched him at sixteen to lodge with a Calvinist minister in Lausanne. The boy tangled himself with the pastor's daughter, and on being summoned home expressed himself later:

. . . I sighed as a lover, I obeyed as a son . . .[1]

But over there he had also met Georges Deyverdun, who joined him for many months in the family home at Beriton when Gibbon, at twenty-eight, was still contemplating his *History* 'at an awful distance'.

When he was forty-six, having abandoned parliamentary life and now absorbed in the fourth volume, Gibbon proposed to his friend that he should join him in Lausanne. Deyverdun, ensconced in a house given by his aunt, gladly accepted and Gibbon sent over his library.

Four years later, in a summer-house in the four acres of beautiful garden, he 'wrote the last lines of the last page' of 'that laborious work'. The acclaim that he began to receive on all sides was shattered by the death of his friend, who in his will had provided for Gibbon to live in the house for the rest of his life. In poor physical shape from a too sedentary life, the broken man himself died within another four years.

'The "prime passion" of TENNYSON's whole existence'[2] was Arthur Hallam, whom he knew 'thro' four sweet years' beginning 'the fifth

---

1 *Miscellaneous Works of Edward Gibbon, Esquire. With Memoirs of his Life & Writings, composed by himself* ed. John Lord Sheffield (1796), i, p. 75.
2 Harold Nicolson: *Tennyson: Aspects of his Life, Character & Poetry* (1923), p. 63.

autumnal slope'.[1] They met at Cambridge, and Tennyson was twenty-four when his friend died of apoplexy in Vienna. Charlotte Brontë, on reading *In Memoriam* published seventeen years later, said that if Hallam 'had been somewhat nearer' – Tennyson's 'brother, instead of his friend' – she 'should have distrusted this rhymed, and measured, and printed monument of grief'.[2] Two generations later, Nicolson drew a distinction between 'that artificially constructed synthesis' of 1850 and 'those lonely, wistful, frightened elegies . . . scribbled in the old account-book, scribbled in odd unhappy moments during the seven years from 1833 to 1840 . . .'[3]

Hallam, eighteen months Tennyson's junior, 'looked up to him as to a great poet and an elder brother'.[4] Tennyson recognized in the meteoric young man who dazzled Cambridge a wonderful and potential statesman. But Hallam was not only the friend, 'more than my brothers are to me',[5] he was engaged to Tennyson's sister, Emily.

> . . . For now the day was drawing on,
> When thou should'st link thy life with one
> Of mine own house, and boys of thine.
>
> Had babbled 'Uncle' on my knee . . .[6]

In one section of his poem, Tennyson supposes that he has received word of Hallam's return:

> . . . And I went down unto the quay . . .
>
> And standing, muffled round with woe,
> Should see thy passengers in rank
> Come stepping lightly down the plank,
> And beckoning unto those they know,
>
> And if along with these should come
> The man I held as half-divine;
> Should strike a sudden hand in mine,
> And ask a thousand things of home;
>
> And I should tell him all my pain,
> And how my life had droop'd of late,

1 *In Memoriam* (1850), p. 37: XXII.
2 To Mrs Gaskell: 27 Aug. 1850.
3 *Op. cit*, pp. 296–7.
4 *Alfred Lord Tennyson: A Memoir by his Son* (1897), i, p. 35.
5 *In Memoriam*, p. 13: IX.
6 *Ibid.*, p. 114: LXXXII.

And he should sorrow o'er my state
And marvel what possess'd my brain;

And I perceived no touch of change,
No hint of death in all his frame,
But found him all in all the same,
I should not feel it to be strange.[1]

The close friendship of MATTHEW ARNOLD and ARTHUR CLOUGH belonged also to youth – at Rugby, where Clough was three years senior, above all as Fellows of Oriel, and during the immediate bachelor years. Arnold's mother helped by bringing the lonely school-boy into the family when his parents had returned to America.

Their views on poetry differed sharply, so that Clough was unimpressed by his friend's first volume of verse, *The Strayed Reveller, and other Poems*. Clough 'valued literal expression more than beauty . . .'

He refused to heighten his feelings; he loved reality . . .[2]

Yet when his friend at thirty-three was crossing to the States, Arnold wrote:

. . . we agree more with one another than with the rest of the world.[3]

From Boston, Clough complained of ways in which he had been left in the cold during the past five years, and Arnold, who was married, defended himself on the grounds that 'being in love generally unfits a man for the society of his friends'. He added:

. . . only remember, *pray* remember that I am and always shall be, whatever I do or say, powerfully attracted towards you, and vitally connected with you . . . by intellectual bonds – the strongest of all.[4]

Five months later, in *The North American Review*, Clough savagely attacked Arnold's second volume, *Empedocles on Etna, and other Poems*. Arnold accepted eleven alterations to one of the poems, 'Tristram and Iseult', and then replied with his first real work of criticism – the Preface to his *Poems* (1853).

Like Hallam, Clough died of a stroke abroad, at Florence, aged forty-three. Arnold confided in his mother:

1 *Ibid.*, pp. 22–3: XIV.
2 Desmond MacCarthy: *Portraits* (1931), pp. 64, 66.
3 28 Oct, 1852.
4 13 Feb. 1853.

. . . poor Clough . . . is a loss I shall feel more and more as time goes on, for he is one of the few people who ever made a deep impression upon me . . .[1]

He wrote to the widow:

. . . our friendship was more important to me than it was to him, and no one will ever again be to me what he was.

He was now Professor of Poetry at Oxford, and in his lectures on translating Homer he quoted Tennyson:

> Dear Friend, far off; my lost desire . . .
>
> Sweet human hand and lips and eye,
> Dear heavenly friend that canst not die,
> Mine, mine for ever, ever mine . . .[2]

He had told his mother:

I shall some day in some way or other, relieve myself of what I think about him.

This was fulfilled five years later in 'Thyrsis', his finest poem.

This pattern of strong friendship dashed by early death can be seen in Thomas Gray and Richard West, Charles Kingsley and Charles Mansfield, Rudyard Kipling and Wolcott Balestier,[3] Vera Brittain and Winifred Holtby. KINGSLEY's love for Mansfield at Cambridge went very deep, and his wife omitted it in her biography. At the time of Mansfield's death, Kingsley wrote:

He was my first love. The first human being, save my mother, I ever met who knew what I meant.[4]

The 'delicately beautiful' Frank Leigh in *Westward Ho!* was based on him.

Sensitive to male beauty were J. K. JEROME ('the male is Nature's favourite'[5]) and GEORGE DU MAURIER ('never a sitting woman among them all who could match for grace . . . of outward form that mighty Yorkshireman – Taffy – sitting in his tub . . .').[6] KINGSLEY told his future wife:

1 20 Nov. 1861.
2 These lines from section CXXVII of *In Memoriam* he inserted in LVI.
3 See p. 94.
4 To J. M. Ludlow. Quoted by Susan Chitty: *The Beast The Monk* (1974), p. 52.
5 *My Life & Times* (1925), p. 182.
6 *Trilby* (1894), p. 96.

There is something awful, spirited, in man's love for each other . . . Had you been a man we should have been like David and Jonathan.[1]

The view of Lady Chitty is that 'whereas with Charles any element of homosexuality remained latent', with his brother Henry 'it became more overt'.

II

When VERA BRITTAIN wrote of her friendship with WINIFRED HOLTBY, 'which continued unbroken and unspoilt for sixteen incomparable years', she reflected that the friendships of women 'have usually been not merely unsung, but mocked, belittled and falsely interpreted', and that such loyalty and affection enhanced 'the love of a girl for her lover, of a wife for her husband, of a mother for her children'.[2]

They met at Somerville College, Oxford, and to begin with did not like each other at all. Winifred's exuberant style and outgoing personality contrasted with Vera's sense of isolation and bereavement following the deaths of her brother and fiancé in World War I. Their divide was exacerbated when Winifred, as secretary of a new debating society, invited her to propose the motion: 'That four years' travel are a better education than four years at a university'. Vera expounded to the younger students the superiority of her harrowing experience as a VAD nurse at the Front. Winifred's speech, containing a quotation from *As You Like It*, was one of the first on the opposite side, and the motion was heavily defeated. Vera believed herself mocked for her war service 'by a number of heartless juniors at Winifred's instigation'.[3]

The following term she was lying mournfully in bed with a chill when Winifred suddenly appeared and promptly vanished, leaving a bunch of grapes. She came back next day, and Vera discovered that Winifred in the WAAC had known 'that *via dolorosa*, the road to Camiers, and had lived beside the same historic railway-line . . .'[4]

1 28 Oct. 1843: Chitty, *op. cit.*, p. 52.
2 *Testament of Friendship* (1940), p. 2.
3 *Ibid.*, p. 93.
4 *Testament of Youth* (1933), p. 491.

After College – both receiving Seconds in History – they spent their 'most perfect' six weeks' holiday in pre-Fascist Italy. The night Winifred returned home to Yorkshire, she wrote a letter to Vera in which she said:

. . . the best thing of all was finding out from day to day how dear you are . . . Thank you, thank you, thank you, for being so completely satisfactory, you most sweet woman. [1]

They shared a working life of journalism, lecturing, and creative writing in a ground-floor studio and then a top-floor flat in Doughty Street, later moving to a spacious mansion flat in Maida Vale. Vera was the first to get articles published, and Winifred a book, *Anderby Wold*. They were continuously together for five years and after that, except during one or two long intervals, remained so to the end of Winifred's life.

Neither had known the joy of coming home at the end of the day after separate experiences, and recounting them to another over late biscuits and tea. Winifred

used to sit on the floor in front of the tiny gas-fire, the light on her hair and her blue eyes sparkling with enjoyment, eagerly imploring: 'Tell me some more!' [2]

They spent three months together in Central Europe. Vera's only personal experience of telepathy occurred in connection with her intimatest friend. She had returned early to the flat and called Winifred's name. Winifred, in Berkeley Street at the time, had been startled to hear her name called but no one behind her, and when she came home asked Vera rather oddly if she had returned early.

On Vera's announcing she was going to marry an American professor who had taken her to see Shaw's *St Joan*, Winifred wrote in her own copy of the play: '*Ave atque Vale*, July 5th, 1924. W.H.' (Her friend saw it for the first time a week after Winifred's death when she was going through her library.) In reply to a letter from her mother, Winifred wrote:

She may drop me, but I don't think that she will dupe me . . . don't you see that long ago I saw that this was inevitable? [3]

1 *Testament of Friendship* (1940), p. 112.
2 *Ibid.*, p. 117.
3 *Ibid.*, pp. 144–5.

Winifred was the only bridesmaid. She wore a blue dress, and Vera described her hair as 'golden, Madonna-like'.[1] When Vera accompanied her husband to America, she spoke of 'remorsefully leaving my parents, who had lost their only son . . .' She added:

It was even harder to leave Winifred, for the past five years my second self.[2]

When Winifred returned to the flat alone, she wrote her poem, 'The Foolish Clocks':

> Oh, foolish clocks, who had no wit for hoarding
> The precious moments when my love was here,
> Be silent now, and cease this vain recording
> Of worthless hours, since she is not near.[3]

She wrote to Vera of walking through the evening streets:

I am, as I said, very very happy, but it's a sort of autumn empty happiness. I miss the feel of your fingers round my left arm . . .[4]

After a year in America, Vera resumed her journalistic career in London, and Winifred and she went back to the flat in Maida Vale. When Vera's husband changed his professorship to a half-time post, Winifred suggested joining the household from which he would so often be absent. There was a move first to an upper maisonette in Nevern Place, Earl's Court, before settling in 19 Glebe Place, Chelsea. There, when Winifred was nearly thirty-two, she experienced the nearest thing to complete happiness – the companionship of her friend and friend's husband, babies, toys – and books in the attic, which they had converted to a top-floor library. Her Friends of Africa came.

Each time a coloured visitor came through the front gate, the children stood at their nursery door wide-eyed and enraptured . . . the exciting information would be conveyed in a tense whisper: 'Daddy! Mummie! Auntie's got an *African* in her room!'

To the interest of surrounding artists, they gave parties which overflowed into the long narrow garden – 'where huge Jamaican negroes and smaller students from Cape Town mingled with Colonel Josiah Wedgwood and Ellen Wilkinson'.[5]

1 *Ibid.*, p. 165.
2 *Testament of Experience* (1957), p. 29.
3 *Testament of Friendship* (1940), p. 166.
4 *Ibid.*, p. 176.
5 *Ibid.*, pp. 292–3.

Even her last illness . . . did not quench the gaiety of our shared home.[1]

Five years after that last move, Vera once more was helping Winifred dress and pack to go into a nursing home.

. . . I did not dream that I should never see her dressed again . . .[2]

Three weeks later, she died.

1 *Ibid.*, p. 291.
2 *Ibid.*, p. 430.

CHAPTER TWELVE

Passion for Youth

I

It was a novelty for GRAY, at thirty-three, to be gadding about the lanes of Stoke Poges in a butcher's cart driven by a young heiress, Miss Henrietta Speed. She had called upon the author of the *Elegy* on one of his summer visits to his mother and sister, but he was out and she had left her card. She lived at the Manor House with Lady Cobham and he had returned the call, describing it all in his comic poem 'A Long Story'. He called in future summers until Lady Cobham died and Henrietta married a foreign baron and lived abroad.

At Peterhouse and Pembroke Hall, the celibate scholar had become too accustomed to male company for his affections seriously to be involved. He was used to sycophantic young men like William Mason and Norton Nicholls, whom he would gently advise, 'Remember I speak from experience!'[1] 'You are a green gosling!'[2] and for whom he would go to any lengths to share his scholarship. But Charles Victor de Bonstetten was different.

At fifty-three, Gray was introduced through Nicholls to the twenty-one-year-old Swiss nobleman and persuaded him to visit Cambridge. Bonstetten was there barely five weeks, yet enough for the poet to be utterly bereft when the young man had gone. From his rooms at Pembroke, Gray informed his 'dearest friend':

I am grown old in the compass of less than three weeks . . .[3]

A week later, he wrote:

My life now is but a perpetual conversation with your shadow – the known sound of your voice still rings in my ears – there, on the corner of the fender,

1 *c.* 1767.
2 *c.* 1770.
3 12 Apr. 1770.

you are standing, or tinkling on the pianoforte, or stretched at length on the sofa . . .[1]

Three weeks afterwards, the sense of loss seemed no less acute:

I am returned, my dear Bonstetten, from the little journey I made into Suffolk . . . The thought that you might have been with me there has embittered all my hours . . .[2]

Gray's feelings for Bonstetten were paralleled in HENRY JAMES'S relations with Hendrik Christian Andersen (a distant relative of Hans Christian Andersen). Andersen, 'of magnificent stature', was twenty-seven, and James fifty-six, when they met in Rome. The young sculptor invited him to his studio, where James bought a small terracotta bust that Andersen had done of Conte Alberto Bevilacqua.

That summer Andersen stayed three days at Lamb House in Rye. As they sat under the mulberry tree and talked, they seemed to have so much in common – sharing the same birthday, both second sons, each with a talented brother – but James went further and projected his inner feelings about art on the flaxen-haired youth. When Andersen had left for New York, James wrote to his friends the Elliotts in Rome:

That most lovable youth . . . whirled himself off into space after making me grow quite fond enough . . . to miss him . . . I would with joy have put him up for ever so much longer.[3]

He wrote to Andersen:

. . . I have *missed* you out of all proportion to the three meagre little days . . . that we had together . . .[4]

As Gray thought with longing of Bonstetten standing on the corner of the fender, so James remembered how Andersen and he had bicycled up Udimore Hill in the evening.

But in spite of the warmth of his letters, they were to have only half a dozen widely spaced meetings.

I wish I could go to Rome and put my hands on you (oh, how lovingly I should lay them!) . . . but I return to Rye . . . and sooner or later to *have* you there . . . and *make* you lean on me as on a brother and a lover . . .[5]

1 19 Apr. 1770.
2 9 May 1770.
3 Leon Edel: *The Life of Henry James* (1953–72), iii, *The Treacherous Years*, p. 294.
4 7 Sept. 1899: *Henry James Letters* ed. Leon Edel (1974–84), iv, p. 118.
5 9 Feb 1902: *ibid.*, iv, p. 226.

Leon Edel urges caution in interpreting this 'physical, tactile language'. While it speaks for 'a certain physical intimacy in their meetings', it can be seen also as 'forms of endearment in one who was overtly affectionate in public'.[1] Shaw recounted a visit to Lamb House and James crossing the length of the garden to kiss him on both cheeks, as if conferring a Légion d'honneur.

Wolcott Balestier, Kipling's friend, was the first of several young men who revered James in middle life. He may have been the prototype for the young admiring doctor who tends the dying novelist in the tale *The Middle Years*.

EDWARD LEAR, at sixty-five, living at San Remo, found a companion in Hubert Congreve whom he had met as a child – now grown up, 'a wonderfully delightful lad'. He saw him as his protégé, learning to paint. When Hubert went to King's College, London, without confiding his plans, the darkness that came down was 'nearer to utter & total madness'[2] than any he had known.

His lifelong friendship with Franklin Lushington, considerably younger than himself, began when Lear was thirty-six and they went together to Greece. A few years later, he opened his heart to Emily Tennyson concerning the Lushington family, and Vivien Noakes says:

... she comforted him as she might have done a young boy in love for the first time.[3]

He accompanied his friend to Corfu when Lushington became Judge to the Supreme Court of Justice in the Ionian Islands. Eventually, after Lushington had come back to England and married, Lear made a friend of his wife.

Another lifelong friend, Chichester Fortescue (later Lord Carlingford), he met at thirty-three, in Rome, when Fortescue was twenty-two; when this friend also married, Lear wrote:

Every marriage of people I care about rather seems to leave me on the bleak shore alone.[4]

On Lear's death, his servant Giuseppe Orsini conveyed to Lushington his last words:

1 Edel: *The Treacherous Years*, cit., p. 296.
2 *Diary*: 2 Aug. 1877. Vivien Noakes: *Edward Lear: The Life of a Wanderer* (1968), p. 277.
3 *Ibid.*, p. 128.
4 22 Aug. 1868: *ibid.*, p. 193.

My good Giuseppe . . . You will render me a sacred service in telling my friends and relations that my last thought was for them, especially the Judge and Lord Northbrook and Lord Carlingford. I cannot find words sufficient to thank my good friends for the good they have always done me . . .[1]

When Dean INGE was a young schoolmaster at Eton, he had a favourite pupil, Charles Calvert. One summer day he took him and two other boys to Burnham Beeches, and said afterwards: 'I think nothing more charming than Calvert was ever created.' Three years later, a midwinter visit there brought 'the beautiful image' to mind.

I think I shall never forget . . . how angelic Calvert looked at the top of a steep bank, his straw hat on the back of his head looking like an aureole, and his eyes dancing like two sunbeams. It was the prettiest sight I ever saw or shall see.

Inge's biographer comments that it is not the language of ordinary experience nor what was characteristic of him: 'It is the language of vision . . .'[2]

II

From the time he was six, T. E. LAWRENCE had known a conventional sweetheart, Janet Laurie, living next door. When he came of age Janet was invited to dinner, and he suddenly bolted the door to shut out the parlourmaid. Without warning, he proposed. Janet's response was to laugh, upon which he said, 'Oh, I see!' Ten years later she married Guthrie Hallsmith, another war hero, and invited Lawrence to give her away. At first he agreed, but then sent a note saying he could not go through with it.

When he was twenty-three, excavating the site of Carchemish, he met a fourteen-year-old water boy or donkey boy, Dahoum (Salim Ahmed). Sir Leonard Woolley, in charge after Hogarth and Thompson, described Dahoum as 'beautifully built and remarkably handsome'.

Lawrence spent three years with the boy, tramping the Syrian desert between digs and nursing him when he nearly died from a dangerous form of malaria. He became possessive if in his absence the

1 *Ibid.*, p. 312.
2 Adam Fox: *Dean Inge* (1960), pp. 40–1.

German railway engineers behaved roughly to Dahoum. At Jebail they spent long hours together in the sea, and for three weeks in Lebanon he dressed in a spare set of Dahoum's clothes, which led at Halfati to his first beating by the Turks. The two were seen as possible deserters and, although Lawrence may have feared ridicule if exposed wearing Arab dress, Desmond Stewart believes the stronger motive for keeping quiet was to identify himself with Dahoum, who could well have been a recruit.

He not only taught him his letters but also photography to practise usefully on the dig. He brought the sixteen-year-old lad, together with the foreman, Sheikh Hamoudi, home to Oxford and they slept in the bungalow which his father had built for Lawrence at the bottom of the garden. Looking back on those two months, Arnold, the youngest member of the family, observed that his brother shaped his protégé like a son.

Back at Carchemish, he worked a sculpture from soft local sandstone of 'a squatting demon of the Notre Dame style', for which Dahoum posed naked. It was set up on his house roof and, when local gossip saw the figure as proof of perversion, Woolley defended a highly amused Lawrence. Dahoum died, about twenty, of typhus, guarding the Carchemish site – ironically still under Turkish rule – before he could be emancipated by Lawrence's Arab Revolt. Gunner T. W. Beaumont remembered Lawrence saying, 'I loved that boy,' and saw he had been weeping.

Seven Pillars of Wisdom is dedicated 'To S.A.'. Lawrence told Liddell Hart that the initials represented a composite idea. J. M. Wilson, and other biographers, believe that 'the personal element in this dedicatory poem could only have been Dahoum':[1]

> I loved you, so I drew these tides of men into my hands and wrote my
>   will across the sky in stars
> To earn you Freedom, the seven pillared worthy house, that your eyes
>   might be shining for me
>
> > When we came.
>
> Death seemed my servant on the road, till we were near and saw you
>   waiting:
> When you smiled, and in sorrowful envy he outran me and took you
>   apart:
>
> > Into his quietness.

1 T. E. Lawrence: *Minorities* ed. J. M. Wilson (1971), Introduction, p. 30.

Love, the way-weary, groped to your body, our brief wage ours for the
moment . . .
Men prayed me that I set our work, the inviolate house, as a memory of
you . . .

In the expedition against Akaba, Daud, a youth who was strange to
Lawrence, appealed to him on behalf of his 'love-fellow', Faraj, who
had burnt their tent in a frolic. It seemed the pair had always been in
trouble, and all Lawrence could achieve from Sharraf ('the severe')
was for Daud to share Faraj's beating. Afterwards they hobbled back
to him, saluted, and said they would follow him 'for company and out
of gratitude'. Faraj,

a beautiful, soft-framed, girlish creature, with innocent, smooth face and
swimming eyes . . . knelt in appeal, all the woman of him evident in his
longing.

At the end he took them both, 'mainly because they looked so young
and clean'.[1]

They were brave and cheerful beyond the average of Arab servant-kind. I
liked their freedom towards myself . . .[2]

When his men led their exhausted camels, Faraj and Daud danced
along 'barefooted, delicate as thoroughbreds'.[3] They saw the presence
of snakes as 'a new and splendid game', sounding the alarm at every
harmless twig and root. Lawrence, who 'had a shuddering horror of
all reptiles', at last ordered them to keep quiet and on the noonday
halt noticed them enjoying a joke. His eyes followed theirs 'to the
neighbouring bush under which a brown snake lay coiled, glittering
at me'.
They had been exasperating the others.

The culprits were abashed when they saw that all the hides and all the sticks
in the party would hardly expiate their account . . .

But Lawrence saved them 'the weight of it' and they were set 'under
the women to gather wood and draw water for the tents'.[4]
He later obtained their release from Sheikh Yusuf's prison after
they had dyed the head of the Governor's 'cream-coloured riding

1 *Seven Pillars of Wisdom* (trade ed. 1935), p. 237.
2 *Ibid.*, p. 243.
3 *Ibid.*, p. 253.
4 *Ibid.*, pp. 270–1.

camel . . . bright red with henna, and her legs blue with indigo, before turning her loose'.[1]

Their sins were elvish gaiety . . . the being happy when we were not; and for such follies to hurt them mercilessly like criminals . . . seemed to me degrading, almost an impiety towards two sunlit beings on whom the shadow of the world had not yet fallen – the most gallant, the most enviable, I knew.[2]

It was a leaden-eyed Faraj, looking old, who came to tell them that Daud had died of cold.

He took punctilious care, greater even than before of my camel, of the coffee, of my clothes and saddles . . .[3]

A month later, he rode straight for the Turkish guns and ignored the decision to make a flanking attack. Lawrence found him terribly wounded and tried to move him but he screamed pitifully. Lawrence realized he had to save him from being burnt alive by the approaching Turks.

I knelt down beside him, holding my pistol near the ground by his head, so that he should not see my purpose; but he must have guessed it, for he opened his eyes, and clutched me . . . I waited a moment, and he said, 'Daud will be angry with you', the old smile coming back so strangely to this grey shrinking face. I replied, 'salute him from me'. He returned the formal answer, 'God will give you peace', and at last wearily closed his eyes.[4]

III

BYRON's sexual ambivalence began at Harrow. Lord Clare ('Little Clare', his favourite, who was jealous),

I never hear the word '*Clare*' without a beating of the heart – even *now* . . .[5]

the Duke of Dorset, Lord Delawarr (Clare's successor), the Hon. John Wingfield – all were boys considerably younger and of exceptional beauty, Lord Delawarr remarkably so, 'almost too much so for a

---

1 *Ibid.*, p. 392.
2 *Ibid.*, p. 311.
3 *Ibid.*, p. 508.
4 *Ibid.*, p. 517.
5 'Detached Thoughts': *The Letters & Journals* ed. Leslie A. Marchand (1973–82), ix, p. 44.

boy'.[1] The first of LYTTON STRACHEY's 'desperate businesses' at Leamington was for one of the larger, older boys.

Byron said:

My School friendships were with me passions . . .'[2]

It is generally thought these were intellectual and sentimental, yet they were enough to alarm Dr Drury, the headmaster. Hobhouse hints that he knew 'the principal cause and motive of all these boyish friendships'. He says that when the fifteen-year-old Byron had stayed as the guest of Lord Grey, who was then tenant of Newstead, 'a circumstance occurred . . . which . . . had much effect on his future morals'. The boy left but would not say why. Byron told Augusta:

I am not reconciled to Lord Grey, *and I never will be* . . . my reasons for ceasing that Friendship are such as I cannot explain, not even to you . . .[3]

At Cambridge he saved fifteen-year-old John Edleston – 'very thin, very fair complexion, dark eyes, & light locks' – from drowning, and heard him singing in Trinity College Chapel. He described his 'love and passion' as 'violent, though *pure*'. Edleston gave him a heart-shaped stone –

> He offer'd it with downcast look,
> As *fearful* that I might refuse it . . .[4]

Byron told Elizabeth Pigot, one of his older confidantes:

I certainly *love* him more than any human being . . . during the whole of my residence at *Cambridge*, we met every day, summer & Winter . . .[5]

In the second year of his Grand Tour, with the heterosexual Hobhouse out of the way, he travelled with a youth he had previously met, 'my dearly-beloved Eustathios' Georgia. He wrote to his old friend:

. . . I found the dear soul upon horseback clothed very sprucely in Greek Garments, with those ambrosial curls hanging down his amiable back, and . . . a *parasol* in his hand to save his complexion from the heat . . . in spite of

1 To Augusta Byron: 2 Nov. 1804.
2 *Ibid.*
3 26 Mar. 1804.
4 'The Cornelian': *Hours of Idleness* (1807).
5 5 July 1807.

the *Parasol* on we travelled [from Vostiza to Tripolitza] very much enamoured . . .[1]

After Eustathios had been returned to his father, Byron took lodgings in a Capuchin monastery below the Acropolis, where a young boy, Nicolo Giraud, was one of six pupils and taught him Italian.

I am his 'Padrone' and his 'amico' and the Lord knows what besides . . . after informing me that he was most desirous to follow me over the world, he concluded by telling me it was proper for us not only to live, but *morire insieme*.[2]

Byron was woken in the morning by the boys and there were 'scamperings, and eating fruit, and peltings and playings: and I am, in fact, at school again . . .' He called them his 'sylphs', organized boxing matches, and was 'vastly happy and childish'. Summoned home by his agent, there was a painful farewell with Nicolo, whom he put in a school in Malta. On his return to England, he made a will leaving Nicolo £7,000, but this was not repeated in another that he made four years later.

He now heard that John Edleston, his beloved choirboy at Trinity, was dead (the young John Wingfield had also died).

> Thou too art gone, thou loved and lovely one!
> Whom Youth and Youth's affection bound to me . . .[3]

The stanza in *Childe Harold* lamenting the death of his own mother and of his friend Skinner Matthews speaks of him:

> . . . The parent, friend, and now the more than friend . . .[4]

A number of poems to Thyrza are of this time:

> Ours too the glance none saw beside;
> The smile none else might understand;
> The whisper'd thought of hearts allied,
> The pressure of the thrilling hand . . .
>
> The pledge we wore – I wear it still,
> But where is thine? – Ah! where art thou? . . .[5]

1 To Hobhouse: 29 July 1810.
2 *Ditto*: 23 Aug. 1810.
3 *Childe Harold*: Canto II: xcv.
4 Canto II: xcvi.
5 'To Thyrza'. 11 Oct. 1811.

'Tis silent all! – but on my ear
The well remember'd echoes thrill . . .[1]

In the last year of his life, on the island of Metaxata, he found a good-looking Greek page, Loukas Chalandritsanos. He brought him to Missolonghi, but his last passionate love met with a mercenary response. To him he addressed the lines 'On This Day I Complete My Thirty-Sixth Year':

'Tis time this heart should be unmoved,
Since others it hath ceased to move:
Yet, though I cannot be beloved,
Still let me love!

My days are in the yellow leaf;
The flowers and fruits of love are gone . . .

With the onset of serious illness and his hopes of the Greek cause failing, he addressed his last tormented poems to fifteen-year-old Loukas:

. . . and yet thou lov'st me not,
And never wilt! Love dwells not in our will.
Nor can I blame thee, though it be my lot
To strongly, wrongly, vainly love thee still.

1 'Away, Away, Ye Notes of Woe!' 6 Dec. 1811.

CHAPTER THIRTEEN
Homosexuality

I

SWINBURNE's obsession with flagellation, and his friendship in his twenties and thirties with men like Milnes (Lord Houghton), Simeon Solomon, George Howell, George Powell and John Thomson, who all shared his fixation, suggest he had homosexual experience. There are stories of Solomon and him chasing each other naked inside 16 Cheyne Walk – with Rossetti calling in vain to them: 'Stop!' In a letter to Solomon, Swinburne put the childish cypher that he and his cousin Mary had used, as if he were trying to substitute his friend for that early love.

Thomson, as a boy, had introduced Swinburne and other clients to 'the mysterious house in St John's Wood'. He introduced Adah Menken to Swinburne when Rossetti deemed thirty was time a maker of voluptuous verse should know the physical embrace of a woman. Rossetti is said to have paid the ex-dancer and circus performer – the talk of the town, appearing in flesh-coloured tights and strapped to a horse – £10 to seduce his friend. Unlikely as this sounds, a photograph of them together was on sale in the shops. But after the frequent nights at Dorset Street the honest woman returned the money, reporting love-bites and nothing else.

When her son was thirty-three, Lady Swinburne wrote to Rossetti:

. . . he again tells us that he is staying with a friend, a Mr Thomson . . . We do most earnestly wish that he would not take lodgings in Town at all events for the present – and we urged him when he was here to have everything he wanted in the way of furniture and books sent down here . . . it is impossible but a mind like his should require the society of persons with minds and pursuits similar to his own, unless he could make up his mind to remain here as a means of conquering his fearful propensity . . .[1]

1 11 Feb. 1871. Quoted by Philip Henderson: *Swinburne: The Portrait of a Poet* (1974), p. 167.

She wrote to Houghton when Swinburne was forty-one:

I fully appreciate the kind feeling which has made you write to me on the subject of the sad state in which you found my poor Son[1] . . . the case is a most grievous one and seems so hopeless. We have done our utmost to make our home a happy one for him . . .[2]

The following year, Watts-Dunton took him to his own rooms, then to his sister's home, and by the end of the month, 'ailing and broken – thought to be nearly dying . . . Swinburne was brought in a four-wheeler to The Pines',[3] Putney Hill, where he stayed thirty years, the rest of his life.

Solomon was now selling personal and incriminating letters, for, under Watts-Dunton's influence, Swinburne had renounced him after his imprisonment on a homosexual charge. Howell, too, was spreading wild reports. Henceforth, Watts-Dunton's legal training would be on hand. He weaned his friend from brandy to port and, eventually, to a small bottle of Bass's pale ale at lunch. There was a promise never to enter a pub in Putney. But Swinburne's interest in flagellation literature went underground. Like his enthusiasm for de Sade, the subject was taboo. Secure in his haven, he published twenty-three more volumes of poetry, prose and drama. J. K. Jerome recalled a discussion at the Marston Club:

The trouble was that Swinburne's genius would persist in following the line of inverse ratio to his moral improvement . . . The general opinion was that Watts would do better to 'let him rip'.[4]

II

WILDE flirted with several respectable girls at Oxford and, during the Long Vacation in Dublin when he was twenty-one, had a serious love affair with Florence Balcombe – 'an *exquisitely pretty girl*. She is just seventeen . . .'[5] Two years later she turned him down in favour of Bram Stoker.

1 i.e., at 25 Guildford Street.
2 23 July 1878.
3 Max Beerbohm: *And Even Now* (1920), p. 74.
4 *My Life & Times* (1925), pp. 1–2.
5 Letter to Reginald Harding: Aug. 1876. Quoted by Vyvyan Holland: *Son of Oscar Wilde* (1954), p. 223.

He married at thirty Constance Mary Lloyd, another Irish girl, and on their honeymoon waxed eloquent to Sherard about the physical joys of marriage. He seems to have continued deeply in love at least until the birth of Vyvyan, their second son. The story that Constance interrupted her husband in his full flow of conversation with 'Oh, Oscar! *Did* you remember to call for Cyril's boots?' has been answered by Vyvyan in his maturity: men of fashion at that time would not be seen to carry a parcel in the street, nor would middle-class wives have imposed such a chore with two or more servants to hand.

My mother . . . was a woman of considerable culture. She spoke French and Italian fluently, and much of her reading was done in those languages. She may not have had much sense of humour, but then she did not have very much to laugh about.[1]

Two years after marriage, according to Sherard and Ross, he suspended physical relations when he discovered that, contrary to a medical opinion before he proposed, he was not clear from a youthful infection. He may have become a practising homosexual at this time, coincident with his meeting Robert Ross. He was introduced to the Ross family through a Canadian artist who painted his portrait, and nineteen-year-old Ross, before he went up to Cambridge, spent two months with the Wildes in Tite Street while his mother wintered in the South of France. Ross admitted to Frank Harris that he was 'the first boy Oscar ever had'.[2]

Towards the end of June, or the beginning of July, 1891, when Wilde was thirty-six, Lionel Johnson, whom he had the misfortune to know, brought Lord Alfred Douglas ('Bosie') in a cab to Tite Street. Douglas had just completed his second year at Oxford. After tea in his study, Wilde introduced him upstairs to Constance. According to Douglas:

She told me, about a year after I first met her, that she liked me better than any of Oscar's other friends.[3]

In November 1891, Wilde dedicated *A House of Pomegranates* to his wife, but he was living more and more now in a world of his own. When he left his wife with the children in Tite Street to spend two

1 *Ibid.*, pp. 33–4.
2 H. Montgomery Hyde: *Oscar Wilde: A Biography* (1976), p. 185.
3 *Ibid.*, p. 143.

months in Paris, completing *Salomé* and meeting among many French writers André Gide, Proust, and the great actor Coquelin, Lady Wilde, who was very fond of Constance, wrote to her son: '*Do* come home. She is very lonely and mourns for you.'[1] At the time that *Lady Windermere's Fan* was about to open at St James's, a rumour of altercations between Wilde and the producer caused Lady Wilde to advise her son:

. . . do try to be *present yourself at the first performance* . . . Constance would like it. Do not leave her all alone.[2]

He rented a box for himself and his wife – who 'looked charming in her pale brocaded gown made after the fashion of Charles I's time'.[3] After his theatrical triumph she went home to Tite Street, while he took Ross, More Adey, Reggie Turner, Maurice Schwabe, Douglas and several other young men to supper at Willis's.

He presently took the cure in Homberg, cutting down on smoking, rising and going to bed early, and Constance wrote, with a flash of humour: 'I only wish I was there to see it.'[4] The following year they were wintering at Babbacombe Cliff, Torquay, and Constance herself went to stay with friends in Florence, leaving Wilde with the children. Douglas was with him. That summer he took The Cottage, Goring-on-Thames, at the behest of Douglas, who quickly moved in. Constance and the children were already there, but after a short while she took them to the seaside at Dinard, leaving her husband with Douglas.

During these eight or nine years it is conjectural how much she understood. According to Hyde, she suspected her husband 'of having a love affair, not with Alfred Douglas, but with an actress . . . possibly Ellen Terry or Lillie Langtry . . .'[5] Douglas's mother was wont to send Wilde 'endless little notes, marked *Private* on the envelope'. Constance 'used to laugh and say we must be collaborating in a society novel or something of the kind'. Wilde wrote to Douglas of 'strange and troubling personalities walking in painted pageants'.[6] He invited the twenty-one-year-old Edward Shelley, who worked at his publisher's (and was to testify against him), to dine with his wife

1 3 Dec. 1891: *ibid.*, p. 133.
2 8 Feb. 1892: *ibid.*, p. 135.
3 *Ibid.*, p. 136.
4 Letter to her brother, Otho Lloyd: *ibid.*, p. 142.
5 *Ibid.*, pp. 152–3.
6 *Ibid.*, p. 147.

and himself at Tite Street. Professional blackmailers called and tried to sell a letter that Wilde had written to Douglas. The Marquess of Queensbury (Douglas's father) came to the home with a prize-fighter, whom Wilde ejected. Wilde told Sherard later:

Fortune had so turned my head that I fancied I could do what I chose.[1]

In the last year of his freedom he went with Gide and Douglas to Algiers, telling Ross 'the Kabyle boys are quite lovely'.[2]

At 4.30 p.m. on 18 February 1895, Queensberry handed to the porter at the Albemarle Club his card inscribed 'For Oscar Wilde posing as somdomite' (*sic*). It was Wilde's misfortune that Douglas hated his own father, for, incited by Douglas, who contributed towards the cost, and against the advice of Ross, he prosecuted Queensberry for criminal libel.

For two days you . . . feasted your eyes with the spectacle of your father standing in the dock of the Central Criminal Court. And on the third day I took his place . . . In your hideous game of hate together, you had both thrown dice for my soul and you happened to have lost.[3]

Even now his wit did not desert him. Two nights before the trial he ordered a box at the St James's, where *The Importance of Being Earnest* was playing. George Alexander, when he went backstage, reproached him for coming:

'Why don't you withdraw from the case and go abroad?'
'I have just been abroad, and now I have come home again. One can't keep on going abroad, unless one is a missionary.'

When Douglas said good-night to Constance at the theatre, he noted she had tears in her eyes.

I felt dreadfully sorry for her . . . although I then believed that Oscar would beat my father . . .[4]

At this first trial beginning 3 April, Sir Edward Carson defended Queensberry. He began by correcting Wilde's age by a year or so but then, with a crowded court pealing with laughter, he found himself as

1 Robert Harborough Sherard: *Oscar Wilde: The Story of an Unhappy Friendship* (1902), p. 171.
2 H. Montgomery Hyde: *Oscar Wilde: A Biography* (1976), p. 177.
3 *De Profundis* ('The Complete Text': 1949), p. 51.
4 H. Montgomery Hyde: *Oscar Wilde: A Biography* (1976), p. 206.

Complicated Love

disadvantaged here as years before when his Trinity-Dublin contemporary had been placed above him in the examination lists. Until:

'Did you kiss him [Grainger]?'
  'Oh, dear no. He was a peculiarly plain boy . . .'

The staccato *'Why, why, why* was ugliness mentioned?' never let Wilde alone.

On Queensberry's acquittal, Ross and other friends, even a message from Constance, urged him to leave the country. When the boat-train had left, the warrant was signed, and at about half past six that evening he was arrested in the Cadogan Hotel. The Bow Street magistrate withheld bail, and while Wilde lay in Holloway Prison his creditors put the bailiffs into the house in Tite Street, described by Sherard as 'a very temple of lettered ease'.[1] Valuable paintings and china went for knock-down sums. Presentation copies he had received from leading writers of the day, Whistler etchings given him by the artist, passed hands for a shilling or two. Some of his manuscripts and even personal letters from his wife were stolen.

After three weeks he made his second appearance at the Old Bailey, his first time in the dock. It says much for the impression Wilde had made, or for his charisma, that Sir Edward Clarke, hitherto a stranger, provided his services free throughout, in spite of being misled by his client in chambers that Queensberry's charges were 'absolutely false and groundless'. Wilde consistently refused to put Douglas on the stand against his father. He made the eloquent speech:

'The Love that dare not speak its name' in this century is such a great affection of an elder for a younger man as there was between David and Jonathan, such as Plato made the very basis of his philosophy, and such as you find in the sonnets of Michelangelo and Shakespeare . . . It is beautiful, it is fine, it is the noblest form of affection. There is nothing unnatural about it. It is intellectual, and it repeatedly exists between an elder and a younger man, where the elder has intellect and the younger man has all the joy, hope, and glamour of life before him.

On the jury being unable to reach a decision, he was now placed on bail. A gang of roughs, hired by Queensberry, followed him around to prevent his admittance to any hotel. Eventually, towards midnight, having managed to shake them off, he came to his mother's house in

1 Robert Harborough Sherard: *Oscar Wilde: The Story of an Unhappy Friendship* (1902), p. 105.

Oakley Street and said to his brother, 'Give me shelter, Willie. Let me lie on the floor, or I shall die in the streets.'[1]

Carson, who refused to have anything to do with subsequent proceedings, had asked the Solicitor-General, Sir Frank Lockwood, if he could not now 'let up on the fellow' who had 'suffered a great deal'. But there was to be a third appearance. Lockwood made his

appalling denunciation of me – like a thing out of Tacitus . . . like one of Savonarola's indictments of the Popes of Rome . . .[2]

On 24 May, he was sentenced to 'be imprisoned and kept to hard labour for two years'. Outside the court-house Sherard said to Ernest Dowson:

'This is a trial in which, out of nine people incriminated, eight have been admitted to act as Queen's Evidence.'[3]

Wilde passed into Pentonville Prison and six weeks later was transferred to Wandsworth, where he wanted to die. The regime still had the treadmill, and clothes with broad arrows. Wilde's industrial employment was oakum picking. Early on, it seems, for talking on exercise he was put into solitary, in a dark cell; he told Frank Harris: 'There is a punishment here more terrible than the rack . . . They can drive you mad in a week, Frank.'[4] He said, later, that 'three permanent punishments' were 'authorised by law in English prisons' – hunger, insomnia (from cold and the initial plank bed: 'The object of the plank bed is to produce insomnia'),[5] and disease (diarrhoea, a consequence of the diet).

On 21 September, Constance was authorized a special visit and travelled from the Continent to see him. She told Sherard it was more awful than she had any conception it could be: 'I could not see him and I could not touch him . . .'[6] Three days later, he was brought to the Bankruptcy Court in Carey Street, where in the corridor, before the crowd, Ross was waiting so

1 Robert Harborough Sherard: *Oscar Wilde: The Story of an Unhappy Friendship* (1902), p. 163.
2 *De Profundis* ('The Complete Text', 1949), p. 131.
3 Sherard: *op. cit.*, p. 200.
4 Frank Harris: *Oscar Wilde* (2nd edn., 1938), p. 233.
5 Letter to *The Daily Chronicle*: 24 Mar. 1898.
6 Robert Harborough Sherard: *Oscar Wilde: The Story of an Unhappy Friendship* (1902), p. 209.

. . . he might gravely raise his hat to me, as, handcuffed and with bowed head, I passed him by.[1]

About ten days after that, accused of malingering by the prison doctor, he was trying to dress himself, when he fell, injuring one of his ears. For several weeks he was in the Prison Infirmary.

On 13 November, from 2.0 to 2.30 p.m., he had to stand on the centre platform of Clapham Junction, in convict dress and handcuffed, before the train arrived to take him to Reading Gaol.

Each train as it came up swelled the audience . . . For half an hour I stood there in the grey November rain surrounded by a jeering mob.[2]

So that he would not hear it from indifferent lips, his wife travelled from Genoa to Reading, ill as she was, to break the news of his mother's death.

A petition for his early release, largely drawn up by Shaw, had to be abandoned for lack of signatures. His own unsuccessful petition to the Home Secretary, when a little more than half his sentence had been served, speaks of 'the three years preceding his arrest', during which time 'he was suffering from the most horrible form of eroto-mania, which made him forget his wife and children . . .'[3] The long letter *De Profundis*, written in prison to Douglas, contains a moving peroration which makes admission of sickness:

. . . but Nature . . . will cleanse me in great waters, and with bitter herbs make me whole.[4]

On release he wanted to go into a retreat for six months, but his request was refused by the priests of Farm Street – tragically, in view of his subsequent regression. He assumed the name of Sebastian Melmoth and, accompanied by More Adey, went to Dieppe, where Ross and Reggie Turner were waiting to greet him. After a week or so he settled at Berneval.

Sherard worked hard to bring about a reconciliation with his wife and children, but her family alienated her from him. When Wilde had exhausted his meagre funds and resumed friendship with Douglas in Naples, she wrote:

1 *De Profundis* ('The Complete Text', 1949), p. 68.
2 *Ibid.*, p. 116.
3 H. Montgomery Hyde: *Oscar Wilde: A Biography* (1976), p. 188.
4 (1949 edn. *cit.*) p. 145.

I forbid you to return to your filthy, insane life. I forbid you to live at Naples.[1]

Douglas had now become for her 'that dreadful person'. Suffering from spinal paralysis, the consequence of a fall down a whole flight of stairs shortly before she had left Tite Street, she died at thirty-eight, the year following his release.

The Marquess controlled his son by stopping his allowance and Wilde came back to Paris, staying at the Hôtel d'Alsace. Laurence Housman met him at the café Vieille Rose, in the company of Ross and other friends:

. . . the impression left upon me from that occasion is that Oscar Wilde was incomparably the most accomplished talker I had ever met.[2]

Three years after leaving prison Wilde died, aged forty-six.

III

On the traumatic death of his mother, twelve-year-old A. E. HOUSMAN found feminine comfort and friendship not with his sisters, who were younger, but with sixteen-year-old Edith Wise, the daughter of his godmother, and with the German governess in their family, Sophie Becker. Miss Becker, then in her early thirties, became a mother figure and when she died at ninety, not long after his seventy-fifth birthday, he told Dr Withers he had possessed only three friends, all associated with youth and early manhood. Deeply shaken, he said he had loved and reverenced Sophie.

His brothers and sisters thought that in his boyhood he was secretly in love with Edith and teased him about his rambles with her on Selsley Hill, but both of them were to remain unmarried. Visiting her, and corresponding with Sophie (then in Germany), were the real pleasures of his life. Edith died when he was seventy-one.

He was at least fourteen when his father decided that the four boys should be circumcised. Alfred's sister Kate thought later that it was not 'to fulfil a scriptural rite . . . but on sanitary mosaic lines'. She considered it 'severe treatment . . . for well-grown boys'. Robert was

1 29 Sept. 1897. Quoted by Wilde in his letter to More Adey. (Hyde, *op. cit.*, pp. 338–9.)
2 *Echo de Paris: A Study from Life* (1923), p. 15.

thirteen, Basil nine and Laurence eight. Richard Perceval Graves uses stronger language in suggesting it was 'particularly traumatic for boys well out of infancy . . . and . . . must have helped to make sexual activity seem dirty to Alfred'.[1]

When he first went up to Oxford, Edith and Sophie were his closest friends and he longed to be with them. During his third year there he met Moses Jackson, almost one year his senior, both scientist and athlete when Housman was neither, yet 'the man who had more influence on my life than anybody else'.[2] In old age he declared that Oxford had not much effect on him, 'except that I there met my greatest friend'. In their last year, they and Alfred Pollard took five rooms together 'in a picturesque old house' nearly opposite St John's. After dining in Hall of an evening, they crossed St Giles to their lodgings for coffee and Pollard usually retired to work in the lower sitting-room, leaving the others talking on the first floor.

Their intimacy was renewed when Housman was working at the Patent Office, like Jackson, who held a higher position. They shared a set of rooms at 82 Talbot Road, Bayswater, a younger brother, Adalbert Jackson, taking the place of Pollard. It was during three years there that Housman's attachment to Moses deepened from affection to love. Kate said that after Oxford her brother's life was very much 'a sealed book' to his family. When his brother Laurence and their other sister, Clem, came to take lodgings in Kennington, Alfred never introduced them to the Jacksons. Moses had no idea that his friend had a brother and sister living in London until they were introduced by Pollard.

When Alfred was twenty-six, he seems to have realized that Moses's feelings towards him were simply of friendship and, after disappearing for a week, he presently moved to 39 Northumberland Place. Perhaps from this time he faced the fact that he was homosexual.

They continued to visit each other often, and then Moses went to become principal of a college in Karachi. Two years later, he returned on leave for his wedding. He came to Alfred at the Patent Office, but it was not until he had taken his bride back to India that Alfred knew the marriage had taken place. He congratulated Moses, and again after a son had been born. A poem declared his love:

1 *A. E. Housman: The Scholar-Poet* (1979), pp. 21-2.
2 From an article by Laurence Housman in *Encounter*, Oct. 1967. Quoted by R. P. Graves: *ibid.*, p. 190.

> . . . But if you come to a road where danger
> Or guilt or anguish or shame's to share,
> Be good to the lad that loves you true
> And the soul that was born to die for you,
> And whistle and I'll be there.[1]

When Housman was forty-nine and Professor of Latin at University College, London, Moses came home briefly on leave, apparently without his family. Pollard, who had also married, invited them to dinner and offered accommodation for the night. The spirit of the old St Giles's days was recaptured and either the Principal or the Professor was responsible for their apple-pie beds.

Thirteen years later, Moses emigrated with his family to Canada. It was now extremely unlikely he and Housman should ever see each other again. They continued to correspond and, a year before he died in a Vancouver hospital, Moses received a copy of Housman's *Last Poems*, its dedication from 'a fellow who thinks more of you than anything in the world'.[2] Laurence Housman in old age told an American biographer that, after Moses had gone to India, Alfred was physically attracted to Adalbert Jackson and his feelings were reciprocated.

On Wilde's release from prison, Alfred sent him a copy of *A Shropshire Lad*, 'with the best wishes of the author'. Laurence, who shared homosexual tendencies, sent his own *All-Fellows: seven legends of lower Redemption*. Wilde replied to Laurence that both their books had arrived by the same post:

Thus, you and your brother have given me a few moments of that rare thing called happiness.[3]

At forty-one, following a holiday in Switzerland Alfred travelled on to Milan and Venice, taking an introduction from his colleague, Walter Ashburner, to Horatio Brown, a long-standing friend of the homosexual writer John Addington Symonds. Alfred followed Symonds's example, and also Byron's, in befriending a gondolier, twenty-three-year-old Andrea. For seven years Alfred visited him in Venice. He then went more frequently to indulge 'the vices of Paris'. A document in his handwriting apparently lists a large number of

1 *More Poems* (1936), no. 30.
2 George L. Watson: *A. E. Housman: A Divided Life* (1957), p. 211.
3 Laurence Housman: *Echo de Paris: A Study from Life* (1923), p. 14.

male prostitutes visited within just over a fortnight, and the prices. He also took an interest in pornographic books banned in England. Then, after a long absence, Andrea, now married and lying seriously ill, sent for Housman. At sixty-seven he came, and provided money regularly until Andrea died four years later.

With photos of Adalbert as a young man and Moses in late middle age above the fireplace in his Tower room at Trinity, the atheist professor thanked God he had lived to know Sophie 'safely laid to rest' and that 'comfortably he could meet death now his three friends were at peace'.[1]

IV

When MAUGHAM was eighty-seven, he told his nephew:

I'm bisexual, but for the sake of my reputation I don't care to advertise the fact . . . I've loved girls and I've loved boys, I've loved women and I've loved men.[2]

He said, the following year, that he was 'a quarter normal and three-quarters queer'[3] but had tried to persuade himself it was the other way round – adding that Syrie, his wife, had thrown herself at his feet and ruined his life.

Beverley Nichols wondered who, other than Syrie, were the women in Maugham's life. Maugham claimed that Rosie had been his mistress for eight years and given him the idea for *Cakes and Ale*. There was also 'Olga X'. His friendship with Barbara Black, probably his happiest, was free from emotional involvement.

For thirty years, even from the time of his marriage, his 'chief care . . . pleasure, and . . . anxiety' had been Gerald Haxton, nearly twenty years younger.

The best years of my life – those we spent wandering about the world – are inextricably connected with him.

Gerald saved his life in Borneo. A 'great mass of water . . . caught the boat and turned it over' – and Gerald gave himself a heart attack

1 Percy Withers: *A Buried Life* (1940), p. 129.
2 Robin Maugham: *Conversations with Willie: Recollections of W. Somerset Maugham* (1978), p. 114.
3 *Ibid.*, p. 140.

getting Maugham to the riverbank. Beverley Nichols stayed at the Le Touquet villa and heard Gerald groaning and staggering about in the night. He found him, always a heavy drinker, naked on the floor being sick and covered with thousand-franc notes won from the casino. Then Maugham came in, his face 'contorted' with rage and jealousy, and shouted to Nicols to get out. When Gerald died in New York, aged only fifty-two – 'and I had every right to think that he would have survived me' – Maugham was 'lost and lonely and hopeless'.[1]

The following year, Alan Searle succeeded him as secretary and devoted companion. They returned from America to Cap Ferrat, and re-established the Villa Mauresque after enemy and allied occupation. He bore with Maugham's increasing melancholy for twenty years, and towards the end found it hard to get away for even half an hour a day. Thirty years younger than Maugham, he told Robin Maugham:

This isn't a life. It's a nightmare . . .[2]

Robin believed that without Searle his uncle would have gone mad or killed himself. Nichols wrote that the Master's devotion to Alan Searle 'was one of the best things in his life . . . in Gerald it was the evil that fascinated him and in Alan the good'.[3] Maugham asked that Searle should follow his body to the crematorium alone and take the ashes to his old school.

Sir OSBERT SITWELL and David Horner, eight years his junior, were together twenty-five years.

V

RADCLYFFE HALL was christened Marguerite, a name abandoned in favour of Peter and then, more permanently, John. She was a beautiful child, but the suspicion that she was not 'normal' may have motivated her mother's dislike. Her mother told her: 'Your hands . . . are just like Radclyffe's [her father] . . .'[4]

From the age of seventeen, she fell in and out of love with members

1 *Ibid.*, p. 81.
2 *Ibid.*, p. 152.
3 *A Case of Human Bondage* (1966), p. 31.
4 Vera Brittain: *Radclyffe Hall: A Case of Obscenity?* (1968), p. 32.

of her own sex. Her long love affair with 'Ladye' began when Mrs George Batten was a beautiful woman of fifty and Radclyffe twenty-seven. There were holidays in Morocco, Corsica, Rome and Monte Carlo. Together they bought White Cottage, Malvern. When she was thirty-two, Radclyffe came to know Ladye's cousin, Una Troubridge, in her twenties. After Ladye's death from a car accident in which Radclyffe had been unhurt, her affection for Una became in the end essential to both. They established a joint home in Chelsea and then Kensington.

At forty-four, having made her name with *Adam's Breed*, she wanted to write an imaginative study of inversion, recognizing that such a book might mean the end of her career. *The Well of Loneliness*, published the following year, was dedicated to 'Our Three Selves', subsequently disclosed by Lady Troubridge as referring to Radclyffe, herself, and Mabel Veronica Batten (Mrs George Batten). It was reviewed by Vera Brittain in *Time and Tide*[1] as 'a plea, passionate, yet admirably restrained and never offensive, for . . . social toleration, compassion and recognition . . .' A week later, after pre-advertisement in its news columns with extracts in leaded type, James Douglas, editor of *The Sunday Express*, wrote that he 'would rather give a healthy boy or a healthy girl a phial of prussic acid than this novel . . . I appeal to the Home Secretary to set the law in motion . . .', and cited Oscar Wilde. Jonathan Cape withdrew the book, and wrote in *Then and Now*:

It is a book for a special public, and in the course of time would have reached that public through the personal recommendation of thoughtful people . . . Serious and fine work has claims on the publisher . . . That the book will pass into oblivion we do not believe . . .[2]

But secretly they sent the moulds to a firm in Paris. The book was reprinted by Pegasus Press and copies were imported into England, to be seized whenever they were discovered. The Director of Public Prosecutions applied for an Order under the Obscene Publications Act of 1857.

The proceedings opened at Bow Street on 9 November 1928. Norman Birkett, KC, represented Cape, and was prevented from calling thirty-nine witnesses including Forster, Desmond MacCarthy, Storm Jameson, Victoria Sackville-West, the Woolfs, Hugh Walpole,

1 12 Aug. 1928.
2 n.d. [no date], pp. 23–4.

Mrs Cecil Chesterton, Victor Gollancz, Vera Brittain, Edward Garnett, Charles Ricketts. Vera Brittain in her study of the case relates how the Chief Magistrate, Sir Chartres Biron, was unimpressed even by Professor Julian Huxley and the Registrar of Durham University – 'I reject them all'.[1] Shaw had declined to give evidence for the reason he was 'immoral' himself. Galsworthy (President of PEN) had disappointingly refused to appear, as had Anthony Hope. Birkett introduced a new plea that the relations between women described in the book represented a normal friendship, and in the lunch interval Radclyffe attacked him for this with 'tears of heart-broken anguish'. Birkett, by now warmly appreciative of her as a person, became acutely distressed that, as the law stood, he could do so little for her.

When the hearing resumed after a week's adjournment, Sir Chartres quoted a passage from the book concerning women ambulance drivers at the Front. 'I protest!' Radclyffe cried. 'I emphatically protest!'

Sir Chartres retorted: 'I must ask you to be quiet.'

'I am the author of this book – '

'If you cannot behave yourself in court, I shall have to have you removed.'

'Shame!' she shouted from her seat at the solicitor's table. Sir Chartres made an order for the seized copies to be destroyed, and on 27 November two hundred and forty-seven were flung into the furnace at Scotland Yard.

At the Appeal,[2] Kipling and Dr Marie Stopes were present. The Chairman, Sir Robert Wallace, announced:

In the view of the Court it is a most dangerous and corrupting book . . . Put in a word . . . this is a disgusting book . . . It is an obscene book . . .

In America, the following year, the book was pronounced 'not in violation of the law'. The Kensington house, which Radclyffe and Una had shared for several years, was sacrificed to help legal costs.

Radclyffe, a convinced Catholic, undertook in *The Master of the House* a study of Christ as a young man. Vera Brittain has pointed out that this book and *Adam's Breed* and *The Sixth Beatitude* contained nothing 'to suggest her sexual peculiarities . . .'

1 *Radclyffe Hall: A Case of Obscenity?* (1968), p. 92.
2 14 Dec. 1928.

Their religious spirit is in poignant contrast to the supposed reputation conferred upon their author by pornographers and scandalmongers.[1]

After several years Radclyffe and Una went to stay in Sirmione, where Naomi Jacob lived. They established themselves at the Albergo Catullo and visited Naomi's villa every morning. A well-to-do woman in her own right, Radclyffe left £118,015 to Una who was directed to destroy her latest book.

VI

In KATHERINE MANSFIELD's life, the ambiguous Ida Baker was as important as Middleton Murry, but Ida had known Katherine from the age of fourteen at Queen's College. The tall blonde girl had shown the Beauchamp sisters their room when they arrived.

Katherine was drawn to another girl in the College, also slightly older, Vere Bartrick-Baker. They would hold literary conversations in the school's dark lower corridor and seem to have been suspected of 'immorality' by the Lady Resident, Miss Camilla Croudace (herself given to favouritism). They once exchanged kisses on the top of Westminster Cathedral.

On the crossing home to New Zealand, her parents noticed she attracted women as well as men. Now, at eighteen, she experienced her first passionate love affairs with girls. One was Maata Mahupuku, a Maori girl – a schoolfriend in Wellington, who had also been to London. Katherine wrote in her *Journal*:

I want Maata – I want her as I have had her – terribly. This is unclean I know but true . . . I feel . . . almost powerfully enamoured of the child.[2]

Among modern authors recommended to Katherine and Vere by their young German professor, Walter Rippman, at Queen's College had been Oscar Wilde. Katherine wrote to an unidentified friend:

In New Zealand Wilde acted so strongly and terribly upon me that I was constantly subject to exactly the same fits of madness as those which caused his ruin and his mental decay . . . I think my mind is morally unhinged . . .[3]

1 *Radclyffe Hall: A Case of Obscenity?* (1968), p. 73.
2 29 June 1907. See Antony Alpers: *The Life of Katherine Mansfield* (1980), pp. 49, 430 Note 15.
3 1909. *Ibid.*, p. 91.

(In his old age, Bowden described to Alpers the second time he met her at a musical party: 'She looked like Oscar Wilde.'[1])

Another of her fascinations in New Zealand was a professional artist of exceptional beauty, Edith Kathleen Bendall, nine years older than she. Katherine wrote in her *Journal*:

She enthrals . . . me . . . her body absolute – is my worship . . . pillowed against her . . . I am a child, a woman, and more than half man.

Again:

I drew close to her warm sweet body, happier . . . than I could ever have imagined being . . .[2]

During this time she also heard 'constantly' from Ida, about whom she wrote to her cousin: 'You know I love her very much indeed . . .'[3] On Katherine's return to England, it was Ida – 'the only person who . . . believes in me'[4] – waiting as the boat-train drew in.

After Katherine had left him on their wedding-night, Bowden rationalized the cause as lesbianism and her own mother concurred, calling in Ida's father, who sent his daughter on a cruise to the Canaries. The two women came together again when Katherine was very ill after an operation. Ida fetched her in a taxi and nursed her in her own flat in Marylebone Road. Later, at 131 Cheyne Walk, she would disconcert visitors by suddenly appearing from a curtained-off bedroom.

Katherine's feelings towards her were ambivalent. In Switzerland with Murry, she called her 'my wife'; at other times Ida was 'an albatross' about her neck. At a party at Hampstead she was made to wait at table. Katherine wrote to Murry from San Remo:

My deadly deadly enemy has got me today . . . Her great fat arms, her tiny blind breasts . . . her eyes fixed on me . . . waiting for what I shall do so that [she] may copy it.[5]

Ida bore insults and rages; she sacrificed her independence because Katie in sickness called: '. . . in my horrid odious, intolerable way I

1 Antony Alpers: *The Life of Katherine Mansfield* (1980), p. 87.
2 1 June 1907. *Journal of Katherine Mansfield* ed. J. Middleton Murry (1954), pp. 12–14.
3 To Sylvia Payne: 4 Mar. 1908.
4 Ida Baker: *Katherine Mansfield: The Memories of LM* (1971), p. 31.
5 20 Nov. 1919. Alpers: *op cit.*, p. 302.

love you . . ." Faithful, indispensable, she became more of a surrogate mother. Back with Murry in Switzerland, Katherine wrote:

The truth is I can't really work unless I know you are *there*.

Six months from her death, she wrote:

I feel I cannot live without you.

VII

At first, RATTIGAN seems to have hoped that his homosexuality at Harrow and at Oxford might be temporary, and then he had the problem of separating his heterosexual friends from the others, and keeping his homosexual friends from the knowledge of his mother who often lived with him at Sunningdale. For most of his life, together with others like him, he lived in fear of criminal prosecution.[2]

The suicide of one of his friends, Kenneth Morgan, inspired the writing of *The Deep Blue Sea*, which in its original version told the story of a homosexual love affair ending in tragedy. Rattigan had begun to be very deeply attracted to this actor six years after they had first met, when Morgan played in the film version of *French Without Tears*. Now thirty-four, Rattigan was breaking away from the emotional possessiveness of a considerably older man, Henry ('Chips') Channon. The affair with Morgan was a similarly unequal relationship, but with roles reversed – Rattigan in pursuit of a younger man of twenty-seven. Morgan, in his turn, felt unable to reciprocate with the same intensity of involvement and turned to another man, who then left him increasingly by himself and was, in fact, bisexual. A few months afterwards, Morgan took an overdose of sleeping tablets and gassed himself. Overwhelmed with grief, Rattigan blamed himself, and the lessons he learnt affected the rest of his life. Never again would he allow himself to be so heavily committed to another man.

In his early forties, a four-year relationship with a young ballet dancer, Adrian Brown, roused jealousy from Michael Franklin, an

1 Baker: *op cit.*, p. 197.
2 The recommendations of the Wolfenden Report (1957), that private homosexual liaisons between consenting adults be removed from criminal law, were implemented in the Sexual Offences Act (1967) when Rattigan was fifty-five.

interior designer, criticized by Rattigan's other friends for showing ingratitude. But Rattigan did not reject Franklin – who, later on, arranged the decor of Rattigan's three properties. Another companion was Robin Maugham, who was persuaded by Rattigan to publish *Wrong People*, a novel with a homosexual theme. At forty-eight, he told Robert Muller in an interview:

I may be a success as a writer, but as a person I am not.[1]

Although his mother used to wonder why there were 'so many young men and so few girls at Terence's parties',[2] and although he claimed that a VD infection from a prostitute when he was at Oxford had finally put him off women, he was not averse to female company. When he was forty-two, Jean Dawnay, a top fashion model played hostess at his house party in honour of the Oliviers. Jean and he became so close that his mother actually contemplated their marriage. At fifty, when he sold his estate in Sunningdale for Bedford House in Brighton, a bedroom was kept for the exclusive use of the actress Margaret Leighton – who provided another talking-point for journalists. It was a restless time for him, during which he began to drink heavily.

When he collapsed with a fever at Eaton Square, Sheila Dyatt, his new secretary, stayed to nurse him throughout an Easter Bank Holiday in the absence of anyone else. She made the discovery that Lady Cynthia Asquith, Barrie's secretary, made, that the celebrated man was often lonely:

. . . lots of people . . . liked him, but no one . . . really cared for him.[3]

Other homosexuals were Henry Kingsley, Sir Edward Marsh, Saki, Lytton Strachey, Rupert Brooke, E. M. Forster, Mary Renault, Auden, Isherwood, and, in our own day, Sir Angus Wilson, Peter Ackroyd and A. L. Rowse. Among those who were bisexual, Sir Harold Nicolson, like Wilde, had two sons; John Addington Symonds and Sir Edmund Gosse each had three children. Gosse was described by Lytton Strachey as not homosexual but 'Hamo-sexual', referring to his lifelong passion for Hamo Thornycroft – a witticism less

1 *The Daily Mail*: 23 Sept. 1959.
2 Michael Darlow & Gillian Hodson: *Terence Rattigan: The Man & His Work* (1979), p. 213.
3 *Ibid.*, p. 274.

offensive than Swinburne's 'Mr Soddington Symonds'. Gosse's biographer hints that his marriage may have reflected in part the Nicolsons':[1]

. . . the very depth of the love that he and Nellie shared seemed to make it possible for him to explore other, more dangerous feelings. She seems to have understood and to have tolerated his passion, sure of his devotion to her.[2]

DAPHNE DU MAURIER, mother of two daughters and a son, saw herself 'a half-breed'.[3] The child – 'so feminine and fair'[4] – believed that inside she was a boy, the son her father, Sir Gerald, was denied. She (like her younger sister Jeanne) dressed in boys' clothes. In early teens she chose an alter ego, 'Eric Avon'. Then, with puberty, this boy in her was 'locked up in a box'.[5] At eighteen he broke out when she was sent to a finishing school near Paris and began to love, with a boy's love, one of the teachers, Fernande Yvon ('Ferdy'). He broke out again, at forty, when she fell in love with Ellen, wife of her American publisher, Nelson Doubleday – but *she* reciprocated her affection not her sexuality. Daphne put her feelings for Ellen in the ambiguous play *September Tide*, and that was how she met Gertrude Lawrence – 'my dearest friend' – who was cast as the star. For a period of eighteen months they were lovers. When Gertie died, she was bereft.

EVELYN WAUGH entered a short, but extreme phase, of homosexuality when he was at Oxford.

1 See p. 135.
2 Ann Thwaite: *Edmund Gosse: a literary landscape* (1984), p. 196.
3 See Margaret Forster: *Daphne du Maurier* (1993), p. 418.
4 Her father's poem to her: 'My very slender one . . .' *c.* 1920 (?). *Ibid.*, p. 13.
5 Her letter to Ellen Doubleday, Dec. 1947. *Ibid.*, p. 28.

CHAPTER FOURTEEN
Sexual Extravagances

Asmall group shared a tormented drive to inflict penance and pain upon their flesh. Before his marriage, CHARLES KINGS-LEY arranged with his future wife a weekly festival and fast. At 11.0 p.m., every Thursday, they imagined 'those thrilling writhings' when they would 'lie in each other's arms'.[1] At 10.0 p.m., every Friday, she 'agonized' in the knowledge that, to allay the guilt of his sexuality (he confessed to have gone with a prostitute at Cambridge), he stripped himself naked and scourged himself. While he waited till he could undress her 'with my own hands and cover you all over with burning kisses', this curate of Eversley went on All Saints' Day 'into the woods at night and lay naked upon thorns and when I came home my body was torn from head to foot'.[2]

In a letter to his 'Dear Woman', he enclosed instruction for the making of a pair of hair shirts: 'the coarsest and roughest [canvas] you can get . . . as tight as you can make them . . . And make yourself two also, of the same pattern . . .'[3]

In the year SWINBURNE, at twenty-eight, published *Atalanta in Calydon*, he became a regular client at a sumptuous brothel, probably at 7 Circus Road, St John's Wood, to be whipped by one of two blonde ladies. A week before that first visit, his cousin Mary Gordon had turned him down for a middle-aged colonel in the 106th Light Infantry, and Swinburne now played out in fantasy his Eton floggings at a cost to his health.

> But you, had you chosen, had you stretched hand,
> Had you seen good such a thing were done,
> I too might have stood with the souls that stand
> In the sun's sight, clutched with the light of the sun![4]

1 Susan Chitty: *The Beast & The Monk: A Life of Charles Kingsley* (1974), p. 81.
2 *Ibid.*, p. 75.
3 *Ibid.*, p. 80.
4 'The Triumph of Time': *Poems & Ballads* (1866).

Gosse pointed out the paradox that Swinburne's arcane life 'existed, as it were, outside his morality'. He never boasted of his excesses, nor did he recommend them to others.

He was a perfectly safe companion for youth, and to those who were temperate and innocent he seemed to have himself preserved both temperance and innocence.[1]

At least two years after Swinburne's arrival at The Pines most of the unpublished *Flogging Block* was written, and 'Eclogue I Algernon's Flogging' at least six years later still. In its harrowing detail, and in spite of the voyeuristic enjoyment of the other boys, always he sides with the victim and not the tormentor. He saw the act as a duel having much to do with honour and calling for heroism which, Randolph Hughes argues, 'sharply differentiates' Swinburne's conception from that of de Sade.[2]

T. E. LAWRENCE, on enlisting in the Royal Tank Corps as T. E. Shaw and being posted to Bovington Camp, Dorset, engaged a tough Scots fellow-trooper, Jock Bruce, to deliver severe flagellation. He paid him £3 a week, and invented a relative – 'the Old Man' – who demanded the punishment on pain of exposing his illegitimacy. It has been conjectured that Lawrence was trying to repeat the Deraa experience, his claimed homosexual assault by the Turks, which may have been the only occasion on which he had abandoned himself sexually. After his death, many of his contemporaries compared his rejection of fame to a mediaeval withdrawal into a monastery. H. Montgomery Hyde has suggested that the beatings were in the nature of a penance rather than a perversion. Langton recounted as an example of JOHNSON's masochism the occasion when they were swimming together near Oxford: he cautioned Johnson against a particularly dangerous pool, whereupon Johnson directly swam into it.

The vagaries of ERIC GILL, sometimes bizarre, were nearly always unabashed. When he was a pupil at the Central School of Arts and Crafts, he recorded in his diary a sexual encounter with an old woman on Clapham Common, which Fiona MacCarthy says 'in retrospect he

---

1 Essay accompanying *The Confidential Papers* lodged by Gosse in BM, 1920.
2 Swinburne: *Lesbia Brandon* ed. Randolph Hughes (1952): 'An historical & critical commentary &c.', p. 505.

seems to slightly shudder at'.[1] At thirty-two, while receiving instruction for his entry into the Roman Catholic Church, he carved a life-size marble phallus modelled on his own 'most precious ornament'. He later made scrupulous drawings of the genitalia of his male friends. When he was forty-seven, he records on two occasions an experiment with a dog, and his discovery that 'a dog will join with a man'.[2] Dr Flood, the chaplain at Pigotts, showed some of Gill's erotica to a psychologist, who said that the man who made them was more than highly sexed – 'he must have had a particular phallic fixation'.[3]

Such intimate aspects of remarkable people speak of the complex nature of human beings, and the mystery of genius in certain individuals.

1 *Eric Gill* (1989), p. 47.
2 *Ibid.*, p. 239.
3 Robert Speaight: *The Life of Eric Gill* (1966), p. 179.

PART FOUR
PARENTHOOD

CHAPTER ONE
Creativity and Children

Meredith's son, Will, was misinformed about Barrie being 'born to a mother – long after the rest of her family',[1] and went on to conclude:

. . . & so often is the case – with genius but little virility.[2]

The childless marriages of Blake, Hardy, Shaw,[3] T. S. Eliot, D. H. Lawrence, and many more – George Herbert, Pepys, Carlyle, Ruskin, Stevenson, the Webbs, Galsworthy, Beerbohm, Chesterton, Barrie himself – seem to be extending what Will Meredith said about genius and virility. There is the childless union of George Eliot and Lewes, father of four; she was thirty-four when they went to Germany together. Johnson married a widow twenty-two years older than he. Disraeli married a widow of forty-six. Leonard Woolf consulted two doctors and they were strongly against Virginia having children.

We followed their advice.[4]

Orwell believed himself sterile, although it was probably due to Eileen that they were unable to have children of their own.

Many maintained a 'passionate celibacy': Swift, Pope, Horace Walpole, Gibbon, Rogers, Jane Austen, Keats, Macaulay, and Henry James; together with Newton, Prior, Gray, Gilbert White, Goldsmith, Cowper, Lamb, Newman, Edward Lear, Anne and Emily Brontë, Palgrave, R. D. Blackmore, Christina Rossetti, Dodgson, *Erewhon* Butler, Pater, Gerard Manley Hopkins, A. C. Bradley, Francis Thompson . . . There is George Moore – although it is

1 Barrie was the ninth child of ten.
2 Letter to Charles Scribner: 9 Nov. 1909.
3 Shaw confided to Thomas O'Bolger: 'There never was any question of breeding; my wife had a morbid horror of maternity; and as she was forty it was too late to begin, without serious risk . . .' 12 Apr. 1916. (*Bernard Shaw: Collected Letters* ed. Dan Lawrence [1965–88], iii, p. 382.)
4 Leonard Woolf: *Beginning Again* (1964), p. 82.

possible that Nancy Cunard was his natural child. Among more recent celibates were Edith Sitwell, Ronald Knox, T. E. Lawrence, Wilfred Owen, R. C. Sherriff, Winifred Holtby. There are those who preferred their own kind.[1]

Yet impressive though all this may be, we have to remind ourselves that Donne fathered twelve children, Sir Thomas Browne the same number, and Richard Lovell Edgeworth twenty-two. Marryat sired eleven, Darwin ten, Dickens eleven. Pursuing these filial stakes we find that Spenser had four children, Shakespeare three, Izaak Walton nine, Evelyn eight, Defoe eight, Blackstone nine, Boswell seven, Scott four, Wordsworth six, Coleridge four, Southey eight, Francis Trollope five, Leigh Hunt seven, De Quincey eight, Shelley five, Mrs Gaskell six, Kingsley four, Sir Leslie Stephen four, Doyle five, Wells five, Belloc five . . . Included in these figures are Wordsworth's illegitimate daughter Caroline, and the assumption of Dickens's illegitimate son, as well as the natural children of Boswell and Wells where known.

Chaucer's family remain obscure, but he compiled his *Treatise on the Astrolabe* for 'Litel Lowis my sone'. Ben Jonson, it appears, was married with several children. Among more modern names can be cited: Churchill with five children, Priestley five, Evelyn Waugh six, Malcolm Muggeridge four, C. Day Lewis four, H. E. Bates four, A. J. P. Taylor six, Nigel Balchin five, William Douglas-Home four, Roald Dahl five, Robert Bolt four . . .

Of those who were bisexual, Wilde, Symonds, Gosse, Maugham and Nicolson all had children.

1 See pp. 215–34.

CHAPTER TWO

Enjoying Their Children

I

I if Wilde is right about cruelty being 'the entire want of imagination',[1] it should not be surprising that writers (and artists generally) make loving parents. RICHARD STEELE wrote to his wife, who was looking after her estate in Wales:

Your son at the present writing is mighty well employed in tumbling on the floor of the room and sweeping the sand with a feather. He grows a most delightful child, and very full of play and spirit.[2]

COLERIDGE, at twenty-four, in the second year of marriage, wrote to his friend John Thelwall:

. . . my little David Hartley grows a sweet boy . . . he laughs at us till he makes us weep for very fondness.[3]

When a daughter came along, following the two boys, Coleridge announced to the Southeys:

I had never thought of a girl as a possible event; the words child and man-child were perfect synonyms in my feelings. However, I bore the sex with great fortitude, and she shall be called Sara . . . I left the little one sucking at a great rate.[4]

He cared tenderly for their differences. He wrote to Matthew Coates:

Derwent is a large, fat, beautiful child, quite the pride of the village, as Hartley is the *darling*. Southey says wickedly that 'all Hartley's guts are in his brains, and all Derwent's brains are in his guts'. From earliest infancy Hartley was . . . a mere dreamer at his meals . . . with little Derwent it is a

---

1 Letter to *The Daily Chronicle*, 28 May, 1897: 'The Case of Warder Martin: Some Cruelties of Prison Life'.
2 16 Mar. 1717.
3 6 Feb. 1797. *Letters of Samuel Taylor Coleridge* ed. Ernest Hartley Coleridge (1895), i, p. 220.
4 Christmas Day, 1802: *ibid.*, i. p. 416.

time of rapture and jubilee, and any story that has not *pie* or *cake* in it comes very flat to him. Yet he is but a baby.[1]

There is a fascinating letter when Hartley, ten, was under his father's sole care, first with the Wordsworths at Coleorton:

My dear Boy,
. . . You are now going with me (if God have not ordered it otherwise) into Devonshire to visit your Uncle G. Coleridge. He is a very good man and very kind; but his notions of right and of propriety are very strict . . . I take, therefore, this means of warning you against those bad habits, which I and all your friends here have noticed in you . . . I am not writing in anger, but on the contrary with great love, and a comfortable hope that your behaviour at Ottery will be such as to do yourself and me and your dear mother *credit*.
. . . never pick at or snatch up anything, eatable or not . . . in the Church Catechism *picking* and *stealing* are both put together . . .
Next, when you have done wrong acknowledge it at once, like a man. Excuses may show your ingenuity, but they make your *honesty* suspected . . . We may admire a man for his cleverness; but we love and esteem him only for his goodness . . . Lastly [and he had put at the beginning: 'I could equally apply it to myself'!], do what you have to do at once, and put it out of hand. No procrastination; no self-delusion . . .
. . . I beg you . . . to remember not to stand between the half-opened door, either while you are speaking, or spoken to. But come *in* or go out, and always speak and listen with the door shut . . . and never to interrupt your elders while they are speaking, and not to talk at all during meals. I pray you, keep this letter, and read it over every two or three days . . . my dear, my very dear Hartley, most anxiously your fond father . . .

P.S. I have not spoken about your mad passions and frantic looks and pout-mouthing; because I trust that is all over.[2]

On his last visit to the Lake District, the estranged father tells John Morgan how he collected the boys from school:

When I went for them from Mr Dawes, he [Derwent, now eleven] came in dancing for joy, while Hartley [fifteen] turned pale and trembled all over, – then after he had taken some cold water, instantly asked me some question about the connection of the Greek with the Latin, which latter he has just begun to learn. Poor Derwent . . . has complained to me (having no other possible grievance) 'that Mr Dawes does not *love* him, because he can't help crying when he is scolded, and because he ain't such a genius as Hartley – and that though Hartley should have done the same thing, yet all the others are punished, and Mr Dawes only *looks* at Hartley, and never scolds *him*,

1 Letter from Greta Hall, Keswick: 5 Dec. 1803.
2 3 Apr. 1807. *Letters, cit.*, ii, pp. 512–4.

and that *all* the boys think it very unfair – he *is* a genius.' This was uttered in low spirits and a tenderness brought on by my petting, for he adores his brother . . . A gentleman who took a third of the chaise with me from Ambleside, and whom I found a well-informed and thinking man, said after two hours' knowledge of us, that the two boys united would be a perfect representation of myself.[1]

It was the time of the celebrated quarrel, when Montagu repeated to Coleridge what Wordsworth had confided about his friend's weakness for spirits, and when the boys saw that their father did not intend to turn aside to visit the Wordworths at the Rectory, opposite Grasmere Church, 'they turned pale and were visibly affected.'[2]

Next year, WORDSWORTH's eldest son, Johnny, joined the two Coleridge boys at Ambleside School. Dorothy gives a cameo of the ten-year-old so anxious to please, yet unable to emulate either of them academically:

. . . he walks every morning and returns at night, with a bottle over his shoulder and a Basket in his hand – he always meets us with smiles . . .[3]

The shock of losing two of his children caused Wordsworth to make a fuss of the youngest, Willy, and talk 'to him just as if he were but a year old' – instead of seven. Even Dorothy had to complain.

I am astonished with his babyishness . . .[4]

Dora, the second child, became his favourite, but seems to have led them a dance when small. Dorothy said:

She *can* do anything but . . . is desirous to master everybody.[5]

Seeking to improve Dora's health, Mr Scrambler, the local doctor, recommended the equivalent of a daily cold bath. Dorothy recorded:

We had one terrible struggle with her; but she now likes it . . .[6]

After six daughters, SOUTHEY had a son, Herbert, who vied with Hartley in his knowledge of Greek, Latin, French and German by the

---

1 28 Feb. 1812: *Letters of Samuel Taylor Coleridge* ed. Ernest Hartley Coleridge (1895), ii, pp. 576–7.
2 Letter from Mrs Coleridge to Poole, 30 Oct. 1812: *ibid.*,, ii, p. 576 Note.
3 To Catherine Clarkson, 23 June 1812: *The Letters of William & Dorothy Wordsworth* ed. C. L. Shaver, Mary Moorman, Alan G. Hill (1967–79), iii, p. 34.
4 Ditto. 2 Mar. 1817: *ibid.*, iii, p. 371.
5 Ditto. 31 July 1812: *ibid.*, iii, p. 40.
6 Ditto. 15 Aug. 1815: *ibid.*, iii, p. 246.

age of nine. The father idolized him and called him his 'moon'. De Quincey recalled an incident in a sailboat on the lake when there was a party 'chiefly composed of Southey's family and his visitors'. On disembarking at one of the islands, a stranger good-naturedly picked up the five- or six-year-old Herbert, 'stepping with him most carefully from thwart to thwart'. A man 'more unaffectedly polite and courteous in his demeanour to strangers' than Southey could not be imagined, but now, 'in a perfect frenzy of anxiety for his boy', he 'rushed forward, and tore him out of the arms of the stranger without one word of apology'. It was the only rude thing that De Quincey had ever known him to do. The stranger's face reflected 'a race of emotions':

. . . a hasty blush of resentment mingled with astonishment: then a good-natured smile of indulgence . . . finally, a considerate, grave expression of acquiescence in the whole act; but with a pitying look towards father and son, as too probably destined under such agony of affection to trials perhaps insupportable.[1]

DE QUINCEY himself loved nothing better than playing with little tots, and Margaret bore him eight of his own. After he had brought his family to be with him in Edinburgh, her health deteriorated so that, helped by a servant, he often had to care for them all. Florence, a delicate child, remembered 'the kind, careful arms' which 'rescued' her from 'a weariful bed'. She remembered being carried to 'the bright warm room, and the dignity and delight of *sitting up* with papa',[2] the sweetened coffee and story, before he continued his writing as she fell asleep. He managed partially to teach his children and, in spite of being 'put to the horn'[3] on nine separate occasions, employed teachers for them. They, in turn, when their father had to go into hiding in the 'Abbey',[4] fetched and delivered his copy. Florence wrote:

On me fell the main burden and I know the north and southbacks of the Canongate, George the Fourth Bride, the cross causeway . . . as hideous

1 *The Collected Writings of Thomas De Quincey* ed. David Masson (1889–90), ii, pp. 331–2.
2 A. H. Japp: *Thomas De Quincey: His life & Writings, With Unpublished Correspondence* (2nd edn., 1890), p. 278. Quoted by Grevel Lindop: *The Opium-Eater: A Life of Thomas De Quincey* (1981), p. 300.
3 After application by a creditor, a Scots court had power to issue a 'royal demand'. If the debtor continued in default, an official in the market-place – on three blasts of a horn – proclaimed him a rebel, and imprisonment could follow.
4 i.e. the debtors' Sanctuary, which contained Holyrood Palace and two or three square miles to the south.

dreams, my heart rushing into my mouth with the natural terrors of footsteps approaching . . . When he turned up it was all right, and I am sure I never told him what I suffered . . .[1]

A Princes Street bookseller recalled 'Mr De Quincey's young fair-haired English laddies'[2] asking for loans on behalf of their father.

Emily, the youngest of six surviving children, was only four when their mother died. The eldest daughter, Margaret, now nineteen, assumed the maternal role, keeping house prudently and also taking charge of her father's magazine payments to help keep him solvent. Two or three years into his widowhood he acquired Mavis Bush Cottage, a little beyond the village of Lasswade. Seven miles outside Edinburgh – for De Quincey a walking distance – it was in a pretty setting and had eight rooms and a garden.

According to Peacock, SHELLEY 'was extremely fond of his children'.

He was pre-eminently an affectionate father.

With his first-born, Ianthe, in his arms, he 'would walk up and down a room . . . for a long time together, singing to it a monotonous melody of his own making, which ran on the repetition of a word of his own making':

His song was 'Yahmani, Yahmani, Yahmani.' It did not please me, but . . . it pleased the child, and lulled it when it was fretful.[3]

Peacock even gave the notes – B, C, D, in the key of A natural; a crotchet and two quavers. Shelley addressed her in a sonnet when she was three months old:

> I love thee, Baby! for thine own sweet sake:
> Those azure eyes, that faintly dimpled cheek,
> Thy tender frame so eloquently weak . . .[4]

Before the right to his children was contested by the Westbrooks on the grounds of his atheistic and revolutionary principles, he wrote to Mary:

1 Horace A. Eaton: *Thomas De Quincey: A Biography* (1936), p. 375 Note.
2 Grevel Lindop: *The Opium-Eater: A Life of Thomas De Quincey* (1981), p. 321.
3 Thomas Love Peacock: *Memorials of Shelley* (1860).
4 *To Ianthe*: Sept. 1813.

Remember my poor babes, Ianthe and Charles. How tender and dear a mother they will find in you – darling William, too! My eyes overflow with tears . . .[1]

JOYCE sang his daughter to sleep with a lullaby '. . . *una bella bambina . . . Lucia . . .*'[2]

II

A favourite saying of TENNYSON's was:

Make the lives of children as beautiful and as happy as possible.[3]

He wished to do this for Hallam and Lionel – he told Thomas Wilson that his own childhood 'had been at times very unhappy'.[4] Thackeray, Kingsley, Edmund Gosse, all had a similar experience and expressed the same motivation with their children.

A photo exists of the Tennyson family, looking very Pre-Raphaelite, walking in the grounds at Faringford. Eight-year-old Lionel contentedly holds his mother's hand, while Hallam, nine or ten, at his father's side, gazes proudly ahead, his hair flowing in imitation of Tennyson's mane. The boys, slightly older in their head-and-shoulders' portrait by G. F. Watts, still wear the tasselled lace ruffs and belted smocks with large buttons. When the boys were eleven and twelve, their parents started with them for their private tutor's, Mr Paul at Bailie, Dorsetshire. Their mother recorded in her diary:

A sorrowful sight to us both – our two boys on the Bailie platform, alone for the first time in their lives as our train left.[5]

Hallam, fourteen, at Marlborough, contracted pneumonia and the parents started off by the next boat. His mother's diary shows Tennyson 'very calm but deeply moved':

At the crisis he said humbly, 'I have made up my mind to lose him: God will take him pure and good, straight from his mother's lessons. Surely it would

1 15 Dec. 1816.
2 Richard Ellmann: *James Joyce* (1959), pp. 319–20.
3 *Alfred Lord Tennyson: A Memoir by his Son* (1897), i,. p. 371.
4 *Ibid.*, i, p. 512.
5 22 May, 1865: *ibid.*, ii, p. 23.

be better for him than to grow up such a one as I am.' He was wrapped up in the boy.[1]

There was a speedy recovery. But Lionel at fourteen was entered at Eton, 'as his health could not endure the cold climate of Marlborough'.[2]

KINGSLEY gave his children pet-names – 'Cocky' for Rose the eldest, then there was 'Morry', Mary was 'Polly', and the youngest 'My Lord Grenville' till he was five. For his three eldest he used to draw pictures, but for Grenville he made a train with nine carriages. His eldest boy, Maurice (named after his father's mentor, F. D. Maurice), looked back on his childhood as a time of 'perpetual laughter'. Philip remembered EDMUND GOSSE as 'the most indulgent' of fathers.

Unlike Dickens, who had more than double again, KINGSLEY positively welcomed every addition, each of which he saw as 'another pledge' of married love. When Fanny, over forty, told him a fourth was coming, he wrote:

– what shall I say of my delight . . . It seems too good to be true.[3]

He let his children dress sensibly in clothes that did not restrict play. He tried not to be partial but at eight Rose had her own pony, bought for £10, and she rode with her father about the parish.

He hired good tutors for the education of his girls at home. When nine-year-old Maurice went to a prep school at Blackheath, Kingsley visited him often and his letters promised holiday treats – a new cricket bat or saddle, or a fishing-trip. When he taught at Cambridge and his son entered Trinity, he wrote:

Maurice walks everywhere with me, like a dog, of his own accord.[4]

Mrs Cowden Clarke, who enjoyed many informal visits to No. 1 Devonshire Terrace as a personal friend, recorded that DICKENS made a good father, especially to his smallest children. In the *Cornhill* article after her father's death, his oldest daughter, Mamey (Mary Angela), wrote:

1 1 Mar. 1867: *ibid.*, ii, p. 42.
2 His mother's *Journal*, 20 July 1868: ibid., ii, p. 56.
3 Susan Chitty: *The Beast & the Monk: A Life of Charles Kingsley* (1974), p. 189.
4 Letter to wife, 11 Feb. 1867: *ibid.*, p. 244.

When any treat had to be asked for, the second little daughter [Kate Macready], always a pet of her father's, was pushed into his study by the other children, and always returned triumphant.

He had a peculiar tone of voice and way of speaking for each of his children, who could tell, without being called by name, which was the one addressed . . .

I can see him now through the mist of years, with a child nearly always on his knee at this time of the evening [before they went to bed]. . . I can hear his clear sweet voice as he sang to those children as if he had no other occupation in the world but to amuse them . . .

He was invaluable in a sick room . . . From his children's earliest days his visits, during any time of sickness, were eagerly longed for and believed in, as doing more good than those even of the doctor himself. He had a curiously magnetic and sympathetic hand, and his touch was wonderfully soothing and quieting.[1]

When at thirty he returned with his wife from the first visit to America, they quickly had their four children out of bed and 'little Charley was so excited that he fell into convulsions'. Mamey continues:

When the move was made . . . to Tavistock House . . . he promised his daughters a better bedroom than they had ever had before . . . but they were not to see 'the gorgeous apartment' until it was ready for their use . . . They found it full of love and thoughtful care . . . not a single thing . . . had not been expressly chosen for them, or planned by their father . . . There were two toilet tables, two writing tables, two easy chairs, &c., &c., all so pretty and elegant . . .

She recalled 'one year . . . in a charming villa, quite out of the town' of Boulogne:

. . . he and his youngest son, 'The Plorn', [Edward Bulwer Lytton] would wander about the garden together admiring the flowers, the little fellow being taught to show his admiration by holding up his tiny arms. It was a pretty sight . . . down the long avenue, the baby . . . in its white frock and blue ribbons, either carried in his father's arms, or toddling by his side with his little hand in his, and a most perfect understanding between them.

There were always anecdotes afterwards, when his father invariably wound up with the assertion that he was 'a noble boy'.[2]

During the times FRANCES HODGSON BURNETT was not occupied

1 *The Cornhill Magazine*, Jan. 1885: 'Charles Dickens at Home: With especial reference to his relations with Children'.
2 *Ibid*.

with her work, she played with her two small sons in the nursery. Her biographer says 'she saw them as temples she was building', but insists that their childhood 'does seem to have been most attractively normal'.[1] She herself maintained:

The one perfect thing in my life was the childhood of my boys.[2]

III

Up to the ages of eight and ten, when Vyvyan and his elder brother, Cyril, were parted from their father for ever, WILDE was 'a real companion' and they always looked forward to his frequent visits to the nursery.

There was nothing about him of the monster that some people who never knew him and never even saw him have tried to make him out to be.[3]

He told them about the family home at Moytara, and the 'great melancholy carp' that had to be called with the Irish songs he had learnt from his father.

I do not think he sang very well, but to us he had the most beautiful voice in the world . . .[4]

    Theodore Wratislaw stayed a weekend at the summer cottage rented at Goring, and was to give a tantalizing glimpse of Wilde sculling his elder son and him on the Thames. Seven- or eight-year-old Cyril, who appeared at Sunday breakfast, having come up from town, was 'possibly the most beautiful child I have ever seen, sturdy and strong with a mass of golden curls . . .'[5] During lunch the young poet let slip a slighting remark on Home Rule, which caused the small boy to flush with anger and violently demand if he were not a Home Ruler. Equally amused but perhaps less astonished by 'the juvenile politician', Wilde gave a diplomatic quip to his audience of two:

Ah! My own idea is that Ireland should rule England.[6]

1 Ann Thwaite: *Waiting for the Party: The life of Frances Hodgson Burnett* (1974), p. 80.
2 *Ibid.*
3 Vyvyan Holland: *Son of Oscar Wilde* (1954), p. 52.
4 *Ibid.*, p. 54.
5 *Oscar Wilde: A Memoir* ed. Karl Beckson (1979), p. 12.
6 *Ibid.*, p. 13.

Vyvyan remembered at seven being taken by his father to see *Once Upon a Time*, a children's play at the Haymarket, and in the interval they went round to see Herbert Beerbohm Tree, who played the chief roles.

Then there was the gold-headed malacca cane which his father always carried in London, and that so fascinated Vyvyan he rushed to take it immediately Wilde came home. He asked if he could have it when he grew up, and received the reply that it would be his as soon as he reached its height. One of Vyvyan's last memories of his father was of greeting him with books tied beneath his feet so that he was taller than the stick. Wilde, very amused, compromised by putting a half-sovereign in his son's money-box. The incident must have happened during the Christmas holiday, two months before Queensberry's arrest.

MASEFIELD was twenty-five when Judith was born, and because his wife was often away running a school with her friend until the child was eight the little girl developed a rapport with her father. He called her variously Judykins, Mouse, Kit, Pusskins, and her teddy bears 'the Boys.' She liked it when he played at shops, impersonating fussy customers. He made her a ship on wheels, in which she could sit. He taught her to read, and after his morning's work she would sit on his knee in the study while he told her thrilling stories in instalments and drew her pictures in coloured ink.

When she was thirteen, and distressed at having to move from her boarding school on the Suffolk coast because of the Zeppelin raids, her father wrote:

I am so very sad to hear of you being unhappy . . . My dear, we do try to give you a happy time . . . and though I know you are very brave and would not be frightened, still you might be hurt . . .[1]

EVELYN WAUGH wrote in a similar strain to his ten-year-old daughter, Margaret, who was unhappy at her boarding school:

. . . believe me, I am very unhappy that you should be unhappy – I will try and find you another school . . . I love you and will not let you be really unhappy if I can prevent it . . .[2]

Lewis ('Timcat') was born when Masefield was thirty-two. The curly-haired, round-faced little boy at nearly seven lived in a fantasy

1 18 Apr. 1917: Constance Babington Smith: *John Masefield: A Life* (1978), p. 171.
2 Whit Sun. 1953: Christopher Sykes: *Evelyn Waugh: A Biography* (1975), p. 453.

world of church ritual, and at one stage his mother reported that his toys – 'the bunnies' – had all become Roman Catholic. She wrote to her husband in France:

Lew talks ceaselessly of you, rather to my discredit. 'Father is never cross with me, you sometimes *are* a *little* cross, Mother.'[1]

When he was small, CHRISTOPHER MILNE belonged to his mother rather than his father. Like Elspeth Grahame, who dressed Alistair in girlish clothes, she gave instructions about the smocks depicted in Shepard's illustrations, and kept his hair long when other boys had it short. But for over eight years no one meant so much to him as his Nanny.

One day at the Garrick Club, A. A. MILNE mentioned to Louis Goodrich, an actor, his little boy's obsession with soldiers, and Goodrich volunteered to dress up. Arrangements were made to hire a scarlet tunic with busby – and a magnificent Guardsman appeared at the door of the nursery. Another day, Christopher sat happily beside his mother on the sofa while his father, who had come in from his study, settled himself and read the story, just finished, *In which Piglet does a very grand thing*. From time to time Milne sat for his small son to draw his profile. Then at the Garrick he would say to Munnings or George Morrow, bringing out his wallet: 'Oh, by the way, you might like to see what my boy did yesterday.'[2]

Then, when Nanny left to get married, 'it was different, very different'. For nearly ten years his father filled that place in his affections.

We were together until I was eighteen, very, very close . . . he was very grateful. And once, a little shyly, he thanked me . . .[3]

His father alone accompanied him in the car when Burnside drove him to school. They did the *Times* crossword and said their goodbyes, still in the car with some way to go.

We said them looking straight ahead. It was easier that way . . .

His mother had said goodbye until the next holidays, but part of his father would still remain 'lovingly and anxiously watching me, through

1 27 Sept. 1916: Babington Smith, *op. cit.*, p. 170.
2 Christopher Milne: *The Enchanted Places* (1974), p. 100.
3 *Ibid.*, p. 122.

the term'. It was his father who 'got something done about the draughty classroom at Gibbs and the over-crowded changing-room at Stowe'.[1] He was the one who invariably came on visiting days and knew the masters.

When Christopher was nine, his father took him to a cricket school in South London, four mornings a week during the Christmas holidays. At about ten or eleven, he first accompanied his father to the Oval, and Woolley was batting. From then on, summer holidays always began with the first two days in London, watching cricket. In the luncheon interval they had their ham sandwiches, egg sandwiches, and there was a paper-bag full of cherries.

IV

Each day at 6.00 p.m., until they started at school, Nigel and his elder brother, Ben, came down from the cottage up the hill, where they lived in the care of a nanny, to Long Barn, the cottage their parents had bought near Knole. Their mother, VICTORIA SACKVILLE-WEST, pleased to see them as they to see her, would look up from the present book she was writing, 'uncertain how to amuse us'. But their father would take them for walks, draw funny pictures for them, read them Conan Doyle, and 'studied us (though we did not notice it), wondering how he could help'.[2]

After they reached thirteen and sixteen respectively, their home was Sissinghurst Castle. They shared a bedroom in one of the cottages, until they were both at Oxford, and their parents had two bedrooms for themselves in another. Each member of the family had a separate sitting-room. Nigel comments that his parents 'had achieved by the accident of the physical separation of the buildings the perfect solution to our communal lives'.[3]

At forty-four, HAROLD NICOLSON ended his *Diary* for 1930:

Few men have been so spoiled by fortune as I have. But all of it – money, fame, health – is of little weight against the scale of my home life. Viti, Ben

1 *Ibid.*, p. 98.
2 Nigel Nicolson: *Portrait of a Marriage* (1973), p. 194 (Amer. edn. pp. 215–6).
3 *Ibid.*, p. 219 (Amer. edn. p. 247).

[sixteen], Nigel [nearly fourteen], home, Sissinghurst, books. These, I hope, will always remain what I really care for.[1]

Nigel said of his father:

His attitude to his sons was one of open enthusiasm for anything that we were doing. He read, for instance, the whole of Aeschylus's *Seven Against Thebes* because it was my set-book at school.[2]

When Nigel had written from Eton about the problem of switching from surname to Christian-name terms with close friends, he received from the United States a six-page letter of advice. Another letter his father wrote, this one to seventeen-year-old Ben at Eton, contained, Nigel considered, his whole nature:

My darling Benzie,
   I thought your sonnet excellent – really good . . .
   . . . I sometimes wish that you did not agree with Mummy and me so much. Of course, *of course*, we are always right. But a boy of your age should sometimes think us wrong.
   . . . I beg you, when you see a person as shy and as unhappy as you were yourself, to give him a kind word, a look of understanding . . . I know that in my case [at Wellington] I found that when I got to your position in my house, the opportunity of being kind to little miseries, made up for all the unkindness and cruelty which I had received myself . . .
   Bless you, my own darling. Your very loving . . .[3]

The following year, Nicolson wrote of Nigel at nearly sixteen:

Niggs is as sensible and hard-working and sweet as ever.[4]

EVELYN WAUGH told Frances Donaldson that he liked to see himself in the role of a father. She remembered how he had followed Hatty out into the garden when the small child told him there were some white animals with horns and they proved to be Cabbage Whites. When his wife gave the children a playroom approached by outside steps, at the back of Piers Court, he fetched a green table so they could write poetry.

His second daughter Margaret, who (partly because for most of one term he had taught her) became 'his official favourite, a position

1 *Diaries & Letters 1930–1939* ed. Nigel Nicolson (1966), p. 62.
2 *Ibid.*, Introduction: pp. 27–8.
3 1931. Nigel Nicolson: *Portrait of a Marriage*, pp. 223–5 (Amer. edn. pp. 253–5).
4 31 Dec. 1932: *Diaries & Letters 1930–1939*, p. 125.

neither resented nor sought by my siblings', wrote a memoir of her father, reminiscent of Mamey's of Dickens:

It was he, not my mother, who wrote the weekly letters to school. It was he who took all the decisions about our education and welfare.[1]

She described their nursery life as 'deliberately old-fashioned', but from about the age of eight, at which stage they joined their elders at the dinner-table, 'one was treated as a grown-up'.[2] If sometimes he was harsh on his sons, when he was angry with the girls they dissolved into tears and he would immediately be contrite and concerned. She concluded:

I would never have chosen a different father.[3]

Even Auberon remembered his childhood as a happy one, due in large part to his father, not in spite of him. Auberon told Christopher Sykes that he criticized his father only for 'a certain emotional capriciousness with all his children except Margaret' – he seemed to regard 'his parental affection as a gift which it was in his power to confer or withdraw'.[4]

A. J. P. TAYLOR said of his firstborn, Giles:

From the moment he arrived I needed no other companion and the arrival of other children increased my detachment from society.[5]

The six children from his two marriages were 'all attractive' and shared their young lives with him. He expresses gratitude to his son Crispin, 'some fifty years younger than myself', who it seems from about the age of ten taught him to read up his sightseeing beforehand and approach it systematically.

They became 'my abiding consolation'. They went together to the cinema and theatre. At sixty-two, he walked a long stretch of the Pennine Way with Sebastian, his second son now twenty-eight. At sixty-five, it was the Offa Dyke with fifteen-year-old Crispin, and the following year Giles joined them to complete it to the sea.

1 Christopher Sykes: *Evelyn Waugh: A Biography* (1975), p. 451.
2 *Ibid.*, pp. 451–2.
3 *Ibid.*, p. 455.
4 *Ibid.*, p. 450.
5 *A Personal History* (1983), p. 132.

When Richard Croucher commented that I saw a lot of my children, I replied, 'They are my only friends' – a remark I have heard denounced as incestuous.[1]

V

Dolly Ponsonby recorded in her diary the BARRIES and Sylvia, with two of her boys, Peter and Michael, coming to tea in Hampshire. She watched three-year-old Michael putting his hand in Uncle Jim's as they walked down the garden path into the field.

His devotion & genius-like understanding of children is beautiful & touching beyond words as he has none himself.[2]

Peter remembered how the morning following his mother's funeral Barrie had taken him, nearly sixteen, and George, seventeen, 'to an old-fashioned shop in the Haymarket' to purchase eight-foot fly-rods, casts and flies, before they went back with him near Exmoor for the rest of their summer holidays:

I dare say it worked well enough, and that the new rods helped, as no doubt J. M. B. with generous cunning knew that they would, to do the trick.[3]

Although one of four guardians, Barrie at fifty, in his inimitable way, appropriated entire charge of the five boys. He told Quiller-Couch: '. . . it is my main reason for going on . . .' He did 'a little writing' in his flat, 'tho' mostly I am with them'.[4] The loyal nurse, Mary Hodgson, who had come to the Llewelyn Davieses just before Peter had arrived, was now to Michael, ten, and Nico, six, 'wholly unique and wholly irreplaceable'.[5] She ran their home at No. 24 Campden Hill Square, but did not like being responsible to Barrie. Theirs was a state of armed neutrality ever since those days in Kensington Gardens. She differed with him over indulging their every wish, and considered it detrimental to their upbringing.

Dolly Ponsonby, an old friend of the family, complained in her

---

1 *Ibid.*, p. 208.
2 21 Aug. 1903. Andrew Birkin: *J. M. Barrie & The Lost Boys* (1979), p. 98.
3 The Peter Davies collection of personal papers. Janet Dunbar: *J. M. Barrie: The Man Behind the Image* (1970), p. 192.
4 7 Mar. 1911. Birkin, *op. cit.*, p. 197.
5 Nico, 1975: *ibid.*, p. 270.

diary that 'in his desire to make up to the boys for all they have lost
. . . nothing is denied them in the way of amusement, clothes, toys
. . .' Barrie took the boys to the best restaurants in their evening
clothes and then on to the stalls or a box at the theatre.

They buy socks costing 12/6 a pair & Michael, aged 11, is given very
expensive lessons in fly fishing.[1]

Indeed, when Michael went to Oxford, Barrie bought him a car and a
country cottage.

In loco parentis, he devoted himself to their education and careers.
Four went to Eton, followed by Oxford, and Jack to Osborne and
Dartmouth. From these contacts with Eton, Barrie said he had come
to believe himself an Old Etonian. He involved himself in all their
ailments, and showed the same possessiveness as his mother had
shown towards him. Ever since Michael was a young child, Barrie
had helped him over his nightmares, sitting by his side, 'doing
something frightfully ordinary, like reading the newspaper'. Barrie
wrote:

I think few have suffered from the loss of a mother as he has done.[2]

To ease the boy's loneliness at Eton, Barrie wrote every day instead
of every week as to George. Michael wrote back every day, and by
the time he left Eton there were two thousand letters between them.
Lady Cynthia Asquith, on first coming as Barrie's secretary, asked
him what to do with them and he said not a single one was to be
thrown away.

When George went to the 1914–18 war, Barrie sent regular hampers
from Fortnum & Mason's:

Wherever you are I hope you see near your bed the flowers I want to place
there in a nice vase, and the illustrated papers and a new work by Compton
Mackenzie which I read aloud . . .[3] A few things to note from your last. For
one thing I enclose four pounds in French money, and for another it is always
a blessed thing for me when you want something. So if you don't want, go
on inventing . . . The one great thing for me is when we are all together
again.[4]

1 7 Aug. (1911): *ibid.*, p. 198.
2 To Elizabeth Lucas: 17 Oct. 1920. *Ibid.*, p. 211.
3 Jan. (?) 1915. Janet Dunbar: *J. M. Barrie: The Man Behind the Image* (1970), p. 208.
4 28 Feb. 1915. *Ibid.*, p. 210.

Nico said, in 1975, they 'all knew that George and Michael were The Ones – George because he had started it all, and Michael . . . because he was the most original, the potential genius . . .' and that Barrie was platonically in love with George and Michael, 'as he was with my mother . . . for myself, Peter and Jack . . . different . . . nearer to normal deep affection'.[1]

On one of the long walks STEVENSON and eleven-year-old Lloyd enjoyed in California, instead of the usual story or ingenious game he spoke seriously, and said he was going to marry Lloyd's mother. After it had sunk in that Luly would be his for keeps, the boy put his hand into Stevenson's and felt it warmly held. Thus linked, they walked on.

VI

LEWIS HIND was sixty when he adopted a three-year-old boy, with yellow hair, whose mother had brought him to the house. His wife, Belinda, told him about the little boy, and he replied: 'We would take in a wet dog. Why not a small child?'

The little boy, coming in, put his small head on Belinda's arm and said, 'Lady, do you love me?' Hind wrote about him in the 'Life and I' series he was doing for *The Daily Chronicle*:

I christened him Julius Caesar . . . He continues to conquer everybody – by love.[2]

After nine years of marriage, by which time his wife felt increasingly cheated of affection, BENNETT fell in with her wish to adopt his brother's eldest son, Richard, already fifteen. There would be no legal adoption but, in return for his education at Oundle followed by university – which his father could not afford – Richard should look upon *them* as his parents and withdraw from his family, of whom he was very fond.

During the summer holiday when Bennett was absent, Richard, now eighteen, was forbidden by his aunt to drive the T-model Ford which he claimed his uncle allowed him to do, and when later he

---

1 Letter to Andrew Birkin: his *J. M. Barrie & the Lost Boys* (1979), p. 130.
2 *Life and I* (1923), p. viii.

showed resentment she sent him to his room as if he were a child. Since a silence then prevailed she wrote word he must apologize, and in future desist from joking when she kissed him good-night or good-morning. He passed down a long letter, in which he said:

. . . When Uncle is here I always feel more free; and always enjoy a holiday when I am here with Uncle as well. When Uncle is away I feel unhappy and not free . . .[1]

Marguerite sent him back to his mother, who, like himself, had never really understood that he was meant to be always separated from his parents.

But Bennett showed the same magnanimity as he did with his 'absurd settlement' on his wife when they separated two years later. He continued to pay his nephew's bills and saw that he went to Clare's, Cambridge. They still wrote to each other almost weekly. In one letter Bennett told him he had taken tea with Virginia Woolf, the day after his *Evening Standard* article:

We got on fine. She undertook to do me in later.[2]

Richard received a brief message from Uncle Arnold just before the end. They were the last words he wrote.

ORWELL, at thirty-six, congratulated Rayner Heppenstall on the birth of his child:

What a wonderful thing to have a kid of one's own, I've always wanted one so.[3]

Four years later he persuaded his wife they should adopt a baby boy, naming him not by his own or his father's name, Eric, which he hated, but after his old publishing friend, Sir Richard Rees.

He spoke of him proudly and frequently. After Eileen's death, the Fyvels thought it wonderful he had Richard to care for, and now other friends began to have certain images of them together. There was one of this very tall man striding down the street towards them, with Richard riding his shoulders, seemingly in peril from every branch or sign. Another was when Orwell and Richard were about to spend Christmas 1945 with the Koestlers in North Wales, and Celia

---

1 Dudley Barker: *Writer by Trade: A View of Arnold Bennett* (1966), p. 200.
2 *Ibid.*, p. 232.
3 Apr. 1940: *The Collected Essays, Journalism & Letters of George Orwell* ed. Sonia Orwell & Ian Angus (1968), ii, p. 22.

Kirwan suddenly saw this 'huge, gaunt figure' waiting on Euston Station, 'in an extra-long shabby military greatcoat, with Richard under one arm and a battered old suitcase in the other hand'. She thought his posture 'conveyed both loneliness and his love for his adopted son which came shining through'.[1] He took a long country walk with Koestler, who noticed he carried the boy Asian-style on the hip.

His first instructions to Susan Watson, whom he employed at the Canonbury Square flat, were: 'You must let him play with his thingummy' and 'Can you make scones?'[2] Herself a young mother with a daughter of seven, she was recently separated from her husband, a Cambridge don, and polio had left her lame. Orwell also engaged a cockney char, whose little boy called his mother 'Mum', and Richard began copying him. 'Can't have Richard calling you "Mum,"' said Orwell to Susan. 'I'd like him to call you Nana.'[3] Richard seems to have expressed a mind of his own – or perhaps it was Susan – for in the end Richard called her by her name.

At that time his workload was heavy and high tea with Richard, always Orwell's favourite meal, was a cherished part of the day, after which he would play with him for half an hour or so until starting work. She thought the highlight of his week came on her day off, every Tuesday, when he had Richard to himself.

He mentioned to Susan, once or twice, his early suffering at St Cyprian's as an experience that Richard would be spared. Later, he wrote to Julian Symons:

. . . I am not going to let him go to a boarding school before he is ten.[4]

Fresh from meeting his old schoolfellow John Strachey, however, 'once nearly Communist' and now boasting of sending his son to Eton, Orwell told Fyvel he was totally against boarding schools and, as a compromise between them and state schools, he had put Richard down as a day-boy at Westminster.[5]

At Barnhill on the Isle of Jura, he with his sister Avril boiled all

1 T. R. Fyvel: *George Orwell: a personal memoir* (1982), pp. 145–6.
2 Bernard Crick: *George Orwell: A Life* (1980), p. 347.
3 *Ibid.*, p. 349.
4 29 Oct. 1948. *The Collected Essays, Journalism & Letters of George Orwell* ed. Sonia Orwell & Ian Angus (1968), iv, p. 451.
5 T. R. Fyvel: *George Orwell: a personal memoir* (1982),. pp. 168–9. See also letter to Julian Symons: 16 June 1949. *Letters, cit.*, iv, p. 503.

milk, and tried to get a tuberculin-tested cow. His concern was 'to prevent Richard getting this disease' and, when Orwell was in bed for several weeks, the little boy had to be kept out of his room for fear of infection. During his seven-month stay in Hairmyres Hospital, Glasgow, he wrote to Mary Fyvel that Richard, now three and a half, was 'blooming' when he had come away.

He is out helping with the farm work all day long, getting himself covered with mud from head to foot.[1]

Avril brought an excited Richard, a big boy for four and a half, to meet him on discharge and, back at Barnhill, Orwell enjoyed six weeks of golden summer – his Indian summer – in relative good health, playing with him more than before although he now got up for half the day.

After the spate of *Nineteen Eighty-Four*, he was in Cranham Sanatorium. He wrote in that last year to his old friend Rees that he didn't see that it mattered 'except for being expensive & not seeing little R.'

I am so afraid of his growing away from me, or getting to think of me as just a person who is always lying down & can't play.

Richard used to come to him and say, 'Where have you hurt yourself?'[2] – injury being the only reason he could comprehend for his father continually in bed. Orwell's thoughts were on Richard and Richard's future when he wrote to Jacintha Buddicom:

. . . he's as keen on fishing as I was and loves working on the farm, where he's really quite helpful. He has an enormous interest in machinery, which may be useful to him later on.

He thought it 'rather a good thing' that Richard was 'such an entirely practical child'.[3]

Their last meeting together was when Avril brought him at five and a half years old, just before it was thought Orwell would be leaving for Switzerland. Andrew Gow also was at the bedside of his old Etonian pupil, and Orwell – always divided about 'bourgeois' standards – was embarrassed for the classical scholar when Richard related a farmyard incident in fruity language.

1 16 Jan. 1948. Fyvel, *op. cit.*, p. 157.
2 3 Mar. 1949. *The Collected Essays, Journalism & Letters of George Orwell* ed. Sonia Orwell & Ian Angus (1968), iv, p. 479.
3 15 Feb. 1949. Jacintha Buddicom: *Eric & Us* (1974), p. 151.

CHAPTER THREE
Non-Olympian

I

any writers were anything but remote and pompous author-
itarian fathers. CHARLES KINGSLEY – with his 'infantry' –
played cricket in the hall and indulged in practical jokes at
breakfast. Once, in his early thirties, they had dined at a neighbour's
and in the garden were two tall leafy trees. Suddenly, he and a young
doctor present flung off their coats and raced each other to the top of
the trees and down to the ground. He took his younger son, at nine,
to inspect a prep school at Winchester, and told his wife:

I left Grenville playing with the boys by himself, and I *ran in the sack race.*[1]

To a little girl who had written to him and whose letter had been
buried under the books and papers on his table, he apologized and
wrote how he longed 'to throw all into the garden and play with all
the little children he can find'.[2] The sentiment would have been
equally characteristic of Chesterton.

The dour editor, and often hack-writer, SMOLLETT was devoted
to his wife Nancy and especially to his 'little Bet'. He wrote in a
letter:

Many a time do I stop my task and betake me to a game of romps with Betty,
while my wife looks on smiling, and longing in her heart to join in the sport;
then back to the cursed round of duty.[3]

We think of MATTHEW ARNOLD's children watching a band from
the window of the dining-room before breakfast, saddened as it went
away – then their father shutting windows and doors and giving an

1 1867. Susan Chitty: *The Beast & the Monk: A Life of Charles Kingsley* (1974), p. 189.
2 Letter to Agnes Alleyne, 1868. *Ibid.*, p. 223.
3 *DNB.*

imitation so that the boys followed suit: Tommy 'playing the Marseil-
laise on a paper knife and Budge dragging the litter-basket round &
round the room to the tune of *Cheer* Boys Cheer'.[1]

CONAN DOYLE devised elaborate games for the three small
children of his second marriage. The Indian game had a ritual of the
Chief of the Leatherskins (very serious and carrying a rifle) lighting
his pipe, which 'was passed . . . from one tiny hand to another,
Laddie taking a hearty suck . . . which set him coughing, while Baby
. . . only touched the end of the amber with her little pink lips'. It
'horrified' the great Queen, who was also 'doubtful' of the fire-water –
'ginger-ale drunk out of the bottle . . . gravely passed from hand to
hand'.[2]

'Now, then, warriors, we go forth on the war-trail. One whoop all together,
before we start . . . Follow me, now, one behind the other . . . If one gets
separated . . . let him give the cry of a night-owl and the others will answer
with the squeak of the prairie lizard.'[3]

Dimples used to startle casual acquaintance by asking: 'Can your
Daddy give a war-whoop?'[4]

A very early memory of TENNYSON's elder son, Hallam, was of
being tossed with his brother in a shawl by his father and the Master
of Balliol, Benjamin Jowett. Since their mother was not able to walk
far, Tennyson harnessed his boys 'to her garden carriage, and himself
pushed from behind; and in this fashion we raced up hill and down
dale'. In cold weather he played football with them 'in an old chalk-
pit, or built castles of flint on the top of the "Beacon Cliff", and we all
then cannonaded from a distance'.[5] A generation later, when grand-
children appeared at Aldworth, William Allingham walking up from
Haslemere came upon Tennyson and 'golden-haired Ally' in the dog-
cart, the child under 'great Alfred's black sombrero', and a little sailor
hat perched high on the poet's forehead – 'and so they drove gravely
along'.[6]

Mamey DICKENS spoke of the funny songs which her father used to
sing to the children before they went to bed.

1 Park Honan: *Matthew Arnold: A Life* (1981), p. 289.
2 Arthur Conan Doyle: *Three of Them: A Reminiscence* (1923), p. 43.
3 *Ibid.*, p. 45.
4 *Ibid.*, p. 4.
5 *Alfred Lord Tennyson: A Memoir by his Son* (1897), i, p. 369.
6 *Ibid.*, ii, p. 259.

One . . . about an old man who caught cold and rheumatism while sitting in an omnibus, was a great favourite, and as it was accompanied by sneezes, coughs and gesticulations, it had to be sung over and over again before the small audience was satisfied.

Very often, on his eldest son's birthday, which fell on Twelfth Night, he dressed as a magician and gave a conjuring entertainment.

Then, when supper time came, he would be everywhere at once, serving, cutting up the great twelfth cake, dispensing the bonbons . . . calling upon first one child and then another for a song or recitation. How eager the little faces looked for each turn to come round, and how they would blush and brighten up when the magician's eyes looked their way![1]

Like Dickens, EVELYN WAUGH sometimes 'played the entertainer and conjurer' for his children. Margaret said her father 'would devise endless jokes . . . play games and invent fantastic stories about our neighbours and friends'.[2]

Mamey and her sister were 'quite tiny' when DICKENS took it into his head that they must teach his friend John Leech and him the polka.

It must have been rather a funny sight to see the two small children teaching those two men – Mr Leech was over six feet – to dance, all four as solemn and staid as possible.[3]

In their chalet at Davos, in a chilly attic 'reached by a crazy ladder . . . so low and so dark that we could seldom stand upright, nor see without a candle', STEVENSON with twelve-year-old Lloyd collaborated in war games which went on for weeks with six hundred lead soldiers spread all over the floor. There were elaborate fixed rules – for example, a 'march was twelve inches a day without heavy artillery, and four inches with heavy artillery'.

Upon the attic floor a map was roughly drawn in chalks of different colours, with mountains, rivers, towns, bridges, and roads of two classes. Here we would play by the hour, with tingling fingers and stiffening knees, and an intentness, zest, and excitement that I shall never forget.[4]

1 'Charles Dickens at Home: with especial reference to his relations with Children': *The Cornhill Magazine*, Jan 1885.
2 Christopher Sykes: *Evelyn Waugh: A Biography* (1975), p. 451.
3 Mamey Dickens, *op. cit.*
4 Lloyd Osbourne: *Scribner's Magazine*, Dec. 1898, p. 709. Quoted by Graham Balfour: *The Life of Robert Louis Stevenson* (1901), i, pp. 197–8.

Vyvyan, WILDE's younger son, remembered his father 'as a smiling giant . . . who crawled about the nursery floor with us'.[1]

Most parents in those days were far too solemn . . . with their children, insisting on a vast amount of usually undeserved respect. My own father was quite different; he had so much of the child in his own nature . . .[2]

He played with them in the dining-room too, where there were more chairs and tables to romp through. At those times he cared nothing for his appearance. Vyvyan said that his father was at his best with them at the seaside. He wore a Norfolk jacket and knickerbockers, no shoes or stockings and a large grey hat that was probably a souvenir from America, and the boys were dressed the same. He took them out sailing and fishing. He excelled in building sand-castles – and Vyvyan used to help him – extensive, rambling ones with moats and battlements, and he would usually pull out of his pocket some lead soldiers to man the walls.

When COLERIDGE began four-year-old Hartley's formal education, they crawled about the vegetable garden of Greta Hall examining antheaps.

II

Three years after BARRIE had first met the Llewelyn Davies boys, the family spent August at a farmhouse only five minutes from the Barries' Black Lake Cottage, near Farnham.

He was forty-one, and for George now eight, Jack seven, and Peter four he peopled the nearby lake with pirates, the pinewoods with Red Indians, and added fairies for Peter's benefit. His dog stood in for fearful beasts, and a character Peter Pan, who had already featured in his verbatim stories, was transplanted from Kensington Gardens. Denis Mackail comments:

. . . the serial adventures weren't only described, but were lived.[3]

It was all extempore, and the children contributed as much as he. Improvised costumes and props appeared. Barrie played a cowardly

1 *Son of Oscar Wilde* (1954), p. 200.
2 *Ibid.*, p. 52.
3 *The Story of J. M. B.: a biography* (1941), p. 315.

Captain Swarthy who made Peter walk the plank. One evening, Michael (No. 4 in a pram) was carried to see the trail, and created Tink by waving his foot 'as our lanterns twinkled among the leaves'.[1]

The parents and his wife capitulated by the sheer force of the happiness being generated. Only the nurse dared to interrupt as she lifted Peter 'bodily out of our adventures' to give him 'a midday rest'.[2]

When it came to an end, Barrie had his action photographs bound up by Constable, with a printed text supposed to be by Peter and edited by Michael. He gave one of two copies to the father – who left it on a train. Then it was seen to be only the beginning, for, two years after *The Boy Castaways of Black Lake Island*, Barrie began the 'inky' part of *Peter Pan*.

Next year, Sylvia brought the boys to visit the play in rehearsal at the Duke of York's, and he let the boys fly about. Later on, because five-year-old Michael, ill in bed, was unable to see a revival, Barrie and Frohman brought it to his nursery at Berkhamsted, complete with scenery and a specially printed programme. The youngest children in the company played the leads.

At Cotchford Farm, from the time he was nine, Christopher MILNE played catch with his father; they looked for birds' nests and fished in the stream. Of an evening, Christopher changed into white flannels – his first long trousers – put on pads and gloves, and batted in the meadow while his father bowled. They did those things as equals.

In front of the house a lawn sloped down to a ditch. Milne, 'a natural games player, at his happiest with a club or bat', had immediately claimed it and laid it out for clock golf. When Christopher was at home he joined him. 'Just time for a quick round before lunch?' They played together, not competitively.

If I wasn't there, he played alone; and if he did a particularly good round, he would proudly tell me. When I was at school or away during the war, he would tell me in his weekly letter.[3]

PRIESTLEY'S son, Tom, allowed that his father 'was always formidable', adding:

But he always found it easy to enter into the world of childhood.[4]

---

1 *Peter Pan* (1928), Dedicatory Preface, pp. xxvii–xxviii.
2 *Ibid.*, p. xvii.
3 Christopher Milne: *The Enchanted Places* (1974), p. 45.
4 Tom's documentary: *Time & the Priestleys*, ITV, 2 Sept. 1984.

He had six children: two girls from his first marriage, three from his second, and an only son. There was a game called Family Coach, in which Priestley would allocate characters and then tell a story. Every time a character was mentioned, he or she had to get up and spin round. Tom remembered a fat cook who seemed to be constantly spinning.

Priestley wrote that 'the most successful game' he ever had with two of his children 'was based on their remembering a monstrous rigmarole of questions and answers . . . that admitted them to some secret order we had cooked up between us'.

Their eyes immense, solemn, shining, they stood before me, night after night . . . poised on the edge of abandon . . . they were sharply disappointed if I happened to be elsewhere; for they could not play this game by themselves, and their mother, like any sensible woman, would have no truck with such solemn piffle . . .[1]

At fifty-five, he dedicated *Delight*, a volume of essays from which the above extract is taken:

FOR THE FAMILY
These small amends
With the old Monster's love.

EVELYN WAUGH's daughter, Margaret, said they 'were often bribed, not to be good, but to taunt his friends or discomfort his acquaintances'.[2] When Cyril Connolly came down to Piers Court, the children (probably trained by Evelyn) kept popping up all over the garden, with 'Mr Connolly, I presume', and succeeded in giving him persecution mania.

When Waugh drove his children round the countryside, he taught them to declaim suitable lines to the houses of people he regarded suspect as well as of those he approved. On passing his next-door neighbour, they recited:

God bless Colonel Brown. They shall prosper that love him. Peace be within his walls and prosperity within his palaces.[3]

This ability of writers to play so naturally with their children is accounted for in a theory held by Andrew Lang:

1 *Delight* (1949), pp. 105–6.
2 Christopher Sykes: *Evelyn Waugh: A Biography* (1975), p. 452.
3 Frances Donaldson: *Evelyn Waugh: Portrait of a Country Neighbour* (1967), pp. 40–1.

... *all* children possess genius, and ... it dies out in the generality of mortals, abiding only with people whose genius the world is forced to recognise.

He saw it illustrated in STEVENSON, whose 'unextinguished childish passion for "playing at things" ... remained with him', and who perhaps had partly suggested 'this private philosophy of mine'.[1]

1 *Adventures Among Books* (1905), p. 53.

CHAPTER FOUR

How They Described Their Children

The images from Nature with which COLERIDGE described the personalities and play of his children are very striking. He wrote to Southey of 'little Hartley, who uses the air of the breezes as skipping-ropes'.[1]

He told William Sotheby:

I have been looking at as pretty a sight as a father's eyes could well see – Hartley and little Derwent running in the green where the gusts blow most madly, both with their hair floating and tossing, a miniature of the agitated trees, below which they were playing, inebriate both with the pleasure – whirling round for joy, Derwent eddying, half-willingly, half by the force of the gust, – driven backward, struggling forward, and shouting his little hymn of joy.[2]

The following year, a few months before he left them to go to Malta, he gave the lovely description of Sara:

Our girl is a darling little thing, with large blue eyes, a quiet creature that . . . seems to bask in a sunshine as mild as moonlight, of her own happiness.

The same letter, to Matthew Coates, points to a reversal of conventional roles of teacher and taught:

Next to the Bible, Shakespeare and Milton, *they* [Hartley seven, Derwent three, Sara one] are the three books from which I have learned the most, and the most important and with the greatest delight.[3]

Such a reversal would find its fullest expression in Wordsworth's *Immortality Ode*, completed in three more years. THACKERAY, after setting up home for his daughters, nine and nearly eight, wrote to his mother:

1 22 July 1801. *Letters of Samuel Taylor Coleridge* ed. Ernest Hartley Coleridge (1895), i, p. 359.
2 27 Sept. 1802 *Ibid.*, i, p. 408.
3 5 Dec. 1803. *Ibid.*, i, pp. 443–4.

They are a noble pair. They do me so much good that I won't brag of it. There is something angelic in Minny's sweetness: and I have almost as much veneration for Anny's brains as you have for your own prodigy of a son.[1]

GOSSE called his children two 'of the three anchors of my life'.[2]

MASEFIELD, with a two-year-old daughter, wrote to Janet Ashbee, who had sought advice about her poetry:

A poem is like a little child; one ought to give it all that one has.[3]

As father of a three-year-old boy as well, he told his brother Harry:

Children are about the best things one gets out of life, and they make all the difference in the world to marriage.[4]

ALDOUS HUXLEY, on the birth of Matthew, acknowledged to Arnold Bennett:

These works of nature really do put works of art in the shade.[5]

Lord CLARK was twenty-four when his son Alan was born. He spoke of him by the age of ten as having 'passed the *reharbitif* stage' and becoming 'the warmhearted intelligent companion he has been ever since'. All three of his children he described as 'the joy of my life, and of the many pieces of good fortune that have been poured out on me I count this as the greatest'.[6] Again, he said:

Our children were always a joy to me.[7]

When Christopher Sykes asked EVELYN WAUGH about his 'famous annulment', he replied:

If things had gone as I wanted, I would never have married Laura and I would have been deprived of the joy I have from my children.[8]

1 6 Apr. 1847. *The Letters & Private Papers of William Makepeace Thackeray* ed. Gordon N. Ray (1945–6), ii, p. 288.
2 1885. Ann Thwaite: *Edmund Gosse: a literary landscape* (1984), p. 255.
3 19 Mar. 1907. Constance Babington Smith: *John Masefield: A Life* (1978), p. 98.
4 9 Oct. 1913. *Ibid.*
5 20 Apr. 1920. Sybille Bedford: *Aldous Huxley: A Biography* (1973–4), i, p. 109.
6 Kenneth Clark: *Another Part of the Wood: A Self-Portrait* (1974), p. 257.
7 *The Other Half: A Self-Portrait* (1977), p. 127. Cf. A. J. P. Taylor, p. 256.
8 Christopher Sykes: *Evelyn Waugh: A Biography* (1975), p. 163.

CHAPTER FIVE

Natural Pride

At Nether Stowey, COLERIDGE worked at night in a room where his sleeping son Hartley (perhaps sometimes Berkeley) lay cradled,

> Whose gentle breathings, heard in this deep calm,
> Fill up the interspersed vacancies
> And momentary pauses of the thought!
> My babe so beautiful! it thrills my heart
> With tender gladness, thus to look at thee . . .[1]

Immortalized in *The Nightingale*, as well as in *Frost at Midnight* and *Christabel*, his first-born was especially cherished.

> . . . my dear Babe,
> Who, capable of no articulate sound . . .
> How he would place his hand beside his ear,
> And bid us listen! And I deem it wise
> To make him Nature's play-mate. He knows well
> The evening-star; and once, when he awoke
> In most distressful mood . . .
> I hurried with him to our orchard-plot,
> And he beheld the moon, and, hushed at once,
> Suspends his sobs, and laughs most silently . . .
> . . . Well! –
> It is a father's tale: But if that Heaven
> Should give me life, his childhood shall grow up
> Familiar with these songs, that with the night
> He may associate joy . . .[2]

As his other children came along, a father's usual pride extended to them:

. . . and fat Derwent, so beautiful, and so proud of his three teeth, that there's no bearing of him![3]

---

1 *Frost at Midnight*, written 1798.
2 *The Nightingale*; Apr. 1798.
3 22 July 1801: *Letters of Samuel Taylor Coleridge* ed. Ernest Hartley Coleridge (1895), i, p. 359.

Another letter to the long-suffering Southey, who had a child of his own, actually begins:

Derwent can say his letters, and if you could but see his darling mouth when he shouts at Q! This is a digression . . .

and ends:

That child [Hartley] is a poet, in spite of the forehead, 'villainously *low*', which his mother smuggled into his face . . .[1]

While his children grew up, he took pride in their intellectual progress. When the boys were boarded at school in Ambleside and spent their weekends with him, he wrote to his wife at Keswick:

Hartley [thirteen] . . . is really handsome; at least as handsome as a face so original and intellectual can be. And Derwent [nine] is 'a nice little fellow', and no lack-wit either. I read to Hartley out of the German a series of very masterly arguments concerning the startling gross improbabilities of Esther . . . It really *surprised* me, the acuteness and steadiness of judgment with which he answered more than half, weakened many, and at last determined that two only were not to be got over . . . Indeed Eichhorn . . . was obliged to give up the two which he had declared as desperate.[2]

RICHARD STEELE wrote to his wife when their small son was still 'tumbling' and in 'frocks':

He is . . . a very great scholar: he can read his Primer; and I have brought down my Virgil. He makes most shrewd remarks about the pictures.[3]

Settled with the Morgans at Hammersmith, Coleridge visited Greta Hall for the last time, and during that month described his daughter's precocity at the age of nine:

. . . little Sara . . . reads French tolerably, and Italian fluently, and I was astonished at her acquaintance with her native language. The word 'hostile' occurring in what she read to me, I asked her what 'hostile' meant? and she answered at once, 'Why! inimical; only that "inimical" is more often used for things and measures and not, as "hostile" is, to persons and nations.' If I had dared, I should have urged Mrs C. to let me take her to London for four or five months, and return with Southey, but I feared it might be presumptuous

1 9 Aug. 1802: *ibid.*, i, pp. 393, 395.
2 Spring 1810: *ibid.*, ii, p. 564.
3 16 Mar. 1717.

in me to bring her to you. But she is such a sweet-tempered, meek, blue-eyed fairy . . .[1]

The children of WORDSWORTH's marriage, despite their advantage of a united home, were nothing like as academic as Coleridge's offspring – 'The Coleridges are all scholars'[2] – although the Words-worths' third child, Thomas, had he lived, might have proved an exception. Wordsworth spent much time teaching his eldest, Johnny, but found him 'for book attainments the slowest Child almost I ever knew'.[3] Dorothy faced reality when she wrote to her sister:

. . . we do not produce scholars.[4]

She said when aunt or mother tried to teach six-year-old Willy, the youngest, the 'lesson was the signal for yawning, and for perpetual motion in one part of the body or another'.[5]

They were cherished none the less for that, their other qualities recognized, and in that closely knit home Dorothy showed as much pride as if she were their mother:

Oh! my dear friend! Johnny [five] *is* a sweet Creature; so noble, bold, gentle, and beautiful . . . D. [Dora, four] is very pretty, very kittenish, very quick . . . but not given to *thought*. Coleridge often repeats to her [altering a line of William's poem of *Ruth*] 'the wild cat of the wilderness was not so fair as she'. To this she replies with a squall, inviting him to some fresh skirmish. C. says that John has all the virtues of a tame Dog, she the qualities of the Cat. God bless them . . . As to little Thomas [two] he is a Darling – but he having spent much of his early time in the kitchen he is never happier than when he is among the pots and pans. Therefore he is called 'Potiphar'. To this name he lustily replies, 'Me no Potiphar, me a good boy.'. . . we are all . . . very proud of him.[6]

In a letter that spoke of 'John [now eleven] . . . without exception, unfortunately the slowest Boy at his books that ever I was acquainted with', she quickly went on to add:

1 To John Morgan, 28 Feb. 1812: *Letters of Samuel Taylor Coleridge* ed. Ernest Hartley Coleridge (1895), ii, pp. 575–6.
2 Dorothy to Catherine Clarkson, 24 Apr. 1814: *The Letters of William & Dorothy Wordsworth* ed. C. L. Shaver, Mary Moorman, Alan G. Hill (1967–79), iii, p. 141.
3 To Christopher Wordsworth, 26 Nov. 1814: *ibid.*, iii, p. 172.
4 To Priscilla Wordsworth, 27 Feb. 1815: *ibid.*, iii, p. 207.
5 To Catherine Clarkson, 4 Apr. 1816: *ibid.*, iii, p. 294.
6 Ditto., 8 Dec. 1808: *ibid.*, ii, p. 283.

. . . yet he has a good understanding, and as just a sense of right and wrong as the best philosopher. He is tall, strong, and well-looking, a good player and well liked among his schoolfellows for his sweetness of temper and his plain honesty. . .[1]

Dorothy knew 'no greater pleasure than to instruct a girl . . . so eager in the pursuit of knowledge' as Coleridge's daughter, Sara (thirteen), and often did she wish that Dora (eleven) 'was like her in this respect', but again she found compensation:

. . . for with all Dorothy's [i.e., Dora's] idleness there are many parts of her character which are much more interesting than corresponding ones in Sara, therefore, as good and evil are always mixed up together, we should be very contented with a moderate share of industry, her talents being quite enough.[2]

CONAN DOYLE celebrated his own in *Three of Them* – 'prepared to believe that England is full of even such children'.[3] He described them as 'all beautiful and all quite different':

The eldest is a boy of eight . . . whom we shall call 'Laddie' . . . His soul is the most gallant, unselfish, innocent thing that ever God sent out to get an extra polish upon earth . . . Dimples is nearly seven when he begins . . . He has a love and understanding of all living creatures, the uglier and more slimy the better[4] . . . Then there is Baby, a dainty elfin Dresden-china little creature of five at the outset, as fair as an angel and as deep as a well.[5]

JOYCE said of his children, to whom he was deeply attached, that Jane Austen had named them 'Sense and Sensibility'.[6] When he invited friends to the flat in Zurich, he would tell them to come early so they could hear his boy Giorgi sing his own favourite Verdi. He told his sister:

The most important thing that can happen to a man is the birth of a child.[7]

---

1 To Priscilla Wordsworth, 27 Feb. 1815: *ibid.*, iii, pp. 207–8.
2 To Catherine Clarkson, 26 May 1816: *ibid.*, iii, p. 320. (Cf. Dorothy's letter, 24 Apr. 1814: *ibid.*, iii, p. 141 – 'There is not one of them [the Coleridges] wholly free from affectation.')
3 *Three of Them: A Reminiscence* (1923), Introduction, p. v.
4 *Ibid.*, pp. 1–3.
5 *Ibid.*, p. 5. He also had a son and daughter from his former marriage.
6 Richard Ellmann: *James Joyce* (revised edn. 1982), p. 204.
7 *Ibid.* (1959), p. 212.

CHAPTER SIX

Providing Educational Treats and Pursuits

In summer, as they passed through London to Lincolnshire, TENNYSON took his boys to Westminster Abbey, the Zoo, the Tower, the Elgin Marbles at the British Museum, or the National Gallery.

In the last he much delighted . . . he always led the way first of all to the 'Raising of Lazarus' by Sebastian del Piombo and to Titian's 'Bacchus and Ariadne'.[1]

There were the 'summer journeys' when he took his family, Hallam and Lionel, nine and seven, to the Auvergne and the Pyrenees – and, four years later, to Waterloo and Weimar.

As DICKENS's children 'grew older, and were able to act little plays', Mamey told that 'it was their father himself who was teacher, manager, and prompter to the infant amateurs':

. . . He would teach the children their parts separately . . . acting himself for their edification.[2]

When KIPLING's children (just like Dan and Una in *Puck of Pook's Hill*) 'did a little piece of *Midsummer Night's Dream*' in the Quarry at Bateman's – seven-year-old John as Puck, and eight-year-old Elsie as Titania – their father played Bottom.

During Fanny's convalescence in Torquay following a grim miscarriage, the family went down to be with her, and KINGSLEY offered to supply marine specimens to his friend Philip Gosse, who sent a hamper of wicker-topped jars. He enlisted the help of Rose and Maurice, who ran 'with proud delight to add their little treasure'. He worked out where to find *chirodata* and the orange-mouthed *actinia*, and they went to Petit Tor, Tor Abbey and Goodrington. Gathered

---

1 *Alfred Lord Tennyson: A Memoir by his Son* (1897), i, p. 371.
2 'Charles Dickens at Home: with especial reference to his relations with Children': *The Cornhill Magazine*, Jan. 1885.

around the mother's sofa of an evening, they put 'the wonders and labours of the long happy day' into the vivarium, 'examining, arranging, preserving and noting down in the diary . . .'[1]

He wrote of Maurice, with him at Cambridge at the time of his history professorship:

Oh, what a blessing to see him grow under one's eyes . . . the father who can finish his boy's education ought to be thankful.[2]

After STEVENSON's marriage, when they were confined indoors by the rain at Braemar he and twelve-year-old Lloyd vied together in putting up a painting or drawing each day on a certain wall in the sitting-room, and to amuse him Stevenson began *Treasure Island* – as Kenneth Grahame to entertain a smaller boy told *The Wind in the Willows*.

At Davos, where they rented a chalet, all three collaborated in preparing productions for Lloyd's toy theatre. In a room called 'The Office' Lloyd kept a toy printing press brought from California, and one day there was a respectful knock and Stevenson handed in to Osbourne and Co. – for so the boy styled himself – a set of verses. Lloyd, overwhelmed and overjoyed, printed an edition of fifty, which he sold in the hotels. Their next venture was a larger edition of more poems, this time illustrated, which sold for ninepence a copy. Jenni Calder suggests that such activities 'prepared the ground for a more creative collaboration later'.[3]

A. A. MILNE and Christopher shared a love of maths. From his father, sitting beside him on the sofa, Christopher learned how to solve simultaneous equations. His father taught him Morse so they could pass messages to each other as Burnside drove them down to Cotchford. He introduced Christopher to *Treasure Island*, encouraging him, when at Stowe, to read Wells, Dickens, and Hardy.

According to his daughter Margaret, EVELYN WAUGH enjoyed most of all the role of educator and instructor to his children. He read to them 'a great deal, mostly Dickens', and grumbled about their posture so that in the end they had to sit absolutely still.

1 Quoted by Susan Chitty: *The Beast & the Monk: A Life of Charles Kingsley* (1974), p. 166.
2 Letter to Fanny, 15 July 1867. *Ibid*, p. 244.
3 *RLS: A Life Study* (1980), p. 160.

However we all loved these reading sessions.[1]

One term he taught her daily in the library, at the age of ten. There was no geography or maths, but much prejudiced history, Victorian literature, the technical processes of prints, and novel-writing.

From about the age of eight, his daughters swept down to the dining-room in long dresses picked from their playbox, and at table he encouraged his children in the art of conversation – to talk not only to grown-ups but with each other. Frances Donaldson's elder daughter (who, like her sister, wore short dresses until sixteen and felt 'absolutely barbaric' beside them) told her later that 'all that talking at meals was very useful when we first grew up'.[2] Then there was the involvement of his children in the ritual that he made of entertaining, for he was always a stickler for form. His youngest child present would have to turn the handle of the musical box as guests took their places. A special guest would listen to a long, previously rehearsed, speech delivered by one of the children.

At a fête in his house and garden to raise money for St Dominic's, Dursley, he got his own and the Donaldson children to assist – Rose Donaldson he trained to be a very original guide speaking his own repartee. When he took his daughter Teresa to St George's Chapel and she asked if that was the tomb of Henry VIII, he said: 'Yes. You may spit on that.'[3] For five years, A. J. P. TAYLOR took Crispin and Daniel, sons of his second marriage, to the North Yorkshire moors where there were five Cistercian abbeys and six castles. He also took his children abroad.

1 Christopher Sykes: *Evelyn Waugh: A Biography* (1975), p. 451.
2 Frances Donaldson: *Evelyn Waugh: Portrait of a Country Neighbour* (1967), p. 41.
3 *Ibid.*, p. 46.

CHAPTER SEVEN

Using Psychology

I

When ten-year-old Hartley was in his care at Coleorton, COLERIDGE described an incident to his wife and found a psychological explanation of his son's behaviour:

. . . when he could get out of the coach at dinner, I was obliged to be in incessant watch . . . He twice ran into a field . . . I was out five minutes seeking him in great alarm, and found him at the further end of a wet meadow, on the marge of a river. After dinner . . . I ordered him to go into the coach and sit in the place where he was before . . . In about five minutes I followed. No Hartley!. . . At length, where should I discover him! In the same meadow . . . close down on the very edge of the water. I was angry from downright fright! And what . . . was Cataphract's excuse! 'It was a misunderstanding, Father! I thought, you see, that you bid me go to the very same place in the meadow where I was.' I told him that he had interpreted the text by the suggestions of the flesh, not the inspiration of the spirit; and *his wish* the naughty father of the base-born Thought. . . . he is a very good and sweet child, of strict honour and truth, from which he never deviates except in the form of sophism when he sports his logical false dice in the game of excuses. This, however, is the mere effect of his activity of thought, and his aiming at being clever and ingenious.[1]

Mrs Cowden Clarke described the DICKENS family and their few guests sitting in the garden at No. 1 Devonshire Terrace on a summer evening:

. . . I recollect seeing one of the little sons draw Charles Dickens apart, and stand in eager talk with him . . .

A few minutes later, Dickens, then in his mid-thirties, came and told her what the child had required:

---

1 25 Dec. 1806. *Letters of Samuel Taylor Coleridge* ed. Ernest Hartley Coleridge (1895), ii, pp. 509–10.

'The little fellow gave me so many excellent reasons why he should not go to bed so soon, that I yielded the point, and let him stay up half an hour later.[1]

KINGSLEY brought the psychology that children had 'their hours of rain, when the quicksilver falls' and at those times, instead of repression, parents should provide a change of activity. CONAN DOYLE ('as every harassed parent knows') found a different type of naughtiness in each of his later three:

Laddie was rarely naughty, but if he was it was in a despairing can't-help-it, very sorry-but-you-will-have-to-put-up-with-it way which it was difficult to deal with. Dimples was cold-blooded and deliberate with a . . . 'I will-now-do-some-mischuff' air, which invited spanking. Baby was seldom obstreperous, but . . . when it did come . . . it was impossible to control, so that a distressed lady and a secretly chuckling Daddy could only wait till the weather cleared.[2]

One day, into one of the WILDES' receptions held in the drawing-room of (then) 16 Tite Street, Chelsea, capered two little boys of six and seven. They had taken off all of their clothes in protest at having to go to a fancy-dress party as Little Lord Fauntleroy and Millais's 'Bubbles'. Vyvyan reports official disapproval – but that his father took the hint. They went in their sailor suits of real naval cloth cut by a naval tailor.

Wilde's letter to *The Daily Chronicle*, in which he defended Warder Martin who had been dismissed by the Prison Commissioners 'for having given some sweet biscuits to a little hungry child', reflects his understanding of the psychology and physiology of small children from experience of his own:

A child can understand a punishment inflicted by an individual, such as a parent or guardian, and bear it with a certain amount of acquiescence. What it cannot understand is a punishment inflicted by society. It cannot realize what society is. With grown people it is, of course, the reverse . . . Anyone who knows anything about children knows how easily a child's digestion is upset by a fit of crying, or trouble and mental distress of any kind.[3]

When she was thirteen, the relations between Judith and her mother became rather strained and MASEFIELD, away in France during World

1 Charles & Mary Cowden Clarke: *Recollections of Writers* (1878), p. 316.
2 *Three of Them: A Reminiscence* (1923), p. 53.
3 28 May 1897. *De Profundis (with Additional Matter), Collected Edition of Wilde's Works* ed. Robert Ross (1908), xi, pp. 167 f.

War I, told his wife that only 'mild and loving joking' would find a response.

You can coax her into being a saint, but that is the only way.[1]

DOYLE said of his own Billie, five years old:

Her will is tremendous . . . Only kind guidance and friendly reasoning can mould it.[2]

JOYCE, who spoilt his daughter Lucia, never chastised either her or Giorgi, although his wife did when they were naughty. He said:

Children must be educated by love, not punishment.[3]

II

A. A. MILNE had an unfailing sensitivity about putting his son right and always tried to give reasons. When young Christopher at dinner put down his fork pointing upwards, and wanted to know why it was wrong, he said:

Suppose somebody fell through the ceiling. They might land on your fork and that would be very painful.[4]

When he observed, from afar, Chistopher altering a cap pistol, which already had an abnormal explosion and now nearly caused an injury, he told him about a boy whom Christopher knew and who had lost an eye, playing with a gun. 'That's why I've never been too happy about your pistol,' he concluded – and Christopher on his own volition threw it away.[5] When the boy made a mistake about a nest under the tiles and said he had seen a blackbird flying in, Milne, instead of contradiction, left a tactful loophole:

Perhaps it's a blackbird visiting a starling.[6]

From the age of eight, Christopher developed a stammer which, aggravated by shyness, had become considerably worse by sixteen. If

1 6 May 1917. Constance Babington Smith: *John Masefield: A Life* (1978), p. 170.
2 *Three of Them: A Reminiscence* (1923), pp. 5–6.
3 Richard Ellmann: *James Joyce* (1959), p. 447.
4 Christopher Milne: *The Enchanted Places* (1974), pp. 120–1.
5 *Ibid.*, p. 155.
6 *Ibid.*, p. 121.

the boy wanted something from a shop, instead of pressurizing him to attempt the purchase his father said, 'All right, let's go and buy it together,' – and Christopher wrote in his maturity:

I blessed him for it and loved him all the more.[1]

During this difficult time he was allowed, when on holiday, 'to enjoy himself in the shallows'. No excessive demands were made on him. If there were visitors, it was enough for him to appear and 'slide silently off . . .'

Alone by the river . . . through the fields . . . yet never lonely. What bliss this was![2]

When Christopher was twenty-four and in Italy, during World War II, a parcel of books that his father sent him had among them Renan's *The Life of Jesus* and Winwood Reade's *The Martyrdom of Man*. It was the latter that Christopher found totally satisfying. In their further correspondence, he learned that his father shared Reade's atheistical views. For twenty-four years his father had allowed the Church to use its influence, 'though never its force, and that was why I had not been christened' – Nanny could teach him to say prayers, and at school he had done Divinity like the other boys and gone to Chapel. But now the time had come to hear the other side. Even then his father 'had wanted to play absolutely fair, and so he had added *The Life of Jesus*'.[3]

Like Barrie with the Llewelyn Davies boys, Milne relived his boyhood vicariously through his son. 'He needed me', Christopher wrote, 'to escape from being fifty.'[4]

At fifty-one, Sir HAROLD NICOLSON attempted an evaluation of his and Vita's relations towards their sons:

We have never imposed any sort of filial duty on either Ben or Nigel. They know that they can make any possible claim on us and that we shall never make any claim on them. That is the only basis for a proper relationship between one generation and another.

It was more difficult for him than for Vita, essentially a solitary soul.

I try to live my own life again in those of my sons.

1 *Ibid.*, p. 141.
2 *Ibid.*, p. 150.
3 *Ibid.*, p. 144.
4 *Ibid.*, p. 159.

He knew that this drove them to fury, and he tried to control his yearning. He acknowledged it to be 'rather grotesque' that with all his activities he loved them so much and thought about their lives instead of his own.

But they understand it. Benzie in a gentle way. Nigel in a dutiful way . . . But I am sometimes terrified by my adoration of them.[1]

To his friend, Julian Symons, ORWELL philosophized:

They're awful fun in spite of the nuisance, & as they develop one has one's own childhood over again.

He is another who showed himself aware of one of the pitfalls of bringing up a child:

I suppose one thing one has to guard against is imposing one's own childhood . . .[2]

When C. S. LEWIS married in late life a dying woman, he had – for the six years and a few months left to him – the responsibility of bringing up two orphan stepsons. He asked Sister Madeleva to pray for help and guidance on his behalf, but added:

I have only one qualification if it is one; those two boys are now facing the very same calamity that befell my brother and myself at about the same age.[3]

1 7 June 1938: *Diaries & Letters 1930–1939* ed. Nigel Nicolson (1966), p. 346.
2 20 Apr. 1948. *The Collected Essays, Journalism & Letters of George Orwell* ed. Sonia Orwell & Ian Angus (1968), iv, p. 415.
3 8 May 1957. *Letters of C. S. Lewis* ed. with *Memoir* by W. H. Lewis (1966), p. 276.

CHAPTER EIGHT

Practicalities

When STEELE's beloved Prue was in Wales, he drew her attention, in a letter, to some practical matters with regard to their small son:

He begins to be very ragged; and I hope I shall be pardoned if I equip him with new clothes and frocks, or what Mrs Evans and I shall think for his service.[1]

It is interesting to discover that COLERIDGE could show a similar concern about such prosaic things. As a young man, when Hartley was a baby, he wrote to Thelwall:

You would smile to see my eye rolling up to the ceiling in a lyric fury, and on my knee a diaper pinned to warm.[2]

He wrote to his wife from Caermarthen:

It is my particular wish that Hartley [six] *and Derwent* [two] *should have as little tea as possible, and always very weak, with more than half milk.* Read this sentence to Mary and Mrs Wilson. I should think that ginger-tea, with a good deal of milk in it, would be an excellent thing for Hartley. A teaspoonful piled up of ginger would make a potful of tea, that would serve him for two days. And let him drink it half milk. I dare say that he would like it very well, for it is pleasant with sugar, and tell him that his dear father takes it instead of tea, and believes that it will make his dear Hartley grow. The whole kingdom is getting ginger-mad.[3]

Five months after, he told her from London:

I will try to bring down something for Hartley, though toys are so outrageously dear, and I so short of money, that I shall be puzzled.[4]

1 16 Mar. 1717.
2 6 Feb. 1797. *Letters of Samuel Taylor Coleridge* ed. Ernest Hartley Coleridge (1895), i, p. 220.
3 16 Nov. 1802. *Ibid.*, i, p. 413.
4 4 Apr. 1803. *Ibid.*, i, p. 421.

Nearly another year, and some weeks before sailing for Malta, he wrote from London:

I should be very unhappy if he [Hartley] were to go to the town school, unless there were any steady lad that Mr Jackson knew and could rely on . . . who would be easily induced by half-a-crown once in two or three months to take care of him, let him always sit by him, and to whom you should instruct the child to yield a certain degree of obedience.

He intended getting for his children the game 'the Spillekins . . . a German refinement of our Jack Straw':

You or some one of your sisters will be so good as to play with Hartley, at first, that Derwent may learn it . . . It is certainly an excellent game to teach children steadiness of hand and quickness of eye, and a good opportunity to impress upon them the beauty of strict truth, when it is against their own interest . . .[1]

Nearer the time, he wrote:

Hartley will receive his and Derwent's Spillekins with a letter from me by the first waggon that leaves London after Wednesday next.[2]

ORWELL's friends may have been sceptical about his carpentry, but were unanimous that he made an excellent father. After his wife's death, he invited Fyvel's wife, who had worked with small children, to advise him about his handling of Richard. So one Tuesday, as Susan left for her day off, the Fyvels came in. His Canonbury Square flat seemed cheerless that early winter of 1946 and Mary proposed that he fit draught excluders to the doors. This he promised to do. He particularly wanted her to watch him bathe Richard, and she suggested that the window of the unheated bathroom should be closed. He shut it at once, saying 'A good idea!' He used plenty of warm water but, afterwards, carried the little boy in a skimpy towel along a draughty passage to dry him before the sitting-room fire. She said he must dry him partly and quickly in the bathroom and wrap him in a proper bath towel. He again seemed grateful, and said: 'A good idea!' But overall she had nothing but praise for his loving and warm relationship with Richard.

1 To his wife: 19 Feb. 1804. *Ibid.*, ii, pp. 461–2.
2 1 Apr. 1804. *Ibid.*, ii, p. 468. (Joyce excelled at the game of Spillikins [jackstraws] when he was at Clengowes Wood College 1888–91. See Richard Ellmann: *James Joyce* [revised edn. 1982], p. 31.)

. . . it was obvious that both father and child were thoroughly enjoying the whole experience.

Orwell told her: 'You see, I've always been good with animals.'[1]

At Holywell Ford, when A.J.P. TAYLOR was tutor at Magdalen, he made his children's breakfast porridge and bathed them in the evening. He read to them tales ranging from Beatrix Potter's to those by Dickens and Scott. He used to take the two girls to their nursery school, carrying first one on his bicycle while the other walked, and then changing about.

Others have been equally down-to-earth when children were not their own. WILDE had seen many children in prison and, in his letter to *The Daily Chronicle* immediately after his release, he wrote that if they had to be there ('Of course, no child under fourteen . . . should be sent to prison at all'), they should be in a workshop or schoolroom by day, a dormitory at night, and 'should be allowed exercise for at least three hours a day'. Their food should not be the same as given to the men – bread and water for breakfast, 'coarse Indian meal stirabout' for dinner, and dry bread and water for supper – but 'should consist of tea and bread-and-butter and soup'.[2]

A. S. NEILL, showing visitors round Summerhill, felt ashamed that he had to unlock the workshop. The shutting out was a denial of freedom, when he and his Australian wife had set out to make a school in which children had freedom to be themselves. But the workshop was locked, by general consent, after elder pupils had ceased to enter because all the tools were spoilt. Neill valued tools. They were among the few things he was possessive about.

We must face the fact that adults are possessive and children aren't. Any living together between children and adults must result in conflict over things material.[3]

1 See T. R. Fyvel: *George Orwell: a personal memoir* (1982), pp. 147–8.
2 28 May 1897. 2nd Collected Edn. of the Works of Oscar Wilde (1909), x, *De Profundis*, p. 135.
3 *That Dreadful School* (1937), p. 148.

CHAPTER NINE

Children Outside Marriage

I

They had their share of children born outside marriage. Even unlikely people such as Wordsworth, and Dorothy L. Sayers, put aside the conventions.

After Cambridge, WORDSWORTH at twenty-one went to France –

> Led thither chiefly by a personal wish
> To speak the language more familiarly,
> . . . At that time,
> . . . the first storm was overblown,
> And the strong hand of outward violence
> Lock'd up in quiet . . .
> . . . and my heart was all
> Given to the People, and my love was theirs . . .[1]

His sympathies tended towards the moderate republican party, the Girondists, but his companions were royalist officers and counter-revolutionaries. 'Young . . . impetuous . . . encompassed with strong temptations',[2] in his lodgings at Orleans he fell in love with Annette Vallon, who tutored him free of charge in French. Her father, a surgeon, was dead, and her mother had married again. She was twenty-five, both Catholic and royalist.

He wrote urgently to his brother Richard in London for £20, but did not mention Annette far advanced in pregnancy. To provide for their child who would be born in two months, he needed to fulfil his intention of becoming a clergyman in the Church of England, for which he would depend on the influence of his guardian uncles who controlled his purse-strings and were clamouring for him to come home.

---

1 *The Prelude* (1805–6 version), Bk. IX: ll. 36–7, 107–10, 124–5.
2 Christopher Wordsworth: *Memoirs of William Wordsworth* (1851), p. 74.

> Reluctantly to England I return'd,
> Compelled by nothing less than absolute want
> Of funds . . .
> (After a whole year's absence). . . [1]

On his way back through Paris, the magnet of a city in ferment held him a while, or perhaps with the increasing danger of arrest he had to move circumspectly. Only the month before, in September, her Jacobin masters – Danton, Marat, Robespierre – had begun the Terror by encouraging the mob in the Massacre of hundreds of suspected royalists. Wordsworth arrived back in England shortly after his daughter was born on 15 December 1792 in Orleans, and she was baptized Anne Caroline Wordwodsth (*sic*).

Immediately he made his sister Dorothy his confidante, who from the first took a great interest in the welfare of mother and child, and became their friend and correspondent. But Uncle William, whom he or Dorothy told, would neither continue relations with the father of an illegitimate child – and a republican – nor help his nephew towards ordination. Within two months, France declared war on England.

In *The Prelude* his own love story is veiled in the anecdote of *Vaudracour and Julia*:

> . . . whether through effect
> Of some delirious hour, or that the Youth,
> Seeing so many bars betwixt himself
> And the dear haven where he wish'd to be
> In honourable wedlock with his love . . .
> Was inwardly prepared to turn aside
> From law and custom, and entrust himself
> To Nature for a happy end of all . . .
> I know not . . . [2]

Post-World War I, a letter by Annette to Wordsworth and one to Dorothy were unearthed by two ingenious scholars, G. M. Harper and Émile Legouis. The letters, confiscated by the Blois police, had lain in the archives of the Department of Loire-et-Cher for a hundred and thirty years.

Annette, known in France as Veuve Williams, wrote that her distress would be lessened were they married:

1 *The Prelude* (1805–6 version), Bk. X; ll. 190–2, 204.
2 Bk. IX: ll. 594–602, 607.

Yet I regard it as almost impossible that you should risk yourself. You might be taken prisoner . . . do your very utmost to hasten your daughter's happiness and mine, but only if there is not the slightest risk . . .[1]

She replied to a letter from Dorothy, who had expressed the hope that one day Annette and Caroline would be with William and herself in the same little cottage:

Oh sister, how happy we shall be! And you, my dear [William]. . . surrounded by your sister, your wife, your daughter, who will breathe only for you, we shall have but one feeling, one heart, one soul . . .

Not only was he separated from the mother of his child, his country was engaged in a life-or-death struggle with her people. Lord Clark described him writing poetry for the next three years 'without a glimmer of comfort or hope' and walking 'for miles alone, on Salisbury Plain and in Wales, talking only to tramps and beggars and discharged prisoners'.[2]

Then, at twenty-five, a legacy following the death of his friend Raisley Calvert enabled him to realize a long-cherished dream of setting up house with Dorothy. But not until seven more years did the brief Peace of Amiens enable him, accompanied by his sister, to spend four weeks in Calais. On the way he composed[3] *Sonnet upon Westminster Bridge*. Ahead of him, on the journey, were his first love and the child he had not seen. Behind him, in her home at Gallow Hill, his childhood sweetheart, whom he had told about Annette, waited to be his bride. Surely only Wordsworth at such a time could have written:

> Ne'er saw I, never felt, a calm so deep!

Mary Moorman believes that the enforced absence must soon have shown him that Annette stood apart from his poetic life. He could not draw inspiration from her as he did from the other men and women to whom he gave his love. Annette

had no conception that such a world even existed as that in which he lived and thought.[4]

In her *Journal*, Dorothy recorded:

1 Hunter Davies: *William Wordsworth: A Biography* (1980), p. 56.
2 Kenneth Clark: *Civilisation: A Personal View* (1969), p. 278.
3 It was not necessarily *written*.
4 *William Wordsworth: Early Years* (1957), p. 182.

We walked by the sea-shore almost every evening with Annette and Caroline, or Wm and I alone.[1]

Nine year-old Caroline is mentioned in a *Sonnet* he composed at this time:

> It is a beauteous evening, calm and free,
> The holy time is quiet as a Nun . . .
> Dear Child! dear Girl! that walkest with me here,
> If thou appear untouched by solemn thought,
> Thy nature is not therefore less divine:
> Thou liest in Abraham's bosom all the year;
> And worshipp'st at the Temple's inner shrine,
> God being with thee when we know it not.

About twelve years later a young French officer, Eustace Baudouin, who had been a prisoner of the English, called at Rydal Mount with firsthand news. Caroline, now twenty-one, was engaged to his brother Jean Baptiste. Under Napoleon, she and her mother had risked their lives helping royalist supporters. Eustace remarked on the physical similarity of father and daughter.

Despite having had no contact for so long, Wordsworth was consulted about the match and gave consent. The wedding was delayed by Napoleon's escape from Elba (causing consternation to Annette's royalist circle) and the Battle of Waterloo. There was the hope at first that Wordsworth would attend; then it was to be Dorothy. In the event, February 1816, neither was present. The marriage certificate described Caroline as the daughter of William Wordsworth: '*demeurant à Grasner Kendan duche de Westmorland, Angleterre*'.

The honouring of a debt by his father's employer – of which Wordsworth and Dorothy's share was about £3,000 – and the cessation of war now made it possible for him to send Caroline £30 annually until in 1835 he gave a lump sum of £400. The names of her first child included that of Dorothée.

Southey, the year after the wedding, was going on a trip that would take him to Paris, and Wordsworth asked him to call on Caroline. He told his friend 'it would not be necessary nor pleasant' for him 'to be acquainted with the story of Caroline's birth'. She spoke with Southey an hour and the whole story unfolded. Next day he breakfasted with

1 The Grasmere Journals, 31 July–29 Aug. 1802.

Caroline and her mother. Their love for Wordsworth was very apparent – they showed no feeling of bitterness. After a tour of Switzerland and the Italian Lakes, when Wordsworth was fifty, he, Mary, Dorothy, and Crabb Robinson, on their way home took lodgings in Rue Chalot, the street where Annette and the Baudouins were living. Caroline, who now had two little girls, called him 'Father'. He paid another visit when he was sixty-seven.

After John Cournos had left England, DOROTHY L. SAYERS brought home at Christmas 'a poor devil' she had chummed up with one weekend. His 'literary intellect' wasn't 'exactly his strong point . . . he knows all about cars . . .'[1] She permitted him the use of contraceptives, denied to the man she loved, and became accidentally pregnant just when she had started her job at Benson's advertising agency. She wrote to Cournos:

If you'd wanted me, you'd have taken me. The Beast did, to do him, justice.[2]

She waited until only two days before the birth and then wrote to 'her best friend', her cousin Ivy, who fostered children:

There's an infant I'm very anxious you should have the charge of.[3]

Anthony was born in a private nursing home in Southbourne and about four weeks later she brought him to Ivy, having admitted 'he was my own!'

According to Janet Hitchman, she went home on her motor cycle (her Ner-a-Car?) when she was 'almost six months advanced in pregnancy', and 'it is probable that she confided in her parents' – who 'would have had to be extremely unworldly had they not eventually noticed her condition'.[4] But James Brabazon declares 'the suggestion that she went back to Christchurch [Cambridgeshire] during her pregnancy is quite without foundation'.[5] He is categorical that to the end of their lives her parents knew nothing of Anthony's birth.[6]

She paid Ivy Shrimpton £3 a month, increasing the sum as time went on. After eight or nine months her visits grew less frequent and

1 Letter to her mother, 18 Dec. 1922: James Brabazon: *Dorothy L. Sayers: The Life of a Courageous Woman* (1981), pp. 96–7.
2 4 Dec. 1924: *ibid.*, p. 97.
3 1 Jan. 1924: *ibid.*, p. 101.
4 *Such a Strange Lady: An introduction to Dorothy L.Sayers* (1975), p. 65.
5 *Op cit.*, p. 100.
6 *Ibid.*, p. 105.

she left her affectionate and eccentric cousin in sole control. Ivy, living as a recluse, taught him until he was ten.

Before Anthony went to school an unofficial adoption took place. Dorothy had now married 'Mac' and the boy called them mother and father, but he was never brought into their home. She paid the bills, dutifully met him on special occasions, and wrote him friendly, humorous and practical letters. She saw he had a watch, a pen and pocket-knife for his prep school in Kent, and when he won a scholarship to Malvern she helped to pack his things. She sent him to Oxford.

II

RICHARD STEELE, as well as four children by his second marriage, had one natural daughter. About 1718 he proposed to marry her to Richard Savage, whose play *Love in a Veil* had caused the two men to be acquainted, but, according to Johnson, Steele was unable to raise the intended dowry of £1,000 and, when he received a report that Savage had 'ridiculed him', the young man was 'never afterwards admitted . . . to his house'.[1]

Just twenty-two, and soon after his arrival in London, BOSWELL heard that he had fathered a son. Before leaving Scotland, he had left instructions for the baptism and £10 with Dr Cairnie for the mother's use. The boy was named after the Royal Martyr and put with a foster-mother. Boswell wrote to his old schoolfellow Johnston:

I am really fond of the character of a father. I feel myself more dignified somehow . . . God bless him . . . By all means let the nurse give my child the surname of Boswell immediately. I am not ashamed of him. And I am not afraid of its being known.[2]

He saw 'Peggy Doig, the mother of my little boy' in town, and 'advised her not to fall into such a scrape again':

I really don't know how to talk on such a subject, when I consider that I led her into the scrape. However, it was not the first time, and she has been well taken care of.[3]

1 *The Lives of the English Poets* (Dublin edn. 1779–81), iii, p. 44.
2 *Boswell's London Journal 1762–1763* ed. Frederick A. Pottle (1951), p. 390 Note.
3 This was 'some time ago' but is entered under Wed. 27 July 1763: *ibid.*, p. 389.

She was probably a servant.

Before leaving England on his Grand Tour, he wrote again to Johnston:

. . . Poor little creature! I wish from my heart that I had seen him before I left England. His resembling me is a most agreeable thing. I am positive that he is my own. He shall always find me an affectionate father . . . I am determined that nothing shall be wanting to accomplish him for whatever his genius leads him to . . .[1]

But in the new year, Charles died, while Boswell was in Utrecht. In the two or three years before he married his cousin, he maintained a liaison with a young grass widow, Mrs Dodds, and a daughter, Sally, was born. Apparently she too died in infancy.

In his love and responsibility for his children, BURNS did not discriminate whether they were born in or out of wedlock. He celebrated his first child, a daughter by Elizabeth Paton, in *Welcome to a Bastart Wean*:

> Welcome, my bonie, sweet, wee dochter!
> Tho' ye come here a wee unsought for,
> And tho' your comin I hae fought for
> Baith kirk and queir;
> Yet, by my faith, ye're no unwrought for –
> That I shall swear!. . .
>
> Tho' I should be the waur bestead,
> Thou's be as braw and bienly clad,
> And thy young years as nicely bred
> Wi' education,
> As onie brat o' wedlock's bed
> In a' thy station . . .

With Jean Armour and Meg Cameron both pregnant by him, he wrote to Robert Ainslie congratulating him on a bastard son:

. . . My ailing child is got better . . . and I shall get a farm, and keep them all about my hand, and breed them in the fear of the Lord and an oatstick, and I shall be the happiest man upon earth . . .[2]

After DE QUINCEY had pruned the rambling hedges around his orchard at Town End (now Dove Cottage), Dorothy Wordsworth and Sarah Hutchinson were horrified, for they considered him 'no more

1 *Ibid.*, p. 390 Note.
2 29 July 1787.

than a caretaker'[1] of their once beloved home. The quarrel lasted six years. But when he married a local dalesman's daughter who had already borne him a son, the Wordsworths cut him completely. Richard Caseby suggests that 'one reason . . . was the expectation that De Quincey would marry Dorothy'.[2] At the time he moved in, Dorothy had loved him 'dearly' and found local women to make his curtains. She had bought him kitchen utensils from Kendal, and commissioned shelves worth £17 17s 8d from a Grasmere carpenter for his twenty-nine chests of books.

William, the first-born, was the pride and joy of the De Quincey household. He grew to share his father's same love of books, and upon him De Quincey 'exhausted all that care and hourly companionship could do for the culture of an intellect . . .'[3] He lived until seventeen, and his father spoke of him – as did Southey of his own young son – as 'the crown and glory of my life'.

In view of BYRON's numerous liaisons it is curious that we do not hear of more natural children. To honour his twenty-first birthday an ox was roasted whole in the courtyard of Newstead Abbey, while he dined abstemiously in London. The youngest maid, Lucy, he was keeping on with another to take care of the house – 'more especially as the youngest is pregnant (I need not tell you by whom) and I cannot have the girl on the parish'. He provided for Lucy with unconventional generosity: £50 for her and £50 for the child annually. In the spirit of Burns, he celebrated William's birth in a poem entitled *To My Son*:

> . . . Why, let the world unfeeling frown,
> Must I fond Nature's claim disown?
> Ah, no – though moralists reprove,
> I hail thee, dearest child of love . . .

Scholars are still divided about the ambiguous birth of Medora. Leslie A. Marchand[4] points out that Medora believed Byron to be her father. However, Byron neither made any direct acknowledgement nor showed more interest in her than in Augusta's other children, and it would have been uncharacteristic of him not to recognize his illegal offspring – although, of course, this would be a special case. The

1 Richard Caseby: *The Opium-Eating Editor & The Westmorland Gazette* (1985), p. 70.
2 *Ibid.*, p. 82.
3 Grevel Lindop: *The Opium-Eater: A Life of Thomas De Quincey* (1981), p. 320.
4 *Byron: A Portrait* (1971), p. 166 Note.

Countess Longford ventures that 'Byron himself probably had doubts'. She shows that Medora never supplanted her eldest sister, Georgiana, undoubtedly Leigh's child, in Byron's affections; he continued to speak of *'my* Georgiana', and never made plans for Medora, as he did for Allegra, or wrote her a poem as he did his illegitimate son.[1]

Seventeen-year-old Claire Clairmont had been sending Byron love-letters for some time, and before he left for Italy when he was twenty-eight, she wrote:

Have you any objection to the following plan? On Thursday evening we may go out of town together by some stage or mail, about the distance of ten or twelve miles. There we shall be free and unknown; we can return the following morning . . .

He proposed a house in Dover Street.

Next month she accompanied Shelley and her stepsister Mary to Switzerland, and Byron came to stay in their hotel by Lake Geneva. As the months passed, Claire, now pregnant, went up to the Villa Diodati to join her lover, returning at dawn to the Shelleys' cottage.

. . . I could not exactly play the Stoic with a woman who had clambered eight hundred miles to unphilosophize me . . .[2]

But Byron was growing weary of the 'foolish girl'.

The child was born in her father's absence, and called at first Alba or The Dawn. When she was baptized along with the Shelleys' two children at St Giles-in-the-Fields, Claire saw that the entry read:

Clara Allegra. Right Hon. George Gordon Lord Byron, the reputed father by Clara Mary Jane Clairmont.

The little girl of unusual beauty was shuttled between her mother, the Hoppners, the Shelleys, and her father.

Claire was intent on her child's rights as the daughter of a personage who was both an English nobleman and a famous poet. Byron said that if Allegra were handed over the parting must be regarded final, and characteristically Shelley intervened protesting at such cruelty. According to Claire, Byron faithfully promised that, if the child came to live with him, he would never give her into the hands of strangers until she was seven. He proposed that Claire should have the title

1 Elizabeth Longford: *Byron* (1976), p. 62.
2 Letter to Augusta, Sept. 1816.

'Aunt' to save any embarrassment when she visited. Shelley warned of the risk she ran of losing her child for ever, but she rejected his advice and sent her 'little darling'. Later, she wrote to Byron:

You answer my request [to visit] by menacing, if I do not continue to suffer in silence, that you will . . . put my child in a convent where she will be equally divided from us both.

He carried it out with the excuse that Allegra, aged four, was 'quite beyond the control of servants'.

Shelley gives a poignant picture of the young girl, a few months before she died of typhus, in the Convent at Bagnacavallo. In a letter to Mary, he described his visit when he took a basket of sweetmeats:

She was prettily dressed in white muslin, and an apron of black silk with trousers.

She had led him all over the garden, and all over the convent, 'running and skipping so fast that I could hardly keep up with her'.[1] She had shown him her little bed and the chair where she sat at dinner.

The twelve-year liaison between DICKENS and Ellen Ternan – according to his daughter Kate – resulted in a boy who died.[2] Dorothy Cheston bore BENNETT a daughter when he was fifty-nine. Being legally separated from his wife, he could not marry, so she changed her name to his by deed poll. He told his brother Frank: 'Dorothy is recognized by all friends as my wife.'

Amber Reeves bore WELLS a child six years after Jane had given birth to their second boy. Wells wrote to Barrie's wife at the time of her divorce:

I've had rather a bad time. Amber & I are being forced never to see or write to each other . . . Anyway we've brought a very jolly little daughter into the world.

From his association with Rebecca West a son, Anthony, was born the day World War I started. It was not in the plan and he, being 'the experienced person',[3] took full blame. Anthony was shifted from school to school; when Rebecca West visited him, sometimes she was his aunt, sometimes his mother, and sometimes his adopted mother.

1 15 Aug. 1821.
2 Peter Ackroyd points out she offered no proof, and that Dickens 'was not "ordinary" in any sense'. (*Dickens* [1990], p. 914.) See p. 193.
3 *H. G. Wells in Love: Postscript to an Experiment in Autobiography* ed. G.P. Wells (1984), p. 96.

CHAPTER TEN
Bereavement

I

If earlier writers seem very modern in the way they treated their children, they also faced losing them on a scale no longer known in the West. Apparently none of BEN JONSON's several children survived him. His 22nd *Epigram* is on the death of his eldest daughter, Mary, at six months, and the 45th is on the death of his eldest son, Benjamin, aged seven. Of Sir THOMAS BROWNE's twelve children only one son and three daughters survived their parents. In the early 1730s, SAMUEL RICHARDSON lost all six children of his first marriage, and his wife. THOMAS GRAY was the only one of his eleven brothers and sisters to survive infancy. EDWARD LEAR's parents produced twenty-one children, many of whom died in babyhood; they named their daughters Sarah, until the third survived – and followed the same practice with their boys, three being Henry.

Perhaps it was no bad thing that MATTHEW ARNOLD spoilt his good-looking children shamefully, for he was to lose three of his four sons within a period of four years. Basil, the last to arrive, did not reach two. The father had his dead baby photographed – 'we should else have had no picture of him whatever'.[1] Sixteen-year-old Tommy died after a term at Harrow, the parents having moved house to care for him there. He had once made free to kiss his father at the door with 'God bless you, Matt!' In sending to Lord Houghton Tommy's setting of 'Good-Night and Good-Morning' (which became quite a popular success), Arnold wrote:

He composed a great deal but wrote hardly anything down . . . We have just this one thing to remind us of his talent for music, which was a very genuine one.

1 Park Honan: *Matthew Arnold: A Life* (1981), p. 289.

Trevenen ('Budge') died at Harrow, two years older. When the boy was small, the exhausted School Inspector used to fall on the bed as he returned home – and 'Budge, who never sits down at any other time, announces that he is very tired and must lie down with Papa . . . and there he reposes asking me from time to time if I love him . . . the fat old duck'.[1] It was noticed, during his bereavement, that Arnold interviewed pupil-teachers with his eyes filled with tears.

In one terrible year WORDSWORTH lost four-year-old Catherine, and Thomas, six and a half. The bereaved father had looked on Thomas as 'the future companion of his studies'.[2] He wrote to Southey:

I loved the Boy with the utmost love of which my soul is capable . . .[3]

The double loss probably explains what Aunt Sarah said when Willy was five:

. . . a pale look of that child has the power to disturb his father. He will scarcely suffer the wind of heaven to come near him and watches him the day through.

The same fear and anxiety are expressed in COLERIDGE's letter from Germany:

My dear Poole! don't let little Hartley die before I come home. That's silly – true – and I burst into tears as I wrote it.[4]

When Hartley was four, his health at times giving cause for alarm, Coleridge wrote to Southey:

If I were to lose him, I am afraid it would exceedingly deaden my affection for any other children I may have.

The enigmatic Conclusion to Part II of *Christabel* is placed at this point in the letter, making it plain that the lines refer to Hartley:

> A little child, a limber elf
> Singing, dancing to itself;
> A faery thing with red round cheeks

---

1 *Ibid.*, p. 288.
2 Dorothy Wordsworth to Catherine Clarkson: 24 Apr. 1814. *The Letters of William & Dorothy Wordsworth* ed. C. L. Shaver, Mary Moorman, Alan G. Hill (1967–79), iii, p. 141.
3 2 Dec. 1812. *Ibid.* iii, p. 51
4 6 May 1799. *Letters of Samuel Taylor Coleridge* ed. Ernest Hartley Coleridge (1895), i, p. 300.

> That always *finds*, and never *seeks*,
> Doth make a vision to the sight,
> Which fills a father's eyes with light! . . .[1]

A matter of weeks before he sailed for Malta, Coleridge makes the aside: 'Oh, my God vouchsafe me health that he may go to school to his own father!'[2]

SOUTHEY lost his beloved Herbert aged ten, and 'the radiant felicity . . . of the unhappy father' died for ever. He told De Quincey that 'for *him*, in this world . . . happiness there could be none; for his tenderest affections, the very deepest by many degrees which he ever knew, were now buried in the grave . . .'[3] Another son, Cuthbert, was born when Southey was forty-seven. Like the Wordsworths, the Southeys lost two young children. The Coleridges lost one.[4]

The DE QUINCEYS' eldest boy, William, nearly eighteen, fell ill of a cancer affecting chiefly the bones of the head and face, and died within three months, suffering greatly. Night after night the parents sat up with their 'poor boy', who had become totally blind as well as totally deaf. De Quincey wrote to an editor who had complained that an article required a different conclusion:

These things have . . . harrowed up my heart with grief and agitation . . . Doubtless you are right . . . and I have repeatedly laboured to write one . . .[5]

When the SHELLEYS' three-year-old, William, named after Godwin, fell ill with an alarming gastric attack, in Rome, Mary wrote:

The misery of these hours is beyond calculation . . . I am well, and so is Shelley, although he is more exhausted by watching than I am.

Shelley remained by his side for sixty hours. He wrote to Peacock:

Yesterday . . . my little William died . . . It is a great exertion to me to write this, and it seems to me as if, hunted by calamity as I have been, that I should never recover any cheerfulness again.

'Willmouse' was buried in the Protestant cemetery. 'This spot', Shelley wrote, 'is the repository of a sacred loss, of which the yearnings of a parent's heart are now prophetic; he is rendered

---

1 6 May 1801. *Ibid.*, i, p. 355. This epistolary version varies slightly.
2 19 Feb. 1804. *Ibid*, ii, p. 461.
3 *Selections Grave & Gay by Thomas De Quincey* (1853–71), i, p. 340.
4 See p. 88.
5 Nov. 1834. Grevel Lindop: *The Opium-Eater: A Life of Thomas De Quincey* (1981), p. 319.

immortal by love, as his memory is by death.' He could not finish a
requiem which began:

> Where art thou, my gentle child?
> Let me think thy spirit feeds,
> With its life intense and mild . . .[1]

When HAZLITT's youngest child died, aged six months, he cut off a
lock of hair and enclosed it in a piece of paper on which he wrote: 'My
dear little John's hair, cut off the day he died.' Lamb's lines *On an
Infant Dying as soon as Born* were prompted by the death of HOOD's first
child. THOMAS MOORE lost two daughters in infancy, and his most
beloved child, Anastasia, died of TB.

SHAKESPEARE lost his twin son Hamnet, his only boy, who was
about eleven years old. His cameos of children, so tenderly drawn,
convey the enormity of that loss.

II

SMOLLETT was 'overwhelmed by the loss of his only child',[2] Elizabeth, at fifteen. Under attack at the time by his enemies, he took his
wife to France and stayed in Nice for eighteen months. Like Southey
and Kipling in bereavement, he was never the same man again.

Lewis Hind remembered a Saturday night with HENLEY and his
'young men' at Chiswick 'when Henley quelled the din, a strange look
in his blue eyes, as he said, "Hush! there's a young lady upstairs
now."'[3] Hind contrasted Henley's 'savage truculence' with the 'infinite
gentleness, when he spoke of the child, that wonder child, Margaret
Emma Henley . . .'[4] Henley wrote two poems about her, one when
she was three, and the other after she had died at six years of age:

> . . . a little exquisite Ghost,
> Between us, smiling with the serenest eyes,
> Seen in this world.[5]

1 Edward Dowden: *The Life of Percy Bysshe Shelley* (1886), ii, pp. 267–8.
2 Thomas Seccombe: *DNB*.
3 C. Lewis Hind: *Naphtali* (1926), p. 54.
4 C. Lewis Hind: *Authors & I* (1921), p. 130.
5 Written three years later, in 1897. See p. 414.

He told Hind 'that his last work would be called A Book of Pity and Death; but he had not the heart to finish it'.

KIPLING lost his first child, Josephine, at the same age. According to his cousin, Angela Thirkell, it changed him:

. . . I feel that I have never seen him as a real person since that year.[1]

Years later, Kipling wrote:

People say that kind of wound heals. It doesn't. It only skins over . . .

He seems to have had a premonition that his little girl would die: 'We worship a baby in a snow temple.'[2] She is in *Merrow Down* and is one of the lost children in *They*.

Dean INGE lost his younger daughter Paula, from diabetes, in her twelfth year – in spite of 'the new insulin treatment'. He had often thought what 'a perfect wife and mother' she would have been 'for some good man'. He wrote in his *Diary*:

There never was a more saintly and beautiful life than hers.[3] . . . Our darling Paula will always be with us in memory . . .[4]

His *Personal Religion and the Life of Devotion* ended, uncharacteristically, with a very private account of her illness and death. The loss seemed to have the effect of breaking down his reserve.

Some knew the equally cruel reversal of Nature when the parent buries an older child. In the closing years of MADAME D'ARBLAY's life came the bereavement of her only son – 'my darling, loved, and most touchingly loving, dear, soul-dear Alex'[5] – who died of influenza shortly after his appointment as minister of Ely Chapel at forty-two.

WORDSWORTH lost Dora from TB at the same age. Five months after her death, he could not hold back his tears while talking to Crabb Robinson. Wordsworth wrote:

Daily used She to come to my bedside and greet me and her Mother, and *now* the blank is terrible . . . She is ever with me and will be so to the last moment of my life.[6]

1 *Three Houses: Reminiscences* (1931), p. 86.
2 Lord Birkenhead: *Rudyard Kipling* (1978), pp. 138–9.
3 29 Mar. 1923. *Diary of a Dean* (n.d.), p. 85.
4 Adam Fox: *Dean Inge* (1960), pp. 184–5.
5 *Diary & Letters of Madame d'Arblay* ed. by her Niece (1842–6), vii, p. 380.
6 Letter to Isabella Fenwick: 6 Dec. 1847.

When he lay dying, nearly three years later, Mary told him: 'William, you are going to Dora.' He did not reply, but next morning, the day he died, her niece entered his room and he asked, 'Is that Dora?'[1]

Lionel Tennyson fell ill in India and died on the boat, at thirty-two. 'The thought of Lionel's death', TENNYSON wrote, 'tears me to pieces, he was so full of promise and so young.'[2]

III

There were some who met a violent death. KIPLING's only son, John, was killed at seventeen in the Battle of Lous, and Lord Birkenhead called it 'the second major blow of Kipling's life.'[3] Four years after the event, Kipling wrote:

Nothing matters much really when one has lost one's only son. It wipes the meaning out of things.[4]

The broken father, with memories of John and himself on skis, found any more holidays in Switzerland impossible. He refused the offer of a bulldog bitch because 'at the Woolsack [the house Rhodes had given them], John, without shoes or stockings, owned and was owned by one "Jumbo", a brindle and white bulldog . . .'[5]

BARRIE received the last letter of George, the eldest of the Llewelyn Davies boys, after he had already received a telegram of sympathy from the King and Queen. George's letter ended:

We go up to the trenches in a few days again.[6]

He was killed next day, aged twenty-one. Barrie never wrote to the dead boy's mother again. He blamed himself for failing her trust.

'Q' was stricken to lose his only son, Bevis, who survived four years of the trenches only to die of Spanish influenza shortly afterwards.

KENNETH GRAHAME was intent his only son, Alistair, in spite of disability, should have the Oxford that had been denied to *him*. The boy, blind in one eye and with a bad cast in the other, had a nervous

1 Mary Moorman: *William Wordsworth: The Later Years* (1965), p. 606.
2 *Alfred Lord Tennyson: A Memoir by his Son* (1897), ii, p. 324.
3 *Rudyard Kipling* (1978), p. 268.
4 *Ibid.*, p. 290.
5 *Ibid.*, p. 270.
6 14 Mar. 1915.

mannerism of waving his arms if he got excited. He had 'stuck it out for six weeks'[1] at Rugby and for over a year at Eton – at the price of a breakdown so serious as to make him almost insane. Now with his eyesight deteriorating, he passed Mods. heroically. On 7 May 1920, a few days short of his twentieth birthday, he dined in Hall at Christ Church and, after an unaccustomed glass of wine, walked by himself across Port Meadow. His decapitated body was found early next morning, lying across the rails. In his pockets were many religious tracts. The Coroner pronounced Accidental Death, but 'Q' and others suspected suicide. Grahame scattered lilies of the valley over the coffin.

Yet surely, as a little boy, 'Mouse' was very privileged. He was first to hear, and helped to create, *The Wind in the Willows*. His father told it to him extempore – the way Dodgson told *Alice's Adventures Under Ground* to the Liddell girls, or Roald Dahl recounted *James and the Giant Peach* to his children. During its completion Grahame had walked a good deal with his eight-year-old son around Cookham, teaching him about the countryside. After Alistair's death, a holiday-maker recalled Grahame in the Italian Dolomites, 'his Inverness cape swirling around him':

On and on he went, solitary, absorbed in his own thoughts, until he vanished in the distance. I think he was deeply grieved over the loss of his son and I hesitated to intrude on his self-imposed isolation.[2]

Six years after George's death, BARRIE came down in the lift at eleven o'clock at night to post his daily letter to Michael, up at Oxford. He was in the hall of Adelphi Terrace when a reporter asked him if he could give any information about the Oxford tragedy. The reporter then realized *he* was breaking the news that Michael – the Llewelyn Davies boy who was the closest of all to Barrie, and who had never learned to swim – had been drowned with his friend, in the Thames at Sandford Pool. In four weeks he would have been twenty-one. Barrie phoned his secretary, Lady Cynthia Asquith, in a voice she did not know. Peter, and Gerald du Maurier, came to him. He was in a state of shock. When Cynthia arrived early next morning she found he had walked up and down all night.

1 Grahame to Austin Purves, 18 Feb. 1915. Peter Green: *Kenneth Grahame: A Study of his Life, Work & Times* (1959), p. 314.
2 *Ibid.*, p. 337.

MASEFIELD lost his only son, Lewis, in World War II, at the same age as Tennyson's Lionel. A conscientious objector serving in the RAMC, 'Lew' was killed in Africa. Five years afterwards, the father wrote of his son's life and ideals concluding:

He was the most delightful, the wisest, and the best man whom I have known well.[1]

J. DOVER WILSON also lost his only son, Godfrey, in that war, in South Africa, and wrote that among the letters he received from his friends 'none was more tender and understanding'[2] than the one by Edwin Muir.

IV

While WILDE was in Reading Gaol his children were taken from him by legal procedure. They were handed over by an order of the High Court to the joint guardianship of his wife and her cousin.

That is, and always will remain to me a source of infinite distress, of infinite pain, of grief without end or limit . . .[3]

On his release, he wrote to Ross that his wife had sent him photographs of the boys –

. . . such lovely little fellows in Eton collars – but makes no promise to allow me to see them: she says she will see me twice a year, but I want my boys . . .[4]

These two photographs, taken at Heidelberg in 1897, and a few letters the boys had written to him from their prep schools before 1895, were his only keepsakes.

Three years later, in Paris, a few months before he died, he regularly dined at a little restaurant at 42 Rue Jacob, where the proprietors kept a table reserved for him. Once, a child who used to come with his mother accidentally spilt something on 'Monsieur Sébastien's' table, and the mother scolded him. Monsieur Sébastien said:

1 Lewis Masefield: *All Passion Left Behind* (1947), Introduction by John Masefield.
2 *Milestones on the Dover Road* (1969), p. 130.
3 *De Profundis* ('The Complete Text': 1949), p. 75.
4 May 1900. *Vyvyan Holland: Son of Oscar Wilde* (1954), p. 103.

'Be patient with your little boy, One must always be patient with them. If, one day, you should find yourself separated from him . . .'

The boy inquired if he had a little boy, and the gentleman told him he had two but they were far away. He then broke down and wept, drawing the boy to him and kissing him on both cheeks. While he did so, he said something in English which next day another customer translated: 'Oh, my poor dear boys!' Lucien, grown up, wrote to Vyvyan Holland after the publication of *Son of Oscar Wilde* and described the incident. He also added:

. . . I realized that I had been given those two kisses vicariously – I was just at the age at which you had last seen him . . . I ask myself whether my clumsiness was not, perhaps . . . an opportunity for him to send you an indirect message.[1]

In a Chancery suit, conducted by Lord Eldon, four-year-old Ianthe and three-year-old Charles were committed into the care of a physician and his wife, even though SHELLEY had legalized his union with Mary – who longed to receive 'those dear children whom I love so tenderly . . . there will be a sweet brother and sister for William . . .'[2]

Leigh Hunt said that Shelley never after 'dared to trust himself with mentioning their names in my hearing, though I had stood at his side throughout the business'. But there was no such inhibition from flaying the Lord Chancellor in his verse:

> I curse thee by a parent's outraged love;
> By hopes long cherished and too lately lost;
> By gentle feelings thou couldst never prove;
> By griefs which thy stern nature never crossed;
>
> By those infantine smiles of happy light . . .
>
> By all the happy see in children's growth,
> That undeveloped flower of budding years;
> Sweetness and sadness interwoven both,
> Source of the sweetest hopes and saddest fears.[3]

Two years later, he immortalized him in *The Masque of Anarchy*:

> Next came Fraud, and he had on,
> Like Lord E——, an ermine gown;

1 Vyvyan Holland: *Time Remembered: After Père Lachaise* (1966), pp. 11–12.
2 Letter to Shelley, 17 Dec. 1816.
3 Edward Dowden: *The Life of Percy Bysshe Shelley* (1886), ii, p. 125.

His big tears, for he wept well,
Turned to mill-stones as they fell;

And the little children, who
Round his feet played to and fro,
Thinking every tear a gem,
Had their brains knocked out by them.

Subsequently, Harriet's sister, Eliza, brought up Ianthe, who married a Somerset banker. Charles was taken into the charge of his grandfather, who sent him to Syon Academy, Shelley's old school, but he died of TB at eleven years old.

CHAPTER ELEVEN

When Their Children Grew Up

I

S ome of their children associated themselves with their father's work. When Sara COLERIDGE was nineteen, her mother brought her to Highgate. She had not seen her father for ten years, but his influence now became strong. Besides her own authorship while he lived, after his death she brought out important editions of *Aids to Reflection* and *Biographia Literaria*. She also collected his leaders to *The Morning Post* and contributions to *The Courier*.

The interests of some future biographer indeed have been present to my mind in all that I have done for editions of my Father's writings . . .[1]

J. S. MILL's stepdaughter collaborated with him in *The Subjection of Women*, his last book. He spoke of his singular good fortune in drawing such 'another prize in the lottery of life' after the loss of his wife. Lady Ritchie, the eldest daughter of THACKERAY, wrote biographical introductions for a new edition of her father's works. KINGSLEY's daughter Mary, after his death, finished a novel, *The Tutor's Story*, that her father had put aside.

VYVYAN HOLLAND was eighteen when his Aunt Nellie told him the 'truth' about his father. On his twenty-first birthday (which would have passed unnoticed by his guardian) Ross gave him a magnificent dinner party at Kensington, and among the twelve at table were his brother Cyril, Charles Shannon, Charles Ricketts, Henry James, Reginald Turner, Ronald Firbank and More Adey. The following year he was at the dinner given to Ross on the publication of his collected edition of Wilde, when the hundred and sixty guests numbered Gosse, Wells, Archer and Binyon. Vyvyan sat next to

1 *Essays on His Own Times: Forming a Second Series of The Friend by Samuel Taylor Coleridge* ed. by his Daughter (1850), i, p. xiv.

Maugham, and Cyril between William Rothenstein and E. V. Lucas. He formed friendships with James, Hardy, Bennett, Beerbohm, and particularly Wells. At Trinity, Cambridge, he became acquainted with Rupert Brooke. He was called to the Bar and practised. During World War I he was mentioned in Dispatches four times and received the OBE. Twenty-five years after the death of his first wife, he married an Australian and they had one son, Merlin. They went out to Australia and New Zealand for just over a year, after which he sometimes worked as historical adviser at Pinewood Studios. In addition to his translations from French, Spanish, Italian, and German authors and his own writing – not least *Son of Oscar Wilde* and a pictorial biography, *Oscar Wilde* – he edited *The Portrait of W. H.* and a much larger text of *De Profundis* (taken from the copy Ross had made of the original MS.).

Nigel NICOLSON, as co-founder of Weidenfeld & Nicolson, edited and published his father's *Diaries and Letters*. He also wrote and published *Portrait of a Marriage*. Anthony West, spoken of by WELLS as 'a very good friend of mine', became his father's biographer.

As one of BARRIE's literary executors, Peter Llewelyn Davies (No. 3 of the Five) commissioned and published Denis Mackail's *The Story of J.M. B.* He published *The Boy David*, *Portrait of Barrie* by Cynthia Asquith, Barrie's *Letters*, his speeches (*McConnachie and J.M. B.*), and a trade edition of *The Greenwood Hat*.[1]

II

Hartley COLERIDGE, at thirty-seven, published a small volume of poems containing sonnets acclaimed by Richard Garnett as 'among the most perfect in the language', also *Leonard and Susan* reprinted from *Blackwood's Magazine*. His unfinished *Biographia Borealis*, appearing the same year, he subsequently retitled *Worthies of Yorkshire and Lancashire*.

The work of Anne, novelist daughter of THACKERAY, influenced her stepniece Virginia Woolf. KINGSLEY's eldest daughter, Rose, wrote several history books for children, as well as the important *Roses and Rose Growing* (1908). EDMUND GOSSE's son, Philip, became with

1 See pp. 14–5.

much else a successful writer and a Fellow of the Royal Society of Literature. Lewis MASEFIELD wrote two novels, one of which appeared posthumously.

SHELLEY's devoted heir, Percy Florence, was only two and a half when his father died, and succeeded to the baronetcy at twenty-four on the death of his grandfather. Residing at Boscombe Manor, he and his wife were responsible for erecting the Shelley monument in Christchurch Priory. Dowden speaks of an alcove in Boscombe Manor lovingly devoted to Shelley MSS. and other of the poet's relics. Sir Percy and Lady Shelley befriended the Stevensons from the time of their Bournemouth days.

Other arts are represented. MATTHEW ARNOLD's eldest son, Richard Penrose, with his wife, helped Elgar to read his music 'as it came in proof'.[1] Dick may have failed his degree and left college with vast gambling debts, yet he achieved immortality as 'R.P.A.': the subject of the fifth *Enigma Variation*. JOYCE's son, Giorgi, began a singing career at twenty-three in Paris. Five years later, he took his wife and child to the United States, where John McCormack gave him some help. He sang on National Broadcasting programmes, his father cabling good wishes before each performance. Giorgi's wife was eventually admitted to a mental hospital at Suresnes; after their divorce, when Giorgi was forty-eight, he married again. BETJEMAN cheerfully accepted his son Paul running a jazz band at Oxford – Betjeman's Beats – and afterwards studying the saxophone at Benny Goodman's old music school in Boston. In his late thirties Paul turned to electronic music.

GOSSE's daughter Sylvia was an artist, and her portrait of Sickert, her teacher, was presented to the Tate by Sassoon. MASEFIELD's daughter Judith became, in late teens, a keen participant in her father's amateur theatricals at Boar Hill. When she was twenty-one, she played The Prayer and Mary Magdalene in his verse-play *The Trial of Jesus*, held in the Music Room. Among others taking part were Lillah McCarthy, Ian Hay, Julian Huxley, and Juliette Huxley. Her chronic asthma prevented a full-time stage career. J. K. JEROME's daughter, Rowena, acted in her father's plays. From the age of nineteen, JOYCE's daughter, Lucia, became a dancer in Paris, a career which lasted three years. She fell into depression and experienced unhappy love affairs,

1 Percy M. Young: *Elgar O. M.: A Study of a Musician* (1955), p. 84.

one with Samuel Beckett. After entreaties by her father to help her, Jung became her twentieth doctor without success. Joyce used her decorative alphabet in *A Chaucer ABC* (1936). He refused to believe her schizophrenic even when she had to be restrained in a strait-jacket. She trusted only her father and he would not certify her.

Whatever spark of gift I possess has been transmitted to Lucia, and has kindled a fire in her brain.[1]

PRIESTLEY's son Tom joined Ealing Films under Sir Michael Balcon. He received a BAFTA award for his work on *Morgan – A Suitable Case for Treatment. Tess* and Michael Radford's *1984* are among his productions; also his film *Time and the Priestleys* for Central Television, just before his father died.

WELLS's daughter, Amber Reeves, became 'a first-class honours B.Sc. and a promising light of the London School of Economics'. Wells did not think a daughter could ever become fully one if you had seen 'nothing of her from babyood to maturity' – his became 'a very dear friendly niece'.[2] They dined out and went to theatres together. GOSSE's elder daughter, Tessa, educated at Newnham (Cambridge) and Bedford (London) was a suffragette.

III

As Vicar of Brigham, WORDSWORTH's eldest son, Johnny, fulfilled his father's own earlier intention. Johnny's four marriages produced six children from his first, and another, a daughter, born of his third.

Most like his father, brilliant in declamation and tragically flawed, Hartley COLERIDGE gained an Oriel fellowship but soon lost it through intemperance. Two years afterwards, he returned permanently to the Lakes. He took a post at Ambleside School, and taught Wordsworth's youngest boy. Dorothy spoke of him as having fourteen scholars. He pronounced Little Will 'a bore'. The last ten years of his life were spent fulfilling his father's prophecy literally:

1 Letter from Paul Léon to Harriet Weaver, quoting Joyce, 19 July 1935. Richard Ellmann: *James Joyce* (1959), p. 663.
2 *H. G. Wells in Love: Postscript to an Experiment in Autobiography* ed. G. P. Wells (1984), p. 86.

But thou, my babe! shalt wander like a breeze
By lakes and sandy shores, beneath the crags
Of ancient mountain, and beneath the clouds . . .[1]

In an upstairs rented room at Nab Cottage, a few hundred yards from Rydal Mount, his younger brother, Derwent, nursed him in his last illness. He died at fifty-two. Wordsworth said to Derwent in Grasmere Churchyard, 'Let him lie by us, he would have wished it.' Then, as he looked up from Dora's grave, he pointed to where Hartley had stood at her funeral, and told him, '*He* was standing there.'[2]

The Rev. Derwent COLERIDGE, like Matthew Arnold, is an important figure in the story of Elementary Education. He went to St John's, Cambridge, and became headmaster of the grammar school at Helston, Cornwall, making it 'the Eton of the West'. At forty-one, he was appointed as the first principal of St Mark's Training College for Teachers, in Chelsea, set up by the National Society (for Promoting the Education of the Poor in the Principles of the Established Church throughout England and Wales), a post he held for twenty-three years. Dean Stanley called him 'the most accomplished linguist in England'; he read not only the European languages (including Welsh) but Arabic, Coptic – even Zulu and Hawaiian.[3]

Among her other activities, Rose KINGSLEY, who never married, founded Leamington High School for Girls. ALISON UTTLEY's son, John, was a form master at Eton and later housemaster of Walpole House, Stowe. Dr Judd writes that after the suicide of her husband, the mother's relations with her good-looking son 'verged on the incestuous'.[4] John married, but after a miscarriage there were no children. He inherited his father's depressions and, at sixty-three, two years after his mother's death, he drove his car over a cliff in Guernsey.

Many, like Dickens's sons – but more voluntarily – went overseas. Maurice KINGSLEY left Cambridge without a degree, studied agriculture, and worked on a ranch in Argentina. He helped to build the narrow-gauge railway from Denver to Colorado Springs, and in Mexico he married an American. Kingsley's 'Lord Grenville' finished

1 *Frost at Midnight.*
2 Henry Crabb Robinson: *On Books & Their Writers* ed. Edith Morley (1927), ii, pp. 685–6.
3 The Rev. William Benham: *DNB.*
4 Denis Judd: *The Life of a Country Child* (1986), p. 118.

his formal education when he left Harrow at sixteen. Some years later, after an unhappy love affair with a married woman, he worked as a drover in Australia.

Richard Penrose ARNOLD, at twenty-three, went out to be a clerk in the Union Bank of Melbourne. His aim was to be very rich. Arnold said that Dick had promised first to 'repay me all I have had to spend on him, and then shall enable me to retire!'[1] At the ship's rail he took off his cap 'and the dear fellow's "yellow mop" was all visible'. Arnold, always supportive of what his boy wanted to do, wrote:

I shall go on as usual, but I shall never have a happy day until I see him again.[2]

Dick came back some four years later to be a Manchester factory inspector and to marry an Australian. The association with Elgar was in his forties, after his father had died.

Only seventeen, Philip GOSSE, as naturalist, joined an expedition which climbed Aconcagua in the Andes for the first time. He qualified in medicine and, as a practising naturalist like his grandfather, supplied specimens and new subspecies to the Natural History Museum. Sylvia Gosse, the artist, was awarded the Order of the Serbian Red Cross after World War I.

After WILDE's death his elder boy, Cyril, at fifteen and a half, replied to a letter from Robert Ross:

It is hard for a young mind like mine to realise why all the sorrow should have come on us, especially so young . . . It is of course a long time since I saw father but all I do remember was when we lived happily together in London and how he would come and build brick houses for us in the nursery.[3]

Vyvyan said that while his own youth 'was filled with perplexity', his brother had 'the weight of knowledge which he was too young to bear'.[4]

Cyril stayed on at Neuenheim College because 'he had already started on his determined mission in life to rehabilitate the family name by sheer force of character and by overcoming all weaknesses

1 22 Oct. 1878.
2 Nov. 1878. Park Honan: *Matthew Arnold: A Life* (1981), pp. 380–1.
3 Vyvyan Holland: *Son of Oscar Wilde* (1954), p. 153.
4 *Ibid.*, p. 139.

and obstacles'.[1] In his last year at Radley, he won the mile, the half-mile, and the steeplechase, receiving a silver medal as *victor ludorum*. He was the best swimmer in the school and head of his house. When he went into the Army – because the Navy wouldn't have him – he won the mile at Woolwich and the two miles against Sandhurst. Like T. E. Lawrence, he punished himself. The 'beautiful child' that Wratislaw had met in The Cottage at Goring-on-Thames, at twenty-eight spent six months' leave trekking to Peking over 'the terrible plateau of Tibet . . . weary and ill with dysentery and alone . . .' In 1914, he wrote to Vyvyan:

All these years my great incentive has been to wipe that stain away . . . the more convinced I became that . . . there must be no cry of decadent artist, of effeminate aesthete, of weak-kneed degenerate.[2]

The following year, he was killed 'in what amounted to a duel with a German sniper'.[3]

1 *Ibid.*, p. 107.
2 *Ibid.*, p. 140.
3 *Ibid.*, p. 144.

CHAPTER TWELVE

The Fury of a Name

I

'What's in a name?' confided Peter Llewelyn Davies to his private papers. 'My God, what isn't?'[1] BARRIE wrote that he had 'made Peter [Pan] by rubbing the five of you violently together . . .'

That is all he is, the spark I got from you.[2]

But Peter, who was No. 3, bore the burden of the first name. He had been teased at Eton because of it. 'That terrible masterpiece' was how he later described *Peter Pan*.

Only nineteen and invalided from the Somme, after another three years Peter was demobbed with an MC. He visited George's grave in 1917 and again in 1945, 'feeling bloody miserable'. On Michael's death in Sandford Pool, Oxford, *The Evening Standard* blazed the headline: THE TRAGEDY OF PETER PAN. The article spoke of the 'original' being 'George . . . killed in action in March 1915'. It stated what amounted to the truth:

Now both boys who are most closely associated with the fashioning of Peter Pan are dead. One recalls the words of Peter himself: 'To die would be an awfully big adventure.'[3]

Three years later, when he was twenty-seven, Peter went to Walter Blaikie in Edinburgh to study typography and book production. With Barrie's support, and assistance from Hodder & Stoughton, he had a practice run in London before setting up a publishing firm of his own. Compton Mackenzie was to call him 'an artist among publishers'. At thirty-four he married, and there were three children.

1 Andrew Birkin: *J. M. Barrie & the Lost Boys* (1979), p. 196.
2 *Peter Pan* (1928), Dedicatory Preface, p. vi.
3 21 May 1921.

On 5 April 1960, when he was sixty-three, he walked from the Royal Court Hotel to Sloane Square Underground Station and threw himself under a train – the third of Barrie's 'five boys' to die tragically. One paper's headline ran: PETER PAN'S DEATH LEAP. Jack had died the previous year. Only 'Nico', the youngest, was left, and *The Sunday Times* photographed him at seventy-four sitting in his garden, holding Roger Lancelyn Green's *Fifty Years of Peter Pan*.

II

FRANCES HODGSON BURNETT included her younger son, Vivian, when she called *Little Lord Fauntleroy* an albatross round both their necks. His death at sixty-one prompted the report:

ORIGINAL 'FAUNTLEROY' DIES IN BOAT AFTER HELPING RESCUE 4 IN SOUND . . . Author's Son who Devoted Life to Escaping 'Sissified' Role, is Stricken at Helm – Manoeuvres Yawl to get 2 Men and 2 Women from Overturned Craft, Then Collapses.[1]

The book sold over a million copies in the English language and there were translations into more than a dozen other languages. Frances had written it when Vivian was eight.

'I will write a story about him,' I said . . . Almost every day I recorded something he had said or suggested.[2]

She had another son, Lionel, two years older, who was the introvert, but he died at sixteen of TB. Both children were exceptionally beautiful. Just as the young Christopher Milne wore the 'curious clothes' that Shepard drew, so *they* wore best suits of black velvet with lace collars.

A. A. MILNE's son would hear from his study at Stowe boys play 'the famous – and now cursed – gramophone record . . . over and over again'.

. . . Christopher Robin was beginning to be what he was later to become, a sore place that . . . would never heal up.[3]

---

1 1937. Quoted by Ann Thwaite: *Waiting for the Party* (1974), p. 91.
2 'How Fauntleroy Occurred': *The Captain's Youngest Piccino &c.* (1894), pp. 157, 159.
3 Christopher Milne: *The Enchanted Places* (1974), p. 164.

On being demobbed after World War II he went up to Cambridge to read English, and at thirty-one opened a bookshop in Dartmouth with his wife. To his acute embarrassment he found that some parents got their offspring to shake his hand so they could afterwards tell their 'little friends'.

CHAPTER THIRTEEN
With Other Children

I

Their love of children extended beyond their own. Sir WALTER RALEGH allowed Cecil's young boy, William, to recuperate at Sherborne. He wrote to the father:

Because I know that yow cann receve no pleasinger newse from hence then to heare of your beloved creture, I thought good to lett you know of his good health . . . His stomake, that was heretofore weake, is altogether amended, and he douth now eat well and digest rightly. I hope this aire will agree exceedingly with hyme. He is also better keipt to his booke then any wher elce.[1]

A letter from William, when his host was away, reveals a side of Ralegh surprisingly 'modern' and non-Olympian – akin to other writers mentioned earlier:

Sir Walter, we must all exclaim and cry out because you will not come down. You being absent, we are like soldiers that when their Captain are absent they know not what to do: you are so busy about idle matters. Sir Walter, I will be plain with you. I pray you leave all idle matters and come down to us.[2]

With such an intimate tie, one might have expected Mr Secretary to act less ambiguously at the time of Ralegh's fall three years away.

Dickens remembered THACKERAY asking him 'with fantastic gravity', after a visit to Eton, 'whether I felt as he did in regard to never seeing a boy without wanting instantly to give him a sovereign?'[3] Dickens's daughter happened to be at a window as Thackeray approached Portland Place, where some poor children were playing.

1 27 Mar. 1600. Edward Edwards: *The Life of Sir Walter Ralegh together with his Letters* (1868), ii, p. 202.
2 Summer, 1600. Modern spelling.
3 'In Memoriam': *The Cornhill Magazine*, Feb. 1864.

She remarked to her friend: 'Watch and see if Mr Thackeray does not give them something.'[1] They saw him feel in his waistcoat pocket and, bending down, say something as he gave each a coin.

Froude tells how CARLYLE 'would drop a lesson' in the way of 'the imps of the gutters . . . sometimes with a sixpence to recommend it'.

The crowds of children growing up in London affected him with real pain; these small plants, each with its head just out of the ground, with a whole life ahead, and such a training![2]

WILDE paid the fines of three children he had seen the day before he left Reading Gaol.

They had just been convicted (for snaring rabbits) and were standing in a row in the central hall in their prison dress, carrying their sheets . . . They were quite small children, the youngest . . . being a tiny little chap, for whom they had evidently been unable to find clothes small enough to fit . . . I need not say how utterly distressed I was to see these children at Reading, for I knew the treatment in store for them.[3]

A month later, at Berneval, to celebrate the Queen's Diamond Jubilee, he gave a party for fifteen small schoolboys, at which they feasted on strawberries and cream, and 'a huge iced cake'.

Every child was asked beforehand to choose his present: they all chose instruments of music!!![4]

II

Certain writers had the charisma that causes small children to steal up uninvited, knowing perfectly well they will be secure. Harriet Martineau described an elderly WORDSWORTH complete with 'cloak . . . Scotch bonnet, and green goggles, attended perhaps by half-a-score of cottagers' children, – the youngest pulling at his cloak, or holding by

1 Gladys Storey: *Dickens & Daughter* (1939), p. 16.
2 J. A. Froude: *Thomas Carlyle: A History of his Life in London 1834–1881* (1884), ii, pp. 255–6.
3 Letter to *The Daily Chronicle*: 28 May 1897. 2nd Collected Edn. of the Works of Oscar Wilde (1909), x, *De Profundis*, pp. 123–4.
4 Alin Caillas (one of the children): *Oscar Wilde tel que je l'ai connu* (1971). Quoted by H. Montgomery Hyde: *Oscar Wilde: A Biography* (1976), p. 329.

his trowsers, while he cut ash switches out of the hedge for them'.[1]
KINGSLEY was another. When he visited his son Maurice at his prep
school in Blackheath the boys followed him about the commons as he
taught them 'about birds and nature'.

Kingsley was very good to us boys . . . I do not remember that he stammered
then.[2]

KIPLING, on the ship to South Africa, had children squatting about
him on the deck while he spun what his daughter Elsie said became
his *Just So Stories*.

FRANCES HODGSON BURNETT may have disappointed Miss Brandt's
guests in Washington (similarly, Charlotte Brontë in Thackeray's
house in Kensington), but, when the nephews and nieces at the far
end of the room begged a story,

Her face changed . . . She sat down upon the floor . . . Her face, her whole
figure, radiant, absorbed . . . each expression reflected in the small faces
about her.[3]

BARRIE was godfather to Captain Scott's son, christened after Peter
Pan, and he took him at four and a half to see the play. Like Dodgson
and Lear to their protégés, he wrote him 'delightful comic letters,
often in rhymes and always full of invention'. Peter Scott frequently
visited No 3, Adelphi Terrace House.

As a very small boy I used to go there for tea, sometimes with my mother,
sometimes alone . . . Barrie knew all about how to get on with children.
Although there were often long silences I cannot ever remember feeling shy
in his company.[4]

Barrie was also godfather to Priestley's son, Tom.
    After Lady Asquith had come as his secretary, he went to Sussex
Place and at once got down on the floor to play games with Michael,
her four-year-old son. On another visit, he held him with his stories
and sleight of hand – doubtless spinning a coin and affixing a penny
stamp to the ceiling, his favourite party trick. On her son's first visit
to the Adelphi flat, she envied 'the licence of his years' when, in

1 Harriet Martineau's *Autobiography* with *Memorials* by Maria Weston Chapman (1877), ii,
p. 236.
2 A nonagenarian's letter quoted by Susan Chitty: *The Beast & the Monk: A Life of Charles
Kingsley* (1974), p. 191.
3 Ann Thwaite: *Waiting for the Party* (1974), p. 61.
4 *The Eye of the Wind* (1961), p. 23.

crystal tones, he said to Barrie: 'Perhaps if you were to take that great pipe out of your mouth, I might be able to hear what you say.'[1]

The charm worked on royal children. At seventy-three, Barrie rented Balnaboth House – twelve miles from Kirriemuir – for his summer entertaining, and the Duke and Duchess of York, with the two Princesses, came to tea. Next day there was a return visit to Glamis, and he sat beside three-year-old Princess Margaret at her birthday tea. On Barrie's pretending to covet a simple toy, she placed it between them and said: 'It is yours *and* mine.' Afterwards he heard that when his name had been mentioned, the little Princess said:

I know that man. He is my greatest friend, and I am his greatest friend.[2]

He lifted this dialogue into *The Boy David*, and told her she should have a penny every time one of her phrases was spoken in the theatre. In default of payment, her father, now King, threatened His Majesty's solicitors. Barrie had a formal agreement prepared and envisaged a handing-over ceremony in which a bag of bright pennies would figure. But he lay dying. He signed the indenture and the Queen, with sympathetic understanding, sent it back countersigned by Princess Margaret.

III

The charisma of A. S. NEILL must have been considerable. His books mark his steps as a teacher. *A Dominie's Log*, written when he was thirty-two, was 'a groping book' and reflected when he taught in his father's fine example of a village school.

I felt that schooling was all wrong, but did not know how to put it right.[3]

At thirty-three, he published *A Dominie Dismissed*. He read a report of a lecture by Homer Lane and next year, in 1917, while a cadet in the artillery school at Trowbridge, he visited Lane's Little Commonwealth in Dorset. Galsworthy had visited three years previously and recorded in his diary:

1 Cynthia Asquith: *Portrait of Barrie* (1954), p. 109.
2 Denis Mackail: *The Story of J.M. B.: a biography* (1941), p. 658.
3 *That Dreadful School* (1937), p. 62.

A most interesting experiment; pure democratics applied to 32 young delinquents, male and female. Awfully jolly atmosphere the result.[1]

Neill wrote:

To Lane love was not a sentimental thing, not even an emotional thing: love to him was being on the side of a person: love was approval.[2]

As joint editor with Beatrice Ensor of *The New Era*, part of Neill's work was to visit progressive schools. At this time appeared *A Dominie in Doubt*. At thirty-eight, he became joint founder of the International School, Helleran, Dresden, and wrote *A Dominie Abroad*. After three years, owing to political events in Germany, he transferred his division of the school to Austria, and later to Lyme Regis, in a big square house with black and orange gates, at the top of a hill. And so there is Summerhill – where six-year-old Vivien was allowed to smash seventeen windows, and its founder made the grandest assertion of all pedagogues: 'Thou shalt be on the child's side.'[3] ROALD DAHL, in a TV book programme, unconsciously echoed Neill:

I see myself totally on the side of children when I write books for them.[4]

One wonders what MATTHEW ARNOLD would have made of Neill. He himself had been criticized for the way he conducted inspections. Once, he put his face to a little girl who had her head bandaged, and found out she had earache.

'Ah,' boomed Arnold, 'I know what that is! I used to have bad ears when I was a little boy. I know how they hurt me. Go home and take that to your mother' – slipping the girl a shilling – 'and tell her to tie your head up in hot flannel, and don't come back to school until you are quite better.'[5]

The teacher at this particular school, at Edmonton, the Rev. John Dymond, said that Arnold's 'patience with the children was wonderful'. Park Honan points out that Arnold, as a School Inspector, 'was to talk to more working-class children than any other poet who has ever lived'.[6]

KINGSLEY, at his son Maurice's prep school, gave a lecture on

1 H. V. Marrot: *The Life & Letters of John Galsworthy* (1935), p. 394.
2 *That Dreadful School* (1937), pp. 63–4.
3 *Ibid.*, p. 66.
4 1985.
5 Park Honan: *Matthew Arnold: A Life* (1981), p. 259.
6 *Ibid.*, pp. 218–19.

coconuts and, when Maurice went to Wellington, lectured and preached there often. Like C. J. Cornish at St Paul's, he helped to found the school museum. He took fifteen-year-old John Martineau, too delicate for Public School, as a resident pupil, and John wrote to his mother: '. . . he is very kind and I like him very much.'[1] The shy, quiet boy was his tutor's constant companion, and Eversley became for him 'the enchanted land.'[2] After nearly a year and a half, his parents took him away because he was becoming too attached to his kindly mentor. The memoir, which he wrote for Mrs Kingsley's *Life* of her husband, includes:

. . . his mind and character left their impression upon mine as a seed does upon wax.[3]

She wrote in a letter: 'A son you were to him, and a son and friend to me.'[4] He lived and died in the adjoining parish, but his and his wife's grave lay 'at the feet of his Master and friend'.

Before his marriage WORDSWORTH cared for Basil, the son of Montagu, his old friend. 'A shivering half starved plant' not yet three, he came to live with them at Racedown and was 'quite metamorphosed'. Dorothy wrote: 'He is my perpetual pleasure,'[5] and again:

Till a child is four . . . he needs no other companions, than the flowers, the grass, the cattle, the sheep that scamper away from him . . . the pebbles upon the road . . .[6]

For two years Montagu paid £50 a year for Basil's board and lodging, but the Wordsworths kept him for nearly another year when his father could not pay.

Basil liked crying (as well as lying 'like a little devil') and they told him that 'if he chose to cry he must go into a certain room . . . and *stay* till he chose to be quiet, because the noise was unpleasant to us'. It is very *Émile* – the child amidst natural scenes; the lecture alongside

1 Jan. 1850. *John Martineau: The Pupil of Kingsley* by his daughter Violet Martineau (1921), p. 5.
2 *Ibid.*, p. 11.
3 Quoted: *ibid.*, p. 4.
4 27 Jan. 1890. *Ibid.*, p. 173.
5 To Mrs John Marshall: 7 Mar. 1796. *The Letters of William & Dorothy Wordsworth* ed. C. L. Shaver, Mary Moorman, Alan G. Hill (1967–79), i, p. 166.
6 To Mrs William Rawson: 13 June & 3 July 1798. *Ibid.*, i, p. 222.

an inevitable course of action.[1] Basil, later, 'when he felt the fretful disposition coming on . . . would say, "Aunt, I think I am going to cry" and retire till the fit was over'.[2] At twenty-one, physically and mentally ill, Basil visited Keswick; Dorothy immediately went to nurse him, and stayed there three months.

Coleridge noticed that HAZLITT, as a young man, was 'very fond of, attentive to, & patient with, children . . .'[3]

IV

The Lakeland writers knew each other's children almost as intimately as their own. After the Coleridges had settled at Greta Hall, Hartley went to stay at Dove Cottage during the time of Derwent's birth. DOROTHY WORDSWORTH wrote:

I shall find it very difficult to part with him when we have once got him here.[4]

The following year she was writing:

Hartley is to stay some time with us and to go to Grasmere school. Dear little fellow! he will be as happy as a young lamb playing upon the grass turf in the church-yard with our bonny little lasses.[5]

She quoted his sayings and made Derwent's frocks. WILLIAM WORDS-WORTH was described as Hartley's second father.

When Coleridge and his son were spending some weeks with Wordsworth at Basil Montagu's house in London, he and SCOTT took the ten-year-old boy to the Tower and, on that April or May day in 1807, 'li'le Hartley' had those men to himself. Hartley later shed a little light:

1 See *Emilius & Sophia or, A New System of Education* trans. from the French of J. J. Rousseau, Citizen of Geneva, by the Translator of *Eloisa* (1762–3), i, 152–3.
2 To Mrs John Marshall: 19 Mar. 1797. *The Letters of William & Dorothy Wordsworth* ed. C. L. Shaver, Mary Moorman, Alan G. Hill (1967–79), i, pp. 180–1.
3 Oct. 1803. *Collected Letters of Samuel Taylor Coleridge* ed. E. L. Griggs (1956–71), ii, pp. 990–1.
4 To Mrs John Marshall: 10–12 Sept. 1800. *The Letters of William & Dorothy Wordsworth, cit.*, i, p. 298.
5 To Mary Hutchinson: 29 Apr. 1801. *Ibid.*, i, p. 330.

The bard's economy would not allow us to visit the Jewel Office, but Mr Scott . . . took an evident pride in showing me the claymores and bucklers taken from the Loyalists at Culloden.[1]

The figures are caught in tableau. One wonders where they sat and whether they brought a snack.

Before he escorted Mrs Coleridge and her children from Bristol to Keswick, DE QUINCEY, twenty-two, had taken eleven-year-old Hartley – 'at the risk of our respective necks – through every dell and tangled path of Leighwood', but Derwent still continued 'my favourite'.[2] On the four-day journey he made such friends with four-year-old Sara that she 'partly believed'[3] she was to be his wife.

As they made the final ascent of White Moss, De Quincey and the boys decided to alight 'as we all chose to refresh ourselves by running down the hill into Grasmere'. On the sharp bend they could see 'a white cottage, with two yew trees breaking the glare of its white walls', and Hartley, who had shot ahead, suddenly turned in at a garden gate. De Quincey was relieved that Wordsworth had to go forward to help Mrs Coleridge and Sara from the chaise, for he was overcome by meeting 'that man, whom, of all the men from the beginning of time I most fervently desired to see . . .'[4]

On the first morning of his stay, which lasted a week, he was awakened early 'by a little voice issuing from a little cottage bed in an opposite corner'.

I soon recognized the words – 'Suffered under Pontius Pilate; was crucified, dead, and buried'; and the voice I easily conjectured to be that of the eldest amongst Wordsworth's children, a son, and at that time about three years old.[5]

'Mr De Quincey', Johnny was to say proudly, 'is my friend.'

A year later, he stayed longer – at Allan Bank, when Coleridge was domiciled with them. Dorothy wrote of De Quincey:

1 *Letters of Samuel Taylor Coleridge* ed. Ernest Hartley Coleridge (1895), ii, p. 511 Note.
2 A. H. Japp: *Thomas De Quincey: his Life & Writings. With Unpublished Correspondence* (2nd edn. 1890), p. 91.
3 *Memoir & Letters of Sara Coleridge* ed. by her Daughter (1873), i, p. 12. Quoted by Grevel Lindop: *The Opium-Eater: A Life of Thomas De Quincey* (1981), p. 148.
4 *The Collected Writings of Thomas De Quincey* ed. David Masson (1889–90), ii, pp. 234–5. At seventeen, and twenty years ahead of public opinion, he had 'addressed a letter of fervent admiration to Mr Wordsworth', whose 'answer was long and full'. (*Ibid.*, ii, p. 59.)
5 *Selections Grave & Gay, from Writings Published & Unpublished*, by Thomas De Quincey (1853–71), ii, p. 316.

We feel often as if he were one of the Family . . . John sleeps with him and is passionately fond of him.[1]

Then, 'upon Miss Wordsworth's happening to volunteer the task of furnishing for my use the cottage so recently occupied by her brother's family, I took it upon a seven years' lease'.[2] The house at Town End (now Dove Cottage) was to remain his headquarters, on and off, for twenty-four years.

Baby Catharine, who walked with a limp and whose facial expression led her father to call her 'his little Chinese maiden', so captivated De Quincey that he made the Wordsworths promise he was to be her 'sole Tutor'. Dorothy wrote to her friend:

. . . you may expect that she will be a very learned lady, for Mr De Q. is an excellent scholar.[3]

She called him 'Kinsey' and often slept with him. When the three-year-old died, De Quincey became demented, stretching himself on her grave every night for two months and claiming he could still see her playing around the gravestones. Dorothy told him: 'She never forgot Quincey – dear Innocent . . .'[4] He was godfather to Willy, and ten-year-old Johnny went to him daily to learn Latin.

After their father had gone to live with the Morgans at Hammersmith, the Coleridge boys, now fourteen and ten, kept up their close ties with Allan Bank. One of their visits, at the time the Wordsworths were preparing to move to Grasmere Rectory,[5] caused Dorothy to express all the anxieties and concerns of a mother:

The storm began an hour ago, and upon the sky clearing we suffered Hartley, Derwent and Algernon Montagu (M's eldest son by his second wife) to set off to Ambleside, and poor things! it now rains dreadfully and the thunder is very loud and frequent. These three boys came yesterday morning for the last time of staying all night this summer as we shall have no beds for them. H and D have hitherto come every week, but Algernon only occasionally; for the noise of our own five with H and D was so much that we could not every

1 To Catherine Clarkson: 8 Dec. 1808. *The Letters of William & Dorothy Wordsworth* ed. C. L. Shaver, Mary Moorman, Alan G. Hill (1967–79), ii, p. 283.
2 *The Collected Writings of Thomas De Quincey* ed. David Masson (1889–90), ii, p. 359.
3 To Catherine Clarkson: 15 June 1809. *The Letters, cit.*, ii, p. 357.
4 (5 June 1812). *Ibid.*, iii, p. 23.
5 i.e., the year before Catharine died.

week have all three; but Algernon has come in the short holidays when H and D were at Keswick.[1]

For much of their childhood, Sara almost entirely so, the Coleridge children with their mother shared the SOUTHEY household, and Coleridge – permanently separated from his wife – includes in a letter to her:

Kisses and heartfelt loves for my sweet Sara, and scarce less for dear little Herbert and Edith [Southey].[2]

Gosse's children called on BROWNING, in Warwick Crescent, to take him flowers on his birthday. They received chocolate from him and a cake from his sister. Teresa was his favourite, and he brought her porcelain lambs from Italy which she put in her Christmas crib.

IV

Sometimes other children had the effect of reminding them of their own when they were absent from them. DE QUINCEY, working in London, had begun to see his 'life of literary toils, odious to my heart – as a permanent state of exile from my Westmoreland home'. His three eldest children were 'at that time in the most interesting stages of childhood and infancy . . .'

and so powerful was my feeling (derived merely from a deranged liver) of some long, never-ending separation from my family, that at length, in pure weakness of mind, I was obliged to relinquish my daily walks in Hyde Park and Kensington Gardens, from the misery of seeing children in multitudes, that too forcibly recalled my own.[3]

KINGSLEY, when recovering at Clovelly from a breakdown, wrote:

How I long after them [Rose and Maurice] and their prattle. I delight in all the little ones in the street for their sake, and continually I start and fancy I hear their voices outside.[4]

1 To Catherine Clarkson: 'Finished at 12 o'clock Sunday night', 12 May [1811]. *The Letters of William & Dorothy Wordsworth* ed. C. L. Shaver, Mary Moorman, Alan G. Hill (1967–79), ii, p. 486.
2 [20 Jan.] 18. [13]. *Letters of Samuel Taylor Coleridge* ed. Ernest Hartley Coleridge (1895), ii, p. 605.
3 *The Collected Writings of Thomas De Quincey* ed. David Masson (1889–90), iii, p 71.
4 To his wife, Aug. 1849. Susan Chitty: *The Beast & the Monk: A Life of Charles Kingsley* (1974), p. 128.

THACKERAY, at thirty-five, told Jane Shawe:

As for me I am child-sick, and when I see in Kensington Gardens or my friends' houses a pair of little girls at all resembling my own, become quite maudlin over them.[1]

1 July 1846. Hester Thackeray Ritchie: *Thackeray & his Daughter* (1924), pp. 22–3.

CHAPTER FOURTEEN

Childless

I

Those writers who were unmarried or childless were not unfamiliar with children. GEORGE HERBERT and his wife, Jane, made a home for their three orphaned nieces in the parsonage at Bemerton. GOLDSMITH, when he was about thirty and lodging at No. 12 Green Arbour Court, used to collect children in the area to dance to his flute.

BLAKE led a friend to a window and, pointing to a group of little children playing, said, 'That is heaven.' Samuel Palmer wrote of him:

. . . he was gentle and affectionate, loving to be with little children, and to talk about them.[1]

In his late sixties Blake spent happy Sundays at the Linnells' Hampstead cottage. One of their children remembered watching for him when she was five or six, and how as he walked over the brow of the hill he made a particular signal. He would take her on his knee and tell stories to all the children. He helped her with her drawing, and one day he brought a sketch-book containing his drawing of a grasshopper, which gave special delight to the family.

At an evening party a beautiful child was presented to him. Blake looked at her tenderly a long while and then, stroking her long curls, said:

May God make this world to you, my child, as beautiful as it has been to me![2]

She marvelled that such a poor old man, dressed in shabby clothes, could ever imagine the world to be as beautiful to him as it must be to her surrounded by riches and elegance.

EDWARD LEAR, in his early twenties, was invited to make drawings

1 Letter to Alexander Gilchrist: 23 Aug. 1855.
2 Alexander Gilchrist: *Life of William Blake* (1863), i, p. 310.

of the animals in Lord Stanley's private menagerie, and the Earl began to notice that his grandsons no longer sat with him after dinner. On his asking them why, they told him that the artist in the steward's room was such good fun. 'In that case,' said Lord Derby, 'he shall dine with us,' and, going to the head of the stairs leading to the servants' quarters, he called: 'Mister Lear, come up here!'[1] The nursery at Knowsley was full of children, and just as Lear's first nonsense poems had been written for the daughter of a Sussex friend, so he continued in this vein with the Stanley family. He wrote in his introduction to *More Nonsense*:

. . . the lines beginning, 'There was an Old Man of Tobago', were suggested to me by a valued friend . . .

At fifty-five and living in Cannes, he took an illustrated copy of *The Owl and the Pussey-cat* to the Symondses' small daughter, Janet, ill in bed. Three years afterwards, staying in Turin, he developed an acquaintance with a little American girl in his hotel (as Stevenson was to do with the little Russian girls in Menton). She had whispered to her mother she would like to have the gentleman sitting opposite for an uncle, and the mother, who knew Lear, confided the secret.

The adoption took place there and then; he became my sworn relative and devoted friend. He took me for walks in the chestnut forests; we kicked the chestnut burrs before us, 'yonghy, bonghy bos', as we called them.[2]

He sang to her *The Owl and the Pussey-cat* to a 'funny' tune of his own. Like Dodgson, he conducted a nonsense correspondence – signing himself 'Adopty Duncle'.

Hubert Congreve remembered their first meeting, when Lear had introduced himself with 'a long, nonsense name, compounded of all the languages he knew', but seeing the little boy's discomfiture he put a hand on his shoulder:

I am also the Old Derry Down Derry, who loves to see little folks merry . . .[3]

According to Ephie Gray, one of the reasons RUSKIN gave for not consummating their marriage was his 'hatred of children'. It is thought she must have meant he did not want the responsibility of his own.

1 Vivien Noakes: *Edward Lear: The Life of a Wanderer* (NE [New Edition] 1985), p. 33.
2 *Ibid.* (1968), pp. 243–4.
3 *Ibid.*, p. 248.

The King of the Golden River was written for her when, at thirteen, she had stayed the second time with the family.

Five years after the marriage had been annulled, Miss Bell invited him to her school at Winnington, where he found the six-year-old girls knew him by that fairy tale, 'as the others do by my larger books'. On his third day, he wrote to his father:

I think I have made them all very happy here by what I have been able to show them, and I haven't enjoyed myself so much anywhere these many years . . .[1]

On subsequent visits, he played 'prisoner's base' with them, invented singing games, wrote nonsense verses, and read to both young and older groups. Georgina Burne-Jones, whom he invited to go along, observed him taking part 'occasionally in a quadrille or country dance'.

He looked very thin, scarcely more than a black line, as he moved about amongst the white girls in his evening dress.[2]

He told his father:

. . . these young children . . . are so beautiful and so good . . .[3]

When he was forty-five, his talks to them became the basis of *The Ethics of the Dust*.

Like Dodgson, Ruskin was enamoured of the Liddell girls, to whom he gave drawing lessons.

II

Children were 'three-fourths' of DODGSON's life. Stuart Collingwood said they appealed to his uncle because he was 'pre-eminently a teacher' and 'a keen admirer of the beautiful in every form'. They appealed also 'to the simplicity and genuineness of his own nature'.[4] Dodgson acknowledged a poem on *Alice* that had been sent to him by Miss M. E. Manners:

1 Mar. 1859: Joan Evans: *John Ruskin* (1954), p. 256.
2 G. Burne-Jones: *Memorials of Edward Burne-Jones* (1904), i, p. 138. Quoted by Evans: *ibid.*, p. 278.
3 Nov. 1863: *The Works of John Ruskin* ed. E. T. Cook & A. Wedderburn (1903), xxxvi, p. 459. Quoted by Evans: *ibid.*, p. 281.
4 Stuart Dodgson Collingwood: *The Life & Letters of Lewis Carroll* (1898), pp. 361–3.

Next to what conversing with an angel might be – for it is hard to imagine it – comes, I think, the privilege of having a real child's thoughts uttered to one.[1]

He preferred little girls to boys:

I am fond of children (except boys) . . .[2]

– whom he thought, on the whole, 'a mistake'.[3] On train journeys he would take a mechanical toy of his own invention, hopefully to engage the attention of a small child travelling with her mother or nanny, while on the beach he carried a helpful supply of safety pins, so that any little girl who wanted to paddle could pin up her dress. Ironically, like the warm and generous actions of Hans Andersen, Dodgson's have seemed more ambiguous to a *permissive* age.

He would have a child friend staying with him during the Long Vacation at Eastbourne; for twenty years it was at No. 7 Lushington Road and then there was a move to No. 2 Bedford Well Road. His landlady, Mrs Dyer, was 'a good motherly creature' and there was also a maid. He insisted on his young guests brushing their teeth after every meal, and sweets were strongly disapproved of. There was a rule about not entering his room in the morning until his newspaper had been withdrawn. One little girl recalled, long after, his displeasure when she had forgotten and burst in to tell him something. He replied to his sister, who had questioned whether it were wise for a single gentleman to have little girls staying with him:

The only two tests I now apply . . . are, first, my own conscience, to settle whether I feel it to be entirely innocent and right, in the sight of God: secondly, the parents of my friend, to settle whether I have their *full* approval . . . any action, however innocent in itself, is liable . . . to be blamed by *somebody*. If you limit your actions in life to things that *nobody* can possibly find fault with, you will not do much . . .[4]

To entertain his guests, his rooms at Christ Church had a wide variety of musical boxes, clockwork toys, and puzzles. Mrs Waterhouse (née Ruth Gamlen) was 'one of Mr Dodgson's little girls' from 'nine years old, nearly ten', and remembers being shown a file where

1 Dec. 1885: *ibid.*, p. 365.
2 Letter to Kathleen Eschwege, 24 Oct. 1879: *ibid.*, p. 416.
3 Letter to Dr G. C. Bell, headmaster of Marlborough: Derek Hudson: *Lewis Carroll: An illustrated biography* (1976), p. 208.
4 1893: *ibid.*, p. 221.

he kept all his menus 'so that no little girl dining with him should ever have the same dinner twice'.[1] Not least, he had a collection of props and a wardrobe of Chinese, Danish, Greek, and Turkish costumes for when he took their photographs.

At nearly forty-seven, he wrote:

. . . photography from life – and especially photographing children – has been . . . [my] one amusement for the last twenty years.[2]

Helmut Gernsheim has acclaimed him 'unhesitatingly' as 'the most outstanding photographer of children in the nineteenth century', and 'after Julia Margaret Cameron . . . probably the most distinguished amateur portraitist of the mid-Victorian era'.[3] Tennyson said that Alice Liddell as a beggar-child was the most beautiful photograph he had ever seen.

But, 'With children who know me well,' he wrote to Mrs Henderson, whose daughters he had already photographed,

and who regard dress as a matter of indifference, I am very glad (when mothers permit) to take them in any amount of undress which is presentable, or even in none (which is more presentable than any forms of undress) . . .[4]

As early as when he was thirty-five, he had taken a photograph of Beatrice Latham, aged three, 'sans habilement'. Three weeks before he died, he wrote:

. . . if I had the loveliest child in the world, to draw or photograph, and found she had a modest shrinking . . . from being taken nude, I should feel it was a solemn duty, owed to God, to drop the request altogether.[5]

Before he died, he destroyed most of the negatives and prints of his nude studies. In his Instructions to his Executors, he said:

Please erase the following negatives: I would not like (for the families' sakes) the possibility of their getting into other hands. They are best erased by soaking in a solution of washing soda . . .[6]

1 Ibid., p. 250.
2 22 Dec. 1878: Morton N. Cohen: Lewis Carroll, Photographer of Children: Four Nude Studies (New York 1979), p. 5.
3 Lewis Carroll, Photographer (1949), p. 28.
4 July 1879: Cohen: op cit., p. 17.
5 To Miss Thompson: ibid., p. 30.
6 Derek Hudson: Lewis Carroll: An illustrated biography (1976), p. 219.

Among the very few that have survived are four hand-coloured photographs, of which one is of seven-year-old Beatrice Hatch, two of her younger sister, Evelyn, godchild of Benjamin Jowett, and one of Annie and Frances Henderson. Annie Henderson's daughter has described how the three girls, of whom her mother was the eldest, all adored 'Lewis Carroll'. Their father had taken Annie and Frances to visit him and they spent the afternoon dressing up. Overhearing him say he would like to photograph them in the nude, they hid under the table, which was draped like a tent with its cloth, and, to the amusement of father and host, came out with nothing on.

Derek Hudson acknowledges that Dogdson was on 'dangerous ground'. Similarly, Peter Wait writes that the Rev. FRANCIS KIL-VERT's 'feelings for little girls may seem rather overheated'.[1]

Kilvert went to read to Sackville Thomas, and describes Polly on her 'tub night . . . with great celerity and satisfaction stripping herself naked before me':

. . . and was very anxious to take off her drawers too for my benefit, but her grandmother would not allow her. As it happened the drawers in question were so inadequately constructed that it made uncommonly little difference whether they were off or on . . .[2]

At Shanklin, he 'stopped to watch some children bathing from the beach below'.

One beautiful girl stood entirely naked on the sand, and . . . was a model for a sculptor . . .

He enumerates 'the supple slender waist, the gentle dawn and tender swell of the bosom and the budding breasts, the graceful rounding of the delicately beautiful limbs and above all the soft and exquisite curves of the rosy dimpled bottom and broad white thigh'.[3]

When Kilvert left the parish of Clyro to help his father, the children 'of their own will saved up their money' and presented 'a beautiful gold pencil case to hang at my watch chain'.[4] Little Polly Nash had been given sixpence to go to the fair but saved it in order to contribute a shilling. Two days after the presentation, Mrs Harris told him:

1 *Journal of a Country Curate: Selections from the Diary of Francis Kilvert 1870–79*: Selected & with an introduction by Peter Wait (The Folio Society, 1977), p. 17.
2 *Kilvert's Diary* ed. William Plomer (1938), p. 325. Sat., 15 Apr. 1871.
3 *Ibid.* (1940), p. 208. 13 July 1875.
4 *Ibid.* (1939), p. 234. 9 July 1872.

'There is great mourning for you at Pen y cae.' . . .

'Why, do the children really care so much?'

'Ay . . . the girl [eleven-year-old 'Gipsy Lizzie'] was crying and dazed all the evening . . . and the boy is worse than her. "There'll be no one to come and teach us now," he says, "Mr Kilvert do come and tell us about all parts."'[1]

As curate, his teaching in the school and assiduous visiting of the scattered parishioners had brought him into frequent contact with the children. When he entered the porch of the little school at Newchurch, he heard their 'eager whispers'.

Janet . . . said she had done five sums, whereupon I kissed her and . . . offered to give her a kiss for every sum . . . As I stood by the window making notes of things in general in my pocket book Janet kept on interrupting her work to glance round at me shyly but saucily with her mischievous beautiful grey eyes. Shall I confess that I travelled ten miles today over the hills for a kiss, to kiss that child's sweet face. Ten miles for a kiss.[2]

He pitied little Mary Thomas whom he found at home 'because the ground was wet and her boots full of holes'. The 'poor child'[3] was trying to work on the floor with a bit of chalk, a broken piece of slate, and a torn leaf of a book.

When he called on Mrs Parker, 'the poor little black dwarf Emily was at home . . . with a bad cold'. Her mother told him that some of the village children laughed at her.

I called her to me and she came and nestled to my side and a beautiful delighted smile flitted over her face as I caressed and kissed her and bade her not to mind.[4]

Mrs Parker told him how deeply attached Emily was to him.

The 'memorable day' he went to Llan Thomas and fell in love with Daisy 'just home from school for good', he told her at supper about Alice Davies and 'what a treat fruit was to the sick child'. She sent the footman for a dish of grapes and put two bunches in a little basket for Kilvert to take away.

'I do like you for that,' I said earnestly, 'I do indeed.'[5]

1 *Ibid.* (1939), p. 237. 11 July 1872.
2 *Ibid.* (1938), p. 123. 3 May 1870.
3 *Ibid.*, p. 131. 12 May 1870.
4 *Ibid.* (1939), p. 126. 26 Jan. 1872.
5 *Ibid.*, pp. 27–29. 8 Sept. 1871.

He sat with little Katie Whitney the night she died.

On nine-year-old Gipsy Lizzie being put into his reading class, he records:

Oh, child, child, if you did but know your own power.[1]

Because of her, Bird's Nest Lane, where sometimes she came down to school, the dingle and fields were 'sweet' to him and 'holy ground'.

But you can never know, and if you should ever guess or read the secret, it will be but a dim misty suspicion of the truth. Ah Gipsy.[2]

The following year he was again 'under the influence of that child's extraordinary beauty':

When she is reading and her eyes are bent down upon her book her loveliness is indescribable.[3]

At the school feast, 'the beauties' were she, Eleanor and Florence Hill, Esther and Pussy of New Barn.

He arranged his yearly children's party to take place on Boosie Evans's birthday. Eight children came to tea in his rooms, at 6.30 p.m. A little shy at first, they stood together at the opposite side of the room.

'Come round here and warm yourselves. You needn't be afraid of me.'
'No, Sir,' replied Sena Anthony . . . 'we're too fond of you to be afraid of you.'

He uncapped 'one of the attar rose bottles' that his sister had brought from Hyderabad, and showed them a lock from the mane which he had cut from the lion at Clifton Zoo when it was asleep. They fed on buns and bread and butter, and Boosie poured out tea. There were crackers, picture books, games, and finally he told them stories.

Dear children, what a pleasure it is to have them. I am never so happy as when I have these children about me . . . I was as sorry when 12 o'clock [!] came as the children, and missed them sadly when all the bright faces trooped out into the dark night together to their homes . . .[4]

In the spring he found the children had brought fresh flowers for his table – 'primroses and the first wood anemone'. After his resig-

1 *Kilvert's Diary* ed. William Plomer (1938), p. 168. 4 July 1870.
2 *Ibid.*, p. 172. 9 July 1870.
3 *Ibid.*, p. 382. 28 July 1871.
4 *Ibid.* (1939), pp. 136–7. Mon., 12 Feb. 1872.

nation, he took charge of the parish for three weeks, and 'the dear children were on the look out for me'.[1] As much as five years afterwards, Florence Hill wrote to him. He received the letter the day there was one from 'dear little Mary Pitchford'.

At Shanklin, emotion came over him 'like a storm' and he turned away,

hungry at heart and half envying the parents as they sat upon the sand watching their children at play.[2]

As Vicar of Bredwardine he boarded and tutored thirteen-year-old Sam Cole. Now thirty-eight, with nearly £400 a year and a very pleasant house, he married Elizabeth Rowland, but after only five weeks he died of peritonitis.

SWINBURNE, a bachelor, not only made much of the young children of his friends but had a passion for the 'race of babies'. His letters frequently described some 'Chick' he had admired on his walks. Beerbohm remembered him describing that he had seen on the Heath 'the most *beaut-iful* babby ever beheld by mortal eyes'.[3] Swinburne enjoyed kissing the toes of the small children of Edmund Gosse, who preserved a memory of him seated on the sofa

– with one of my small girls perched on each of his little knees, while my son, just advanced to knickerbockers, having climbed up behind him, with open palm was softly stroking his bald cranium . . .[4]

Soon after Swinburne had arrived at The Pines, five-year-old Bertie, Watts-Dunton's nephew, came to live there with his parents. 'Of all the children out of arms,' Swinburne assured the little boy's mother, Bertie was 'the sweetest thing going at any price'.[5] Swinburne bought '*our* little boy' gingerbread and currant biscuits, and showed him illustrated books in his library. Watts-Dunton had to be away two nights every week visiting the declining Rossetti, and that may have helped Swinburne 'to *over do*' his emotion for Bertie. Mollie Panter-Downes suggests that when the ever-protective Watts-Dunton noticed what was happening, he may have worked behind the scenes, for his nephew went away on a visit. Swinburne, at forty-four,

1 *Ibid.*, p. 330. 3 Mar. 1873.
2 *Ibid.*, (1940), p. 206. 7 July 1875.
3 *And Even Now* (1920), p. 69.
4 *The Life of Algernon Charles Swinburne* (1917), p. 305.
5 Mollie Panter-Downes: *At the Pines: Swinburne & Watts-Dunton in Putney* (1971), p. 87.

deprived of this seven-year-old boy, found his world 'a cultureless island, my spirit a masterless slave'. He wrote *A Dark Month* – thirty-one poems of lamentation:

> When my King
> Took away
> With him spring . . .
> He is nearer to-night
> Whose coming in June
> Is looked for more than the light . . .

Bertie returned, delayed by five months, and the relationship settled down. On the boy's twelfth birthday, Swinburne ordered Leech's *Drawings from 'Punch'* for him, or, as second choice, Scott's *Waverley Novels* in half morocco, price twelve guineas.

III

STEVENSON wrote to his mother from Menton:

Kids are what is the matter with me.[1]

Staying at his hotel were two little Russian girls of two and a half and eight, who captivated him and like all children delighted in his company. It intrigued him that they thought they were cousins when in reality they were sisters, for their mother confided she had dedicated the second to her childless sister 'before it was conceived'. He struck up a great friendship, especially with the younger, Nelitschka, and for three months his letters were full of this 'little polyglot button'[2] who spoke fragments of six languages. There was an eight-year-old American girl, talented, mischievous, and irresistible.

On the train crossing America he helped a Dutch widow look after her many small children. He also made friends with a newsboy who brought him papers and the best fruit when he was ill – who sat with him when he could and did his best to cheer him.

In the hills near Monterey where the ranchers had nursed Stevenson to health, the mother of the two little girls became too ill to care for them and he took charge, teaching them to read and playing games.

1 7 Jan. 1874: *The Letters of Robert Louis Stevenson to his Family & Friends* ed. Sidney Colvin (1899), i, p. 70.
2 *Ibid.*, i, p. 69.

While he awaited the divorce, his kind landlady's little boy, Robbie, of whom he was very fond, caught pneumonia and Stevenson helped to nurse him, until he himself became very ill as the child recovered.

In Samoa, Fanny at fifty suffered a miscarriage; this sorely disappointed them, for the doctor had assured him the child would have been free of his complaint. When Fanny's daughter Belle and family came to live with them, he enjoyed the company of their young son, Austin, who was sometimes put in charge of the two strong pack horses bringing up supplies from Apia. After Belle's divorce, Stevenson became Austin's guardian, sending him to school in California.

The shabby and gaunt FRANCIS THOMPSON, living in dreams, loved the Meynells' children, who inspired many of his poems which were addressed to them. The son Everard wrote his life.

Before his marriage (which was childless), when he stayed with Lucian Oldershaw's sister, married to Dr Nash, CHESTERTON used to 'walk about with their baby daughter in his arms'.[1] At Overroads every Christmas, the Chestertons held a children's party with the stipulation that no parent or nurse was allowed to be present. His toy theatre came out, and there would be an infinite variety of games worked out by Frances and himself beforehand.

Maisie Ward tells a charming story of the doctor's little boy running along the top of his wall and, looking down at Chesterton, making the spirited remark: 'I think you're an ogre.' The boy's nurse threatened dire punishment if he didn't get down instantly, but the ogre sprang to his defence:

'This wall is meant for little boys to run along.'[2]

On his second visit to America, at fifty-six, he lectured at the University of Notre Dame, and the chauffeur in Indiana was asked if Chesterton had taken 'the lecture business' seriously.

'No. He just wanted five minutes on the porch when he would talk to no one but the kids . . .'[3] He'd walk on the porch and all the children came.'[4]

He talked to children on the road, and always had a smile. He was always calling them over to talk to him. The four- or five-year-olds were the ones he noticed most.

1 Maisie Ward: *Return to Chesterton* (1952), p. 88.
2 *Gilbert Keith Chesterton* (1944), p. 222.
3 *Ibid.*, p. 496.
4 *Ibid.*, p. 493.

'He'd touch one with his stick to make him look round and play with him
. . . The kids were always around him. He liked to ask them things and then
if they gave a good answer he could get a good laugh at it.[1]

A poem in his Notebook ends:

> And I say that if a man had climbed to the stars
> And found the secrets of the angels,
> The best thing and the most useful thing he could do
> Would be to come back and romp with children.[2]

During World War II, in the midst of translating the Scriptures, a
celibate scholar, Monsignor RONALD KNOX, had humbler duties
running concurrently as chaplain to a girls' school evacuated from
London to Shropshire. Every Sunday he preached to them and, with
the simplicity of true scholarship, handled the Mass, the Creed, and
the Gospel in terms of their own imagery:

Do you ever get taken out to lunch at a restaurant by an uncle? . . . don't you
find that he sits down, pulls out his spectacles, and looks through the menu
. . . ? The *Introit* is a bit like that . . .[3]

. . . when the priest has got to the end of the *Gloria*, he seems to get a sort of
scruple that he's not behaving quite like a gentleman . . . There is Mary Jane
behind him . . . so he turns round to bring her into the conversation. Before
turning round, he . . . kisses the altar . . . it is a kind of polite gesture . . .
'Excuse me one moment; I must just turn around and say Dominus vobiscum
to my friends . . . I am leaving a kiss on the altar to show you that I love you
[Almighty God] better than anything or anyone else.'[4]

. . . when you see me . . . all dressed up in silk like a great pin-cushion . . . I
am standing there . . . for you to stick pins in me – all the things you want to
pray about . . . all the worries that are going on at home, are part of the
prayer that I am saying . . .[5]

IV

KATHERINE MANSFIELD never fulfilled her wish to 'sit and read aloud
to my little son'.[6] Overwhelmed by her miscarriage at the Pension

1 *Ibid.*, p. 495.
2 *Ibid.*, p. 223. Cf. Kingsley's letter on p. 263.
3 *The Mass in Slow Motion* (1948), p. 17.
4 *Ibid.*, pp. 25–6.
5 *Ibid.*, p. 104.
6 *Journal of Katherine Mansfield* ed. J. Middleton Murry (1954), p. 41. 29 Apr. 1909.

Müller in Bavaria, she asked her loyal friend for an English child to look after and Ida found eight-year-old Charlie Walter, a shopkeeper's son in a Welbeck Street mews, convalescent from pleurisy. She 'got him a ticket, tied a label on him, and sent him across . . .'[1] Katherine kept him for the summer holidays and made him call her 'Sally'. He is the prototype of Lennie in *The Life of Ma Parker*.

Believing him to be the one who was infertile, she sent Murry to the doctor, and from San Remo at thirty-one she wrote to her husband:

. . . we must have children, we must.[2]

At Le Prieuré, three weeks before she died, she gathered the children to make Christmas decorations.

WINIFRED HOLTBY believed that people who had no contact with children lived in an artificial world, and Vera Brittain claimed that no childless spinster ever had better acquaintance with babies than Winifred. She helped to care for the little girls of her elder sister Grace. At the birth of Vera's son, John, she came in and said to her, 'Oh, darling! you are *clever!*' On her next visit, she picked him up and studied him closely: 'His head's just like a pussy-willow . . .' She became his 'discreet but devoted slave'.[3]

At thirty-one, she took charge of him and his nurse while Vera and her husband were in Geneva. When Shirley (who became the Rt. Hon. Shirley Williams, MP) was born, Winifred helped the nurse. She had always wanted to witness a birth. As the child grew, she would cradle Shirley's head against her shoulder and remark, 'She's caught her hair from me.'[4] She made herself late for *Time and Tide* Board dinners by helping Vera to bath the babies and put them to bed. After the first of her severe headaches, she took charge of the children and their nurse so that the parents could have a holiday, as *she* had done, on the French Riviera.

Vera and five-year-old John met her at Waterloo after she had spent a few weeks in a Devonshire convalescent home. She had written: 'I want to . . . sit about with you and the dear silly children.'[5] Her

1 Ida Baker: *Katherine Mansfield: The Memories of LM* (1971), p. 52.
2 23 Nov. 1919: *Katherine Mansfield's Letters to John Middleton Murry 1913–22* ed. J. M. Murry (1951), p. 407.
3 Vera Brittain: *Testament of Friendship* (1940), p. 277.
4 *Ibid.*, p. 379.
5 *Ibid.*, p. 319.

affection for John and Shirley seemed to grow even more after she had heard from her doctor that, if she were to marry, the attempt to have children could kill her. She said, '. . . who knows what sort of an academic busybody I might be without them!'[1]

Perhaps the loveliest image of her is when Vera, one summer afternoon, watched her push John along the Cromwell Road to Kensington Gardens. She was dressed in light-blue crêpe and a white hat over her golden hair –

Blue, white and gold, the fairy-like cavalcade soon vanished into the warm shadowy distance.[2]

Two weeks from death, she helped – 'as their second mother' – Edith de Coundourff to look after the Brittains' children.

SHAW and his wife treated T. E. Lawrence and Harley Granville-Barker as surrogate children. They did the same with their head gardener and housekeeper. Henry Higgs said:

Mrs Shaw looked upon my wife almost as a daughter. They were like a father and mother to us.

Lawrence joined the Royal Tank Corps under the name of 'Shaw', and legalized the change four years later by deed poll. His motor bike was a present from his adoptive father.

Asked about the encouragement she had given to so many young writers, Dame EDITH SITWELL replied: 'I always have a tenderness for the young.' She said that Dylan Thomas had never behaved anything but impeccably in her presence:

He always behaved with me like a son with his mother.[3]

Because he had been presented by his most intimate friend, Richard Bathurst, JOHNSON regarded the Jamaican Francis Barber almost as a son. Frank came as a boy of nine or ten,[4] and Bathurst's father, the Colonel, had given him his freedom. At fourteen, because it was the boy's wish, Johnson articled him to an apothecary, but at sixteen Frank ran away to sea and, worried at the rigorous conditions then prevailing in the Navy, Johnson was able to get him released two

1 *Ibid.*, p. 404.
2 *Ibid.*, p. 279.
3 BBC TV interview with John Freeman: *Face to Face*, 1959.
4 Assessment by the Curator of Johnson's House, Gough Square. Barber's precise age is not known.

years later. For five years, when Frank was in his later twenties, Johnson paid £300 to have him educated at the grammar school in Bishop's Stortford. The rest of the time, Frank took his place among the other privileged dependants in that household. His slight duties were those of a personal manservant or valet: answering callers, waiting at table on the few formal occasions that arose, and ordering provisions. Johnson interceded when, according to Frank, the authority that the blind lady, Anna Williams, 'assumed over him' was 'exercised with an unwarrantable severity'. After his marriage to an English girl, Betsey, at thirty-four, he lived next door, but they moved back after Mrs Williams's death. They now had two infant daughters, and after Johnson died a son was born, whom they named Samuel.

Johnson asked Dr Brocklesby 'what would be a proper annuity to a favourite servant', and on hearing that a nobleman might leave to such a one £50 a year, he replied:

Then I shall be *nobilissimus*, for I mean to leave Frank seventy pounds a year . . .[1]

Said one of JANE AUSTEN's nieces:

She seemed to love you, and you loved her in return.

Also, she told spontaneously 'the most delightful stories'.[2] When she was living at Southampton in a joint household with her brother Francis (who was in the Navy) and his wife, the sons of another brother, Edward, arived from Winchester, their mother having just died. The kindness, these thirteen and fourteen-year-old boys so desperately needed, they found in 'Aunt Jane'. MACAULAY regarded the children of Hannah, his sister, as his own.

---

1 James Boswell: *The Life of Samuel Johnson, LL D* (1791), ii, p. 571. *Aetat.* 75: 1784.
2 Rev. James Edward Austen-Leigh: *A Memoir of Jane Austen* (1971), pp. 112–3.

CHAPTER FIFTEEN

Exceptions

I

B oswell had the 'whimsical' thought to put to JOHNSON:

'If, Sir, you were shut up in a castle, and a new-born child with you, what would you do?'
JOHNSON: 'Why, Sir, I should not much like my company.'

After Boswell had pressed him, he said he would wash it 'with warm water to please it, not with cold water to give it pain'. He did not advocate 'the hardy method of treating children'.

BOSWELL: 'Would you not have a pleasure in teaching it?'
JOHNSON: 'No, Sir, I should *not* have a pleasure in teaching it.'[1]

Writing of Johnson's early attempt to run a school, Boswell said a temper, easily 'irritated by unavoidable slowness and errour in the advances of scholars',[2] disqualified his friend from being a successful teacher. Dining with the Thrales, Johnson said: 'I myself should not have had much fondness for a child of my own.' When Mrs Thrale rebuked him with 'Nay, Sir, how can you talk so?' he replied: 'At least, I never wished to have a child.'[3]

Such sentiments place him here, yet his attitude to children – witness his care of Francis Barber – was as ambivalent as Evelyn Waugh's. Boswell, elsewhere, speaks of 'Johnson's love of little children' – his 'calling them, "pretty dears", and giving them sweet-meats'.[4] He was much pleased with the boy rowing the sculler from Temple-stairs to the Old Swan, for, to settle a point with Boswell, he called to him:

1 James Boswell: *The Life of Samuel Johnson, LL D* (1791), 1, pp. 324–5. *Aetat*. 60: 26 Oct. 1769.
2 *Ibid.*, i, p. 45. *Aetat*. 26: 1735.
3 *Ibid.*, ii, p. 59. *Aetat*. 67: 10 Apr. 1776.
4 *Ibid.*, (2nd edn. 1793), iii, p. xx (*Addenda*).

'What would you give, my lad, to know about the Argonauts?'
'Sir, (said the boy,) I would give what I have.'[1]

They gave him double fare. The last words he spoke were to 'a Miss Morris, daughter to a particular friend', who had entreated Francis that she might see the Doctor and 'earnestly request him to give her his blessing'. Johnson turned himself in the bed, and said: 'God bless you, my dear!'[2] Ernest Shepard gave a beautiful rendering of the scene, depicting a child,[3] although she may in fact have been older.

BYRON made a more damaging admission to Augusta:

I don't know what Scrope Davies meant by telling you I liked Children, I abominate the sight of them so much that I have always had the greatest respect for the character of *Herod*.[4]

Again there are contradictions as we think of his enchantment with the children of Lady Oxford. But when the Hunts landed in Italy, to be installed on the ground floor of the Palazzo Lanfranchi, Byron posted his bulldog on the main stairs to keep the 'six little blackguards' away from his quarters above, and he referred to the children Hunt doted on as 'dirtier and more mischievous than Yahoos'.[5]

CHARLOTTE BRONTË was happier in the company of adults. Mrs Gaskell gave an explanation when she wrote of Charlotte's sufferings as a private governess:

It was a perpetual attempt to force all her faculties into a direction for which the whole of her previous life had unfitted them . . . the little Brontës had been brought up motherless . . . from never having experienced caresses or fond attentions themselves – they were ignorant of the very nature of infancy, or how to call out its engaging qualities . . . The hieroglyphics of childhood were an unknown language to them.[6]

But when, at thirty-five, Charlotte visited the Gaskells in Manchester, she lost her heart to their youngest daughter, Julia, and marvelled at their little girls perpetually. Mrs Gaskell 'could not persuade her that they were only average specimens of well brought up children'.

1 *Ibid.*, (1791), i, p. 249. *Aetat.* 54: Sat., 30 July 1763.
2 *Ibid.*, 11, p. 579. *Aetat.* 75: Mon., 13 Dec. 1784.
3 *Everybody's Boswell* (1930), pl. 54.
4 To Augusta Leigh: 30 Aug. 1811.
5 To Mary Shelley: 4 Oct. 1822.
6 E. C. Gaskell: *The Life of Charlotte Brontë* (1857), i, p. 187.

She was surprised and touched by any sign of thoughtfulness for others, of kindness to animals, or of unselfishness on their part; and constantly maintained that she was in the right, and I in the wrong, when we differed on the point of their unusual excellence.[1]

After her return, Charlotte wrote:

. . . to what children am I not a stranger? They seem to me little wonders; their talk, their ways are all matter of half-admiring, half-puzzled speculation.[2]

A mystery surrounds J. K. JEROME's stepdaughter Georgina ('Elsie'), whose mother he married nine days after her divorce, Elsie then five. Unlike their own child, Rowena, who acted in her father's plays and became his secretary, she was kept so successfully in the background it was as though she did not exist. That she married, and died sixteen years later, at thirty-eight, is practically all we know. Joseph Connolly assumes it likely that as early at an age as possible she moved away from the family.

It is strange that so liberal-minded a man as Jerome seems to have gone to such lengths . . . and it remains a point of conjecture for whose sake this course was followed.[3]

Ever since Nigel and Ben had been babies, a gap existed between VICTORIA SACKVILLE-WEST and them. When they were at Summer Fields and Eton, she always visited them at half-term – dressed, as their father once said, in the sort of clothes that Beatrice would have worn had she married Dante. She 'was always sweet to us', but after the garden and the dogs her topics of conversation were virtually exhausted. When the Nicolsons lived at Sissinghurst Castle, few were ever admitted to her sitting-room on the first floor of the Elizabethan tower.

We would go to the foot of the staircase in the opposite turret and shout that lunch was ready . . . but by an unspoken rule we never mounted it.[4]

Talking of children one weekend with Barbara Reynolds, DOROTHY L. SAYERS expressed amazement for her friend's interest in 'these

1 *Ibid.*, i, p. 225.
2 Undated letter to Mrs Gaskell (Aug. 1851 ?): *ibid.*, ii, pp. 228–9.
3 Joseph Connolly: *Jerome K. Jerome: A Critical Biography* (1982), p. 129.
4 Nigel Nicolson: *Portrait of a Marriage* (1973), p. 219 (Amer. edn., p. 248).

creatures with unformed minds'. She wrote to her cousin Ivy, into whose care her own child had been entrusted:

. . . maternal affection is by no means my strong point . . .[1]

Yet during World War II, when she and her husband were living at Witham, an evacuee boy from London was billetted with them, whose mother wrote on his return of the 'care and kindness' shown to him. It had been 'a great blow to him when he was recalled'.

He was quite sad about it, saying he had spent two happy years with you . . .

She and her girls were quite sure 'he would never convey to you half the nice things he's said about you and the Major . . .'[2] Mac's health and drinking were obviously not an insuperable problem. There was love to be extended and one wonders why Dorothy's own son could not have had more.

Certainly not a permissive father, EVELYN WAUGH encouraged the image of a tyrannical one.

The presence of my children affected me with intense weariness and depression.[3]

But Frances Donaldson, one of the few who knew the family well, said he was 'much beloved by children who, although they found him rather terrifying, appreciated his quality'.[4] He told her he liked to see himself in the role of a father. She had known his children from the time they were five lovely little ones. If they entered his room unasked, he shooed them away with 'Out, out, out', but she thought they accepted his familiar method of restraint.

II

DICKENS seems to have been less successful as a parent when his sons grew older. At Christmas, when he was fifty, he spoke of Gad's Hill

1 13 May 1927. James Brabazon: *Dorothy L. Sayers: The Life of a Courageous Woman* (1981), p. 141.
2 Letter from Alice M. Long: 29 Sept. 1941. *Ibid.*, pp. 209–10.
3 'The Waugh Trilogy': Nicholas Shakespeare's film biography. *Arena* programme: BBC2, Apr. 1987.
4 Frances Donaldson: *Evelyn Waugh: Portrait of a Country Neighbour* (1967), p. 39.

'pervaded by boys' whose trampling boots, whistling and shouts meant he could write nothing at all.

With their futures in mind, and in the fashion of his day – which he did not follow in other respects – Dickens consigned his sons to early exile. Kingsley wrote to his own eldest son before going up to Trinity:

India is a very fine opening. So is Queensland, though I should prefer India for you.

Dickens's second boy, Walter Landor, was the only one of his sons who might have wanted to be a writer, but Dickens wrote to Walter's tutor:

. . . the less he is encouraged to write the better . . . and the happier he will be.

Through Miss Coutts, the father secured for this very immature seventeen-year-old a cadetship in the East India Company, and Walter died in Calcutta five years later. Alfred Tennyson d'Orsay went to Western Australia. The youngest, Plorn, protesting to no avail, was shipped out to join him – this last eviction called by Una Pope-Hennessy 'the most peculiar' and 'the most cold-blooded'.[1]

But Mamey states that the office housekeeper, who saw Dickens after he had taken leave of the boy, told 'how she had never seen the master so upset, and that when she asked him how Mr Edward went off he burst into tears and couldn't answer her a word'.[2] In a letter to Plorn before his departure, Dickens wrote:

I hope you will always be able to say in after life that you had a kind father.

Similar to Dickens's with his sons, PRIESTLEY's relations with Tom as he grew older were more difficult.

It wasn't so much that we had arguments, but he was . . . very grand . . . distant.[3]

In contrast to both Dickens and Priestley, A. A. MILNE was closest to his son between the ages of eight and eighteen. He had not the gift of

1 *Charles Dickens: 1812–1870* (1945), p. 445.
2 'Charles Dickens at Home: with especial reference to his relations with Children': *The Cornhill Magazine*, Jan. 1885.
3 'Tom Priestley talks to Elisabeth Dunn': *The Sunday Times*, 19 Aug. 1984.

playing with Christopher when he was small, so he wrote about him instead.

One of the most endearing writers on childhood, Milne was not drawn to children in general:

I am not inordinately fond of . . . children . . . I have certainly never felt in the least sentimental about them . . .[1]

Lewis Hind noticed KENNETH GRAHAME on a station platform welcoming friends and behaving like the 'Olympians' he had satirized:

. . . a little fussy, bothering about wraps and a carriage, ignoring two children who were of the party, but studiously polite to their parents.[2]

There was the occasion when his American friends the Purveses arrived to spend a holiday with the Grahames in Fowey, and his little godchild had put his face up to be kissed. Austin Purves Jr. described the incident to Peter Green:

G. said in effect, Pierre it is all right this once, but men don't kiss. Pierre, then aged six, received, for a child, something of a shock.[3]

ANTHONY HOPE attended the first night of *Peter Pan* – sitting unmoved while the audience clapped so hard for fairies that Nina Boucicault wept. After the standing ovation, he let slip: 'Oh, for an hour of Herod!'[4]

III

Caitlin says that DYLAN THOMAS looked upon their first baby as 'a rival':

. . . he didn't want to gaze at him or touch him, and he never dreamt of picking him up.[5]

When Dylan got a job in films and started staying in London for days at a time, 'we abandoned Llewelyn, leaving him with my mother'. Caitlin describes the parting as 'quite the most painful thing that ever

1 *Autobiography* (Amer. edn. of *It's Too Late Now*, 1939), p. 282.
2 *Authors & I*, p. 106.
3 Peter Green: *Kenneth Grahame: A Study of his Life, Work & Times* (1959), p. 311.
4 Denis Mackail: *The Story of J.M. B.: a biography* (1941), p. 368.
5 Caitlin Thomas with George Tremlett: *Caitlin: A Warring Absence* (1986), p. 62.

happened to me', but she felt if she 'didn't do it Dylan would drift back into that pub life that he had before he met me, and would soon forget all about me'. Llewelyn, two years old at the time, did not return to them until after the war when he was five or six.

Even now I have terrible feelings of guilt.[1]

When their daughter Aeron was born, Dylan didn't visit the hospital until a week later, nor did he collect them when the time came for her to be discharged. Of an evening the children were left alone so she could go drinking with Dylan.

. . . I still feel guilt about it.[2]

But she adds that the children never saw their father drunk.

He never drank heavily during the day . . .[3]

He wrote *This Side of Truth* for Llewelyn, and she imagines that with Dylan 'there must have been a certain amount of guilt'. She thinks he was disappointed that Llewelyn was 'always brooding and introspective, sensitive and vulnerable' and that 'he wasn't more of a natural boy'.

Dylan wanted a straightforward boy who kicked a ball. (Our third child, Colm, was much more like that . . .)[4]

Colm was his favourite 'because he used to play and laugh, and this was Dylan's idea of how a baby ought to be'.

Colm inherited all Dylan's charm.

Dylan didn't cuddle him much. He was never very physical towards the children but he used to carry their photographs around with him in his wallet.

I think he must have been proud of them . . . Dylan was very sentimental about them when he was far away.[5]

As the children of Priestley and Evelyn Waugh had to *tiptoe* around certain parts of the house when their father was working, so Caitlin

1 *Ibid.*, pp. 75–7.
2 *Ibid.*, p. 86.
3 *Ibid.*, p. 129.
4 *Ibid.*, p. 93.
5 *Ibid.*, p. 113.

with the children at Laugharne used to go along the cliff and 'tiptoe past the shed as we heard his voice, booming, muttering and mumbling as he wrestled with each word'.[1] Caitlin made sure he was not interrupted.

In order that they could go to the States together, since he had missed her the first time, she had an abortion. 'Naturally, Dylan avoided all the unpleasantness.' He accompanied her to the clinic but wouldn't go in.

> . . . he went to the pub on the opposite side of the road . . . At six months it was very late: the baby was already well formed, and they chopped it up as they were pulling it out . . .[2]

DAPHNE DU MAURIER was a reluctant mother to her daughters when they were small. Tessa was four and Flavia less than a year when she left them with their nanny for Christmas. This was ten days after a five-months absence with her husband and his battalion in Egypt. She indulged 'Kits', who at three was allowed to stay in her writing room provided he played quietly by himself. Even with her husband away for long periods during the war, the children did not have their meals with her – a privilege which must wait until the age of twelve. They came together of an afternoon, rambling through the woods around Menabilly, always a happy time of day. Unlike Dickens, whose relations with his sons became more strained as they grew older, she looked forward to the time when her daughters would be 'of a decent, companionable age'.[3]

1 Caitlin Thomas with George Tremlett: *Caitlin: A Warring Absence* (1986), p. 116.
2 *Ibid.*, pp. 151–2.
3 Letter to Maud Waddell, 'Tod', her own childhood governess. Margaret Forster: *Daphne du Maurier* (1993), p. 145.

CHAPTER SIXTEEN

The Secret

At Grèz-sur-Loing, STEVENSON allowed eight-year-old Lloyd to sit in the canoe that had just completed the *Inland Voyage*. He even went to the trouble of setting up the little masts and sails.

I was very flattered to be treated so seriously – RLS always paid children the compliment of being serious . . .[1]

Bert Coote, through his juvenile acting, got to know DODGSON and paid a tribute all the more remarkable in view of Dodgson's antipathy to little boys:

He was one of us, and never a grown-up pretending to be a child in order to preach at us . . .[2]

When FRANCES HODGSON BURNETT had the children of Cyril Maude and Winifred Emery staying with her at Maytham Hall, Pamela, who was not quite eight, remembered later how Frances 'saw things in the same way as ourselves'.[3]

'Nico' Llewelyn Davies, in his seventies, recalled that BARRIE 'always tried to offer advice as a friend, not as a parent, even when I was very young (which, incidentally, is one reason why he got on so well with children – he always treated them as equals)'.[4] EDWARD THOMAS treated twelve-year-old David Garnett 'from the first moment . . . as an equal'.

I was therefore encouraged to tell him exactly what I was thinking.[5]

ROALD DAHL's daughter spoke of her father:

1 'An Intimate Portrait of RLS by his Stepson, Lloyd Osbourne': *Scribner's Magazine*, Nov. 1923, p. 515.
2 Langford Reed: *The Life of Lewis Carroll* (1932), p. 95.
3 Ann Thwaite: *Waiting for the Party* (1974), p. 200.
4 Andrew Birkin: *J. M. Barrie & the Lost Boys* (1979), p. 282.
5 David Garnett: *Great Friends: Portraits of seventeen writers* (1979), p. 62.

He talks to children as equals which very few adults do.[1]

KINGSLEY allowed his undergraduates at Cambridge to talk to him on equal terms. Leonard Woolf said of SHAW that 'like the Webbs, he seemed never to resent or to be offended by anything which a younger person said or did to him'.[2] Mrs Hinton, a neighbour in Ayot St Lawrence, said: 'He always talked to my children as an equal, so they liked him and looked upon him as a favourite uncle.'

A.S. NEILL believed that to joke with a child gives him or her an assurance of being loved – provided our humour is not 'cutting' or 'critical'. The beautiful anecdote that follows shows how one child's sense of humour grew at the school, and it epitomizes Neill's secret and success.

When David Barton was three (and he 'was practically born in Summerhill'), Neill pretended to be a visitor and said: 'I want to find Neill. Where is he?' The little boy looked at him scornfully and said: 'Silly ass, you're him.' But when David was seven, Neill stopped him in the garden one day and said: 'Tell David Barton I want to see him. He's over at the Cottage I think.' David grinned, and went over to the Cottage. After two minutes he returned.

'He says he won't come.'
   'Did he give a reason?'
   'Yes, he said he was feeding his tiger.'[3]

1 Interview with Sue Lawley: 'Saturday Matters': BBC1, 9 Sept. 1989.
2 *Beginning Again* (1964), p. 122.
3 A. S. Neill: *That Dreadful School* (1937), p. 163.

PART FIVE
PUBLIC FIGURE

CHAPTER ONE

Decorations and Honours

I

A large number of our writers were decorated or honoured one way or another. Bacon, Disraeli, Tennyson, and Kenneth Clark were elevated to the peerage – BACON in the year he became Lord Chancellor, DISRAELI on retiring from the Commons. KENNETH CLARK was created a life peer after more than thirty years' public service in the arts.

TENNYSON, at seventy-four, did not like 'this cocked-hat business at all'. The prospect of taking his seat worried him considerably. He said to Canon Rawnsley:

I did not want it. What can I do? How can I take off a cocked hat and bow three times in the House of Lords?[1]

C. V. WEDGWOOD and IRIS MURDOCH are Dames of the British Empire; IVY COMPTON-BURNETT and DAPHNE DU MAURIER were among the few woman novelists to receive this distinction. Rewarded by five honorary doctorates and a Dame, EDITH SITWELL insisted this did not make her a member of the Establishment.

Had he lived, DICKENS would have been Sir Charles Dickens of Gad's Hill, for he accepted a baronetcy three months before his death and that was how he wished to be styled.[2] P. G. WODEHOUSE was conferred a knighthood six weeks before he died at ninety-three. DOYLE was knighted at forty-three for his work as Senior Physician at the Langman Field Hospital during the Boer War. Five of the sixteen

---

1 Harold Nicolson: *Tennyson: Aspects of his Life Character & Poetry* (1923), p. 212.
2 On account of 'the divine William and Falstaff', ran his letter of 5 Mar. 1870, to the Clerk of the Privy Council, accepting the Queen's offer. (See Una Pope-Hennessy: *Charles Dickens* [1945], p. 461.) Cf. Peter Ackroyd on Dickens's audience with the Queen: 9 Mar. 1870. 'There were rumours afterwards that Dickens had been offered a knighthood or even a peerage, but there was nothing to them . . .' (*Dickens* [1991], p. 1066.)

authors of *The Oxford History of England* (1936–65) received the accolade, but no such honour was offered to A. J. P. TAYLOR.

I have received a greater honour. *English History 1914–1945* became a best-selling paperback in Penguin, which none of the other volumes in the series have done.[1]

A Companion of the Bath at sixty-two, EDMUND GOSSE, at seventy-five, was offered the choice by Asquith of a Companion of Honour or a knighthood, and he chose the latter. He received six honorary degrees – St Andrews, Gothenburg, Oslo, Cambridge, Strasbourg (where an audience of two thousand acclaimed him), and Paris – but he told his son that it was the Sorbonne degree he valued most. GALSWORTHY acquired seven honorary doctorates, Sir JAMES MURRAY nine, Lord CLARK thirteen, ELIOT eighteen – British, American, French, and German. ALISON UTTLEY received an honorary doctorate from her own university of Manchester, at eighty-five.

PEPYS was elected President of The Royal Society when he was fifty-one, and again the following year. When KIPLING accepted the Gold Medal of The Royal Society of Literature, it had been awarded only to Scott, Meredith, and Hardy. In 1961, the same society elected CHURCHILL, FORSTER, MASEFIELD, and MAUGHAM, all in their eighties, to be the first Companions of Literature; the following year, ALDOUS HUXLEY was elected at sixty-seven.

ANTHONY POWELL, a Commander of the British Empire, was made a Companion of Honour at eighty-two – the third living writer, after Graham Greene and Sir Sacheverell Sitwell, to receive this distinction. FORSTER, when he was seventy-four, had been similarly honoured, also MAUGHAM, who reflected that at eighty the recognition had come too late.

To extend the European colouring that has already appeared, CARLYLE's *History of Frederick the Great* was rewarded with the Prussian Order of Merit (founded by his hero), which elicited the comment:

. . . had they sent me a quarter of a pound of good tobacco, the addition to my happiness would probably have been . . . greater.[2]

EDMUND GOSSE was made Knight of the Royal Norwegian Order. DOYLE received an Italian knighthood as well as his English one. The

1 *A Personal History* (1983), p. 244.
2 To his brother, John Carlyle: 14 Feb. 1874.

King of Servia conferred upon SAMUEL SMILES Knight Commander's Cross of Royal Order of St Sava. The King of Belgium bestowed upon GALSWORTHY, for services to Belgian Relief, Palmes en Or de l'Ordre de la Couronne. ELIOT was Officier de la Légion d'honneur, and Commandeur Ordre des Arts et des Lettres; West Germany awarded him Orden Pour le Merite, and Florence the Dante Gold Medal. H. V. MORTON was Commander of the Order of the Phoenix (Greece), and Cavaliere, Order of Merit (Italy). CYRIL CONNOLLY was a Chevalier, and Lord CLARK a Commandeur, de la Légion d'Honneur. Clark was also Commander of the Lion of Finland, and held the Austrian Order of Merit: Grand Cross, Second Class.

BELLOC and CHESTERTON received Papal honours, Knight Commanders of St Gregory with Star. Chesterton was also cited posthumously in a cable from the Vatican to Cardinal Hinsley:

Holy Father deeply grieved death Mr. Gilbert Keith Chesterton devoted son Holy Church gifted Defender of the Catholic Faith.

According to Maisie Ward, the secular press did not print the telegram in full 'because it bestowed upon a subject a royal title',[1] the first to receive it being Henry VIII.

H. M. TOMLINSON managed to be Officer of the Brazilian Order of the Southern Cross. HENRY WALTER BATES was Chevalier of the Brazilian Order of the Rose.

II

The Laureateship – 'profaned by Cibber and contemned by Gray' – was held first, unofficially, by BEN JONSON, who at forty-four received a pension of a hundred marks from James I. In 1630, he petitioned Charles I to make those marks as many pounds. New letters patent were issued, appointing him for life the annual pension of £100, together with

. . . one terse of Canary Spanish wine . . . out of our store . . . in our cellers . . . belonging to our palace of Whitehall.[2]

1 *Gilbert Keith Chesterton* (1944), p. 553.
2 *The Works of Ben Jonson* ed. Peter Whalley (1756), i, pp. xlv–xlvi, lx.

Among those given the official *title* were DRYDEN at thirty-seven (later taken from him at the Revolution of 1688), SOUTHEY at thirty-nine, WORDSWORTH at seventy-three, TENNYSON at forty-one, BRIDGES at sixty-nine, MASEFIELD at nearly fifty-two, C. DAY LEWIS at sixty-three, BETJEMAN at sixty-six, TED HUGHES at fifty-four. The emolument has stayed at £97 per annum.

Macaulay had encouraged LEIGH HUNT to expect the Laureateship on the death of Southey, and Hunt's hopes were dashed again when Tennyson succeeded Wordsworth. Mrs Browning thought on that occasion Hunt should have had it, for 'he has condescended to wish for it'. At first, WORDSWORTH had declined on his inability to discharge the duties, but Peel assured him that no official verses would be required. A letter to TENNYSON from Windsor Castle made it clear:

The ancient duties of this Office, which consisted of laudatory Odes to the Sovereign, have been long, as you are probably aware, in abeyance . . .[1]

According to his son, Tennyson used to joke:

In the end I accepted the honour, because during dinner Venables told me, that, if I became Poet Laureate, I should always when I dined out be offered the liver-wing of a fowl.[2]

When his poem on the wedding of Princess Anne had met with a lukewarm reception, BETJEMAN commented:

One knows poetry can't be written to order. One just waits for something to come through from The Management upstairs and The Management can be very capricious.

The following received the Order of Merit:[3] Bridges, de la Mare, Priestley, and Graham Greene in their eighties; Meredith, Hardy, James, J. W. Mackail, and Bertrand Russell in their seventies (James lying ill and near death); Barrie, Galsworthy, and Eliot in their sixties; Masefield, Dame Veronica Wedgwood, and G. M. Trevelyan (the youngest writer) in their fifties. PRIESTLEY said in a radio interview:

I've only two things to say about it. First I deserve it. Second, they've been too long about giving me it. There'll be another vacancy very soon.[4]

1 Signed C. B. Phipps: 5 Nov. 1850. *Alfred Lord Tennyson: A Memoir by his Son* (1897), i, p. 335.
2 *Ibid.*, i, p. 336.
3 Founded by Edward VII, and limited to 24 British members at one time.
4 Oct. 1977.

The Nobel Prize for Literature[1] was awarded to Churchill, Bertrand Russell, and William Golding in their seventies; Shaw, Galsworthy, and Samuel Beckett in their sixties; Yeats at fifty-eight, and Kipling (the youngest English writer) at forty-two. SHAW used the money to establish the Anglo-Swedish Literary Foundation for translating Swedish literature into English. GALSWORTHY, with his £9,000 Prize money, made a Trust Fund for the benefit of the PEN Club, of which he had been the first President – a post he held thirteen years.

1 Nobel Prizes began in 1901. Kipling received the first British award for Literature in 1907.

CHAPTER TWO

Royal Favour

I

CHAUCER served the courts of Edward III and Richard II. He knew the patronage of three successive kings and two royal dukes, yet if this makes his life seem tantalizingly remote it can only highlight his achievement in creating characters to which we relate. From the age of seventeen he was trained as a page in the household of Lionel, Duke of Clarence, Edward III's second son. When he was captured in France, at twenty, his ransom was partly paid by the King. His marriage to Philippa, through her connections with that family, gave him a patron in John of Gaunt, another son of Edward III.

Yeoman of the chamber – ambassador abroad – surveyor of royal palaces, the images of him are few. The popular one, in the painting by Ford Madox Brown, should be transposed with a younger Chaucer: one of Edward's forty esquires, reading perhaps his *Boke of the Duchesse* or *The Hous of Fame*. His masterpieces were read to the court of Richard II. When Henry IV took the throne, Chaucer addressed to him 'A Compleynt to his Purs' and the King doubled his pension, confirming also the grants Richard had made.

At a time of life when Shakespeare retired to Stratford, CAXTON began the career that would earn his immortality. His best years were spent trading wool at Bruges, where the other English merchants elected him Governor of their gild. Now, in his late forties, encouraged by Margaret, Duchess of Burgundy, sister to Edward IV, he translated *Le Recueil des Histoires de Troge*. To save the tedious task of copying – for 'age creepeth on me daily and feebleth all the body, and also because I have promised to divers gentlemen and to my friends to address them as hastily as I might'[1] – he learnt to use the new

1 *The Recuyell of the Histories of Troy* (1474?), Preface.

360

movable types, in Cologne. Then, with the help of Colard Mansion, he set up his press at Bruges 'to ordain this said book in print':[1] the first book printed in English.

In 1476, when he was about fifty-four (an old man in mediaeval times), he brought his press to the precincts of Westminster Abbey. Under the protection of volatile kings and nobles oscillating between culture and the sword, he proceeded to print nearly a hundred books, many in folio, and twenty of them his own translations. Earl Rivers and the Earl of Worcester translated some. Several were printed under the patronage of Edward IV, who possessed a copy of *The History of Godfrey of Boulogne* (1481), translated and printed by Caxton. He dedicated his *Order of Chivalry* (1484?) to Richard III. He printed *Fayts of Arms and Chivalry* (1489) at the behest of Henry VII, and dedicated *Eneydos* (1490) to Arthur, Prince of Wales, a small child. When the length of *The Golden Legend* (1484?) made him 'half desperate' to finish the paraphrase and ready to 'lay it apart', the Earl of Arundel, to spur him on, promised a buck every summer and a doe every winter after its completion. (Among Chaucer's rewards was a pitcher of wine daily, granted by Edward III, and an annual tun of wine by Richard II.)

As Master of Requests, as knight, as one of the Privy Council, THOMAS MORE was advanced by Henry VIII. The King took such pleasure in More's company that after he had made him Chancellor of the Duchy of Lancaster he 'would on the suddaine go up to his howse at *Chelsey*, to be merry with him',

whither on a tyme comming to dynner, he walked in *Syr Thomas Mores* garden by the space of an houre, and held his arme about *Syr Thomas Mores* necke.

When Roper commented on this afterwards, More replied:

I thanke our Lord God, Sonne *Roper* . . . I find his Grace my very good Lord indeed. And I thinke he doth as singularly favour me, as any subiect within this Realme . . .[2]

On Sundays Henry would send for him to come to his private study, where they would sit and confer. Sometimes at night, Henry had the author of *Utopia* up on his leads to talk about the stars. The King and

---

1 *Ibid.*
2 (William Roper:) *The Mirrour of Vertue in Worldly Greatnes. Or The Life of Syr Thomas More* (1626), pp. 31-2.

Queen Catherine would 'send for him, at tyme of dinner and supper, as also many other tymes, to come & recreate with them'.

But when he perceyued the King to take so much delight in his company, that he could not scarce once in a moneth get leave to go home to his wife and children . . . he . . . did thereupon begin, somewhat to dissemble his merry nature . . .[1]

On Wolsey's death, More succeeded as Lord Chancellor.

The Duke of *Norfolke* in the audience of all the people . . . shewed, that he was from the King himselfe straightley charged . . . to publish there openly . . . how much all *England* was beholding to *Syr Thomas More*, for his good service; and how worthily he deserved the highest roome in the Kingdom; and further how deere his Maiesty loved & trusted him . . .[2]

At first, on the matter of the annulment of the King's marriage ('divorce'), Henry respected More's conscience. As the business proceeded, More voluntarily gave up the chain of office and the Great Seal. Within two years he was in the Tower. Save for the order he was not to be racked, the friend in the King's 'favour and . . . service twenty years and above' was abandoned.

II

RALEGH was about twenty-seven when he found favour with Elizabeth at Greenwich. Within five years, with splendid appointments as he climbed, he became Captain of the Guard responsible for her personal safety. To these years at court most of his poetry belongs, written in the convention and inspired by the Virgin Queen:

> Out of that mass of mirakells, my Muse,
> Gathered thos floures to her pure sences pleasinge . . .
>
> Her regall lookes my rigarus sythes[3] suppressed,
> Small dropes of ioies sweetned great worlds of woes . . .
>
> When shee did well, what did ther elce amiss? . . .
> Shee gave, shee tooke, shee wounded, shee apeased.[4]

1 *Ibid.*, pp. 14–15.
2 *Ibid.*, p. 62.
3 sighs.
4 The 11th: and last booke of the Ocean to Scinthia: *ll.* 45–6, 49–50, 53, 56: *The Poems of Sir Walter Ralegh* ed. Agnes M. C. Latham (1951), pp. 26–7.

When he was forty, Elizabeth discovered his secret marriage to a lady-in-waiting and dispatched both to the Tower; she released Ralegh first, and Lady Ralegh after a few more months. But it was five years before Cecil brought him to the Queen, who gave him back his old place. The same evening, 'he rid abroad with the Queen, and had private conference with her . . .'[1]

Someone observed that the courtiers of Elizabeth were like a suit of clothes made for her and worn out with her. Ralegh, the most glittering of her paladins, was stripped on the accession of James I. By the end of the year, his Captaincy of the Guard, his Lord Wardenship of the Stannaries, his Governorship of Jersey, his patent of wine licences, his London residence of Durham House, all had gone and he was back in the Tower – on a charge of treason. After his attainder the rest of his offices followed, a flaw even being found in the deed conveying Sherborne Castle and Park to the trustees of his son.

During the thirteen years that Ralegh spent in the Bloody Tower, he occupied himself in study; and when a kindlier keeper allowed him the use of a hen-house he conducted scientific experiments. For six years his wife and two children lived with him – at other times in a house on Tower Hill. Lady Ralegh knelt to James for her husband's freedom; she knelt again for recompense over the loss of Sherborne. One Lieutenant of the Tower complained about her coach rattling over the drawbridge regardless of times; also that Ralegh, from what is now known as his Walk, paraded to passers-by.

Prince Henry, a year younger than Ralegh's elder boy, was a frequent visitor and the Vice-Admiral, who had built the *Ark Royal*, designed for him a model boat. As he grew older, the Prince consulted the illustrious prisoner on affairs of state, including his future marriage. He made the spirited remark: 'Who but my father would keep such a bird in a cage?' The Queen supported Ralegh, who petitioned her in prose and verse:

> Cold walls to you I speake but you are senslesse . . .
> Then vnto whom shall I vnfold my wrong . . .
> To her who is the first and maye alone
> Be justlie called the empresse of the Brittaines
> Who should have mercye if a Queene have none?[2]

1 Rowland Whyte to Sir Robert Sydney, 2 June 1597. Quoted by Edward Edwards: *The Life of Sir Walter Ralegh together with his Letters* (1868), i, p. 226.
2 'S. W. Raghlies Petition to the Qveene: 1618': *ll.* 16, 19, 22–4. *The Poems of Sir Walter Ralegh* ed. Agnes M. C. Latham (1951), p. 70.

Twice she pleaded with James to set him free. When she was unwell, she sent for his Great Cordial and found it efficacious. She sent again on behalf of her dying son.

Prince Henry was only eighteen when he died. He had obtained a promise for Ralegh's release; he had purchased Sherborne from its new owner, intending, it is said, to return it to the man he revered. On the dashing of his hopes, Ralegh completed only the first of the three intended folios of his *History of the World*.

It was for the service of that inestimable Prince Henry . . . that I undertook this work. It pleased him to peruse some part thereof, and to pardon what was amiss.

As a leading member of the Lord Chamberlain's Company, SHAKE-SPEARE frequently performed before Elizabeth's court at Richmond, Greenwich, and Whitehall. At Christmas 1597, when he was thirty-three, the Queen witnessed *Love's Labour Lost*, and the following Christmas *The Merry Wives of Windsor*. According to tradition, *The Merry Wives* was written at her 'Command' and 'she commanded it to be finished in fourteen days'.[1] Gildon adds that the Queen had obliged Shakespeare 'to write a Play of Sir *John Falstaff* in Love, and which I am very well assured he perform'd in a Fortnight . . .'[2]

In the first year of his reign,[3] while he was staying with the Earl of Pembroke at Wilton, James I summoned Shakespeare's company to perform before them. When the King eventually made his state entry into London, the Company appeared in the royal train:

. . . each of them was presented with four yards and a half of scarlet cloth, the usual dress allowance to players belonging to the household.

They were granted a licence to perform both in town and the provinces, and now became known as the King's Men, taking 'rank at court amongst the Grooms of the Chamber'.[4]

PEPYS, at twenty-seven, was taken aboard the *Naseby* as the private secretary of Lord Sandwich, his father's cousin, to bring back Charles II – the year Pepys began the *Diary*.

1660. May 23rd. The King with the two Dukes and Queen of Bohemia, Princess Royal, and Prince of Orange, came on board, where I in their

1 John Dennis: dedication to George Granville of *The Comical Gallant* (1702).
2 1710.
3 Dec. 1603.
4 J. O. Halliwell-Phillipps: *Outlines of the Life of Shakespeare* (1881), i, p. 212.

coming in kissed the King's, Queen's, and Princess's hands . . . All the afternoon the King walked up and down, very active and stirring. Upon the quarterdeck he fell into discourse of his escape from Worcester, where it made me ready to weep to hear the stories that he told of his difficulties that he had passed through.

Shortly afterwards, due to his cousin's influence, Pepys was appointed Clerk of the Acts in the Navy Office, and had in fact become Secretary of the Navy Board. He attended the King at Whitehall ('White Hall') in his Cabinet Council:

1664. November 9th . . . I was called in, and demanded by the King himself many questions, to which I did give him full answers. There were at this Council my Lord Chancellor, Archbishop of Canterbury, Lord Treasurer, the two Secretarys, and Sir G. Cartaret. Not a little contented at the chance of being made known by these persons, and called often by my name by the King.

1665. July 26th. To Greenwich to the Park, where I hear the King and Duke are come by water this morn from Hampton Court. They asked me several questions . . . The King having dined, he come down, and I went in the barge with him, I sitting at the door. Down to Woolwich . . . and back again with him in the barge, hearing him and the Duke talk, and seeing and observing their manner of discourse. And God forgive me! though I admire them with all the duty possible, yet the more a man considers and observes them the less he finds of difference between them and other men, though (blessed be God!) they are both princes of great nobleness and spirits.

He found royal favour and was approved:

1666. January 28th . . . and so . . . to Hampton Court . . . I went down into one of the Courts . . . And the King come to me of himself and told me, 'Mr. Pepys,' says he, 'I do give you thanks for your good service all this year, and I assure you I am very sensible of it.' And the Duke of Yorke, did tell me with pleasure that he had read over my discourse about pursers and would have it ordered in my way, and so fell from one discourse to another. I walked with them quite out of the Court into the fields.

On the day of the Great Fire, he went to Whitehall 'and there up to the King's closett in the Chappell, where people come about me and I did give them an account dismayed them all, and word was carried in to the King':

1666. September 2nd. (Lord's Day.) . . . So I was called for and did tell the King and Duke of Yorke what I saw, and that unless his Majesty did command houses to be pulled down nothing could stop the fire. They seemed much troubled, and the King commanded me to go to my Lord Mayor from him and command him to spare no houses, but to pull down before the fire every way. The Duke of York bid me tell him that if he would have any more soldiers he shall . . .

Later that day he 'met with the King and Duke of York in their barge, and with them to Queenhithe'. After the national shame 'of the Dutch breaking the Chaine at Chatham' and burning 'our ships, and particularly *The Royal Charles*', Pepys was called to give an account to Parliament. The following year, he was called again to defend his Office:

1668. March 5th. So we were called in, with the mace before us, into the House, where a mighty full House; and we stood at the bar . . . After the Speaker had told us the dissatisfaction of the House and read the Report of the Committee, I began our defence . . . and continued at it without any hesitation or losse, but with full scope, and all my reason free about me as if I had been at my own table, from that time till past three in the afternoon, and so ended, without any interruption from the Speaker; but we withdrew. And there . . . all the world that was within hearing did congratulate me . . .

The following day, he received royal congratulations:

. . . and I to the Duke of York's lodgings, and find him going to the Park, it being a very fine morning, and I after him and as soon as he saw me he told me with great satisfaction that I had converted a great many yesterday . . . And by and by overtaking the King, the King and Duke of York come to me both; and he said, 'Mr. Pepys, I am very glad of your success yesterday . . .'

III

When George III was informed of JOHNSON's occasional visits to the library at the Queen's House,[1] he asked to be informed next time he came. In due course, Mr Barnard, the librarian, brought the message that Dr Johnson was in the library, and the King entered by a private door. Mr Barnard whispered to Johnson, who was reading by the fire: 'Sir, here is the King,' and Johnson at once stood up. They discussed libraries in general, and then the King asked if he was writing anything. When Johnson said 'he thought he had already done his part as a writer', the King paid a handsome compliment:

1 i.e., Buckingham House (Buckingham Palace). This library was sold to the British Museum, by George IV, in 1823.

I should have thought so too, if you had not written so well.

The King went on to inquire about the extent of his reading. Johnson praised the learning of Warburton which 'resembled Garrick's acting, in its universality'. They discussed other authors and literary journals. Afterwards Johnson told his friends:

I found his Majesty wished I should talk, and I made it my business to talk. I find it does a man good to be talked to by his Sovereign.[1]

For five years in her late thirties, FANNY BURNEY, as Assistant Mistress of the Robes to Queen Charlotte, led a life that Thackeray records 'well-nigh killed her'. When a cold lunch was provided for their Majesties at Oxford,

We . . . untitled attendants, stood at the other end of the room . . . facing the royal collationers . . . absolutely famished . . . as we had breakfasted early, and had no chance of dining before six or seven o'clock.

Kindly Major Price and the ever-practical Colonel Fairly arranged for one at a time to eat, all the rest backing very near and forming a screen. Even the Duchess of Ancaster, dismissed after the first serving, 'drew a small body of troops before her, that she might take a few minutes' rest on a form . . . "Poor Miss Burney! . . . She does not know yet what it is to stand for five hours following, as we do."'[2]

But she saw, and enabled us to see, the domestic side of J. R. Green's George III.[3] She captured the pathos of his personal tragedy. Once, she was with the Queen when he entered:

'She used to copy for her father,' said the Queen; 'indeed, I think her father has a great loss of her.'. . .
  'And who copies for him now?' cried the King.
  'I don't know, Sir.' . . .
  'What does he do then?'
  'I fancy he copies for himself!'[4]

On another occasion, she was with others playing with 'the sweet little Princess Amelia', when all stopped at the King's entry:

1 1767. James Boswell: *The Life of Samuel Johnson, LL D* (1791), i, pp. 292–3, 295. *Aetat.* 58.
2 13 Aug. 1786. *Diary & Letters of Madame d'Arblay* ed. by her Niece (1842–6), iii, pp. 99–101.
3 'In ten years he reduced government to a shadow . . . In twenty he had forced the American colonies into revolt . . . He had a smaller mind than any English king before him save James the Second.' *A Short History of the English People* (illus. edn. 1892–4), iv, p. 1665.
4 Letter to Dr Burney: 16 Oct. 1786. *Op. cit.*, iii, p. 189.

The little Princess . . . grew extremely impatient . . . and distressed me most ridiculously by her innocent appeals. 'Miss Burney! – come! – why don't you play? – Come, Miss Burney, I say, play with me! . . . Why don't you, Miss Burney?'

. . . as she kept pulling me by the hand and gown, so entirely with all her little strength, that I had the greatest difficulty to save myself from being suddenly jerked into the middle of the room: at length, therefore, I whispered 'We shall disturb the King, ma'am!'

. . . she flew instantly to his Majesty, who was in earnest discourse with Mr Smelt, and called out, 'Papa, go!'
  'What?' cried the King.
  'Go, papa, – you must go!' repeated she eagerly.

The King took her up in his arms, and began kissing and playing with her; she strove with all her might to disengage herself, calling aloud 'Miss Burney! Miss Burney! take me! – come, I say, Miss Burney! – O Miss Burney, come!'[1]

At Kew, the King brought the Princess Amelia to the parlour during tea:

'Here,' cried he, 'we shall all be jealous of Miss Burney! Amelia insists upon coming to her again; and says she won't go to bed if Miss Burney does not take her!'

The sweet little child then called upon me to play with her . . . 'Come, Miss Burney,' she cried, 'come and sit down with me . . . why won't you sit down?'

Nothing can be so pretty as this innocence of her royal station and her father's rank: though she gave me a thousand small distresses, I longed to kiss her for every one of them.[2]

When Fanny's father visited her in her apartment at Windsor the King came in and 'began immediately upon musical matters'. The King stayed an hour, unconcerned that Dr Burney in his enthusiasm broke the rules by coming close and thereby entering the 'distant and respectful circle, in which the King alone moves'.[3] Next day, 'after coffee, the sweet Princess Amelia was brought by the King himself':

The King showed her to my father, who could not but most unaffectedly admire so lovely a child.

1 4 Nov. 1786: *ibid.*, iii, pp. 208–9.
2 7 Nov. 1786: *ibid.*, iii, pp. 216–7.
3 29 Dec. 1786: *ibid.*, iii, p. 261.

Then, sportively pointing to my father, the King whispered her, 'Do you know who that is, Emily?'

'No.'

'Is it Miss Burney's papa?'

'No!'

'Why not? is he too young?'

'Yes!'[1]

When the King's health began to break, Fanny met him 'in the passage from the Queen's room' at Windsor:

... he stopped me, and conversed upon his health near half-an-hour ... He is all agitation, all emotion, yet all benevolence and goodness ... that makes it touching to hear him speak.[2]

She was present when the King, sensible of the change in himself, saw Lady Effingham: 'My dear Effy,' he cried in the hoarse voice now common to him, 'you see me all at once, an old man.'[3]

There was the day when she walked in Kew Gardens, having been told the King (undergoing the barbarous treatment of the insane in those times) was in Richmond. Suddenly she saw two or three figures through some trees. She ran off, the King pursuing her and calling hoarsely, 'Miss Burney! Miss Burney!'

One of the attendants implored her: 'Dr Willis begs you to stop! You must, ma'am; it hurts the King to run!'

When the King came up to her, he asked, 'Why did you run away?' He embraced her and kissed her cheek. They walked together for a while. He assured her he was quite well, and inquired after her father. He related many anecdotes of Handel, including the one about himself when Handel had said, 'While that boy lives, my music will never want a protector.' He attempted to sing several airs and choruses, but the sound was terrible on account of his hoarseness. When Dr Willis told him to let the lady go on her walk, he cried:

'No, no! I want to ask her a few questions; – I have lived so long out of the world . . .'[4]

On the King's temporary or partial recovery, it was Fanny's own health that broke down, and her father gave his support that her

1 30 Dec. 1786: *Diary & Letters of Madame d'Arblay* ed. by her Niece (1842–6), iii, p. 263.

2 26 Oct. 1788: *ibid.*, iv, p. 273.

3 1 Nov. 1788: *ibid.*, iv, p. 275.

4 2 Nov. 1789: *ibid.*, iv, pp. 401–6.

position should be relinquished. During her last week at court, the King, who was reading Boswell's *Life of Johnson*, came into the Queen's dressing-room every night and 'detained Her Majesty's proceedings' by wanting certain points clarified:

He was eager to inquire of me who was Mrs Lennox?[1] . . . He told me once, laughing heartily, that, having seen my name in the Index, he was eager to come to what was said of me; but when he found so little, he was surprised and disappointed.[2]

On her last day, the King came into the room to speak to her, but 'perceiving me quite overcome he walked away, and I saw him no more'. They were going to Kew. For the last time she put the cloak over the Queen's shoulders, 'and slightly ventured to press them . . . "God Almighty bless your Majesty!"' The three eldest Princesses ran in. Two held her hands, the Princess Royal putting hers over them; they repeated again and again: 'I wish you happy! – I wish you health!'[3]

IV

SHERIDAN, known to the Prince of Wales since soon after entering Parliament at twenty-eight, became his personal adviser. On receiving a copy of *The Lord of the Isles*, the Prince directed his librarian to write to SCOTT:

. . . the Prince Regent particularly wishes to see you whenever you come to London; and desires you will always, when you are there, come into his library whenever you please.[4]

When Scott was next in town, the Prince got up a snug little dinner. Croker said:

The Prince and Scott were the two most brilliant story-tellers . . . I have ever happened to meet . . .

1 5 June 1791: *ibid.*, v, p. 212.
2 July 1791: *ibid.*, v, p. 214.
3 7 July 1791: *ibid.*, v, p. 226.
4 19 Jan. 1815. John Lockhart: *Memoirs of the Life of Sir Walter Scott, Bart.* (1837–8), iii, p. 340.

Towards midnight the Prince toasted 'with all the honours . . . the Author of Waverley' and looked significantly at Scott. When Scott said, 'Your royal highness looks as if you thought I had some claim to the honours of this toast. I have no such pretension . . .' there followed another: 'to the Author of Marmion' – and the Prince, picking up the end of a story Scott had told them, exclaimed: ' – and now, Walter, my man, I have checkmated you for *ance*.' Even at their first dinner, the Prince addressed him 'Walter'. Before Scott returned to Edinburgh, he again dined at Carlton House, and 'the Regent sent him a gold snuff-box . . . with a medallion of his Royal Highness's head on the lid, "as a testimony [writes Mr Adam, in transmitting it] of the high opinion his Royal Highness entertains of your genius and merit"'. Croker says that on all subsequent visits to London, Scott 'was a frequent guest at the royal table'.[1]

Two years after his appointment as Poet Laureate, WORDSWORTH, at seventy-five, accepted an invitation to attend the Queen's State Ball,[2] and afterwards a levee, for which he borrowed a court dress from Rogers. 'It was a squeeze,' wrote Benjamin Haydon, who disapproved of 'Nature's high priest' with 'bag-wig and sword, ruffles and buckles'. TENNYSON was squeezed into the same coat when he attended as Wordsworth's successor. Thackeray wrote to Allingham:

He [Tennyson] has just been here much excited about his court dress and sword (he says his legs are very good . . .) and as much pleased and innocent about it as a girl or a page.[3]

After publication of EDWARD LEAR's first volume of *Illustrated Excursions in Italy*, Queen Victoria wanted its creator to give her twelve lessons in drawing. He went to Osborne and Buckingham Palace. He liked to stand in front of the fire, facing her, but after the Lord-in-Waiting had repeatedly called him over to see something the other side of the room he realised it was not for a subject to take that position. She wrote in her diary:

Mr Lear . . . teaches remarkably well . . .[4]

1 *Ibid.*, iii, pp. 341–4.
2 May 1845.
3 29–30 Nov. 1850. *The Letters & Private Papers of William Makepeace Thackeray* ed. Gordon N. Ray (1945–6), ii, p. 711.
4 15 July 1846.

The seventeen-year-old Prince of Wales visited him in Rome, and spent an hour one afternoon looking at his 'Greek pictures, & all the Palestine oils, – & the whole of the sketches'.[1]

DICKENS, like Shakespeare, performed before his Queen. On Saturday, 4 July 1857, Queen Victoria, Prince Albert, and the King of the Belgians attended a private performance of *The Frozen Deep* at the Gallery of Illustration in Regent Street when Dickens with his amateur players put on a revival to benefit Douglas Jerrold's widow. Hans Andersen, staying at the time at Gad's Hill, was very surprised that Dickens was able to excuse himself from being presented.

In his fortieth year, KINGSLEY preached at Buckingham Palace and was immediately appointed Chaplain in Ordinary to preach once a year at the Chapel Royal, St James. Later that year, he preached at the private chapel at Windsor, borrowing a 'very thin' pair of tights from the Dean. After dinner he was presented to the Queen and Prince Albert, and to the Crown Prince and Princess of Prussia. The Queen told him she liked *Hypatia* 'best of all . . .'

Then the Prince Consort came up to me and talked for I should think half an hour, about St Elizabeth . . .[2]

When he was forty-six, Queen Emma of the Sandwich Isles accepted his invitation to come to Eversley Parsonage, where she spent twenty-eight hours. (She also stayed at Faringford with the Tennysons.) She spoke 'of the delight with which she and the late King, her dear Husband, had read *The Water-Babies* to their little Prince . . .'[3]

Kingsley's first royal gift was the Regius History Professorship at Cambridge, and three months after taking it up he was appointed history tutor to the Prince of Wales. The Prince attended a class held by Kingsley twice a week, and went each Saturday to revise at Kingsley's private address. When his old tutor lay in his last illness, a concerned Prince sent his own physician.

Four months after the death of the Prince Consort, TENNYSON, at fifty-two, was summoned to Osborne, where the Queen stood pale before him and said:

1 Lear's diary: 29 Mar. 1859. Vivien Noakes: *Edward Lear: The Life of a Wanderer* (1968), p. 169.
2 Susan Chitty: *The Beast & the Monk: A Life of Charles Kingsley* (1974), p. 203.
3 *Ibid.*, p. 240.

'Next to the Bible *In Memoriam* is my comfort.'[1]

The following year she asked him what she could do for him, and he said: 'Nothing, Madam, but shake my two boys by the hand. It may keep them loyal in the troublous times to come.'

So on the 9th[2] Her Majesty sent for us all to Osborne. We lunched with Lady Augusta Bruce, and drove with her in the grounds.

After returning to the Palace we waited in the drawing-room, and the Queen came to us. All the Princesses came in by turns, Prince Leopold also.

Mrs Tennyson wrote: 'We talked of everything in heaven and earth.'[3]

Queen Victoria and Tennyson exchanged a considerable correspondence, in which they shared intimate details of their respective families. He wrote to her with refreshing freedom:

I will not say that 'I am loyal' or that 'Your Majesty is gracious', for these are old, hackneyed terms, used or abused by every courtier, but I will say that during our conversation I felt the touch of that true friendship which binds human beings together, whether they be kings or cobblers.[4]

She signed her letters to him: 'Always yours affectionately'. He had many audiences both at Osborne and Windsor. After he had visited her at Osborne, when he was seventy-four, she wrote in her Journal:

After luncheon saw the great Poet Tennyson in dearest Albert's room for nearly an hour . . . I told him what a comfort 'In Memoriam' had again been to me, which pleased him . . . When I took leave of him, I thanked him for his kindness, and said I needed it, for I had gone thro' much, and he said, 'You are so alone on that terrible height; it is terrible. I've only a year or two to live, but I shall be happy to do anything for you I can. Send for me whenever you like.'

I thanked him warmly.

She also included 'He is grown very old, his eyesight much impaired' and she 'Asked him to sit down'.[5] Disraeli similarly enjoyed this very rare 'chair informality', but Dickens in the last year of his life had to stand; he spoke with the Queen for one and a half hours, while she to honour him remained standing too.

1 Apr. 1862. Written down by Mrs Tennyson immediately after his return. *Alfred Lord Tennyson: A Memoir by his Son* (1897), i, p. 485.
2 9 May 1863.
3 *Alfred Lord Tennyson: A Memoir by his Son* (1897), i, pp. 490–1.
4 Aug. 1883: *ibid.*, ii, p. 434.
5 7 Aug. 1883: *ibid.*, ii, p. 457.

After the Queen had presented DISRAELI with her *Leaves from the Journal of Our Life in the Highlands*, he liked to preface his remarks to her: 'We authors, Ma'am . . .'[1] When he visited Balmoral and fell ill, the Queen came to his room. He wrote to Lady Chesterfield:

What do you think of receiving your Sovereign in slippers and a dressing-gown?[2]

When he lay dying, the Queen's last letter read:

Dearest Lord Beaconsfield, I send you a few of your favourite Spring flowers . . .[3]

His simple burial was attended by the Prince of Wales and a few friends. On his coffin were two wreaths sent by the Queen. The one of primroses carried the slogan 'His favourite flower', while on the other she herself had written: 'A token of true affection, friendship, and respect.' She visited his grave, and paid for a monument in the church:[4]

THIS MEMORIAL IS PLACED BY
HIS GRATEFUL SOVEREIGN AND FRIEND
VICTORIA R.I.

As KIPLING lay in his pneumonia crisis, the Kaiser sent an expression of concern. Kipling wrote George V's speeches, and corresponded with Theodore Roosevelt.

V

BARRIE, at seventy-three, rented Balnaboth House for a month as a sequel to his house parties at Stanworth, and the Duke and Duchess of York, with the two Princesses, came over from Glamis to tea. Cynthia Asquith noted:

1 André Maurois: *Disraeli: A Picture of the Victorian Age* (1927), p. 228.
2 *Ibid.*, p. 258.
3 *Ibid.*, p. 323.
4 See p. 393. Her lessons from Lear; the session with Dickens; her relations with Kingsley, Tennyson, and Disraeli, suggest Lytton Strachey may have been unduly severe: The Prince 'would have liked to summon distinguished . . . literary men to his presence', but Victoria knew 'that she was unequal to taking a part in their conversation'. *Queen Victoria* (1921), p. 115. She did not join those who attacked *Jane Eyre*. She thought it 'most interesting, though very peculiar in parts . . . really a wonderful book . . . such a fine tone in it, such fine religious feelings'.

Barrie's court manners very queer. He kept sweeping in front of the Duke.

But in spite of the *faux pas* of preceding the Duke through a doorway, next day there was a return visit to Glamis and he sat beside three-year-old Princess Margaret at her birthday tea.[1]

MASEFIELD occasionally met George V and his family. He presented to the King a model of HMS *Conway*, not his own but carved by the ship's carpenter and cadets. Once, during the 1930s, he stayed at Windsor Castle.

Shortly after the publication of *Brave New World*, Albert I of the Belgians expressed a wish to meet the author, and this was arranged through an uncle of Maria's. HUXLEY bought a pair of white kid gloves and he and Maria dined with the King and Queen in their palace at Brussels. Maria had come to England with her sisters and mother when the Germans invaded Belgium. Her aunt had been a playmate of Princess Elisabeth of Wittelsbach, the future Belgian Queen.

The appointment of DAPHNE DU MAURIER's husband to Comptroller of the Queen's household meant there were times when she had to socialize, which she detested. She nervously accompanied him to spend a week at Balmoral. When Daphne was fifty-five, they entertained the Queen and Prince Philip to tea at Menabilly; the Prince had been brought by her husband twice before.

The Queen Mother is said to read WODEHOUSE when she needs cheering up, and is believed to have been instrumental in getting him his knighthood.

In 1920, WELLS at fifty-four had an interview with Lenin in Moscow. In 1933, Franklin Delano and Mrs Roosevelt entertained him privately to dinner. That same year, Stalin agreed to see him for forty minutes in the Kremlin. By Stalin's wish, their conversation was prolonged to three hours, through an interpreter. Afterwards Wells related that he had tried (without success) to interest Stalin in the PEN Club.

1 See p. 320.

CHAPTER THREE

Refusal of Honours

I

A group were coy about accepting honours. At forty-one, on the death of Colley Cibber, GRAY was offered the Laureateship, which he, a private man composing very little, immediately refused. He wrote to his friend William Mason, who had mediated on behalf of the brother of the Lord Chamberlain:

If you hear who it is to be given to, pray let me know; for I interest myself a little in the history of it, and rather wish somebody may accept it that will retrieve the credit of the thing . . .[1]

Four years later, in one of his pocket-books, he wrote:

> Too poor for a bribe, and too proud to importune;
> He had not the method of making a fortune . . .
> A post or a pension he did not desire,
> But left church and state to Charles Townshend and Squire.

He declined an honorary doctorate from Aberdeen on the grounds that he did not wish to slight his own university of Cambridge, where, as bachelor of laws, he had 'neglected to finish my course, and claim my doctor's degree'.[2]

Both Rogers and Scott declined the Laureateship on the death of Wordsworth. But ROGERS was eighty-six, and described by Thackeray as

. . . all but extinct and flickers so feebly that you would fancy that old lamp must go out with a puff.[3]

---

1 19 Dec. 1757. It went to William Whitehead.
2 Letter to Mr Beattie: 2 Oct. 1765.
3 To James Spedding: 5 Jan. 1850. *The Letters & Private Papers of William Makepeace Thackeray* ed. Gordon N. Ray (1945–6), ii, p. 629.

(Thackeray would still be breakfasting with him, three years on.) SCOTT was only forty-two, and seems to have inflated the value of the pension, for, at first, on receiving the offer, he wrote to Ballantyne:

Were I my own man . . . I would refuse this offer (with all gratitude); but as I am situated, £300 or £400 a-year is not to be sneezed at upon a point of poetical honour . . .[1]

Three weeks later, he wrote to Joanna Baillie:

. . . it would be high imprudence in one having literary reputation to maintain, to accept of an offer which obliged him to produce a poetical exercise on a given theme twice a-year; and besides, as my loyalty to the royal family is very sincere, I would not wish to have it thought mercenary.[2]

Disraeli, in a letter to CARLYLE when he was seventy-nine, offered to recognize 'the position of High Letters' by a baronetcy or the Grand Cross of the Bath,[3] adding: 'It is not well that in the sunset of your life you should be disturbed by common cares.' Disraeli sounded him out on a state pension, which 'the great spirit of Johnson and the pure integrity of Southey' had 'cheerfully accepted'. Carlyle replied that he would carefully preserve the 'magnanimous and noble letter . . . as one of the things precious to memory and heart', but that 'titles of honour are . . . out of keeping with the tenour of my own poor existence hitherto', and he disclaimed the need of money, signing himself: 'With thanks more than usually sincere'.[4]

GALSWORTHY, offered a knighthood at fifty-one, wrote to Lloyd George:

I am indeed grieved to appear . . . priggish for refusing what is . . . accepted by much better men. But I have long held and expressed the conviction that men who strive to be artists in Letters, especially those who attempt criticism of life and philosophy, should not accept titles.[5]

SHAW, offered a knighthood or peerage by Ramsay MacDonald,[6] said his works had given him all the distinction he required. He declined an OM on the grounds that 'the nature of my calling is such that the

1 24 Aug. 1813. John Lockhart: *Memoirs of the Life of Sir Walter Scott, Bart.* (1837–8), iii, p. 75.
2 12 Sept. 1813. *Ibid.*, iii, p. 94.
3 At that time, the highest distinction for merit.
4 29 Dec. 1874.
5 1 Jan. 1918. H. V. Marrot: *The Life & Letters of John Galsworthy* (1935), p. 437.
6 1924.

Order of Merit in it cannot be determined within the span of a single human life'. A. E. HOUSMAN quoted Admiral Cornwallis:

I am unhappily of a turn of mind that would make my receiving that honour the most unpleasant thing imaginable.[1]

KIPLING declined the Laureateship (on the death of Tennyson), a KCB, a KCMG, a Companion of Honour, and the OM. When Kipling was fifty-one, Baldwin came from Bonar Law informally to say that the Prime Minister was willing to give him 'pretty much' any honour he would accept. His wife wrote in her diary:

Rud says he will not accept any.[2]

No one seems to have refused to deliver so many distinguished lectures: the Romanes at Oxford, the Leslie Stephen at Cambridge, the Gifford at Edinburgh, the Lord Reith of the BBC. Shortly after BENNETT's service with the Ministry of Information in the last six months of World War I (the last two of which he was Director of Propaganda), he was sounded out on a knighthood. He felt obliged to refuse on account of his satirical play *The Title*. He would have liked the OM.

MAUGHAM told his niece that a knighthood had been suggested at one point but he had declined. When she asked the reason, he said:

Because if I went into a party and they announced Mr Arnold Bennett, Mr H. G. Wells, Mr Hugh Walpole, Mr Rudyard Kipling – and Sir William Somerset Maugham – I thought I'd look rather silly.[3]

T. E. LAWRENCE wanted none of it:

Contempt for my passion for distinction made me refuse every offered honour.[4]

In a private audience with George V, he declined the Order of Companion of the Bath, for Aqaba, also the DSO:

He hoped the King would forgive any want of courtesy on his part in not taking these decorations.

1 Feb. 1929.
2 28 May 1917. Lord Birkenhead: *Rudyard Kipling* (1978), p. 378.
3 Robin Maugham: *Conversations with Willie: Recollections of W. Somerset Maugham* (Amer. edn. 1978), pp. 99–100.
4 *Seven Pillars of Wisdom: a triumph* (trade edn. 1935), p. 563.

Whether he added 'it was impossible for him to receive any honour from his Majesty while Britain was about to dishonour the pledges which he had made in her name to the Arabs who had fought so bravely' is a matter for conjecture. He turned down the King's offer of the OM. He refused from Churchill the post of High Commissioner in Cairo or any colonial government he wanted.

It's as good to serve in the RAF as it is to govern Ceylon. I'd say it was much better.

He refused to allow the Croix de Guerre with palms (equivalent to the VC) be conferred on him openly. He declined an honorary Doctor of Laws from St Andrews University, also from Glasgow. It has even been said that he declined the offer of Secretary of the Bank of England. He accepted, three years before his death, nomination by Yeats for membership in the Irish Academy of Letters.

c. s. lewis refused a CBE offered by Churchill in 1951. 'Jack', according to his brother, felt that his appearance, in a Conservative Honours List, might strengthen the ill-founded case of those who identified religious writing with anti-leftist propaganda. In declining a CBE in 1949, joyce cary wrote to Attlee's Secretary:

. . . I should be embarrassed by a distinction which seems to grade writers according to merit.

evelyn waugh refused a CBE – in his case believing he was worth a Companion of Honour. dorothy l. sayers had the rare offer of a Lambeth Degree. In September 1943, William Temple, the Archbishop of Canterbury, offered her a Doctorate of Divinity:

. . . in recognition of what I regard as the great value of your work, especially *The Man Born to be King* and *The Mind of the Maker*.

She was the second woman ever to be proposed and, had she accepted, would have been the first recipient. James Brabazon conjectures that she feared being 'bound up with the ecclesiastical propaganda machine', and that what she regarded as personal sinfulness might have brought dishonour to her Church.[1] In 1962, edmund blunden and robert graves declined their election as Companions of Literature.

priestley explained:

1 *Dorothy L. Sayers: The Life of a Courageous Woman* (1981), p. 215.

If I have refused various honours, it is chiefly because my name has been able to stand alone, without any fancy handles to it.[1]

It was the year he received the OM.[2] Seven years previously, he had turned down Harold Wilson's offer of a peerage.

II

After his personal triumph at the Congress of Berlin when he was seventy-three, DISRAELI refused the Queen's offer of a dukedom and received the Insignia of the Order of the Garter. TENNYSON declined a baronetcy three successive times, from the age of sixty-three.

I had rather we should remain plain Mr and Mrs, and that, if it were possible, the title should first be assumed by our son . . .[3]

Then, when he was seventy-four, still regretting 'my simple name all my life',[4] he accepted a peerage. BARRIE, too, was canny. At forty-nine he refused a knighthood from Asquith, but four years later accepted a baronetcy.

1 *Instead of the Trees: A Final Chapter of Autobiography* (1977), p. 151.
2 See p. 358.
3 To Gladstone: 30 Mar. 1873. *Alfred Lord Tennyson: A Memoir by his Son* (1897), ii, p. 145.
4 *Ibid.*, ii, p. 300.

CHAPTER FOUR
Unofficial Titles

Their most endearing titles were unofficial. Ben Jonson called SHAKESPEARE 'Sweet Swan of Avon'; ANNA SEWARD was known as the 'Swan of Lichfield'. Betjeman referred to KILVERT as 'the Nightingale of the Wye' – a translation of 'Eos Gwy': the signature Kilvert had put on an autobiographical poem the year he died. Byron admiringly called SHELLEY 'The Snake' – his bright eyes, slim figure, and noiseless movements reminding him, he said, of a serpent (pre-Fall?) that walked on the tip of its tail. A. E. HOUSMAN, to college servants, was 'The Walrus' because of his moustache. Pound named ELIOT 'Old Possum'; while among his friends Hayward, Morley, and Faber, all with nicknames, Eliot was 'Elephant' who never forgot; at Faber's, Eliot became known as 'The Pope of Russell Square'. 'The Sage of Chelsea' belongs to CARLYLE, who called COLERIDGE 'The Oracle of Highgate'.

Chaucer called GOWER 'the moral Gower'. SPENSER was, for Lamb, 'the poets' poet'. After the popularity of *Enoch Arden*,[1] TENNYSON began to be called 'The Poet of the People'. Lord Derby called KIPLING 'the soldiers' poet', but Malcolm Muggeridge said of him:

If ever there was a People's Laureate, it was he.[2]

RICHARD SAVAGE assumed the title 'Volunteer Laureat' after Queen Caroline, sending him £50 for a poem of that name, had requested he should write annually on the subject of the King. (Colley Cibber grumbled a man might just as well call himself a Volunteer Lord, or Volunteer Baronet.) BRIDGES was 'the silent Laureate', in view of his non-existent output in wartime.

Smollett, probably, laid on JOHNSON 'The Great Cham of Literature'. Women called AINSWORTH, on account of his good looks, 'the

---

1 60,000 copies were sold in a very short time.
2 Lecture to the Kipling Society, on the centenary of his birth. *The Listener*: 30 Dec. 1965, p. 1067.

Antinous of literature'. Scott, visiting MADAME D'ARBLAY in her eighties, described her as 'a living Classic'. The Samoans gave STEVENSON his name 'Tusitala' – the Teller of Tales. The inscription on ALISON UTTLEY's grave reads 'a Spinner of Tales'. Saintsbury called HAZLITT 'the critics' critic as Spenser is the poets' poet'; a bicentenary at the National Portrait Gallery described Hazlitt as 'the Reluctant Journalist'. Carlyle called G. H. LEWES 'the prince of journalists'. Wells found for GOSSE: 'the official British man of letters'. David Cannadine described G. M. TREVELYAN as 'Britain's unofficial Historian Laureate, the Hereditary Keeper of the Nation's Collective Memory'. BRIDIE was called 'the Puck of British drama'. JOHN MORTIMER's self-evaluation was 'the best playwright ever to have defended a murderer at the Old Bailey'.

Nashe called SPENSER 'the Virgil of England'. HENRY MACKENZIE has been referred to as 'the Addison of the North'. SAMUEL PARR was regarded 'the Whig Johnson'. SHERIDAN's *The School for Scandal* prompted 'the modern Congreve'. An older *Sun* newspaper paid tribute to THACKERAY as 'the Fielding of the nineteenth century'.[1] BRIDIE was both flattered and irritated when he found he was being labelled 'the Scottish Shaw'. Robert Speaight called ERIC GILL 'a Catholic D. H. Lawrence'. LEIGH HUNT took pride in being known as 'the Friend of Shelley'. Sassoon, on the death of ROBERT ROSS, addressed him: 'O friend of friends!' THOMAS SOUTHERNE, because of his kindness, became known as 'the Nestor of poets'.

Wordsworth called CHATTERTON 'the Marvellous Boy'. James called KIPLING 'the infant prodigy' and 'the young Bard'; and, with the same affection, 'the infant monster' and 'the little black demon'. SCOTT's anonymity was penetrated by reviewers, who played along with 'the Wizard', 'the Magician', and 'the Enchanter of the North'. 'The Inimitable' was DICKENS's reply to a spate of mimicry. JOHN FORSTER was 'Fuz' – another one of Carlyle's. 'The divine amateur' reflected ANDREW LANG's versatility. ELIOT evoked more than his share – Ottoline Morrell may have given him 'the undertaker'; Virginia Woolf dubbed him 'Great Tom'.

The Daily Mail was first to call W. R. INGE 'the gloomy dean'.[2] On

---

1 Charlotte Brontë wrote: 'He resembles Fielding as an eagle does a vulture' and substituted 'the son of Imlah' coming 'before the throned Kings of Judah and Israel'. (*Jane Eyre* [2nd edn. 1848], i, p. xi, Preface.)
2 1911.

Chesterton's second visit to America, he was asked: 'Why is Dean Inge gloomy?' He replied:

'Because of the advance of the Catholic Church. Next question, please.'[1]

Shaw called him 'our greatest Churchman and our greatest Free-thinker'.[2] DARWIN has been acclaimed 'our greatest intellectual'.

LILBURNE's insistence on the legal rights of Englishmen earned him the title 'Free-born John'. BORROW's gypsy friends affectionately knew him as 'the Romany Rye'. The gypsies of Eversley Common called KINGSLEY 'Patrico-rai', their Priest King. 'The uncrowned King of Arabia' was the way Ronald Storrs introduced T. E. LAWRENCE to Lowell Thomas; Lawrence was also 'Prince of Mecca'. Thornton Hunt nicknamed JOHN FORSTER 'Beadle of the universe'. Another phrase James used for KIPLING was 'star of the hour'. STEPHEN SPENDER has been called 'the conscience of his generation'. Elizabeth Bowen mourned KATHERINE MANSFIELD as 'our missing contemporary' – a phrase later applied to SYLVIA PLATH.

The distinction of 'Master' was given to HENRY JAMES by Conrad ('*Cher Maître*'). It was given to BEERBOHM, MAUGHAM and NOËL COWARD. Kingsley addressed F. D. MAURICE this way, and later extended the title to DARWIN. Milton, Dryden, Pope, and Keats acknowledged SPENSER as their master. Masefield and other young writers who gathered on Monday evenings at his Bloomsbury lodgings revered YEATS as master, and saw themselves as disciples. C. S. Lewis 'never concealed the fact' that he regarded GEORGE MACDONALD as 'my master':

. . . indeed, I fancy I have never written a book in which I did not quote from him . . .[3]

After World War II, the publication of the Gestapo List – two thousand persons who would have been immediately arrested after a Wehrmacht victory – 'was . . . regarded almost as a Roll of Honour', and the names of VERA BRITTAIN and her husband appeared alphabetically on the same page as CHURCHILL.

This page . . . answered the war-time heresy-hunters more effectively than any argument. Our inclusion brought a sudden spiritual catharsis . . .

---

1 Maisie Ward: *Gilbert Keith Chesterton* (1944), p. 500.
2 *The Nation*, 9 Dec. 1922. *The Works of Bernard Shaw* (1930–1), xxix, p. 162.
3 *George Macdonald: an anthology* (1946), Introduction.

Himmler's addition of conspicuous pacifists to the list of Nazism's arch-enemies showed also how clearly the Gestapo realized that the advocates of non-violent resistance were at least as dangerous to their authority as the belligerent politicians who fought Fascism by its own methods.

The Catlins ('the Brittains') procured a copy of the page from *The News Chronicle* and for some time hung it on their dining-room wall, before eventually banishing it to the lavatory, 'which seemed more appropriate'.[1]

1 *Testament of Experience* (1957), pp. 398–9.

CHAPTER FIVE
Unusual Benefits

Among unusual privileges must be the frigate placed at SCOTT's disposal, by the government, a year before he died. It took him on a Mediterranean cruise in search of health, but the nine months saw further strokes and he was brought home to Abbotsford. As history tutor to the future Edward VII, KINGSLEY was permitted to use, which he did, the Prince of Wales's feathers embossed upon his writing-paper.

With their own hands, the Mataafa chiefs made for STEVENSON a worthy road to his house in Samoa. For them to perform manual labour was entirely without precedent in their traditions. A board, carrying twenty-two signatures, was set up:

> We bear in mind the surpassing kindness from Mr. R. L. Stevenson and his loving care during our tribulations while in prison. We have therefore prepared a type of gift that will endure without decay forever – the road we have constructed.

It became known as the 'Ala Loto Alofa': the Road of the Loving Heart.

BARRIE was given his own key to Kensington Gardens. The request came through Viscount Esher, his reason being that Barrie had written so enchantingly about the place in *The Little White Bird*. The Duke of Cambridge, who was Ranger of the Gardens, had the key specially cut and presented.

Among unusual honours, DOYLE took immense pride in being appointed Deputy Lieutenant of Surrey (Pepys was Deputy Lieutenant for Huntingdonshire), but found the uniform which had gold epaulettes and a fore-and-aft hat rather overdone. Of all ELIOT's honours, the drollest must surely be Honorary Deputy Sheriff of Dallas County – complete with badge and a ten-gallon hat.[1] The most unexpected was when he travelled with his wife to receive an honorary

1 Apr. 1958.

degree in Rome, and Italian students lined the road to the university, shouting 'Viva Eliot!'[1] In a basketball stadium in Minnesota, he was accorded an audience approaching 14,000 to hear him pontificate on literary criticism.[2]

DOROTHY L. SAYERS felt honoured when the Essex Society of Change Ringers made her a life member. At fifty-six, she succeeded Chesterton as President of the Detection Club and ruled austerely. She had already introduced candles and skulls into the initiation ceremony, and also composed an oath for candidates to renounce 'Divine Revelation, Feminine Intuition, Mumbo-Jumbo, Jiggery-Pokery, Coincidence or the Act of God'.

A. J. P. TAYLOR declared that his election as President of the City Music Society, when Sir Arthur Bliss died, was the honour he most cherished. Dr DESMOND MORRIS was vice-chairman of Third Division Oxford United.

Even a postal address is rendered superfluous by literary fame. After the publication of the first two volumes of *The Life and Opinions of Tristram Shandy* a wager was laid in London that a letter addressed to 'Tristram Shandy in Europe' would reach STERNE at Sutton-in-the-Forest, outside York, and a letter so addressed was safely delivered. When *Yeast* was published, letters seeking KINGSLEY's advice began to arrive at Eversley, and some were addressed: 'Charles Kingsley, England.' SHAW received a letter which bore on the envelope his portrait with an arrow 'To' and the words:

LONDON or – where – ever – he – happens – to – be – at – the – moment![3]

Shortly after *Down the Garden Path* was published, the Post Office had to accept 'Allways' as a proper address – the name that BEVERLEY NICHOLS calls the village of Glatton in Huntingdonshire.

1 Mar. 1958.
2 30 Apr. 1956.
3 F. E. Loewenstein: *Bernard Shaw Through the Camera* (1948), p. 61.

CHAPTER SIX

The Abbey and St Paul's

I

A mong the writers buried in Westminster Abbey are: Chaucer, Camden, Spenser, Drayton, Ben Jonson, Beaumont, *Hudibras* Butler, Cowley, Dryden, Prior, Congreve, Addison, Gay, Johnson, Sheridan, Campbell, Macaulay, Dickens, Darwin, Tennyson, Browning, Hardy, and Kipling. A. J. P. Taylor, in his *English History 1914–1945*,[1] interred Meredith there:

I got it into my mind that Meredith had been buried in the Abbey. Who was the last before Hardy? Tennyson – no he was buried at Freshwater, surely.[2]

The only professional woman writer buried in the Abbey is APHRA BEHN, in the east cloister.

CHAUCER was buried in the Cloisters but in 1555, on removal of his body to the south transept, he became the nucleus of what would come to be known as Poets' Corner. He was given the magnificence (now defaced) of an altar-tomb within a recess, beneath an elaborate canopy. In 1868, above his tomb was set a brilliantly coloured window incorporating the Canterbury pilgrims, a scene from his diplomatic life, and an illustration from *The Floure and the Leafe*; there were portraits of Chaucer, Edward III and Philippa, Gower, John of Gaunt, Wyclif, and Ralph Strode. Its base carried a quotation from *Balade of Gode Counsaile*:

> Flee fro the prees, and dwell with soth-fastnesse,
> Suffise unto thy good though it be small . . .
> That thee is sent receyve in buxomnesse;
> The wrestling for this world asketh a fall.

---

1 *English History 1914–1945* (1965), p. 178.
2 Unpublished letter to Author: 15 Nov. 1974.

Unhappily, like some of the memorial windows in Southwark Cathedral, it was shattered in World War II and there is now plain glass.

'EDMOND SPENCER' (*sic*) was buried at Essex's expense, close to Chaucer:

> THE PRINCE OF POETS IN HIS TYME
> WHOSE DIVINE SPIRIT NEEDS NOE
> OTHER WITNESSE THEN THE WORKS
> WHICH HE LEFT BEHINDE HIM.

The smallness of the surface occupied by BEN JONSON's gravestone, in the north aisle, is explained by the fact that the coffin was placed upright, possibly to reduce the fee. His epitaph

> O! rare Ben Jonson

is said to have been cut by a mason for eighteenpence, paid by a passer-by. He also has a marble monument, in Poets' Corner. MATTHEW PRIOR was buried, as he desired, at the feet of Spenser.

When JOHNSON was buried, a journalist noted only one man of hereditary title among the mourners, but added that he who was followed by Reynolds and Burke did not go unhonoured to the grave. SHERIDAN died in penury, but his funeral was followed by royal dukes and by the players of Drury Lane. They laid him beside Garrick. DARWIN was buried next to Newton.

DICKENS's wish to be buried near Gad's Hill was set aside when first the Archdeacon offered Rochester Cathedral and then, it is believed, Lord Houghton promoted an article in *The Times* demanding Abbey burial. But John Forster insisted that otherwise the privacy and simplicity sought by his friend should be respected. So with no public announcement and without the conventional Victorian paraphernalia, three plain carriages accompanied the hearse, and twelve mourners were received by Dean Stanley. The organ played; there was no choir. By the time reporters began to be busy it was all over, save that for two days the grave with its plain oak coffin was left uncovered. When Lewis Hind was taken for the first time to the Abbey, his mother read to him 'some of the long, laborious descriptions inscribed on the monuments of Worthies'. Then they came to a different slab:

CHARLES DICKENS
Born 7th February 1812
Died 9th June 1870

And I said, 'They didn't have to tell who he was and what he had done.' My mother kissed me and whispered, 'You have learnt your lesson, my boy,' and ever afterwards I seemed to know the difference between real fame and a fame that has to be explained.[1]

BROWNING died in Venice. His body was taken on board ship by the Venice Municipal Guard and received by the Royal Italian Marines. His publisher, George Smith, had made arrangements for the funeral in Westminster Abbey, and was one of the pall-bearers. The choir sang Mrs Browning's poem *The Sleep*. TENNYSON was laid in front of the Chaucer monument, next to Browning. His son tells:

We placed *Cymbeline* with him, and a laurel wreath from Virgil's tomb, and wreaths of roses, the flower that he loved above all flowers, and some of his Alexandrian laurel, the poet's laurel.[2]

On the evening of his funeral, the coffin had been set upon their waggonette 'made beautiful with stag's-horn moss and the scarlet Lobelia Cardinalis . . . we covered him with the wreaths and crosses of flowers sent from all parts of Great Britain'.[3] Villagers and schoolchildren followed to Haslemere, by which time it was night. The nave of the Abbey was lined by men of the Balaclava Light Brigade and the London Rifle Volunteers, and by boys of the Gordon Boys' Home (which he had initiated). Among his pall-bearers were Jowett, Lecky, Froude, and Lord Salisbury. The two anthems were settings of his own words: *Crossing the Bar* and *Silent Voices*, the latter being a melody composed by Mrs Tennyson.

On HARDY's death, Barrie asked the Dean for an Abbey burial, which was immediately agreed. Barrie, after fifty years of hero-worship, was making the arrangements, including the choice of pall-bearers, when he heard that Hardy had asked to be buried with his family and first wife at Stinsford. This explains what A. J. P. Taylor called 'this macabre occasion', for in a compromise Hardy's heart was buried at Stinsford while his ashes were interred in Poets' Corner.

1 C. Lewis Hind: *Naphtali* (1926), pp. 4–5.
2 *Alfred Lord Tennyson: A Memoir by his Son* (1897), ii, p. 429.
3 *Ibid.*, ii, p. 430.

A. J. P. Taylor gatecrashed. He showed his visiting-card at the north transept door and was ushered into a choir stall just where the coffin halted. The pall-bearers or chief mourners were 'an odd assembly'. He noticed that Ramsay MacDonald, paired with Baldwin, 'was much at sea': that Galsworthy, walking with Shaw, 'behaved impeccably' while Shaw kept 'looking around'.[1] Then came Gosse and Barrie, Kipling and Housman. The Vice-Chancellors of Oxford and Cambridge also formed the rear of the procession. Shaw hinted at a consummate Lifeman:

But Barrie was the most impressive of all of us. He made himself smaller than ever.[2]

When KIPLING's turn came, his ashes were committed beside those of Hardy and the grave of Dickens. The funeral followed two days after the death of George V. Baldwin was one of the pall-bearers; a bronchial attack prevented Barrie from being among them. The Dean spoke the Committal, standing beside Addison's statue, and afterwards the great congregation joined in singing *Recessional* – 'softly instead of with the usual pompous violence'.[3] Vera Brittain, who was present, 'concluded that the crowd . . . was not a literary crowd at all but chiefly soldiers & civil servants'.[4]

In 1947, owing largely to a letter by Shaw in *The Times*, BEATRICE WEBB's ashes, mingled with Sidney's, were interred in Westminster Abbey. The Prime Minister, Clement Attlee, gave the address. She was the first woman, apart from royalty, to have her ashes buried there. Dan Laurence has pointed out this was the first time in its history that husband and wife had been buried together at the same ceremony.

At least three were rejected by the Dean: Byron, Meredith, and Galsworthy – in Meredith's case, despite the expressed wish of Edward VII. It is curious that Galsworthy's agnosticism should have presented a barrier when Darwin's, declared in his later years, did not.

The Abbey had been offered to CARLYLE, who was buried at his

1 *An Old Man's Diary* (1984), p. 115.
2 Denis Mackail: *The Story of J. M. B.: a biography* (1941), p. 613.
3 23 Jan. 1936. Vera Brittain: *Diary of the Thirties 1932–1939: Chronicle of Friendship* ed. Alan Bishop (1986), p. 245.
4 *Ibid.*, p. 246.

birthplace, Ecclefechan. BARRIE, too, had given instructions that he was to be buried with his parents, his sisters and brother, in Kirriemuir. BENNETT's ashes were put in his mother's grave at Burslem. According to Dorothy Cheston, Beaverbrook tried hard to persuade the Dean that Bennett's burial in the Abbey would be proper.[1]

II

GOLDSMITH's debts prevented Abbey burial and he was laid in the graveyard of Temple Church. His monument in the Abbey was erected at the expense of The Club, who sent a round robin to Johnson that 'the memory of so eminent an English Writer ought to be perpetuated in the language to which his Works are likely to be so lasting an Ornament', but the Doctor was adamant:

he would never consent to disgrace the walls of Westminster Abbey with an English inscription.[2]

The epitaph that Johnson composed in Latin reads (in English):

There was almost no branch of literature that he did not attempt; none that he attempted, and failed to adorn.

Many more are commemorated in the Abbey: Caedmon ('who first among the English made verses'; his stone laid in the 900th year of the foundation of the monastery), Shakespeare (the statue designed by William Kent and executed by Peter Scheemakers),[3] Milton (a Rysbrack bust), Dryden, Shadwell (another Rysbrack memorial), Thomson, Gray:

> No more the Graecian Muse unrival'd reigns:
> To Britain let the Nations homage pay;
> She felt a Homer's fire in Milton's strains,
> A Pindar's rapture in the Lyre of Gray,

Blake ('Artist – Poet – Mystic'):

> To see a World in a grain of sand,
> And a Heaven in a Wild Flower

1 Frank Swinnerton: *Arnold Bennett: A Last Word* (1978), p. 87.
2 James Boswell: *The Life of Samuel Johnson, LL D* (1791), ii, p. 92. 1776: *Aetat.* 67.
3 1740.

> Hold Infinity in the palm of your hand
> And Eternity in an Hour,

Wordsworth (Thrupp's seated statue of the poet meditating), Coleridge, Jane Austen, Shelley, Keats, Keble, Thackeray, Dodgson ('Is all our life then but a dream?'), Gerard Manley Hopkins ('Immortal diamond'), James, Masefield, Eliot:

> the communication
> of the dead is tongued with fire beyond
> the language of the living,

Auden:

> In the prison of his days
> Teach the free man
> how to praise.

There is a plaque devoted to sixteen World War I poets – the Very Reverend Edward Carpenter's own idea – with names such as Binyon, Blunden, Brooke, Graves, Grenfell, Robert Nichols, Owen, Read, Sassoon, and Edward Thomas, edged with a quotation from Owen in red:

My subject is War, and the pity of War, The Poetry is in the pity.

The BRONTË memorial, set in the wall, giving the sisters' names and dates:

WITH COURAGE TO ENDURE

has an added poignancy when one thinks of them going round the dining-room table of an evening, discussing their future plans. After she was lionized, Charlotte may have had just an inkling such an honour was possible, but what would Emily or Anne have made of it? A bust of Longfellow is placed by 'the English Admirers of an American Poet'. Charles Knight thought that the giver of this felicitous name 'Poets' Corner' deserved a monument among them.

KINGSLEY's marble bust by Woolner lies at the back of St George's Chapel, beside one of F. D. Maurice, his mentor, whose affection for him was, according to John Ludlow, 'unspeakable', and to whom Kingsley, in his times of deep depression when he doubted the existence of God, opened his heart. COWARD's memorial stone ('Playwright Actor Composer' and his own epitaph, 'A talent to amuse') lies a few paces away from Poets' Corner, in what is developing into a theatrical one. DISRAELI stands in marble in the complementary Statesmen's Corner, beside his rival, Gladstone. In the name of the government, Gladstone offered a public funeral and a tomb in the Abbey, but Disraeli was buried according to his wish at Hughenden, near his wife.

Some had to wait many years – BYRON, approximately one hundred and forty. The Byron Society, formed for the purpose of winning him this honour, had been disbanded by the time his memorial became acceptable in the 1960s:

> But there is that within me which shall tire
> Torture and time, and breathe when I expire.

D. H. LAWRENCE's memorial was laid by the Lawrence Society on the centenary of his birth:

> Homo sum! the adventurer

with his symbol of a phoenix above. EDWARD LEAR's ('Painter & Poet') waited until the centenary of his death; similarly, GEORGE ELIOT's:

The first condition of human goodness is something to love; the second is something to reverence.

DYLAN THOMAS's was put twenty-nine years after he died:

> They held me green and dying
> Though I sang in my chains like the sea.

Outside the door to Poets' Corner, a tablet marks where CAXTON's printing-press stood.

III

DONNE was buried in Old St Paul's. He had ordered a monument to represent him in his grave clothes as he would rise the Last Day; it was the only survivor of the Fire and stands in the present Ambulatory. The ashes of DE LA MARE ('Onetime choir-boy of St Paul's') are laid in St Faith's Chapel:

> Where blooms the flower when her petals fade,
> Where sleepeth echo by earth's music made,
> Where all things transient to the changeless win,
> There waits the peace thy spirit dwelleth in.

The following have commemorative plaques in the Crypt: Wyclif, part-translator of the first English Bible ('Morning star of the Reformation'), Sidney (*'Quo fata vocant'*), Beerbohm ('Caricaturist and Writer'), E. V. Knox, editor of *Punch*:

> Still are thy pleasant voices
> Thy nightingales awake

A tribute to Dean INGE was 'erected by the publishers of his writings'. BLAKE, like Bunyan and Defoe, was buried in Bunhill Fields; his friends laid him in a 'common grave' that would be 'used again' after fifteen years. In his posthumous fame he has a bust here, as well as in Westminster Abbey. A bust by Eric Kennington bears: 'Lawrence of Arabia'.

CHURCHILL was brought to St Paul's Cathedral in a funeral which Bernard Levin described as

. . . one of the great public ceremonies of history, comparable with the Field of the Cloth of Gold, the coronation of Peter the Great, the funerals of Wellington and of Lincoln.[1]

Afterwards his body was taken to Bladon Churchyard for family burial.

1 *The Pendulum Years: Britain and the Sixties* (1970), p. 407.

CHAPTER SEVEN

What Happened to Others

I

Sir THOMAS MORE's body, as customary after execution, was flung under the floor of the Church of St Peter ad Vincula in the Tower, and his head placed on London Bridge; but this may have been purchased by his daughter Margaret nearly a month after exposure and, preserved in spices, either buried with her in Chelsea Church or laid in the Roper vault in St Dunstan's, Canterbury. Sir WALTER RALEGH's decapitated body is thought to lie beneath the altar of St Margaret's, Westminster. According to Cayley:

The head, after being shown on either side of the scaffold, was put into a leather bag, over which Sir Walter's gown was thrown, and the whole conveyed away in a mourning coach by Lady Raleigh.

She had his head embalmed, and for her twenty-nine remaining years kept it with her in a case; it is supposed to have been buried with their son, Carew, at West Horsley, Surrey.

JOHN GOWER has a splendid tomb in Southwark Cathedral (at that time the Church of St Mary's Overie). The head of the effigy rests upon his three books. In the choir, JOHN FLETCHER and PHILIP MASSINGER have stones next to Shakespeare's brother, Edmond; they were all buried in the church (her dedication then St Saviour's), but their graves are unknown. SHAKESPEARE is buried in the chancel of Holy Trinity, Stratford-upon-Avon:

> GOOD FREND FOR IESVS SAKE FORBEARE,
> TO DIGG THE DVST ENCLOASED HEARE:
> BLESTE BE Y^E MAN Y^T SPARES THES STONES,
> AND CVRST BE HE Y^T MOVES MY BONES.

On the wall is the Gerard Johnson half-length statue, erected not long after his death; this is the earlier of the credited likenesses, for the

First Folio – containing the Droeshout portrait – makes reference to the 'Stratford Moniment'.

IZAAK WALTON died at his son-in-law's house in Winchester, and was buried in the Cathedral. JANE AUSTEN moved to Winchester to be near Mr Lyford, a doctor well regarded. She was buried in the Cathedral – without fuss, as she would have approved. But Brian Vesey-FitzGerald suggests this was 'not because of any expressed wish but because the Cathedral authorities had no interest in Jane'.[1] A petty-canon took the service.

SWIFT directed that his body be 'deposited in any dry part of St Patrick's Cathedral'. He composed a plaque to be cut in large, deep, gilded letters:

> Hic depositum est Corpus
> IONATHAN SWIFT S.T.D.
> Hujus Ecclesiae Cathedralis
> Decani,
> *Ubi* sa va Indignatio
> Ulterius
> Cor lacerare nequit.
> Abi Viator
> Et imitare, si poteris,
> Strenuum pro virili
> Libertatis Vindicatorem.[2]

II

Quarantine laws required that the bodies of SHELLEY, Edward Williams, and the sailor-lad, which had washed ashore, should be buried in quicklime, but two months later Trelawny was able to arrange a cremation to permit removal of the ashes. Shelley's turn came on 16 August 1822, four miles from Viareggio, towards the Gulf of Spezzia, and proceedings began in the heat of noon. The blueness of sea and sky highlighted the colour of the sand, and the snow on

1 *Hampshire & The Isle of Wight* (1949), p. 375.
2 'The body of Jonathan Swift, Doctor of Sacred Theology, Dean of this Cathedral Church, is buried here, where fierce indignation no more can lacerate his heart. Go, wayfarer, and imitate, if you are able, one who strove with all his strength to vindicate liberty.' His dates follow.

distant mountains. A solitary sea-bird refused to go away. As on the previous day for Williams, a Health Officer was present, and soldiers uncovered the grave; they then withdrew, keeping back local fishermen and children.

Exposed parts of the body had been badly eaten by fish. In one pocket of the jacket was a volume of Sophocles, but the 1820 volume of Keats found in the other – given him by Leigh Hunt before he sailed – was past saving.

A pyre was prepared making use of nearby pinewood, and then the same iron furnace that had been used for Williams[1] was put in place, 'with fagots all around'. Into this the carbonized remains were laid. Trelawny, Byron, and Hunt poured oil and wine over their dead friend, and again when the pyre was alight. André Maurois comments drily that 'more wine was poured over Shelley's dead body than he had ever consumed during life'.[2] The men also threw frankincense and salt into the flames. Sensitive of a Hellenic rite, Medwin claims that without such 'accessories'

. . . it would not only have been dangerous to have assisted at the ceremony, but from the state of the body it would have been intolerable.[3]

Three hours were to pass before the body separated across the breast. It was then Trelawny heroically seized the heart.[4] Overcome, Byron stripped and swam to his yacht. The sensitive Hunt, long retired to the coach, gazed in a state of prostration. Trelawny, his hands 'blistered and scorched', cooled the furnace in the sea, and gathered the ash and pieces of bone into a velvet-lined oak box, which had a brass plate and Latin inscription.

By the end of the year, enclosed in a coffin, this was buried in the Protestant cemetery of Rome. A few months later, Trelawny had the box laid in a niche in the old Roman wall immediately under the pyramid of Caius Cestius. The stone bore Hunt's line 'Cor Cordium', with Trelawny's addition below:

1 It was man-sized and made at Leghorn under Trelawny's directions.
2 *Ariel: A Shelley Romance* (illus. edn. 1925), p. 307.
3 Thomas Medwin: *The Life of Percy Bysshe Shelley* (1847), ii, p. 289.
4 See p. 21. The heart was eventually buried in Bournemouth beside his son – a separation of remains anticipating the funeral of Hardy (see p. 389). An urn containing Byron's lungs was placed in the church of St Spiridion; his other remains lie at Hucknall. Cf. also the disposal of Sir Thomas More's remains and Sir Walter Ralegh's (p. 395).

> 'Nothing of him that doth fade,
> But doth suffer a sea-change
> Into something rich and strange'.[1]

Not far away, under the same pyramid, lay KEATS, a lyre cut on the stone, and his own inscription: 'Here lies one whose name was writ in water'. Joseph Severn, who accompanied him to Rome and tended him, lies near his side. Trelawny reserved an accompanying niche near Shelley.

STEVENSON's death scene was as exotic as Shelley's by 'the blue Mediterranean'. Samoans filed past his bed, kissing his hand, and laying many 'parting presents of rich fine mats' on his body, according to their custom. They spent the night watching beside him. An old chief said:

'When Mataafa was taken, who was our support but Tusitala? We were in prison, and he cared for us. We were sick, and he made us well. We were hungry and he fed us.'[2]

A meeting of chiefs organized the work of cutting a path to the summit of Vaea, where Stevenson had once expressed the wish to lie. A body of powerful Samoans carried the coffin shoulder-high on its difficult ascent – and then, in the presence of nineteen Europeans and sixty Samoans, he was buried like a King. Lloyd Osbourne recorded:

No stranger's hand touched him. It was his body-servant that interlocked his fingers and arranged his hands in the attitude of prayer . . . even the coffin was the work of an old friend. The grave was dug by his own men.[3]

Denied the Abbey, GALSWORTHY's ashes were scattered on the Downs from the top of Bury Hill far from the road. Some years earlier he had written:

> Scatter my ashes!
> Let them be free to the air,
> Soaked in the sunlight and rain,
> Scatter with never a care
> Whether you find them again . . .
>
> Scatter my ashes!
> Hereby I make it a trust:
> I in no grave be confined,

1 *The Tempest*, I: 2.
2 Graham Balfour: *The Life of Robert Louis Stevenson* (1901), ii, p. 156.
3 *Ibid.*, ii, p. 158.

Mingle my dust with the dust,
Give me in fee to the wind!
Scatter my ashes![1]

MAUGHAM's body, according to his wishes, was taken by Alan
Searle alone to the mortuary in Marseilles. The ashes were buried at
his old school, in the centre of the lawn, in front of the library he had
donated. Present were a small group of his family, the headmaster,
and a semicircle of boys in school uniforms, aged fourteen to eighteen.
The Dean conducted the service. A plaque is let into the library wall:

WILLIAM SOMERSET MAUGHAM
K.S.C.[2] 1885–1889
BORN 1874 – DIED 1965

II

'A vast concourse of persons assembled' at Dumfries Town Hall for
the funeral of BURNS, and from there the procession moved through
streets lined by the Angusshire Fencibles and the Cinque Ports
Cavalry. At its head marched a firing-party of his fellow-volunteers:
behind them the Cinque Ports Cavalry band playing the Dead March
from *Saul*. The bier was supported by the Volunteers. His relatives
and 'a number of the respectable inhabitants of the town and country'
followed. Other Volunteers and a guard of Fencibles brought up the
rear.

. . . the great bells of the churches tolled at intervals . . . at the churchyard
gate, the funeral party formed two lines and leaned their heads on their
firelocks pointed to the ground.

Three volleys were fired over the coffin in the grave. On his deathbed
Burns had requested playfully that it should not be done by the
'awkward squad' of his Volunteer Company.[3]

The line of carriages at SCOTT's funeral stretched for over a mile,
followed by the Yeomanry 'in great numbers' on horseback. All the
precincts of Abbotsford were crowded with uncovered spectators. His
pall-bearers were his family, ranging from the chief to his little

1 Quoted by H. V. Marrot: *The Life & Letters of John Galsworthy* (1935), pp. 650–2.
2 King's School, Canterbury.
3 See Robert T. Fitzhugh: *Robert Burns: The Man & the Poet* (1971), p. 386.

399

grandson. On the journey to Dryburgh Abbey, the whole population of towns and villages appeared at their doors, almost all in black.

KINGSLEY was given a funeral which Brian Vesey-FitzGerald says 'can never have been accorded to a small country parson before and has certainly never been repeated since'.[1] There was a representative of the Prince of Wales, as well as local gypsies; his squire and labourers, colonial governors and members of the Services, leading Nonconformists and devoted curates, peers, Members of Parliament, authors, publishers – and huntsmen dressed for the field. Dean Stanley of Westminster Abbey read the service, and the Bishop of Winchester gave the blessing. Six of his parishioners, three wearing the Victoria Cross, carried him to his grave.

GEORGE ELIOT's hearse was pulled by four horses and followed by eight mourning carriages, but these were joined by many more on the way to Highgate. MATTHEW ARNOLD was buried at Laleham, attended by Browning, Jowett, James, Lord Coleridge, and four Members of Parliament. His old school friend, George Bradley, now Dean of Westminster, took the service. Arnold's widow was moved by the enormous wreaths sent from schoolteachers who could hardly afford them.

All Beaconsfield went out to honour CHESTERTON; so the funeral procession, instead of taking the direct route, passed through the old town. Later, Monsignor RONALD KNOX preached to his memory in Westminster Cathedral.

III

It was appropriate at the funeral of ANNA SEWELL that her mother, over eighty-one, should make the undertaker remove the bearing-reins from all the horses in the train. HOUSEMAN's coffin had laid upon it white cherry blossom from the avenue of cherry trees in Trinity Backs. On the Great Gate the College flag flew at half-mast, and at the service in the chapel his own hymn – composed eleven years previously for the occasion – was sung. The congregation included academic colleagues, his brother Laurence, two nephews, and Moses Jackson's son.

1 *Hampshire & The Isle of Wight* (1949), p. 11.

WILLIAM MORRIS's coffin was covered with a piece of Broussa brocade which had been in his possession, and a wreath of bay. Waiting at Lechlade Station a yellow farm wagon, with bright red wheels, had been prepared with vine and willow boughs over a carpet of moss. Its roan mare was led to the little church by a Kelmscott carter, while behind, through the country lanes, came family and friends, workmen from Merton Abbey and Oxford Street, Socialist comrades, students of the Art Workers' Guild, and local villagers. He was buried by his schoolfellow, the Rev. W. F. Adams. Of the 'set' or Brotherhood, Faulkner, at least, was dead; among the few survivors at the head of the grave stood Burne-Jones, who watched 'a great part of his own life lowered into earth'.[1]

After a Requiem Mass at Pigotts, ERIC GILL's coffin was closed and placed on a farm cart which had a bed of straw. Wreaths from the Royal Academy, the BBC, and the Monotype Corporation, with many other bunches of flowers, were piled around it. Hilary Pepler immediately followed, carrying the cross, surrounded by grand-children, then Mary Gill and other members of the family. On the way, the choir, including Dr Flood and three Dominican Fathers, sang 'In Paradisum'. A local builder, Gill's friend, led the horse down the steep hill to the cemetery at Speen.

IV

DODGSON, like Dickens, wanted simplicity – 'no hat-bands or scarfs . . . no plumes . . . Also that the Coffin be not . . . covered'.[2] His coffin was carried from the home of his sisters to St Mary's, Guildford, and the Dean of Christ Church and the Rector of St Mary's took the service; it was then brought on a hand-bier to the cemetery. As well as family and friends, G. L. Craik of Macmillan's was there. There were wreaths from his child-friends, including one from Mrs Har-greaves (née Alice Liddell).

SWINBURNE was buried on the Isle of Wight, next to his family. A compromise was made with his irreligious views by holding no

1 J. W. Mackail: *The Life of William Morris* (1899), ii, p. 349.
2 Just one illustration that the 'great' Victorians were great because they dissented against Victorianism.

preliminary service in the church, but the Rector of Bonchurch (in spite of Watts-Dunton's telegram that Swinburne's wishes must be carried out) insisted on paying 'the utmost respect to . . . a baptized member of our Church' and read the burial service over the grave. Among those who joined the coffin at Portsmouth were Sir John Swinburne, Clara Watts-Dunton, May Morris, Bertie Mason, and Andrew Chatto; among those who joined them in the churchyard were Hallam Tennyson, Colonel and Mrs A. H. Leith, and the Mayor of Newport. 'A crowd of villagers . . . lined the path . . . and perched themselves on the tombstones'[1] and rocks. Among the wreaths were those from Eton College, La Princesse de Monaco, the Ranee of Sarawak (whose small son Swinburne had visited at Wimbledon), and two other little boys he had befriended.

For KENNETH GRAHAME's funeral, the church at Pangbourne looked like a cottage garden, with masses of delphiniums and roses, and freshly gathered willows. Children sent flowers from all over the country with cards saying how much they loved him. Thousands of sweet peas lined his grave. After his body had been permanently transferred to Holywell Churchyard, an inscription was composed by Anthony Hope:

To the beautiful memory of Kenneth Grahame, husband of Elspeth and father of Alistair, who passed the River on the 6th July 1932, leaving childhood and literature through him the more blest for all time.

The day following her Memorial Service at St Martin-in-the-Fields, WINIFRED HOLTBY was buried in the churchyard of All Saints' Church, Rudston, where she had worshipped as a little girl. Her father's old shepherd, with whom she used to go on pony rides, led the coffin out of the church. A journalist wrote that only at Ellen Terry's funeral had she seen so many flowers sent to honour a distinguished woman. 'She has come home,' said one of the villagers, 'bringing her laurels with her.'[2]

Two days after STERNE's burial, his body seems to have been 'resurrected' and sold to Charles Collignon, Professor of Anatomy at Cambridge. A friend standing by the dissecting table is said to have recognized the features. BYRON was another whose privacy was

1 Report in *The Times*. Quoted by Philip Henderson: *Swinburne: The Portrait of a Poet* (1974), p. 283.
2 Vera Brittain: *Testament of Friendship* (1940), p. 439.

invaded in death. On 15 June 1938, the family vault was opened at the behest of the Vicar, 'to clear up all doubts as to the Poet's burial place and compile a record of the contents'. It was found, when the inner shells of the coffin were opened, that the body was not decomposed. The lame right foot had been severed and was lying at the bottom of the coffin. It was noted: 'His sexual organ shewed quite abnormal development.'[1]

1 'Notes by A. E. Houldsworth, People's Warden 1938–42, Hucknall Parish Church.' Quoted by Elizabeth Longford: *Byron* (1976), p. 217.

CHAPTER EIGHT
Memorial Services

B ENNETT's Memorial Service took place appropriately in St Clement Dane's, at the head of Fleet Street. For GALSWORTHY's, the Dean insisted on conducting it in Westminster Abbey.[1] Vera Brittain and Winifred Holtby sat opposite Ramsay MacDonald and Barrie, in the enclosure reserved for writers and politicians. Three years later, Vera Brittain reflected:

. . . in the crowd at Kipling's funeral I didn't see a soul I knew, whereas at Galsworthy's Memorial Service I seemed to know every second person.[2]

Hearing, as for the first time, the familiar words from Ecclesiasticus – 'And some there be, which have no memorial; who are perished as though they had never been . . . But these were merciful men, whose righteousness hath not been forgotten . . .' – she decided to put them below her dedication of *Testament of Youth*.[3] At T. E. LAWRENCE's Memorial Service in St Paul's Cathedral, seven months after his death, the Kennington bust was unveiled. BARRIE's Memorial Service was held in the Old College Quadrangle of Edinburgh University, and another took place in St Paul's Cathedral, with an address by the Archbishop of Canterbury.

Lascelles Abercrombie gave the address at JOHN DRINKWATER's,[4] and Dick Sheppard conducted WINIFRED HOLTBY's,[5] both at St Martin-in-the-Fields. Winifred's was crowded not only with writers – Rose Macaulay, E. M. Delafield, Storm Jameson, Phyllis Bentley, Henry Nevinson, as well as W. A. R. Collins, Lady Rhondda, and almost the whole staff of *Time and Tide* – but with representatives of the countless interests she had served. Her coffin lay between Harry

---

1 9 Feb 1933.
2 *Chronicle of Friendship: Diary of the Thirties 1932–1939* ed. Alan Bishop (1986), p. 246.
3 Vera Brittain: *Testament of Experience* (1957), p. 84.
4 2 Apr. 1937.
5 1 Oct 1935.

Pearson ('Bill') one side of the aisle and Vera Brittain the other: 'the two people whom I think she loved best'.[1] The service began with a hymn she had sung every morning at Queen Margaret's School: 'My heart is inditing of a good matter'; then came Bunyan's 'He who would valiant be', which Vera had chosen. After the lesson – 'The souls of the righteous are in the hands of God' – Winifred's cousin sang Tennyson's *Crossing the Bar*. The service ended with Blake's *Jerusalem*. All stood at the end while Chopin's Funeral March was played. After the Holtby family had left, the congregation waited for Vera Brittain to follow – 'a tribute to my friendship . . . which moved & touched me when I recalled it afterwards'.[2]

After WELLS's death, a service of Public Homage to his memory, held at the Royal Institution on 31 October 1946, overflowed into adjoining rooms to which speeches made by Professor G. D. H. Cole, Priestley, and David Low were relayed. Lord Beveridge was in the chair, and a message from Desmond MacCarthy was read. Tributes were passed by Attlee, as Prime Minister, and by Churchill.

The Memorial Service for DOROTHY L. SAYERS in St Margaret's, Westminster, was attended by six bishops – Chichester, Peterborough, Lichfield, Chelmsford, Kensington, and Colchester – as well as the Dean of Canterbury, Dr Hewlett Johnson. The panegyric by C. S. Lewis was read by the Bishop of Chichester, and the service ended with the singing of Abelard's '*O quanta qualia*', which had been a favourite of hers when she was a member of the Bach Choir.

In accordance with his wishes, ALDOUS HUXLEY's body was cremated by an undertaker with nobody present at the funeral service. A month later,[3] a Memorial Service was held in Friends' House, when Yehudi Menuhin played Bach's *Chaconne*, and Julian Huxley, Lord David Cecil, Sir Stephen Spender, and Lord Kenneth Clark spoke.

Old and deaf, Pound attended ELIOT's Memorial Service, which was at Westminster Abbey on 4 February 1965. Sir Stephen Spender gave the address at CYRIL CONNOLLY's, on 20 December 1974, at noon, in St Mary-le-Strand. Betjeman, as Poet Laureate, read the lesson from the Wisdom of Solomon, and Peter Levi gave a reading from *The Unquiet Grave*. 'In Paradisum', from Fauré's *Requiem*, and

---

1 Brittain: *Diary, cit.*, p. 223.
2 *Ibid.*
3 17 Dec 1963.

The Russian Contakion of the Departed were sung by the choir. After the Blessing, while the congregation remained kneeling, the choir sang Michael Berkeley's *Requiem Aeternum*, its first performance 'In Memoriam C.C.' A Requiem Mass was celebrated for EVELYN WAUGH in Westminster Cathedral, the Latin rite dear to his heart being followed after some protest by the Church authorities. At the end, the Last Post was sounded by trumpeters of the Blues.

Prince Charles and Princess Margaret led the thanksgiving at BETJEMAN's Memorial Service in Westminster Abbey on 29 June 1984. There was a jazz band for PHILIP LARKIN's in the Abbey, for 'Poetry was his first duty but Jazz his first love'. Jill Balcon read from his poems, and Kingsley Amis, Michael Frayn, and Harold Pinter were in a congregation numbering one thousand, two hundred.

CHAPTER NINE
Statues

S HAKESPEARE stands in white marble[1] in the centre of Leicester Square. A monumental SCOTT sits above the finest thoroughfare in Europe – Princes Street, Edinburgh. With an open book in his hand, JOHNSON stands in front of Fleet Street, behind St Clement Dane's that keeps his pew. A seated CARLYLE faces the river at Chelsea, and BYRON sits brooding over Hyde Park. DISRAELI and CHURCHILL stand in Parliament Square. On less strategic sites, TYNDALE stands in Victoria Embankment Gardens, a formidable BURNS sits, while further along, nearer the Temple, is a seated J. S. MILL.

The Memorial at Stratford shows SHAKESPEARE in reverie with Prince Hal, Hamlet, Lady Macbeth, and Falstaff. Cast in 1888, it originally stood behind the Memorial Theatre; George Augustus Sala and Wilde spoke at the unveiling. A professorial KINGSLEY stands in Kingsley Road, Bideford; it has been suggested that the town is grateful to him for overstressing, in *Westward Ho!*, the part it played in the defeat of the Armada. Brock's fine statue of THOMAS HUGHES is in the grounds of Rugby School. Eric Kennington's statue of HARDY was unveiled by Barrie in Dorchester, three years after Hardy's death. Swansea has a statue of DYLAN THOMAS uneasy on the edge of a chair.

They grace our public buildings. Roubillac's statue of SHAKESPEARE, commissioned by Garrick, was bequeathed by him to the British Museum; it is based, like the one designed by Kent in the Abbey, on the popular Chandos portrait. In Southwark Cathedral is the Shakespeare monument designed by Henry McCarthy and erected in 1912. Above the shoulder of the meditating figure is his parish church: to the left, Winchester Palace, and further over is the Globe Playhouse; to the right can be seen the entrance of old London Bridge. 'The Fishermen of England', in 1888, subscribed to Mary Grant's

1 An exact replica by Fontana of the statue in the Abbey.

statue of IZAAK WALTON, which was placed in the great screen of Winchester Cathedral. In Christchurch Priory, in marble, SHELLEY's drowned body is embraced by his wife. Hamo Thornycroft was commissioned for the TENNYSON memorial at Trinity College. For St Martin's Church, Wareham, Eric Kennington carved an effigy of T. E. LAWRENCE, who is buried in the churchyard.

In Central Park, New York, FRANCIS HODGSON BURNETT is commemorated by statues of a boy and girl standing in a garden. In Kensington Gardens is Sir George Frampton's statue of Peter Pan, which was commissioned at BARRIE's own expense. Erected to W. H. HUDSON's memory, in the bird sanctuary of Hyde Park, is Epstein's statue of Rima – the half-bird, half-human character in *Green Mansions*.

For WILDE's tomb at Père Lachaise, Mrs Carew paid Epstein to carve a vast winged figure – 'the concept of a poet as a messenger' – which the authorities covered with tarpaulin even after Ross, with the sculptor's eventual consent, had a bronze plaque fitted like a fig-leaf. The tarpaulin was removed in 1914, and some years later students tore away the plaque. A giant nude, sculptured by Tombros and symbolizing youth, was unveiled on the Island of Skyros in 1931, after a Belgian philanthropist had launched an appeal. It was dedicated

TO RUPERT BROOKE
1887–1915
And Immortal Poetry.

CHAPTER TEN

Other Ways in which They are Remembered

I

Many of their portraits hang in the National Portrait Gallery near those of Kings and Queens. As in the Abbey, art is not always commensurate with merit. COLLEY CIBBER – enthroned by Pope as King of the Dunces – is given a wonderful likeness in plaster, a life-sized, flesh-tinted bust from the workshop of Sir Henry Cheete. The BRONTË sisters gaze from their brother's immature and now badly creased canvas, which was 'brought down' by Charlotte to show to Mrs Gaskell. The second wife of the Rev. Arthur Nicholls found it folded on top of a cupboard. In the Council Chamber of Chelsea Town Hall is a mural by George Woolway of local writers – Swift, Smollett, Carlyle, Leigh Hunt, Saint-Évremond, Wilde, George Eliot, and Kingsley.

Their busts scatter the land. In 1878, in St Mary's, Stafford, where IZAAK WALTON was baptized, a marble bust by Belt was put up by public subscription. A Roubillac bust of POPE is in Saltwood Castle. William Kent's Temple of British Worthies, at Stowe, blazons many by Michael Rysbrack, including Shakespeare, Milton, Locke, and Newton. In DICKENS house in Doughty Street are at least four – one from his first visit to Boston, executed by Henry Dexter. Ten years after LEIGH HUNT's burial in Kensal Green, a bust by Joseph Durham was put over the grave:

Write me as one who loves his fellow-men.[1]

CHESTERTON's life-sized bust by Marie Petrie, in the National Portrait Gallery, bore for exhibition: 'A Man of Letters'. A splendid number grace the Athenaeum.

Their monuments are not confined to places of burial. Seventy

---

1 *Abou-ben-Adhem.*

years after CHATTERTON's body had been enclosed in a parish shell, a modest cenotaph was set up by public subscription where he was born. It was re-erected, in 1857, in Redclyffe Churchyard, the place of his dreams. The BURNS Monument in Edinburgh is a copy of the Temple of Lysistrates. STEVENSON has a monument on the wall of St Giles, while in the Plaza of San Francisco a granite pedestal supports a bronze galleon in his honour. Eric Gill cut RUPERT BROOKE's sonnet that begins 'If I should die . . .' below the relief profile by Harvard Thomas on the plaque in Rugby Chapel.[1] Swansea have put a memorial stone in the park where DYLAN THOMAS played as a boy.

Jesus College, Oxford, has five memorials to T. E. LAWRENCE: a tablet at the entrance, a copy of the Augustus John portrait in the hall, James McBey's pencil sketch in the Senior Common Room, a replica of the Kennington bust in the chapel, and the Lawrence Brothers' Memorial Scholarship. Gill cut the GALSWORTHY tablet which is in New College cloisters. In Somerville College Chapel is a tablet to WINIFRED HOLTBY.

Perhaps the most beautiful memorial to any artist is found in Embankment Gardens, behind the Savoy. A weeping Muse in bronze clings to a white plinth bearing Sullivan's bust; theatrical paraphernalia lie around the base. The left-hand side commemorates W. S. GILBERT:

> Life's a boon
> If so it must befall
> That death whene'er he call
> Must call too soon.[2]

Gilbert also has a bronze memorial on the Embankment near Charing Cross. Below a relief bust is inscribed:

PLAYWRIGHT & POET

HIS FOE WAS FOLLY

& HIS WEAPON WIT.

C. S. LEWIS has a living memorial, for since his death former colleagues in Oxford and Cambridge, and friends and admirers, have gathered each summer at Oxford.

The nave of Southwark Cathedral is rich in commemorative win-

---

1 Gill also designed the monument on Chesterton's grave at Beaconsfield, and carved Francis Thompson's tomb, which is in the Catholic cemetery at Kensal Green.
2 *The Yeomen of the Guard* (1888).

dows. The SHAKESPEARE Window over his memorial originally showed the Muse of Poetry sitting beneath the Dove, which symbolized Divine inspiration. To the left stood Shakespeare with copies of *Hamlet* and *Richard III* at his feet. On the right of the central figure stood SPENSER holding a copy of *The Faerie Queene*. In the small quatrefoil opening between Shakespeare and the Muse appeared the head of Shakespeare's actor-brother Edmond. An inscription read:

To the glory of God, in gratitude for His good gifts to men in the genius of William Shakespeare . . . whose greatest works were mostly written while he was connected with and resident near the Globe Theatre, once standing on Bankside in this Parish . . .

This window, gift of Sir Frederick Wigan and dedicated in 1897, was destroyed by a bomb in 1941; a new window, designed by Christopher Webb, was unveiled by Dame Sybil Thorndike in 1954. It now depicts characters from the Comedies and Tragedies, and the Seven Ages of Man. Prospero's farewell speech is quoted in two of the quatrefoils.

Adjacent on this south side, a PHILIP MASSINGER Window commemorated his best-known work, *The Virgin Martyr*, a FLETCHER Window his *Knights of Malta*, and a BEAUMONT Window the theme of Friendship, recalling his devotion to Fletcher. These also were destroyed in World War II.[1] On the north side can still be seen the GOLDSMITH Window, commemorating his favourite theme of Family Life; the JOHNSON Window, Truth; the CRUDEN Window, Scripture; the BUNYAN Window, *The Pilgrim's Progress*; and the CHAUCER Window, Pilgrimage to Canterbury. All these lancet windows came from the studio of Charles Eamer Kempe, with the exception of the Goldsmith Window.

CAXTON, MILTON, and RALEGH have commemorative windows in St Margaret's, Westminster, the Frampton window of Caxton being used for a commemorative postage stamp. IZAAK WALTON and JANE AUSTEN have commemorative windows in Winchester Cathedral. KINGSLEY's church at Eversley celebrated the centenary of his ordination with a *Water-Babies* window. SHAW, with Anatole France, appears in a stained-glass window of Joan of Arc in the Ethical Church, Bayswater. 'The ultimate idolatry', suggests A. N. Wilson, is the

1 The windows destroyed are described by the Rev. T. P. Stevens: *The Story of Southwark Cathedral* (1924), pp. 24–8.

eight-foot-high window of C. S. LEWIS in St Luke's Episcopal Church, Monravia, California.

II

Potters, too, have preserved our literary tradition. Derby and Staffordshire, from 1765 to 1770, were fond of pairing figures of Shakespeare and Milton. In the early nineteenth century, Staffordshire paired Shakespeare ('a figure of a writer') with Newton ('a figure of an astronomer'). Falstaff seems to have been a favourite of Derby, Bow, and Staffordshire. Wedgwood made busts of Bacon and Ben Jonson in black basalt (1768–80), and about this time Staffordshire produced a bust of Addison. In the early nineteenth century, Staffordshire modelled a fine, standing Chaucer. The V. & A., from which these examples are taken, displays a small Worcester vase (c. 1815) that depicts 'Ariel attiring Prospero'.

In the twentieth century, Doulton continued this delightful practice – with Dickensian characters – and Wedgwood produced commemorative Dickens plates. More recently, Doulton have issued Sherlock Holmes ('The Detective', 1976), Tom Brown (with cricket bat), Little Lord Fauntleroy (without Dougal!), and their Beswick 'Alice Series' of 1974. In the 1930s, the Gosse factory repeated a bust, in Parianware, of Sir Isaac Pitman taken from an earlier mould.

Learned societies spring up around individual writers.[1] One thinks of the earnest meetings of The Browning Society – the butt of Beerbohm's cartoon. The Burns clubs, the Dickens Fellowship, even Francis Kilvert societies, are world-wide. IAN MACKAY, who had been 'a vague unpaid-up member of the Baker Street Irregulars', was so delighted to receive his membership form from the Musgrave Ritualists of New York – 'the Scion Society of the Baker Street Irregulars' – that he expressed his intention of joining the Speckled Band of Boston, the Red-Headed League of Pittsburgh, the Dancing Men of Denver, the Noble Bachelors of Scranton, the Crooked Men of Cleveland, and the Scandalous Bohemians of Philadelphia.[2]

With impressive dioramas and sets of worksheets, the Dickens

---

1 See Appendix B.
2 'Ian Mackay's Diary', *The News Chronicle*: 15 Jan. 1952.

Centre at Rochester reaches out to innumerable parties of schoolchildren.

III

They appear on money we use and stamps we lick. They penetrate national occasions. They turn up unexpectedly. SHAKESPEARE decorated the back of a twenty-pound note, and DICKENS is currently on the ten-pound.[1] KIPLING is quoted above the door to the Centre Court at Wimbledon:

> If you can meet with Triumph and Disaster
> And treat those two impostors just the same . . .[2]

On a Night, without precedent, given to BURNS, Scots toast the 'immortal memory'. BINYON's lines 'They shall grow not old . . .'[3] are recited wherever a British Remembrance Day is held. BLAKE's *Jerusalem* is part of Last Night of the Proms. Schubert composed *Ave Maria* as a setting to SCOTT's 'Hymn to the Virgin'.[4] The Savoy serves an Omelette ARNOLD BENNETT (smoked haddock, gruyère cheese, Mornay sauce).

British postage stamps, in recent years, have commemorated Peter Rabbit, Toad, Winnie-the-Pooh, Alice (International Year of the Child); GEORGE ELIOT, the BRONTËS, MRS GASKELL ('Famous People': UN International Decade for Women); EDWARD LEAR (centenary: four limericks and drawings); TENNYSON (centenary: four portraits, superimposed on Victorian illustrations of his poems); W. S. GILBERT (alongside Sullivan and five of their operas).

Their names are used for schools, and to identify blocks of flats. Our very streets bear testimony. In the London *A–Z*, nineteen are named Shakespeare, eighteen Tennyson, fifteen Chaucer, eleven Burns,[5] five Dickens, while KINGSLEY musters twenty-four. Swansea has named several streets after DYLAN THOMAS, and there is the Dylan Thomas Theatre. But Beerbohm would be unimpressed:

1 May 1992.
2 'If . . .: *Rewards and Fairies* (1910), p. 175.
3 *For the Fallen* (1914).
4 *The Lady of the Lake* (1810), canto III: xxix. It was translated by P. A. Storck.
5 Some of these may celebrate the socialist M. P. John Burns. Curiously neither Burns nor Scott appear in names of Edinburgh streets.

Of all the streets that have been named after famous men, I know but one whose namesake is suggested by it . . . Regent Street . . . The mere plastering-up of [a] name is no mnemonic.[1]

Every Wendy owes her name to BARRIE and his befriending of Henley's little daughter Margaret, who called Barrie 'Friendly', then 'Friendy-wendy' or just 'Wendy' – the sex being changed for *Peter Pan*. In December 1988, a 72-foot panoramic mural of the play, painted by Edmund Caswell, was unveiled at Great Ormond Street Children's Hospital.[2] In the year of DODGSON's death, £1,000 was sent by subscribers to endow the *Alice in Wonderland* Cot – an idea initiated by one of his child-friends. On the centenary of his birth, The Lewis Carroll Ward was endowed at St Mary's Hospital, Paddington, as the result of a letter to *The Times*[3] – signed by, among others, Ramsay MacDonald, Baldwin, Barrie, A. P. Herbert, E. V. Lucas, de la Mare, A. A. Milne – and of a special matinée at St James's Theatre. From the twenty-six cots, children could see majolica panels of *Alice in Wonderland* characters by F. V. Blunderstone.

In honour of their illustrious Old Boy, the Harrow School Drama Society is now The RATTIGAN Society, while, in recognition of theirs, Dulwich College has a WODEHOUSE Library with a re-creation of the study in Remsenburg. At the Festival of Britain in 1951, the Abbey Road Building Society (on the mythical site of No. 221B Baker Street) re-created the famous room – an idea repeated, in 1986, by a Tokyo department store. At Wheaton College, Illinois, can be seen the wardrobe to C. S. LEWIS's Nania, and MALCOLM MUGGERIDGE's portable typewriter.

Stratford-on-Avon is not alone in commercializing its famous son. Haworth has its *Villette* tea-room, Heathcliffe Café, and BRONTË Cinema; Bideford a KINGSLEY Café, and the Kingsley Service Station flanking his statue. In Eastwood, a TV rental shop is called Lawrence-ville, and a café in Walker Street *The White Peacock*; a men's outfitters advertises its stock 'for sons and lovers'. Swansea has a *Milk Wood* Café and Dylan Bar. In 1986, when it staged its first Festival of DYLAN THOMAS, the Wales Tourist Board advertised a £200 package; for £80 per head a week, visitors could hire the house on the hill and wake up

1 'The Naming of Streets': *Yet Again* (1910), p. 213.
2 Barrie's copyright had run out. The royalties from *Peter Pan*, bequeathed to the hospital, had reached £1 million.
3 Mar. 1932.

in Dylan Thomas's bedroom. In Canterbury is the House of Agnes Hotel (after Agnes Wickfield in *David Copperfield*) – not to mention the adopted Shakespeare Inn, Falstaff Hotel, and Ben Jonson Restaurant.

STEPHEN POTTER was remembered in the advertisements of Dunsmanship, Tuborg Gold's 'Pure Draughtsmanship', and Chrysler on 'Dodgemanship means providing the vans or trucks you need.' BETJEMAN's last public appearance was when he named his own Pullman at St Pancras. The Victorian dining-room of Charing Cross Hotel had already been renamed after him.

III

In 1967, when the BBC televised *The Forsyte Saga* and *A Modern Comedy*, a posthumous GALSWORTHY caused some churches to bring forward evening services to enable their congregations to return home to their TVs in time. He had been dismissed by the literary establishment,[1] yet these programmes appealed to an entire cross-section of the public (reminiscent of Shakespeare's audience at the Globe Theatre), and they aroused similar enthusiasm in America and a number of Continental countries.

In the 1980s, a posthumous VERA BRITTAIN was also rehabilitated. Her courageous pacifism during World War II had lost her the rank of a best-selling author, and after her death in 1970 she became almost forgotten because virtually all her books were out of print. When *Testament of Youth* was reprinted as a paperback[2] and televised as a serial, a panel in the TV programme *What the Critics Say* spoke for a new generation in agreeing unanimously that she must have been 'a remarkable woman'.

James Bridie once wrote:

This solemn ticketing by self-appointed inspectors of our Barries, our Galsworthies and our Kiplings has always been ridiculous, and has lately become idiotic. There is, no doubt, a place reserved in Heaven for those who have given their fellow-creatures great pleasure. The solemn chaps who write

1 Cyril Connolly put him in a group of writers who were 'dead and out of fashion . . . as if they had never been'; a new Forsyte 'would be a nightmare . . . these writers were unnaturally praised'. (*Enemies of Promise* [1938], p. 5.)
2 Subsequently followed by a reprint of other titles, as well as by the publication of her Diaries.

for reviews seem to be greatly exercised lest the Keeper of that place shall make any mistake about the status of his recent admissions.

He went on:

The truth is that there are only two times to judge a man of letters. The first is while he is still living, moving and having his breakfast. That judgement will probably be wrong. The second time is two, three or four centuries after he and all his friends and enemies are dead. That judgement, too, may be wrong. But both these judgements are more likely to have a trace of truth in them than any formed within a few years of his funeral.[1]

ORWELL and HAROLD PINTER have joined DICKENS in getting their names into the Dictionary; DODGSON has the title of his book there. *Dickensian* has come to denote 'squalor, poverty, repressive working conditions'; *Orwellian*: 'of or characteristic of Orwell's writings'; *Pinter-esque* is defined as 'menacing ambiguities'; *Alice-in-Wonderland* means 'fantastic, absurd'.

1 *A New Judgment* on Barrie, made for BBC Radio: included in *Tedious and Brief* (1944), pp. 151–2.

CHAPTER ELEVEN

Literary Shrines

Plaques in marble, in Minton, in Doulton chocolate-brown terracotta, in Doulton (now Carter) blue glaze[1] are scattered throughout London, from Holly Lodge, Wimbledon Park Road, Southfields, where GEORGE ELIOT wrote *The Mill on the Floss*, to houses in The Grove, Highgate, where A. E. HOUSMAN and COLERIDGE lived. Plaques even exist where original houses have come down – for example at Scott's birthplace in Edinburgh, or Elizabeth Barrett's home in Wimpole Street.

Houses such as Johnson's (Gough Square), Keats House (Hampstead), Carlyle's (Cheyne Row), Dickens House (Doughty Street), Abbotsford, Dove Cottage, the Coleridge Cottage (Nether Stowey), Haworth Parsonage, Max Gate, Lamb House (where James lived at Rye), Bateman's, Shaw's Corner, Monk's House (the home of the Woolfs), Cloud's Hill – many of them now under the National Trust – are places of pilgrimage: their collections and specialist libraries often offering research facilities. Carlyle's House was opened in 1895 by the Carlyle Memorial Trust, and given to the National Trust in 1936. Keats House was rescued from impending demolition in 1920/1 by public subscription, largely American, 'and is now vested in the Hampstead Borough Council, who undertook to maintain it in perpetuity'.[2] The title deeds of old Haworth Parsonage were handed over in 1928 to Lord Brotherton, President of the Brontë Society.

SHAKESPEARE fittingly has a town for his shrine ever since Garrick inaugurated the birthday celebrations.[3] But, until The International Shakespeare Globe Centre (inspired by an American), his commem-

---

1 Public plaques were proposed for London by William Ewart, and implemented the following year by the Royal Society of Arts. The LCC took over in 1901, using Doulton from 1921; blue plaques began in 1937. (See Caroline Dakers: *The Blue Plaque Guide to London*, 1981, Introduction.)
2 *Historical & Descriptive Guide* (4th edn., revised).
3 1769.

oration in the Borough was slight. Harry Williams could not contain his anger:

. . . the Borough spits in his face with a bronze plaque on a brewery wall.[1]

Certain writers endeared themselves to a locality. One thinks of The Ettrick Shepherd, JAMES HOGG; of WHITE of Selborne; the LAKE POETS; the BRONTËS and Haworth, with its 'still higher background of sweeping moors'; BLACKMORE and the Somerset valley of the Doones; RUPERT BROOKE and Grantchester. Many could not mention Stoke Poges without the association of GRAY's *Elegy*, or Bredon Hill without 'the coloured counties' of A. E. HOUSMAN. The Yorkshire Dales are JAMES HERRIOT Country. The DU MAURIER Country in Cornwall is preserved by the National Trust. Frank Delaney has identified a BETJEMAN Country ranging from seaside golf-clubs, cottage hospitals, chintzy tea-shops, and branch lines – with the caution that 'it is also a place in the mind'.[2]

Tourists went to the Trossachs to see the scenery SCOTT had described in *The Lady of the Lake* and *Rob Roy*. HARDY, in *Far From the Madding Crowd*, 'disinterred' the extinct kingdom of Wessex, and within two years he noticed in *The Examiner* an article entitled 'The Wessex Labourer':

. . . the appellation which I had thought to reserve to the horizons and landscapes of a merely realistic dream-country, has become more and more popular as a practical provincial definition . . .[3]

BENNETT is inseparable from the Potteries he hated.

A. A. MILNE causes otherwise sensible adults to play Pooh-sticks over a little Sussex stream. Tourists invade fifty square miles of north Hampshire on account of RICHARD ADAMS and *Watership Down*.

DARWIN has gone beyond a geographical boundary and been given the nineteenth century as his own.

1 *South London* (1949), p. 101.
2 *Betjeman Country* (1983): Introduction, p. 8.
3 *Far From the Madding Crowd* (NE 1895): Preface, pp. v–vi.

CHAPTER TWELVE

Contemporary Reaction

Their contemporaries were affected by their deaths. At SPEN-SER's burial, it is recorded that many poets threw into the open grave their elegies and pens; Charles Knight thought it 'tolerably sure' that 'Gentle Willy' (as Spenser styles Shakespeare) was among them. While SWIFT lay in his open coffin in the Deanery, crowds of the Dublin poor came to weep for their most generous benefactor. Burke wept on news of GOLDSMITH's death, and Reynolds threw down his brushes for the day. When SHERIDAN died, the Prince Regent in grief shut himself up in his room.

Five years after CHATTERTON's death, Johnson and Boswell visited Bristol, where Catcott, his friend, showed them 'the chest' in the Church of St Mary Radcliffe. Johnson said:

This is the most extraordinary young man that has encountered my knowledge. It is wonderful how the whelp has written such things.[1]

Hannah More made a point of visiting Mrs Chatterton for the sake of her dead son. Keats 'inscribed' *Endymion* to his memory and, only three years later, Shelley in *Adonais* sang of Chatterton, Sidney, Lucan rising from their thrones to welcome KEATS.

James Hogg wept on the death of BURNS, and asked himself what was to hinder him from being a successor: 'But then I wept again because I could not write.'[2] Charles Lamb was so paralysed by COLERIDGE's death that for weeks afterwards he could be heard murmuring to himself: 'Coleridge is dead, Coleridge is dead.' On BYRON's death, twelve-year-old Edward Lear wept, and Tennyson, a boy of fourteen, carved on a sandstone rock in the wooded hollow of Holywell: 'Byron is dead.'

. . . a day when the whole world seemed to be darkened for me.[3]

1 1776. James Boswell: *The Life of Samuel Johnson, LL D* (1791), ii, p. 70. *Aetat.* 67.
2 *Autobiography: The Works of the Ettrick Shepherd* ed. T. Thomson (1865), ii, p 444.
3 *Alfred Lord Tennyson: A Memoir by his Son* (1897), i, p. 4.

It was darkened for Jane Carlyle, who likened it to the sun or moon falling from heaven. Numbers of French youth went into mourning.

The story is reported that when DICKENS died, a small boy asked: 'Is Mr Dickens dead? And will Father Christmas die too?'[1] On KINGSLEY's death, Queen Victoria noted in her journal:

Poor Canon Kingsley . . . died to-day, and is a sad loss! . . . He was full of genius and energy, noble and warm-hearted . . . much attached to me and mine . . . and most kind and good to the poor.[2]

Cardinal Newman said a mass for the man who had challenged him to public debate.

Kipling could not write for three weeks after STEVENSON had died. Henry James wept when told of the death of RUPERT BROOKE. When SHAW died, the Indian Cabinet adjourned, and the lights on Broadway were put out for a few moments as a token of respect. Priestley said:

Now that we have lost Shaw, the world will seem a smaller and drearier place.

Leonard Woolf wrote that his friend LYTTON STRACHEY 'had (in life and conversation though not always in his books) a great purity of intellectual honesty and curiosity':

That was why his death shocked and saddened us so painfully: it was the beginning of the end, for it meant that the spring had finally died out of our lives.[3]

His body was left for a day on the bed, and Carrington put on his head a crown of evergreens she had picked in the garden.

If the passing of some has been almost theatrical, it was no less sincere for that. The light of a full moon streamed through the oriel window at Aldworth as the old clergyman of Lurgashall stood by TENNYSON's bed. 'Lord Tennyson,' he cried, 'God has taken you who made you a prince of men! Farewell!'[4] Father Vincent picked up the pen beside CHESTERTON's bed and kissed it.

On Sunday afternoon, the day following ALDOUS HUXLEY's unattended funeral, family and friends including Isherwood assembled for tea, and went on his favourite walk – a path by the canyon

1 André Maurois: *Dickens* trans. by Hamish Miles (1934), p. 3.
2 Osborne: 23 Jan. 1875.
3 *Downhill All the Way* (1967), p. 251.
4 *Alfred Lord Tennyson: A Memoir by his Son* (1897), ii, p. 429.

overlooking the Hollywood hills and a stretch of tree-edged water. There were eleven of them, young and old, and this quite lovely and original idea came from his son Matthew.

Perhaps the most incredible tribute to any writer was in 1931 when BENNETT lay dying in Chiltern Court, Baker Street Station. Police made other drivers slow down, and Marylebone Borough Council laid straw for a hundred and fifty yards to deaden noise.[1]

1 Carlyle had straw, but the practice was common fifty years previously.

APPENDICES

Poets Laureate

	Appointed	
Ben Jonson[1]	1616	James I
Sir William D'Avenant	1638	Charles I
John Dryden[2]	1668	Charles II
Thomas Shadwell[3]	1689	William III
Nahum Tate	1692	
Nicholas Rowe	1715	George I
Laurence Eusden	1718	
Colley Cibber	1730	George II
William Whitehead	1757	
Thomas Warton	1785	George III
Henry J. Pye[4]	1790	
Robert Southey[5]	1813	Prince Regent
William Wordsworth	1843	Victoria
Alfred Lord Tennyson	1850	
Alfred Austin	1896	
Robert Bridges	1913	George V
John Masefield	1930	
Cecil Day Lewis	1968	Elizabeth II
Sir John Betjeman	1972	
Ted Hughes	1984	

'The credit of the thing' was lacking only throughout the eighteenth century when, except for Rowe and Warton, they really are an astonishing collection. Even if Johnson needed wooing, Gray had

1 Pension conferred for continuing poetic services and, in 1630, cask of wine added.
2 First to receive official title.
3 Began custom of New Year and birthday odes.
4 At his request, wine discontinued and additional payment in lieu.
5 Royal odes no longer obligatory by 1820, and abolished by Queen Victoria.

declined, Pope was Catholic and Blake a dissenter, one thinks of available names: Prior, Swift, Congreve, Addison, Steele, Gay, Thomson, Collins, Goldsmith, Cowper, Sheridan, Crabbe, Bowles.

APPENDIX B

Literary Societies

The International Arthurian Society[1]
W. H. Auden Society[1]
The Jane Austen Society (1940)[1]
The Francis Bacon Society (1886)[1]
Arnold Bennett Society (1954; revived 1976)[1]
The E. F. Benson Society (1984)[1]
E. F. Benson: The Tilling Society (1982)[1]
Bewick Society (1985)[1]
The George Borrow Society (1991)[1]
Brontë Society (1893)[1]
The Browning Society (1881[2]; revived 1969)[1]
The John Buchan Society (1979)[1]
The Bulwer-Lytton Circle (1973)
The Burns Federation (1891)[1,3]
The Byron Society[4]
Byron Society (International) (1971)[1]
The Camden Society (1838)
The Carlyle Society of Edinburgh (1929)[1]
The Lewis Carroll Society (1969)[1]
Daresbury Lewis Carroll Society (1970)[1]
The Chaucer Society (1868)[2]
The Chesterton Society (1974)[1]
Agatha Christie Society (1984)

1 Extant.
2 Founded by F. J. Furnivall. Apart from others mentioned here, he founded The Early English Texts Society (1864), The Ballad Society (1869) &c.
3 This body oversees the Burns clubs and societies around the world. H. V. Morton wrote: '. . . to a stranger the Scotsman's habit of forming literary societies is, at first, puzzling. There are Burns Societies, Stevenson Societies, Scott Societies . . . the Scots have a genius for national memorials. The mind of every Scotsman is a national memorial.' (*In Search of Scotland* [1929], pp. 270–1.)
4 See p. 393.

The Churchill Society
The John Clare Society (1981)[1]
The William Cobbett Society (1976)[1]
Friends of Coleridge (1986)[1]
Wilkie Collins Society (1981)[1]
The Conrad Society (1951)
The Joseph Conrad Society (UK) (1973)[1]
The Cowper and Newton Society (1900; last revived 1979)[1]
The De Vere Society (1986)[1]
Dickens Fellowship (1902)[1]
The Arthur Conan Doyle Society (1989)[1]
The British Sherlock Holmes Society (1934)[1]
The Sherlock Holmes Society of London (1951)[1]
The George Eliot Fellowship (1930)[1]
The Gaskell Society (1985)[1]
The Gilbert and Sullivan Society
The Neil Gunn Society (1985)[1]
The Rider Haggard Appreciation Society (1984)[1]
Hakluyt Society (1846)[1]
The Thomas Hardy Society Ltd. (1967)[1]
The Henty Society (1976)[1]
Hopkins Society (1990)[1]
The Housman Society (1973)[1]
W. W. Jacobs Appreciation Society (1988)[1]
Henry James Society (USA)[1]
The Richard Jefferies Society (1950)[1]
Jerome K. Jerome Society[1]
The Johnson Society (1910)[1]
Johnson Society of London (1928)[1]
Keats – Shelley Memorial Association (1903)[1]
The Kilvert Society (1948)[1]
The Kipling Society (1927)[1]
The Charles Lamb Society (1935)[1,2]
The D. H. Lawrence Society (1974)[1]
The T. E. Lawrence Society (1985)[1]

1 Extant.
2 Its first President was Sir Arthur Quiller-Couch, his immediate successors Lord David Cecil in 1944 and Professor Geoffrey Tillotson in 1955. Membership, as with many, is world-wide.

The Wyndham Lewis Society (1974)[1]
The Arthur Machen Society (1986)[1]
The Malone Society (1906)
The Marlowe Society (1955)[1]
William Morris Society (1955)[1]
Newtonian Society
Wilfred Owen Association (1989)[1]
Elsie Jeanette Oxenham Appreciation Society (1989)[1]
Thomas Paine Society (1963)[1]
The Mervyn Peake Society (1975)[1]
Samuel Pepys Club (1903)
The Percy Society (1840)
Beatrix Potter Society (1980)[1]
Powys Society (1967)[1]
Arthur Ransome Society (1990)[1]
The Ruskin Society of London (1985)[1]
The Dorothy L. Sayers Society (1976)[1]
Edinburgh Sir Walter Scott Club (1894)[1]
The Selborne Society (1885)
The Selden Society (1887)
The Shakespeare Society (1840)
The New Shakespere Society (1873)[2]
Shakespearean Authorship Trust[1]
The Sunday Shakespeare Society (1874)[1]
Bernard Shaw Society (*fl.* 1978)
The Shaw Society (1941)[1]
The Shelley Society (1886)[2]
The Spenser Society (Manchester) (1866)
Laurence Sterne Trust
The Surtees Society (1834)
Tennyson Society (1960)[1]
Angela Thirkell Society (1980)[1]
The Dylan Thomas Society of Great Britain (1977)[1]
The Edward Thomas Fellowship (1980)[1]
The Francis Thompson Society (1963)[3]

1 Extant.
2 Founded by F. J. Furnivall.
3 Now The Eighteen Nineties Society (1972).

Russell Thorndike Association (1992)[1]
The Tolkien Society (1969)[1]
The Trollope Society (1987)[1]
Edgar Wallace Society (1969)[1]
The Walmsley Society (1985)[1]
Mary Webb Society (1972)[1]
The H. G. Wells Society (1960)[1]
The Oscar Wilde Society (1990)[1]
Charles Williams Society (1975)[1]
The Henry Williamson Society (1980)[1]
The Wyclif Society (1881)[2]
Francis Brett Young Society (1979)[1]

1 Extant.
2 Founded by F. J. Furnivall.

Index to Writers

ABERCROMBIE, Lascelles
(1881–1938): 404.

ACKROYD, Peter (1949–): 77, 193,
233.

ADAMS, Richard (George) (1920–):
418.

ADDISON, Joseph (1672–1719): 185,
382, 387, 390, 412.

AINSWORTH, William Harrison
(1805–1882): 381.

ALLINGHAM, William (1824–1889):
264, 371.

AMIS, Kingsley (1922–): 147, 406.

ANDERSEN, Hans Christian
(1805–1875): 24, 206, 331.

ARCHER, William (1856–1924): 307.

ARNOLD, Matthew (1822–1888): 5,
22, 36, 117–8, 199–200, 263–4,
297–8, 309, 312, 321, 400.

AUDEN, W(ystan) H(ugh)
(1907–1973): 233, 392.

AUSTEN, Jane (1775–1817): 116,
241, 342, 392, 396, 411.

BACON, Francis, Baron Verulam,
Viscount St Albans (1561–1626): 5,
355, 412.

BALCHIN, Nigel (Martin) 1908–):
242.

BARRIE, Sir J(ames) M(atthew), Bart.
(1860–1937): 5, 84, 105, 121–4,
128–9, 132, 174, 185n., 194–5, 233,
241, 257–9, 266–7, 282, 302–3, 308,
314–5, 319–20, 348, 351, 358,
374–5, 380, 385, 389–91, 404,
407–8, 414–5.

BATES, Henry Walter (1825–1892):
357.

BATES, H(erbert) E(rnest)
(1905–1974): 242.

BATESON, F(rederick Noel) W(ilse)
(1901–1978): 137–8.

BEAUMONT, Sir Francis
(1584–1616): 387, 411.

BECKETT, Samuel Barclay (1906–):
309–10, 359.

BEERBOHM, Sir Max (1872–1956):
33, 151, 241, 308, 383, 394, 412–4.

BEHN, Mrs. Afra or Aphra (née
Johnson?) (1640–1689): 387.

BELLOC, Hilaire (1870–1953): 27,
242, 357.

BENNETT, (Enoch) Arnold
(1867–1931): 106, 129, 131–2, 141,
195, 259–60, 271, 296, 308, 378,
391, 404, 413, 418, 421.

BENTLEY, Phyllis (1894–1977): 404.

BETJEMAN, Sir John (1906–1984):
136, 309, 358, 381, 405–6, 415, 418.

BINYON, (Robert) Laurence
(1869–1945): 36–7, 307, 392, 413.

BLACKMORE, Richard Doddridge
(1825–1900): 241, 418.

BLACKSTONE, Sir William
(1723–1780): 242.

BLAKE, William (1757–1827): 12–16,
30, 97, 140, 241, 328, 391–2, 394,
405, 413.

BLESSINGTON, Marguerite,
countess of (1789–1849): 163.

BLUNDEN, Edmund Charles
(1896–1974): 3, 379, 392.

BOLT, Robert Oxton (1924–): 3,
242.

431

Selected Topics

Interesting Links

Matthew Arnold – and A. H. Clough: 199–200; his son Dick and Elgar: 309, 312.

Jane Austen and Captain John Wordsworth (?): 116.

Sir James Barrie – and Princess Margaret: 320; godfather to Peter Scott and to Tom Priestley: 319; *Mary Rose* cf. Mrs Thackeray: 84.

Arnold Bennett and Virginia Woolf: 260.

Vera Brittain and Winifred Holtby: 201–4.

Fanny Burney and George III: 367–70.

Hartley Coleridge – and Wordsworth: 310–11, 323–4; and Scott: 323–4.

Thomas De Quincey and Dorothy Wordsworth: 293–4.

Charles Dodgson and Ellen Terry: 195–6.

Sir Edmund Gosse – his marriage cf. Nicolsons': 234; his daughter Sylvia and Walter Sickert: 309.

Kenneth Grahame – his wife and Emma Hardy: 108.

Radclyffe Hall and Naomi Jacob: 230.

A. E. Housman and A. W. Pollard: 224–5.

Laurence Housman and Oscar Wilde: 223, 225.

Samuel Johnson and George III: 366–7.

James Joyce – and John McCormack: 30; and the Murrys: 170; his daughter Lucia – and Samuel Beckett: 309–10; and Jung: 310.

Charles Kingsley and Philip Gosse: 276.

D. H. Lawrence and Katherine Mansfield: 166–9.

Sir Thomas More and Henry VIII: 361–2.

William Morris and D. G. Rossetti: 144–5.

Samuel Pepys and Charles II: 364–6.

Sir Walter Ralegh – and Elizabeth I: 362–3; and Prince Henry: 363–4.

Sir Walter Scott – and Robert Burns: 176; and Prince Regent: 370–1.

Bernard Shaw – and H. Granville-Barker: 341; and T. E. Lawrence: 341.